D1356295

THE ESCAPERS

THE
ESCAPERS

A Chronicle of Escape in Many Wars
with Eighteen First-hand Accounts
arranged and introduced
by
ERIC WILLIAMS

COLLINS
with
EYRE & SPOTTISWOODE
1953

First impression September 1953
Second impression September 1953

*Printed in Great Britain for Collins (Publishers), 14 St. James's
Place, London, S.W.1 and Eyre & Spottiswoode (Publishers), Ltd.,
15 Bedford Street, London, W.C.2, by The Thanet Press, Union
Crescent, Margate, Kent.*

To the memory of
RICHARD MICHAEL CLINTON CODNER
the staunch companion of
my secret journey

Acknowledgments

A BOOK of this kind entails considerable research, and I should particularly like to acknowledge the help and information readily given by the Librarian and his Staff at the Imperial War Museum.

My thanks are also due to the following authors and publishers who have granted permission for the use of works of which they hold the copyright:

The Reverend Philip Caraman, S.J. and Messrs. Longmans Green – *John Gerard*.

Messrs. Eyre & Spottiswoode – for one episode (*Casanova*) from F. Yeats Brown's *Escape*

Messrs. Edward Arnold – *My Adventures during the Late War 1804-1814* by Donat Henchy O'Brien

Messrs. William Blackwood – *How We Escaped From Pretoria* by Captain Aylmer Haldane, and *450 Miles to Freedom* by M. A. B. Johnston and K. D. Yearsley

Colonel H. A. Cartwright and Messrs. Edward Arnold – *Within Four Walls*

Messrs. Christy & Moore – *Prisoners of the Red Desert* by R. S. Gwatkin-Williams

The Hon. T. C. F. Prittie and Messrs. Hutchinson – *South to Freedom*

Mr. Roy Farran and Messrs. William Collins – *Winged Dagger*

Mr. Robert Kee – *A Crowd is not Company*, published by Messrs. Eyre & Spottiswoode

Mr. F. Spencer Chapman and Messrs. Chatto & Windus – *The Jungle is Neutral*

Messrs. Michael Joseph – *Farewell Campo 12* by Brigadier James Hargest

Mr. William L. Newnan and The University of Michigan Press – *Escape in Italy*

Mr. George Millar – *Horned Pigeon*, published by Messrs. William Heinemann.

Further thanks are due to the following authors and publishers who have kindly allowed me to quote short passages in my introduction :

Sir Thomas White – *Guests of the Unspeakable*, published by John Hamilton

Sir Edward Keeling – *My Adventures in Turkey and Russia*, published by John Murray

Cambridge University Press – *The Tunnellers of Holzminden* by H. G. Durnford

Mr. Quentin Reynolds – *Officially Dead, The Story of Cdr. C D. Smith, U.S.N.*, published by Messrs. Cassell

Messrs. Sidgwick & Jackson – *Comrades in Captivity* by F. W. Harvey

Mr. Charles Codman and Messrs. Little, Brown & Co., N.Y. – *Contact*

The Executors of Colonel Vladimir Peniakoff and Messrs. Jonathan Cape – *Private Army*

Mr. Russell Braddon – *The Naked Island*, published by Messrs. Werner Laurie.

The story of Sir Winston Churchill's escape is reprinted from *My Early Life* by Sir Winston S. Churchill, K.G., O.M., C.H., M.P., by permission of the publishers and proprietors of the copyright, Odhams Press Ltd.

CONTENTS

The Second World War, 1939-1945

CHAPTER ONE

Moments of Truth

THE SPATE of escape books which followed the First World War convinced many people that in any future war escape would be impossible. Letters were written to *The Times* by these experts protesting that the escapers had given away so many secrets, laid bare so many methods of communication and illustrated the prisoner's attitude to captivity so well that all future attempts were doomed to failure.

When I was a boy I read and re-read all the well-known escape books of the First World War; books such as *The Escaping Club, Cage-Birds, The Road to En-Dor* and *The Tunnellers of Holzminden*. I entered into their strange world of improvisation, derisive laughter and unity against the common enemy. I forged passports and made civilian clothes, toiled for hours underground or, heart in mouth, scaled the walls of formidable ancient castles. Finally, alone or with a staunch companion, I crawled exhausted across the border into neutral Holland or stowed away in a ship for Sweden. In those days my hero (for a boy must have a hero) was not a famous cowboy, nor yet a musketeer; he was not even Tarzan of the Apes. He was a dirty, bedraggled British officer stalking the border on hands and knees or hanging furtively around the barrier to a Baltic port.

When I was taken prisoner in the recent War the memory of those early escapes was a source of inspiration to me as it was indeed to many of my fellow-captives. In German prison camps I found the unity, the warm but antiseptic laughter that I had known in books. I was lucky, because I found also the staunch companion and with him made that dreamed-of secret journey.

The average age of the successful escapers of World War II is fairly high. The Earl of Cardigan,[1] Spencer Chapman,[2] Sir Basil Embry,[3] George Millar,[4] Oliver Philpot[5] and Patrick Reid[6] are only some of those who were over thirty at the time of their escape. The whole catch of Generals who escaped from Campo 12 in Italy were in their fifties. These men had had the opportunity to read the escape books of the earlier War,

---

[1] *I Walked Alone.*   [2] *The Jungle is Neutral.*   [3] *Wingless Victory.*
[4] *Horned Pigeon.*   [5] *Stolen Journey.*   [6] *The Colditz Story.*

most of which have long been out of print. Moreover, many modern
escapers pay tribute in their own books to the inspiration of these early
stories, whose authors in their turn were indebted to even earlier books.
Johnston and Yearsley in *450 Miles to Freedom* acknowledge their debt to
Colonel Rose of the American Civil War, and T. W. White in *Guests of
the Unspeakable* mentions the encouragement he received from reading of
the adventures of that redoubtable eighteenth-century escaper, Baron von
Trenck.

The more "advanced" our civilisation becomes the more difficult is the
escaper's task and the more does he depend on the inspiration and experience of his predecessors. It was not until I decided to make a collection
of escape books that I realised how meticulously and vividly that experience has been recorded. Among the great escapers in fiction, *The Man
in the Iron Mask* and *Peter Simple* are both based on fact. Among the
great escapers in history, Charles II, Casanova, Latude and Louis XVIII
have recorded their own accounts of their adventures. From the time of
the Napoleonic Wars onwards soldiers and sailors and later airmen of
every nationality have been escaping and writing books about it.

The escaper in Napoleonic times had only the gendarmes to fear. The
villages through which he passed were so outside the world of war and
politics that to the local innkeeper or peasant he was merely a foreign
traveller. Even in World War I the peasants were still parochial, and the
police network as it was known in the recent War had not developed. The
prison camps themselves were less escape-proof, and the guards, if not
more venal, were less frightened of a swift and final retribution.

But with the increased difficulties came greater unity among the
prisoners. Up to and including the 1914 War the escapers were usually a
small esoteric clique who kept their plans secret even from their friends.
In World War II each escape became the property of the whole camp and
was jealously guarded by men to whom its success could bring only discomfort and reprisals. Under the splendid guidance of such men as Wing-
Commander Day, for instance, in *Stalag-Luft III*, who though unsuccessful was one of the most persistent escapers of them all, the whole camp
very often worked for the success of one or two men.

It was "Wings" Day who welded the haphazard nuisance value of the
prisoners into a powerful weapon with which to browbeat the German
Commandant into fulfilling his obligations under the Geneva Convention.
If the Commandant was cooperating, the order "Be polite" would go
out and the prisoners would return the German salutes, parade properly
dressed and behave generally as Royal Air Force officers should. If the
wing-commander was not getting his own way we would be told, "Show

resistance", and all the natural high spirits and contumacy of the prisoners would be given full rein. We would go on *appel* with pipes in our mouths, unshaven and unkempt. The Germans would refuse to take the count until we paraded in proper order, and the *appel* would drag on for hours. Such deadlocks would occupy the whole day, keeping us from our normal camp routine; but it was more unpleasant for the Germans than for their prisoners, and in the end the wing-commander would get his way. These "blitzes" as we called them were fun for a while but all of us, prisoners and guards, were glad when they were over and we could return once more to the steady rhythm of our lives.

It has been said, "Yes, that was all right for you, you were in a position to browbeat the Germans. But what about the Russian prisoners?"

I admit that we had food from England and we knew that our Government and the International Red Cross were behind us, jealously watching and ready to take up the cudgels on our behalf. But it was not only food and the knowledge of his rights that kept the British prisoner going. We also had a tradition of freedom and unity, and the best leadership we could have had. Our power, for such it was, was a thing that fed upon itself and each victory made the next more possible. The enemy is very apt to accept you at your own valuation.

In World War I captivity in Turkey was often as hungry and precarious as captivity in the Far East in World War II, when the prisoner had no rights and very little food; but the same spirit of resistance is typified in this song bowdlerised by Sir Thomas White, who tells the story of his escape from Constantinople in *Guests of the Unspeakable*[1]:

> *"We won't be bothered (?) about,*
> *Wherever we go we'll always shout –*
> *We'll be bothered if we'll be bothered about,*
> *We won't be bothered about . . ."*

It is this spirit that makes so many of us look back with some warmth on the time of our captivity.

*   *   *   *   *   *

Most men who were prisoners in Germany during World War II are aware of the debt they owe to the International Red Cross. Their wives and mothers remember the kindly help and advice freely given in those anxious days by the Society's workers. The debt is not often acknowledged because every ex-prisoner feels that for the time of his captivity he

---

[1]The story is also told by his companion Alan Bott in *Eastern Nights—And Flights.*

was an object of charity, and the acknowledgment is not an easy one to make.

Soon after 1854 when Florence Nightingale had first made the British public aware of the appalling treatment of the sick and wounded in the Crimea, Jean Henri Dunant in Switzerland published his book *Un Souvenir de Solférino*, which gave the same publicity to the fate of the unfortunate victims of that battle. As a direct result of this book the first Red Cross Convention was called in Geneva in 1863, and was followed a year later by the Geneva Convention which laid down the first international laws of war regarding the care of the wounded. This Convention was revised in 1906 to include rules for the treatment of prisoners of war. It was further revised in 1929, and again in 1949 to extend some protection to the civilian population and members of organised resistance groups in occupied territories.

Among the rights, privileges and obligations of the prisoner of war under this Convention are:

(*a*) He is the captive of the Government and not of any individual person or military unit. He shall be protected by the Government from violence, insults and public curiosity. If interrogated he is obliged to reveal only his name, rank and serial number; no pressure may be brought to bear to force him to give any other information. All his personal belongings other than arms and military equipment remain his property, and money may only be taken from him on the orders of an officer and on the issue of a receipt. Identity discs, badges of rank and decorations may not be taken from him.

(*b*) He must be removed from the fighting zone as soon as possible but must not be forced to march more than twenty kilometres a day unless this is necessary to reach food and water.

(*c*) His permanent place of captivity must not be in a district which is unhealthy, nor in an area where he will be exposed to the fire of the fighting zone. He may be reasonably restrained there, but he must not be strictly confined except under absolute necessity. He must be properly housed, and the dormitory accommodation and food must be the same as for depot troops of the detaining power. All collective disciplinary measures affecting his food are prohibited. He shall be clothed and shod by the detaining power. The camp in which he is kept must be hygienic, and he must have facilities for washing and the benefit of being out-of-doors. Each camp shall have an infirmary and seriously sick prisoners shall be placed in any military or civil institution qualified to treat them.

(*d*) He shall be given freedom of religious worship.

(*e*) He shall be treated with due regard to his rank and age. He is required to salute all officers of the detaining power, but if of commissioned rank himself he must salute only his equals and superiors in rank. If he is an officer he cannot be obliged to work, and if an N.C.O. can only be obliged to work in a supervisory capacity. A working prisoner must not work longer hours than a soldier of the detaining power and must be paid the same rate of wages.

(*f*) He shall be allowed to correspond with home and to receive parcels of food, clothing and books.

(*g*) Attempts at escape shall be punished only by disciplinary action. All forms of corporal punishment, confinement in premises not illuminated by daylight and all forms of cruelty whatsoever are prohibited as disciplinary punishment, nor may the prisoner he deprived of his rank.

When a fighting man is captured he both loses and gains certain rights and privileges. Before capture he may kill an enemy in uniform and if captured cannot be punished for this. Once he has been captured he forfeits his combatant status and becomes liable to the civil code of the detaining power for his subsequent conduct – and then such an act becomes one of murder and punishable with death.

Since the fighting man loses his combatant status when taken prisoner he may endeavour to escape in civilian clothes and will not be accused of espionage unless definite proof is brought forward that such was his object. On gaining neutral territory he will, since he is now a civilian, be returned to his own country where he resumes his combatant status. If after this he is captured a second time he cannot then be punished for his first escape.

A combatant entering neutral territory is regarded as violating its neutrality and is interned there for the duration of hostilities.

Although the maximum disciplinary punishment for an escape attempt is thirty days in the cells, the prisoner of war, being subject to the laws, regulations and orders of the detaining power, is punishable under the civil code for any crime, such as theft, committed while he is at liberty. In this way a simple escape with additional trumped-up charges – damage to government property for example – can be made to incur a sentence of several years' imprisonment. If the aggregate punishment for an escape is more than thirty days however, three days must elapse between each period of imprisonment.

*　　*　　*　　*　　*

Although the first Geneva Convention relating to prisoners of war was

not signed until 1906, British captives in the Napoleonic Wars were
granted certain privileges due to their military status. A set scale of pay
was drawn up according to rank, and officers were allowed to live on
parole in the towns. Parole was treated by these prisoners with the same
scrupulous respect it was accorded in the later wars, and when intending
to escape they first made certain that they were put in gaol for some minor
offence so that they would, by virtue of this confinement, be temporarily
freed from their bond. Technically, I suppose, a prisoner should not have
used the privilege of parole even to survey the surrounding countryside
and so prepare the way for a future escape attempt; but generally speaking
this was allowed by the rules of the game and, provided the prisoner
formally returned his parole before making his escape, he was free of blame.

During the Napoleonic Wars escaped British prisoners were subject to
a court of inquiry on their return, to make sure that the privilege had not
been abused. On one occasion a British naval officer, Lieutenant Sheehy,
who had 'roken his parole and escaped from Verdun, was returned to
France b the British Government under a flag of truce.

In the early part of World War I parole was given by some British
officer prisoners in Turkey, but there was a growing feeling among them
that this was wrong. E. H. Keeling, who made good his escape from
Turkey after a long trek, recapture and an amazing rescue by outlaws,
discusses the question in *Adventures in Turkey and Russia:*

"Soon after we reached Kastamuni a roll call twice daily was
introduced, to make sure that no one had run away, and we were
individually photographed, to aid the pursuit of anyone who did. But
our new Commandant was not content with these precautions. Three
weeks after he arrived, he announced that orders had come from
Constantinople to stop all games and walks and to keep us in close confinement, but he added that if we would promise not to escape he
would, on his own responsibility, continue our existing privileges, and
even extend them. Our senior officer, though he gave no order, urged
us to give the promise. He argued that the escape of a few was of no real
use to the allied cause, and would make the lot of the remaining
prisoners harder; that to get clear away was, in any case, hardly feasible,
owing to the position of Kastamuni in the interior of Anatolia, hundreds
of miles from any allied force or neutral frontier; that if escape should
ever become possible the promise could be withdrawn; and that in the
meantime the health and comfort of the majority ought to be considered.

"Most officers accepted these views and gave the promise; not unnaturally they deemed themselves entitled, or even by military discipline compelled, to follow the advice of their superior officer. But eleven of us refused. We were not satisfied that escape would always be impossible, and we declined to tie our hands. True, the parole, if given, could be withdrawn should a chance to get away occur later, but a withdrawal would obviously put the Turks at once on the alert. Moreover, the promise would make it unnecessary for the enemy to guard us, and would therefore be tantamount to assisting him. On the other hand, the Commandant had said that refusal to give parole would lead to an increase in the number of sentries. Such an increase would alone, we held, justify our refusal, for we should be detaining in Kastamuni a number of the enemy who would otherwise be released for duty at the front or on the lines of communication. If each prisoner kept even two men to guard him, he would be accounting for as many as he could reasonably expect to kill if he were in a front-line trench. . . .

"The question came up subsequently at another camp, the senior officer of which got a message through to the War Office in London asking for a ruling. After several months the reply arrived that the War Office considered a promise not to attempt to escape opposed to the traditions of the service. The point had arisen in previous wars, and it seems strange that the King's Regulations contained (and still contain) no pronouncement on this matter. An Expeditionary Force routine order eventually forbade the giving of parole, but prisoners captured before its issue could only look for guidance to their senior officers, who should never have been burdened with the responsibility of deciding such a question of principle."

In Germany in World War I parole was approved only for walks outside the camp, and the prisoners' attitude to this is clearly given by H. G. Durnford in *The Tunnellers of Holzminden*:

"In the Great War it was the wish, rightly and clearly expressed by Lord Grey, that officers should use the privilege of parole to take walks outside the camp only when they could not get sufficient exercise within it to keep themselves fit. When, therefore, in previous camps the British had availed themselves of this privilege, they had been in the habit, before starting on the walk, of handing in a signed card to the Germans on which it was stated that they undertook not to do two things: to escape or in any way to facilitate future escape, or to damage German property. The arrangement had proved perfectly satisfactory.

"But in Holzminden, when the cards were produced for us to sign, there was a whole charter of other things that we must or might not do when we went out for walks. We were required, for instance, to sign to the effect that we would unhesitatingly obey the orders of the German officer or N.C.O. accompanying us; this hit at the whole basis of the parole idea. We were asked to append our names underneath a clause which stated that we *knew* that the breaking of our parole was punishable with the death penalty; this merely insulted our intelligence. We were determined that we would either take walks on parole on the terms of heretofore or not take them at all. This spirit of dogged conservatism when there was so clearly everything to lose and nothing much to gain might seem petty and unreasonable, were it not remembered, firstly, that any attempt to interfere with our parole was in honour bound to be furiously contested, and secondly, that if in the course of business you conceded the German an inch, he was pretty certain shortly to make overtures for an ell.''

In Germany in World War II the giving of parole was forbidden except for such brief occasions as a visit to a hospital or to attend the funeral of one of the prisoners who had died. Although this order assisted the British war effort by keeping more guards on duty, it also meant that the would-be escaper was not able to gain a knowledge of the local country as had been possible before. In fact most officer prisoners of World War II were totally ignorant of what to expect once they had broken from their camp.

There were however several amenities in the prison camps in Germany which came under the heading "on parole" and could not be used for escape purposes. Tools, make-up and costumes for use by the camp amateur dramatic society would have been of untold value to the escapers, but they were strictly taboo and it never occurred to us to use them.

In the Japanese camps the position was rather different, as can be seen in the following extract taken from *Officially Dead*, the story of Commander C. D. Smith, U.S.N., told by Quentin Reynolds. The scene is Woosung prison camp, Commanders Smith, Cunningham and Woolley are the senior American officers and Sir Mark Young, late Governor and C.-in-C. of Hong-Kong, is spokesman for the British. The Japanese commandant, Colonel Yusei, had just ordered the prisoners who are lined up on the parade ground to sign their parole not to escape. Sir Mark Young steps forward:

" 'We, the officers, have ordered our men not to sign,' he said simply. 'Do not blame them. You cannot force them to sign an agreement which no military man has a right to sign.'

" That was all. We went back into our barracks, impressed by Sir

Mark's courage and admiring his dignity. A few days later, Sir Mark, Woolley and I went to see Yusei. Sanitary conditions were such that we were in deadly fear of an epidemic or a plague. Sir Mark complained about the conditions and then, always courteous, his speech clipped and cold, he said a few words to Yusei that had the little man a quivery mass of indignation and fear.

" 'Forever your name will smell in the nostrils of mankind,' Sir Mark said. 'You will be linked with those who ordered men into the black hole of Calcutta. I may not live to see your shame but others will come after me and they will know you. They will curse you. And you will suffer.

" 'During the last war I fought the Germans. I was captured and when I tried to escape I was caught. The German officer who questioned me said, "I do not blame you for attempting to escape. A true soldier will try to escape." That is the officers' code the world over, Colonel Yusei. A soldier is bound to fight until he is dead. As long as he is alive he must make every effort to get back to his men and fight again. That is all, sir.'

" ... Two weeks later, Yusei, in a desperate effort to save face, ordered us to sign the non-escape agreement again. We would have no food or bathing privileges or exercise until we did sign. Woolley, Cunningham and I took counsel. Signing the agreement obtained under such duress would mean nothing. It was sign or die. Unless you signed an agreement of your own free will it was not an agreement. You were not giving your word if a gun was held at your neck. We decided to tell the men to sign and they did. Sir Mark held out for two days. His sense of honour would not permit him to sign an agreement he might be tempted to break. I argued heatedly with him. Finally, when I told him of the suffering he would cause his own men if he didn't allow them to sign, he capitulated—but he did it reluctantly.

"Woolley and I were brimming over with plans for escape now."

* * * * *

It seems from the earlier escape books that the relationship between the prisoner and his European guard has changed but little since the time of Napoleon. "The day may come when you may think yourself happy in having been prisoners," the remark with which Midshipman Boys[1] and his friends were greeted by their kindly gaoler, has been modernised into the more succinct German, "For you the war is over!"; but the sentiment is the same, there is the same touch of envy in the consolation.

The damage done by Napoleon's prisoners during their captivity at

[1]*Narrative of a Captivity and Adventures in France and Flanders.*

Verdun was assessed by the French at £520. The French – always intract-
able prisoners and great escapers – did £2,000 worth of damage to
Liverpool Gaol during their imprisonment there. I wonder how much
damage our prisoners did in Germany in World War II? Apart from the
normal burning of furniture in cooking stoves and the use of bed-boards
as shoring for tunnels, the British other ranks who were working in the
fields and factories of the Third Reich carried out a regular campaign of
sabotage (such as the scooping of eyes from seed potatoes before planting
them, mixing sand with engine oil and tampering with military equipment) which must have done untold damage to the German war machine.

This spirit and intractability of the prisoner of war has precedent in
Napoleonic times. It warms my heart to read that when Midshipman
Boys, eighteen years of age, was being marched to prison after capture by
the French in 1803, he found time for a practical joke during a halt for
food in a village inn:

> ". . . I entered an adjoining bedroom, and observing on the mantel-
> piece various little images in plaster of paris, in the midst of which was
> the bust of the adored Buonaparte, and no one being near, I could not
> resist the temptation of placing its head downwards, in a vessel which
> was no ornament to a mantelpiece, nor usually found there."

Retribution followed several days later when the whole party was locked
up by a guard nearly hysterical with rage:

> "'You are in prison by a counter-order lately received from Auch,
> for having put Buonaparte's head into a *pot de chambre*.' A silent gaze of
> astonishment was followed by sudden gusts of laughter, which so
> thundered through the prison as to drown the voice of the incensed
> orator; and nothing could be heard but '*Buonaparte*' and '*diable*'. The
> louder he spoke the more boisterous was our mirth, until, frantic with
> rage, he drew his sword, rushed forward and thrust it through the
> grated hole in the door, stamped, and swore in such a foaming passion,
> that when the storm of derision was over he could scarcely articulate."

This story reminds me of a day in Germany in 1943. A tunnel break had
succeeded, a number of prisoners had escaped, and the remainder were
locked in their rooms. The camp commandant had summoned the Gestapo.

Entering one of the rooms the Gestapo chief, sinister in his pulled-down
felt hat and belted raincoat, noticed pinned to the wall a caricature of
Hitler hanging by the neck from a gibbet. "Every prisoner in this room
will be shot!" He intended it as a plain statement of fact, but instead of
inspiring the terror he had expected the announcement brought nothing

but a shout of laughter. Fortunately the camp was directly under the command of the German army, and the Gestapo had no power to carry out the threat. When they had this power they did not hesitate to use it and the tragedy of *Stalag-Luft III*, when fifty recaptured prisoners were shot in cold blood, is evidence of that. The military prison camps were run more or less according to the Geneva Convention. We should have had a different story to tell had it been otherwise.

Stalag-Luft III, utterly without character, bare, drab, uncompromising in its "fitness for purpose", was typical of hundreds of camps which dotted Europe in World War II. The flat grey dust of the compound was broken only by squat wooden huts raised on piles above the surface of the ground. Round the huts the double twelve-foot fence of bristling barbed wire made a stark barrier, punctuated at intervals by high wooden sentry towers armed with machine-guns and searchlights. Between these sentry boxes were arc lamps suspended from poles above the fence, while below it, sunk deep into the ground, were the seismographs which recorded the vibration caused by tunnelling. At a distance of thirty feet inside the main fence ran the trip-wire, a single strand a foot above the ground. For the prisoners this was the main boundary of the camp, and anyone stepping over it was shot at by the guards. There were white coats hanging at the goalmouth of the football pitch and these were always put on by players crossing the trip-wire to retrieve a ball. Outside the wire fence, sentries armed with rifles patrolled between each pair of watchtowers, and at night when the prisoners were locked in their huts these guards were doubled and savage police dogs, occasionally visible in the searchlight beams, roamed the deserted compound.

Sooner or later nearly every prisoner to arrive at one of these camps thought about getting out again. The problem, simply set, offered three solutions – the three-pronged Morton's Fork of escape. He could go under the wire, through the wire or over the wire.

The obvious way under the wire was through a tunnel; what was not so obvious was the tunnel's starting-place. It is to the everlasting credit of the prisoners of *Stalag-Luft III* that during its brief history over one hundred different tunnels were started there. Only six men returned to England as a result, but that was because the break from the camp was merely the beginning of an escape. From then onwards the escaper depended entirely on his luck.

He could go through the wire in many different ways; disguised as a German, tied up in a bundle of laundry, clinging to the underside of a German lorry. Some brave spirits cut their passage, by night and by day, with wire-cutters, usually pushing before them a sort of snow-plough made of wood to protect them a little from the coiled barbed wire. These men were brave beyond the normal run of bravery. They were, all the time they were cutting the wire, in the field of fire of machine-guns and rifles. While I was a prisoner in *Oflag XXIB* two R.A.F. officers, Toft an Irishman, and Nicholls a member of the American Eagle Squadron, got out this way. Shortly afterwards a Polish flight-lieutenant was taken out, stark naked with his clothes in a mackintosh bundle on his head, sitting in the galvanised iron "night cart" which pumped out the open-trench latrines. This man's desire to fight again was a burning white-hot political fanaticism fanned by German atrocities in Warsaw. He was caught outside the gates, but later he made a successful escape and got clean away. I do not know what became of him.

To go over the wire was no safer. Daring attempts were made with scaling-ladders and planks, rehearsed again and again until each action became automatic and time was cut to a minimum. At least one of these attempts was successful, and is described by A. S. B. Arkwright in *Return Journey*.[1] Prisoners climbed the wire at night or, while the sentries' attention was distracted, in daylight. Some enthusiasts, possibly inspired by Gambetta's escape from Paris in a balloon, designed gliders which were to carry them across the wire; but I do not know of any that were ever completed. Attempts were made to swing out over the fences on ropes, or leap them with vaulting-poles, and on one occasion an acrobatic prisoner was flung over the wire by an equally athletic companion.

As I have said, the break from the camp was only the first step on the escaper's journey. He now had to make his way through many miles of enemy territory before he could begin to think about his exit from the country. As soon as the escape became known and his identity established, his personal description would be flashed to every police station, every Gestapo, Home Guard and Hitler Youth headquarters in Germany. Not only had he to avoid all those who were looking expressly for him, but also the thousands of officials who would ask for his identity card or travel permit and, not being satisfied, arrest him on suspicion that he was a foreign worker on the loose or a German of military age dodging the column. At that time one half of the German population was busy checking up on the other half, and no one was free from interrogation.

Once outside the camp the problem facing the escaper was not how long he could stay out but, rather how far he could travel. To go by train seemed at first to be most dangerous; travel permits were necessary, and special inspectors whose sole duty was to check these permits were everywhere. But the time required to do the journey on foot seemed to weigh

[1]Published by Seeley Service Ltd.

heavily in favour of the more speedy method of travel. Every hour the escaper spent on the journey was another hour in which discovery became more likely. The traveller on foot could rarely carry sufficient food and drink to last the whole journey, and any attempt to steal or beg was fraught with danger. The natural hazards of the sleeper-out – the cold and wet in winter, thirst, mosquitoes and the short hours of darkness in summer – are exactly the same to-day as they were in the days of Napoleon. The advance of science has done very little to help the escaper on his way.

* * * * *

I am sometimes asked, "Why did you try to escape?", and always I find it difficult to reply. Quite apart from the fact that it was our duty to make the attempt, the urge to escape was for most of us a purely personal one, and there must have been as many reasons for escape as there were es- capers. No one in his right mind imagined that his particular absence from the battle could make the slightest difference to the course of the war. For some, escape meant a wiping-out of the disgrace of capture; for others, wine and women – we had plenty of song. Most of us would concede that we had little hope of getting back, but it was good for our self-respect to have a crack at it, and anyway it gave us something positive to do.

If I am honest I must admit that I did not try to escape only in order to be free; the chance of getting away with it was altogether too remote. It was rather like trying to win a rugger match, the opposition was there and one did one's best to overcome it. The outcome, for the escaper, was very much more important than for the footballer, but I think that funda- mentally the incentive was much the same.

The real value of the escape attempt was in its general effect on the morale of the escaper, his fellow-prisoners and, in an inverse ratio, his guards. Recapture was not necessarily failure. The experience gained was useful in the next attempt and especially when pooled, as in this extract from a note written during the 1914 War by a recaptured prisoner and smuggled into the camp from which he had escaped:

"... On five occasions we passed right by a man unchallenged, saying either "*Guten abend*" or nothing. Once we were stopped, but got off by a little German and by having an ugly-looking stick. When we ran into anyone it was nearly always before midnight, and it was very dangerous to leave lying-up positions before 11 p.m. During the day we were several times lying within twenty yards of workers or passers- by, and it pays to have a bit of loose heather ready to scatter over self and belongings. Rye at this moment makes the very best cover, though bad if discovered, no doubt. Walk up furrow between it and another corn-crop, or between two plants of rye, turn in and walk quietly, keeping impediments high, then turn right or left and lie down. But it's fearfully hot midday, and water is essential. Damp woods – e.g., alder, spruce, oak – have so many mosquitoes as to interfere with sleep and rob you of vitality. Young pines, heather, and juniper the best possible combination. Never fail to get water to take into hiding, and drink plentifully also at night. Seed spuds are all right raw (always found close to houses). Everything in a mackintosh is a good idea. We only had one wet night, good weather helps enormously, and especially north star.

"Another time I should never pass through a village till after midnight, and before 3.15 a.m. Fifty kilos from the frontier I should leave all roads and villages and use tracks. I should put into my map the name of every village; it helps so with the signposts. I should make for the Dutch re-entrant north of the Ems-Vecht canal, and on the lines given I should reckon twenty nights inclusive, allowing a course of two hundred kilos. Our best night we did twenty to twenty-two, the canal towpath was easily the best going, and deserted until Recke.

"Twenty nights means a lot of food. I could have just done twenty to twenty-one on what I took, but at first I ate painfully little. Now, after four days' rest, I am, however, much better than when I started. I was weakest the third and fourth nights out. One has no spirit at the end, but one's legs will keep trudging well on a level surface. Men on bicycles are dangerous, and often, I fancy, telephone ahead instead of stopping one. Civilian kit would be a great help. Wear a hat – a 'Gor'blimy' is better than nothing.

"As to routes, I am not sure I wouldn't go the same until three or four kilos west of Recke. Then turn due north, ten kilos. Then north-west and into re-entrant. On the other hand I might try the trolley-line and Hademsdorf rail-bridge for speed. Then, avoiding stations, to Stolzen bridge, thence Drakenberg; try to boat the Weser near there, and take a line north of the big swamp that lies east and north-east of Recke, and so avoid the canal.

"The lieutenant here says west or south-west from this camp is impossible! A straight line west and good going like the canal is very tempting, but on the big heaths and reclaimed land the tracks run beautifully straight. Take change of socks, three big handkerchiefs, spare shorts, plenty of cord, and cut sticks. I shall probably get out to you temporarily in a few days. Love to the whole room. Keep this in cache."

I do not know who wrote this (the letter is quoted by another escaper,

F. W. Harvey, in his *Comrades in Captivity*) but I can imagine the man enduring his solitary confinement, full of the joy and achievement of his journey even though it had ended in recapture, bursting to let his friends know how he had fared and to give them the valuable information he had gathered. I can imagine him scribbling the note on a scrap of paper and smuggling it out of his cell in the cover of a book or hidden in a bundle of dirty laundry.

There is an amusing account of the return of just such a recaptured prisoner in Charles Codman's *Contact*. Codman, a pilot of an American bomber squadron, was captured by the Germans in 1918 and imprisoned at Rastatt, where he notices "the superb prison technique of the British". Describing the return of the escaper he says:

"Against the angles of the prison wall, the British, with an old tennis ball and home-made bats, had improvised a sort of two-dimensional squash game. One brisk autumn afternoon a tournament was in progress. Unseen by the players and the gallery watching them, an arresting group advanced slowly across the courtyard from the entrance building. Two German guards with fixed bayonets. Between them a young British lieutenant. His tattered uniform was deeply stained and encrusted with dirt. The left trouser leg completely torn away. From knee to ankle, ugly scratches and contusions. Above a reddish stubble of beard, a mud-smeared smiling face. Green-grey. Obviously in the last stages of exhaustion. Two weeks previously he had 'gone over the wall' in an attempt to make the Rhine. For fourteen days, we learned later, he had travelled by night, hiding in haystacks by day. For food, beetroots and grass. As he and his escorts approached the tourney, one of the players made a difficult back-hand get.

" 'I say, Bailey, that was jolly well played,' the returned prisoner called in clear tones. At the sound of his voice they all turned. For a moment no one spoke. The other player, a Captain, took a step forward.

" 'Hard lines, Holbrook,' he said, 'but cheer up, there'll be bully-beef stew waiting for you'.

" 'Right-o, sir,' said the prodigal smiling, as the guards led him off in the direction of the punishment cells.

"They watched him in silence until he had disappeared through the archway. Then Bailey turned to the Captain. 'I believe it's your serve, sir,' and play was resumed."

* * * * *

There is magic for me in these tales of personal adventure and individual achievement in the vast impersonal cataclysm of war, a never-failing tonic in the thought of the stubborn struggle of the prisoner, unarmed, ill-equipped and hungry, against the forces of Organization. So far I have collected nearly two hundred escape books, and it is typical of the ingenuity of the escaper that in all this list there is only one repeated title. It is astounding how many variations there are on the theme of captivity and escape. There cannot be many successful escapers of recent years who have not written their story in some form or other, whether it be as a book, a radio script or an article in a regimental magazine. As my collection grew I admired more and more the literary skill of the escapers. Then I realised that the same qualities of ingenuity, originality and above all stubborn perseverance are required in the successful writer as in the successful escaper. One tackles the long arduous task of writing a book in much the same frame of mind as one begins to pick one's way under a thick stone wall or burrow through yards of hard unyielding clay.

When I came to make the selection of escape stories for this book I found that I wanted to include passages from them all; each one in its own way says something worth repeating. In the end I decided that each story must be told in the first person by the escaper himself. I did this to create a "short list", and because I wanted to select that part of each story, not necessarily the climax, which held for me the *moment of truth*.

This term, which I have borrowed from the bull-fight, is used to describe that moment when the combined efforts of the matador, picadors and banderilleros have reduced the bull to such a condition of rage and fatigue that he may be finished by a sword-thrust. So far in the *corrida* it has been possible for the matador, by discreet handling of his cape, and aided by his team, to make his personal danger seem greater than it really is. But this moment admits of no bluffing. Bareheaded, alone with the bull in the centre of the ring, the matador must thrust his sword into exactly the place, the only place, where it will do its work. To do this he must either incite the bull to charge or must himself move forward, so that his arm, passing over the sharp horns, can drive the sword between the shoulderblades. You may not approve of bull-fighting. You may have no sympathy with the man, perhaps no more than a boy for bull-fighters die young, who is of his own choice out there in the ring with the maddened and wounded beast. But in that moment of truth he knows that he is alone, and that his self-respect, his reputation and his life depend on the coolness and skill that he can command in the next few seconds.

Most of us at times of crisis know this moment of truth. It is the moment when one says to oneself, "This is me, this is it." There is a sudden strong acknowledgment of one's own identity. Small details become vividly etched on one's mind, so that while straining every nerve to meet and overcome the danger one is at the same time aware of the fly buzzing against the window, the ticking of the clock on the wall, or the warmth and friendliness of the sun shining on one's hands.

So acute are our senses at this moment, so vivid the impression made on our minds, that for ever afterwards a particular sound or smell will bring back with startling reality the scene and all the emotion that we felt at the time. The mingled smells of sea air, tarred rope and hot engine oil always remind me of waiting apprehensively in the pitch darkness and cramp of a stuffy cubbyhole for the German police to search the ship, while on the other side of a thin wooden bulkhead a young Danish seaman tries to distract the attention of their dog.

Intense fear is usually the background to the moment of truth, and with this fear comes a feeling of elation. This may be caused, my doctor tells me, by the sudden discharge of adrenalin into the bloodstream as our glands respond to the stimulus of fear. It may be caused by the fact that our animal instinct, designed to cope with far more danger than most of us experience in our civilised daily lives, takes control and swamps our inhibitions. Whatever the reason, in this moment every sense is alert yet time seems to have slowed down, and in telling about it afterwards if we do not fog the description with literary decoration, nor state what we think we should feel instead of what we felt, the account is almost bound to be a vivid one. This is how Robert Kee[1] describes being shot down while dropping parachute mines in the North Sea:

"The guns and the searchlights were on to us at once. One of the first shells hit the port engine.

"I was trying to continue the turn so as to get away as soon as possible. For a moment I could not think why the turn seemed peculiar. Then, when I tried to straighten up, nothing happened. It was like trying to walk straight in a fit of giddiness. Before I had completely realised that the port engine was out of action, we had spun. Our height was about eight hundred feet.

"I ceased to notice whether we were still being shot at or not. Out of the past a voice spoke clearly in my brain. 'You must push the stick well forward. It's a Hampden's only chance in a spin.' I pushed the heavy stick forward until it almost touched the instrument panel, pressed the full strength of my leg on to the rudder opposite the spin and waited. There could be no chance at this height. The snow and the frozen sea which had been waiting so patiently below came up to meet us.

"There was no panic. I thought: 'This is death. I am going to die.'

[1] *A Crowd is not Company.* Eyre & Spottiswoode (Publishers) Ltd.

Certainty brought calm. At the same time I felt that I had never lived so
intensely before. Death was the climax, not the end, of life. This feeling
was so strong that the force inside me seemed to overflow my personality. I thought that something from inside me that was not me
would watch me die and would go on.

"Then my ordinary little personality spoke:

" 'If you ever get out of this you'll have a story to tell in the Mess.'

"But it was too late. Already through the perspex glass of the cockpit
I could see the smoothness of the white beach and the powdered
whiskers of the dunes racing towards us.

"Butch's voice came clear and worried over the inter-com.:

" 'What the bloody hell are you doing now?'

"I had no time to answer.

"In a childish gesture of self-defence I pulled back the stick.

"The darkness shattered all round me like a great black plate."

In a different idiom, but with the same exactness, the same careful
honest recollection that conveys to the reader the information necessary
and no more, Corporal B. J. Owen[1] of Popski's Private Army describes a
jeep patrol behind the German lines in Italy:

"... At about four o'clock in the afternoon a civilian came with the
news that the Germans had evacuated Scheggia. I thought this unlikely
and so did the Skipper (Bob Yunnie). 'We'll go in and see, just the one
jeep,' he said. From the second that we sat in that jeep, the Skipper
driving, myself as gunner and Gino sitting between us with a tommy
gun, I knew that we were running into a trap. I was as sure as I have
ever been sure of anything in my life that we were driving into an
ambush. We drove round P.P.A. Corner. ... For the first time no
mortars greeted us. Then suddenly to me everything in the world,
except the jeep we were driving in, stood still. The valley stretched out
in front of us – the winding road along which we were travelling towards the waiting Germans – the jeep and my two companions
comprised the whole of my world. Not a sound anywhere, not a
movement, not even a breath of air.

"I had forgotten my pals – the unit – my people back home. My life
seemed to have started the moment we came round the Corner, and
how long it would last depended on how much I concentrated on my
gun and that white house. Every time it was the house – the house – the
house. My .50 was cocked and aimed at the enemy positions. I sat forward in my seat, my nose almost against the gun. Glancing at the

[1] Quoted in *Private Army*, by Vladimir Peniakoff.   Jonathan Cape.

Skipper, I said to him: 'They are waiting for us, Skipper – they are sitting there waiting for us.' He said, 'I don't think so,' but by his tone I could tell that he knew just as well as I. What a man! I hoped they would miss with their first burst. I could see the haystacks, the cemetery, the white house; nearer and nearer we came. Houses on the left shut out our view. We stopped. Gino said, 'I think it is all right to carry on.' Then he said something about having nothing to worry about as there was a cemetery ready down there. We carried on – slowly – slowly. A high bank on the right hid the haystacks – the cemetery disappeared below a rise in front of us. The Skipper said, 'We'll stop here.' We were hidden from the haystacks and the cemetery but the white house – now with its gable end towards us – was on our left, a little more than a hundred yards away. There was one window facing us – an upstairs window, open.

"I stepped out of the jeep, swinging the .50 towards the house. My right foot had hardly touched the ground when the awful stillness was shattered by the rattle of a spandau. Something seemed to pluck at my hair and bury itself in the bank behind me. I ducked instinctively, at the same time pressing the trigger of my gun. Now I was all for it, I had come back to earth. I absolutely splattered the house with bullets, not forgetting the bushes around it, while the Skipper started reversing the jeep. I walked sideways along with it, still firing, with Gino spraying the vicinity with his tommy gun. Something began to smoke at the house as the Skipper shouted: 'Jump in, Ben.' I jumped into the jeep – still firing the gun with one hand. As Bob backed I held on to the seat with my left hand and fired the gun at right angles to the jeep with my right.

"Bob turned the jeep right hand down into a gateway, which brought the house immediately in front of me. I aimed the gun quickly and pressed the trigger – flashes of light shot off the walls. . . . Another gun opened at us from the red roofs of the cemetery as we began to move forward. I just had time to give him a burst from the .30 before we were hidden by the houses on the roadside. 'Get that .30 going, Ben,' the Skipper shouted. I didn't say anything but waited until the house, haystacks and cemetery came into view again. They did, with a bang, as mortars fell in front of us. . . . I dimly heard the crashes of the mortar shells as they exploded all around us, but was too busy to look where they were falling. We roared up the road and round P.P.A. Corner. . . . We breathed again as we pulled up in Villa Colle di Canale. . . . The rest of the patrol were there. . . . Then we went in search of the man who had informed us that the Germans had evacuated Scheggia,

but, as we had expected, he could not be found. Another Fascist who
had almost caused our downfall. . . . It wasn't till I sat talking to Popski
and Lieutenant Reeve-Walker that I realised how near a thing our latest
escape had been."

I think all the stories in this book were written by men who were afraid.
There are of course men who have never been afraid but this very fact
would prevent them from knowing the moment of truth, which can be
experienced only in the imagination.

      *   *   *   *   *

Sudden action after inactivity, sudden change of scene after close confinement, combine with fear to make every minute of the escaped
prisoner's journey especially memorable and worth recording. He knows
that he is gambling not only for his life but for his freedom too. The
bomber crew or the soldier in action may well say, "Christ, if my love
were in my arms and I in my bed again!" For the escaper to be in *his* bed
again would be defeat; he would be back in the prison camp. So with his
fear goes an intensified exultation because he is not yet caught.

Escaping can at times he desperately funny, but the laughter – a nervous
giggle rather than a loud guffaw – acts in the escaper more often than not
as a safety valve for strained nerves. It requires a highly developed sense of
the ridiculous to find humour, as Robert Kee did, in lying head to foot
with fifty other men in a slimy damp tunnel dug from the side of an open-
trench latrine, fifteen feet below the surface of the ground, suffocating
from lack of air and with the expectation of a bullet in the back as he
crawled from the open end. Yet laughter is the prisoner's best defence,
sometimes his only defence, against his guards. He must cultivate his sense
of humour or go under. Conditions in the Japanese camps were far worse
than in even the most notorious concentration camp in Germany and yet,
in *The Naked Island*, Russell Braddon is able to record the following
scene:

"River Valley was only a brief interlude in our prisoner life: it was
not, however, a dull one. The I.J.A. demanded 'volunteers' to broadcast their propaganda to the Allies. Unanimously we refused. They
threatened: we still refused. They cajoled, offering us the dubious
privilege of a monthly visit to their Army-issue geisha girls (rather
battered-looking pre-war models): we refused. The matter was then
dropped.

"In an effort to soften us up, though, the Guard Commander came into our hut one night and announced: 'Rockhampton, boom, boom, boom.' This meant that Japan had bombed Rockhampton.

" 'Go on, eh, Nippon?' he was queried as a knot of men gathered round, 'Rockhampton, eh?'

" 'Hei,' agreed the Guard Commander.

" 'And Sydney?' asked someone else. 'Sydney, boom, boom, boom?'

" 'Hei, Sydney, boom, boom, boom,' agreed the Nip.

" 'Melbourne?'

" 'Hei,' said the Nip, 'Melbourne, boom, boom, boom.'

" 'Wagga?'

" 'Hei,' confirmed the Nip. 'Wagga, boom, boom, boom.'

" 'Garbo?'

" 'Hei,' he stated. 'Garbo, boom, boom, boom.' It was obvious that there was no place and no person Nippon had not bombed.

" 'Tokyo?' Harry asked, his smile wicked.

" 'Tokyo hei,' said the guard, 'boom, boom, . . .' and then realised how he had been caught.

" 'Tokyo NEI,' he denied. 'Boom, boom, boom NEI Tokyo,' and swept out in high dudgeon."

This time it ended there, but it was more likely to have ended in a "bashing" or even in decapitation for the mocking Australians. The white prisoner did not often bait the Japanese guard with impunity. This scene, to my mind, is typical of the courage and humour which illuminate so much of Russell Braddon's book.

The Japanese P.O.W. camps were in fact practically escape-proof. That cooperation among the prisoners which did so much to foster escape in the European camps prohibited this adventure in the Far East. Not only was the recaptured prisoner beheaded, but all the remaining men in his working-party were also executed. This knowledge proved a greater barrier than all the searchlights and machine-guns in the world. The only exception that I know of was an R.A.F. air-gunner, Sergeant Charles McCormac, whose story is told by Paul Brickhill in *Escape – Or Die*. McCormac escaped from the Pasir Panjang cage, and he took the whole of his working-party with him.

*   *   *   *   *

There are other ways of escape from captivity, ways that sometimes call for more resourcefulness than is needed to solve the merely material problem of getting out; I mean the escape into the imagination – or into the arts, or social service within the camp (many a prisoner found self-expression in becoming Camp Shower Officer, or in serving on the Entertainments Committee).

E. E. Cummings in *The Enormous Room*, Theodore Kroeger in *The Forgotten Village* and Odd Nansen in *Day After Day* all found diversion in their fellow-prisoners and in recalling it give to us something of the warmth and wonder that they discovered. Christopher Burney, one of our agents who was caught by the Gestapo and imprisoned in the notorious Fresnes gaol in Paris, tells in *Solitary Confinement* of eighteen months alone in a cell without the possibility of physical escape, and of how by delving down into his own personality he not only made life bearable but turned his imprisonment into a valuable experience.

*   *   *   *   *

When I began to write this introduction I intended to say something more of the mechanics of escape and to describe some of the ruses of the prisoners and the precautions of their guards. But you will find all this in the stories which follow, told by the escapers themselves. They are a gallant and cheerful crowd, and I am sure that you will enjoy their company as much as I have done, both during the time of my captivity and between the pages of their books.

CHAPTER TWO

THE PROBLEM facing the escaper in the early days was mainly how to pass the immense stone walls and strong iron bars of his prison. Once outside, he could count himself a free man.

Either this early prisoner was fettered hand and foot in a dark dungeon, from which escape was almost impossible; or he was allowed considerable latitude, having his meals sent in from outside and surrounding himself with many of his own possessions. It was under the latter conditions that Sir Walter Raleigh was able to write his *History of the World*.

Another seventeenth-century scholar who did much of his work in captivity was Grotius, the Dutch author of *De Jure Belli*, that early attempt to establish the laws of war and the precursor of the Geneva Convention which has meant so much to military prisoners. Perhaps Grotius would have been content to remain in prison for life; he had his books and the time to pursue his studies, and his wife was with him in captivity. But that resourceful woman would have him free, and arranged for him to be carried out of prison in the wooden chest in which the books he no longer required were sent away.

A hundred years later Lady Nithsdale, another gallant wife, rescued her husband from the Tower of London. Having done everything in her power to effect his release by petition, she decided to rescue him on the eve of his execution. She visited him in the Tower, accompanied by two other women, one of whom carried a change of clothing under her cloak. Shortly afterwards Lady Nithsdale's two accomplices left separately, one of them disguised in the clothing that had been smuggled in. Later, Lady Nithsdale herself left, ushering out her husband dressed in the disguised visitor's cloak and weeping bitterly into her handkerchief. To keep the guards out of the now empty room, Lady Nithsdale told them that she was returning immediately and was only taking the visitor, who had been overcome with grief, a short way on her journey. All this time the prisoner kept his handkerchief before his eyes and over the beard which he had not had time to shave. When she had seen her husband off the premises Lady Nithsdale bravely returned to his room and engaged in simulated conversation with him, mimicking his manly voice and replying in her own, until she was certain that he was clear of the environs of the Tower. Then, bidding him a fond farewell from the door, she told the guards that he would spend the next few hours in prayer and would need no candles.

*   *   *   *   *

John Gerard, who made an earlier escape from the same prison, was one of the many young Catholics who, in the reign of Elizabeth I, were trained in France as Jesuit priests and smuggled back to England to preach the faith and convert the Protestant. He landed on the coast of East Anglia in November 1588, and evaded capture many times before he was caught six years later. After spending some time in the Clink near Blackfriars Bridge he was imprisoned in the Tower of London. Although he was not a prisoner of war he was regarded as an enemy of the State and not as a common criminal; and like so many of the escapers in this book he used his freedom to go on fighting.

The story of John Gerard will be strangely familiar to this generation, more familiar probably than it would have been at any time during the three hundred and fifty years since it was enacted. There is nothing unusual to us in the idea of the patriot, the saboteur, being landed secretly at night on the shores of his own country to work against the enemy in occupation. John Gerard's work was the sabotage of ideas rather than of power plants and military equipment, but he ran the same risks, faced very much the same tortures, as the men and women who were dropped by parachute or landed in folding canoes from submarines during the recent war. Even Topcliffe, Gerard's torturer, is familiar, and so are the interrogation and the prisoner's fear that he will incriminate those who have assisted him. John Gerard survived his ordeal without betraying his helpers and was placed in solitary confinement awaiting trial. His first move was to communicate with his friends outside, and to this end he bribed the warder to bring him oranges and, later, a quill "to use as a toothpick". Comparing the merits of orange and lemon juice as invisible ink, he says, ". . . and lemon juice has this property, that it comes out just as well with water or heat. If the paper is taken out and dried, the writing disappears but it can be read a second time when it is moistened or heated again. But orange juice is different. It cannot be read with water—water, in fact, washes away the writing and nothing can recover it. Heat brings it out, but it stays out, so a letter in orange juice cannot be delivered without the recipient knowing whether or not it has been read."

John Gerard

I TRIED my best to reconcile myself to God's will, and accept all the restrictions imposed on me.

It was the last day of July and the feast of our blessed Father. I was making my meditation and was longing to have the opportunity of saying Mass again, when the thought suddenly came to me – I might be able to do it in the cell of a Catholic gentleman in the tower opposite me. There was only a garden between his cell and mine.

He had been in prison there for ten years and lay under sentence of death, but the sentence had not yet been carried out. Every day he used to go up on to the lead roof above his cell where he was allowed to walk up and down for exercise. From there he used to greet me and wait on his knees for my blessing.

When I turned the idea over in my mind later, I thought it might be done, if only the warder could be persuaded to let me go over. The gentleman's wife was allowed to visit him on fixed days and bring him clean linen and other things he needed. She carried them in a basket, and as she had now been doing this for years the warders had got out of the way of examining its contents. With her help I hoped we might be able little by little to bring in everything we needed for Mass. My friends, of course, would supply them.

I decided to try. So I signed to the gentleman to watch the gestures I was going to make – I dared not call to him because it was a good distance across and I might easily be overheard. He watched me as I took a pen and paper and pretended to write; next, I placed the letter over the coal fire and held it up in my hands as though I were reading it; then I wrapped up one of my crosses in it, and went through the motions of despatching it to him. He seemed to follow what I was trying to indicate.

The next step was to get the warder to take one of my crosses or rosaries to my good fellow-prisoner – the same man had charge of us both. At first he refused, saying that he could not risk it as he had no proof that the other man could be trusted to keep the secret.

"If the man said something to his wife and it became known, it would be all up with me," he said.

But I put heart into him and told him that this was most improbable. Then I placed some money in his hand as I always did, and he agreed. My letter was taken and delivered, but the gentleman wrote nothing back as I had asked him to do. The next day, when he came out for his walk on the roof, he thanked me by signs, holding up in his hands the cross I had sent him.

When at the end of three days he had not replied I began to suspect the reason for it. So I went through the whole series of signs again with greater precision, showing him how I squeezed the juice out of an orange and dipped my pen into the juice; and then, to bring out the writing, held the paper to the fire. This time he understood and held my next letter to the fire and read it. In his reply he said that the first time he thought I wanted him to burn the paper, because I had scribbled a few words in pencil on it, and he had done this.

He answered my query, saying he thought the scheme was practicable, provided the warder allowed me to visit him in the evening and stay over the whole of the following day; his wife would bring all the Mass requisites that were given her.

The next step was to sound the warder – would he allow me over to see my fellow-prisoner just once? I said I wanted to dine with him and promised to let him share the feast. He refused absolutely: he was frightened lest I might be seen walking across the garden or lest the Lieutenant should choose that very day to pay me a visit. But I pointed out that this had never happened and was most unlikely to happen and, to end the argument, I produced the golden reason – I promised to pay him cash for his kind offices. He agreed.

I fixed the day for the feast of the Nativity of Our Blessed Lady.[1] In the meantime I arranged for the prisoner's wife to go to a certain place in the city. There she would meet John Lillie, who, following the instructions in my letter, would hand her the things needed for Mass. I had also told Lillie to bring a number of small hosts and a pyx as I wanted to reserve the Blessed Sacrament.

Lillie collected everything and the woman brought them in.

When the evening arrived, I went across with my warder and stayed with the gentleman all that night and the following day. According to the promise we had made with the warder, not a word was said to the gentleman's wife.

That morning I said Mass. I felt very great consolation and I gave Communion to the noble confessor of Christ, who had been so many years without this comfort. I also consecrated twenty-two hosts and placed them in a pyx with a corporal and brought them back with me to my own cell, and renewed the divine banquet for many days afterwards with fresh relish and delight.

When I went across that evening I had no thought of escape – I had only looked to the Lord Jesus, prefigured as our Redeemer in the ashbaked loaf of Elias, to give me the strength and courage I still needed to

[1] 8th September 1597.

journey the rest of my hard way to the mountain of the Lord. But while we were passing the time of day together, it struck me how close this tower was to the moat encircling the outer fortifications, and I thought it might be possible for a man to lower himself with a rope from the roof of the tower on to the wall beyond the moat. I asked the gentleman what he thought about it.

"Yes, it could be done easily," he said, "if we only had some really good friends who were ready to run the risk of helping us."

"We have the friends all right," I said, "if only the thing is practicable and really worth trying."

"As far as I am concerned," he said, "I am all for attempting it. I would be much happier if I could live in hiding with my friends, and with the consolation of the sacraments and with pleasant companions, instead of passing my days like a solitary between these four walls."

"Good," I said. "Now, we'll pray about it, and meanwhile I'll put the matter to my Superior and do whatever he thinks best."

For the rest of the time we were together we discussed the details of the plan we would follow, if we decided on the attempt.

When I got back to my cell that night I wrote to my Superior through John Lillie and laid all the details of the scheme before him. Father Garnet replied that I certainly ought to attempt it, but I was not to risk my neck in the descent.

I then wrote to my former host and told him that we were going to attempt an escape, and warned him to mention it to as few people as possible. If the plan got out, it would be all over. Then I asked John Lillie and Richard Fulwood (he was attending Father Garnet at the time) whether they were prepared to take the risk, and, if they were, to come on a certain night to the far side of the moat, opposite the squat tower I had described, near the point where Master Page had been seized. They were to bring a rope with them and tie it to a stake; we would be on the roof of the tower and throw them an iron ball attached to a stout thread, the kind used in stitching up bales. They must listen in the darkness for the sound of the ball touching the ground, find the cord and tie it to the free end of the rope. This done, we would draw up the rope by pulling the other end of the cord which we held in our hands. I told them to pin a piece of white paper or a handkerchief on the front of their jackets, for we wanted to be sure of their identity before throwing the cord. Also, they were to bring a rowing boat so that we could make a quick get-away.

When everything was arranged and the night fixed, my former host, who was afraid of the risk I was taking, was anxious that I should first see whether the warder could be bribed into letting me walk out of the prison, as I could easily do in borrowed clothes. Therefore, in the name of a friend of mine, John Lillie offered the warder a thousand florins down and a yearly allowance of a hundred florins for life. The warder would not hear of it. If he allowed it, he said, it would mean that he would be an outlaw for the rest of his life, and he would be hanged if he were caught. So the matter was dropped and we went ahead with our first plan.

I begged the earnest prayers of all who were let into the secret. One gentleman, the heir to a large estate, bound himself by vow to fast one day in the week for life, if I got away safe.

The night came. I begged and bribed my warder to let me visit my fellow-prisoner. I walked across. The warder locked the pair of us in the cell, barred the door as he always did, and went off. But he had also bolted the inside door which gave on to the stairs leading up to the roof, and we had to cut away with a knife the stone holding the socket of the bolt. There was no other way out.

At last we climbed silently up the stairs without a light, for a guard was posted every night in a garden at the foot of the wall, and when we spoke, it was in a faint whisper.

At midnight we saw the boat with our friends approaching. John Lillie and Richard Fulwood were at the oars and a third man sat at the tiller. He was my old warder in the Clink and he had obtained the boat for us. As they pulled in and got ready to land, a man came out from one of the poor dwelling-places on the bank to do something. When he saw the boat draw up, he started talking to the men, thinking they were fishermen.

He went back to bed. But the rescue party were afraid to land until the man had been given time to get to sleep again. So they paddled up and down. Time passed. It became too late to attempt anything that night.

They rowed back towards the bridge, but by now the tide had turned and was flowing strongly. It forced their little boat against the piles driven into the bed of the river to break the force of the water. It stuck, and it was impossible to move it forward or back. Meanwhile the water was rising and was striking the boat with such force that with every wave it looked as if it would capsize and the occupants be thrown into the river. They could only pray to God and shout for help.

We were on the top of the tower and heard their shouts. Men came out on to the bank, and we were able to watch them in the light thrown by their candles. They rushed to their boats and pulled off to the rescue. Several boats came quite near, but they were afraid to pull alongside – the current was too strong. Forming a semi-circle round them, they stayed like spectators watching the poor men in their peril without daring to assist.

Amid all the shouting I recognized Richard Fulwood's voice.

"I know it," I said. "It's our friends in danger."

My companion would not believe that I could pick out anyone's voice at such a distance, but I recognized it only too well, and I was miserable at the thought that such devoted men were in danger of their lives for my sake.

We prayed fervently for them. Though we had watched many people go out to help them, they were not saved yet. Then we saw a light lowered from the top of the bridge, and a kind of basket at the end of a rope. If only they could get into it, they could be pulled up. However, God had regard to the peril of His servants, and at last a powerful sea-going craft came along with six sailors aboard and hazardously drawing up to the craft in danger, pulled on deck Lillie and Fulwood. Then immediately the small boat capsized before the third man could be rescued – as though it had only been kept afloat for the sake of the Catholics it carried. However, by the mercy of God, the man who was washed over into the river was able to grasp the rope let down from the bridge; and he was hauled to safety.

So all were rescued and got back to their homes.

The next day John Lillie sent me a letter as usual through the warder. I might reasonably have expected him to say something like this: "Now we know – and our peril last night has taught us – God does not want us to go ahead with the escape." But quite the contrary. The letter began:

"It was not God's design that we should succeed last night, but He mercifully snatched us from our peril – He has only postponed the day. With God's help we will be back to-night."

Determination like this and the man's devout sentiments, reassured my companion. He felt certain we would succeed. But I had great difficulty in getting leave of the warder to stay a second night out of my cell, and we were very much afraid he might notice the loosened stone when he came to bolt the door in the evening. However, he did not see it.

Meantime I had written three letters which I intended to leave behind in the cell. The first was to my warder, justifying myself for contriving my escape without letting him know. I said I was merely exercising my rights – I had committed no crime and was wrongfully held in prison. I told him I would always remember him in my prayers, if there was no other way I could help him. The purpose of this letter was to put him less at fault, in case he was imprisoned for our escape.

The second was to the Lieutenant. In this letter I made further excuses for the warder, protesting before God that he was not privy to my escape and would never have allowed it if he had known. And to prove this, I mentioned the attractive offer we had made, which he had refused. As for my going across to another cell, I had extorted his permission only with the most persistent entreaties and it would be wrong to put him to death for this.

The third letter was to the Lords of the Council. In the first place I stated my motives for regaining the freedom that was mine by right. I did it not from love of freedom for its own sake, but from love of souls – souls who were being daily lost in England. I wanted to get out and reclaim them from sin and heresy. Concerning the affairs of state they knew my clear record and could count on my not soiling it in the future. Finally, I protested and proved that neither the Lieutenant nor the warder could be charged with connivance or consent. They had known nothing about it: my escape was entirely due to my own exertions and my friends.

I left these letters to be picked up by the warder. One last letter I wrote and took with me. It was delivered to the warder (as you shall hear) next morning – but not by John Lillie.

At the right time we went up on to the tower. The boat came along. No one interfered and it pulled in safely to the bank. The schismatic stayed in the boat, the two Catholics got out with the rope. It was a new one, as they had thrown the old into the river when they ran into trouble the previous night. Following my instructions they fastened it to a stake, and then listened for the sound of the iron ball we threw down to them. It was found without difficulty and the cord fastened to the end of the rope. But it proved very difficult indeed to pull up – it was a good deal thicker and doubled. This was Father Garnet's instruction, to guard against the rope snapping under the weight of my body. But actually he had increased the hazards.

Now a fresh difficulty arose which we had not foreseen. The distance between the tower at one end and the stake at the other was very great and the rope, instead of sloping down, stretched almost horizontally between the two points. We had therefore to descend by working our way along the rope – it was impossible to slide down with our own weight, and this we discovered by making up a bundle of books and other things which we wrapped in my cloak and placed on the double rope to see whether it would go down of its own accord. It didn't. Fortunately, it stuck before it got out of our reach, for if it had gone beyond recovery we would never have got down ourselves. We hauled the bundle back and left it behind.

My companion now changed his mind: he had always said it would be the simplest thing in the world to slide down. Now he saw the hazards of it.

"But I shall certainly be hanged if I remain here," he said. "If we throw the rope back now it will fall into the moat and the splash will betray us

and our friends as well. I'll go down and God help me. I'd rather take a
chance of escape than stay locked up here with no chance at all."

So he said a prayer and took hold of the rope. He got down fairly easily
for he had plenty of strength and the rope was still taut. But his descent
slackened the rope and made it much more difficult for me. I only noticed
this when I started to descend.

I commended myself to God and Our Lord Jesus, to the Blessed Virgin,
my guardian angel and especially to Father Southwell, who was imprisoned near here until he was taken out to martyrdom; and to Father
Walpole and to all our martyrs. Then I gripped the rope with my right
hand, and took it in my left. To prevent myself falling I twisted my legs
round the rope leaving it free to slide between my shins.

I had gone three or four yards face downwards when suddenly my body
swung round with its own weight and I nearly fell. I was still very weak,
and with the slack rope and my body hanging underneath I could make
practically no progress. At last I managed to work myself as far as the
middle of the rope, and there I stuck. My strength was failing and my
breath, which was short before I started, seemed altogether spent.

At last, with the help of the saints and, I think, by the power of my
friends' prayers below drawing me, I moved along a little way and then I
stuck again. Now I thought I would never be able to get down. But I was
determined not to fall into the moat as long as I was still able to hold the
rope. I tried to recover a little strength and then, using my legs and arms
as well as I could, I managed, thank God, to get as far as the wall on the far
side of the moat. But my feet just touched the top of the wall and the rest
of my body hung horizontally behind, with my head no higher than my
legs – the rope had become so slack. I don't know how I would have got
over the wall, if it had not been for John Lillie. Somehow or other (he
could never say how he did it), he got up on to the wall, seized hold of my
feet, pulled me over and put me safely down on the ground. I could not
stand upright, I was so weak. So they gave me cordial waters and restora-
tives which they had taken care to bring with them, and I was able to
reach the boat. Before getting in they untied the rope from the stake, cut
off part of it and let the rest hang down against the wall of the tower. Our
first plan had been to pull it away altogether and we had accordingly
passed it round a big gun on the roof without knotting it. But providentially we could not tug it loose; had we done so it would almost
certainly have dropped into the moat with a big splash and we would
have been in trouble.

We stepped into the boat and thanked God "who had snatched us from
the hands of our persecutors and from all the expectation of the Protestant

people". We also thanked the men who had done so much and undergone such risks for us.

We rowed a good distance before we brought the boat to land. Then I sent my fellow-prisoner with John Lillie to my house, where Mistress Line, that saintly widow, was in charge, while I took Richard Fulwood and went with him to Father Garnet's house. It was on the outskirts of the city, and horses were there ready for us. "Little John," Father Garnet's servant, was holding them, and before dawn broke "Little John" and I were in the saddle.

Father Garnet was in the country at the time. We rode straight to his place and had dinner with him. The rejoicing was great. We all thanked God that I had escaped from the hands of my enemies in the name of the Lord.

Meanwhile I had sent Richard Fulwood to a place we had decided on beforehand, where he was to hold a horse and be ready to fly with my warder if the man was prepared to make off at once. As I said, I had written a letter to be delivered to the warder when he came for his usual morning meeting with John Lillie. But it was not Lillie who came that morning. I had ordered him not to stir out of doors until the storm that was to be expected had blown over. In his place I chose another messenger whom the warder knew. He was surprised, of course, to find another man, but he said nothing. Just as he was turning back, as he thought, to deliver the letter in his usual way, the messenger seized hold of him.

"The letter is for you; no, not for anyone else," he said.

"For me? Who sent it?"

"A friend," replied the other man, "but I don't know who he is."

The warder was dumbfounded.

"But I can't read. If it is urgent, please read it for me."

The man read the letter he had brought. In it I informed the warder that I had escaped from prison, and, in order to put his mind at rest, briefly explained why I had done so. Then I pointed out that, though I had no obligation in the matter – I had merely made use of my rights – yet I would see to his safety. He had always been faithful in his trusts, and I would stand by him now. If he wanted to save his skin I had a man ready with a horse to take him to a safe place a good distance out of London. I would give him two hundred florins a year and he could lead a decent life. But I added this condition. If he accepted the offer he must settle his affairs in the Tower quickly and go off at once to the place to which the messenger would lead him. He was on his way back to the Tower to settle his business and see his wife safely away, when a fellow-warder ran into him.

"Off with you, as fast as you can make it," he said. "Your prisoners have escaped from the small tower. The Lieutenant is searching the place for you. If he catches you, God help you."

Shaking all over the man rushed back to the messenger. He begged him for the love of God to take him to the place where the horses were waiting. The messenger took him and found Richard Fulwood waiting with two horses.

He rode off and Richard took him to the house of one of my friends about a hundred miles from London. Already I had sent a letter asking this gentleman whether he would be so kind as to put the warder up and look after him, should he come. But I warned him not to confide in him or let him know that he knew me. Richard Fulwood, I said, would reimburse him for all his expenses. If the warder wanted to talk about me or about his own affairs, he should refuse to listen.

All went off as I had planned. My friend was not troubled, and the warder was safely away in his house. After a year he moved into another county. There he became a Catholic and lived comfortably with his family on the annuity which I sent him regularly according to my promise. And there too he died after four or five years. By this flight for dear life God had snatched him from the temptation of sin, and, I trust, given him a place in heaven. While in prison I had probed him frequently on his faith – his mind was made up, but I could not work on his will. My escape from prison was, I hope, in God's kind disposing, the occasion of his escaping from hell.

When the Lieutenant discovered that his prisoners and their warder had made off, he went to the Council, taking with him the letters I had left behind. The Lords of Council were amazed at the way I had escaped. One of them, a leading Councillor, said to a gentleman in attendance (as I was told afterwards) that he was glad I had got away. The Lieutenant asked for authorization to search the whole of London and any place suspected but the others told him it would be no use.

"You can't hope to find him," they said. "If he has friends who are prepared to do all this for him, you can count on it, they will have no difficulty in finding him horses and a hiding-place and keeping him well out of your reach."

A search was made in one or two places. As far as I could discover nobody of note was taken.

The Inquisition, 1756

CHAPTER THREE

GIOVANNI GIOCOMO CASANOVA de Seingault was, in a sense, a political prisoner like John Gerard. He too was destined for the church, but he found the call of the great world irresistible and preferred to live by his wits. This he did with varying success until the age of thirty, when he was arrested by the Tribunal of the Inquisition and imprisoned in the attics beneath the lead roof of the Ducal Palace in Venice. He was charged with profligacy and the practice of black magic.

Casanova's description of his solitary confinement is moving and exact, from his early frenzy and pounding on the door, through a period of dull acquiescence, to an increasing determination to escape.

His first attempt, by means of a hole in the floor under his bed, was interrupted at frequent intervals when he was made to share his cell with other prisoners; but in those periods when he was alone he managed to dig through the double wooden floor until he reached a sub-floor made of hard terrazzo. This he tried to soften with vinegar and at length succeeded in piercing. The hole he had made opened into the room below, and all he now required was a rope made of bed sheets with which to lower himself to freedom. Unfortunately for Casanova he was at this moment moved to a larger, lighter cell. He protested vehemently that he had grown fond of his present one, but the gaoler, Lorenzo, merely laughed and told him not to be foolish as the new cell was much more pleasant; and Casanova was forced to move. The iron bar with which he had made the hole went with him hidden in the stuffing of a chair. "I should much have liked," he says, "to have been able to take the hole".

Once in his new quarters and through the offices of the venal Lorenzo, Casanova was able to make contact with a monk named Balbi who, together with a lawyer, Count Asquino, was imprisoned in a nearby cell. They communicated by writing on the flyleaves of books which they sent to one another through the gaoler. Casanova did not, like John Gerard, write with orange juice, but used the juice of mulberries and wrote with his fingernail cut to form a pen.

By means of this correspondence Casanova persuaded Balbi to break through the ceiling of his own cell, crawl across the roof space and make a hole in the ceiling of Casanova's cell. This he was unable to do for himself as, following the discovery of the hole in the floor, his new cell was searched daily. He sent the monk the iron bar hidden under a dish of macaroni and promised that once they were together he would lead him and Count Asquino safely out of the building.

Balbi agreed, but before the plan could be carried out another prisoner, a half-witted informer named Soradaci, was put in to share Casanova's cell. Feeling that the newcomer could not be trusted with the full plan, but determined to carry on with the escape, Casanova talked him into a state of religious terror, swore him to secrecy and told him that an angel of heaven would descend through the roof and set them free.

Although he had reduced Soradaci to a condition bordering on hysteria, Casanova was still frightened of his wagging tongue and made him swear to feign sleep whenever the gaoler Lorenzo entered the cell. He then wrote to the monk Balbi telling him of the addition to the escape party and giving him the exact time at which to break through the ceiling.

All this, with the escape which follows, is told by Casanova in his *Memoirs*. Much has been done since to discredit these memoirs, and the escape from the Leads has come under special scrutiny. Measurements have been taken and Casanova's heights and distances proved much exaggerated. But this does not to my mind prove that the whole account is false. A man may be forgiven some exaggeration when he is scrambling over a slippery roof at night. It may very well have seemed to him that he lowered his companion fifty feet when it was in fact a mere nineteen.

Casanova

ON THE next day the monk wrote that the communication was complete, and there was no more for him to do but to get out on the top of my cell and break through the lowest surface, which could be done in five minutes.

Soradaci was faithful to his word, making believe to be asleep; Lorenzo did not even speak to him. I never took my eyes off him, and I believe I should have killed him if he had made the smallest attempt to look at Lorenzo; for a mere treacherous wink would have been enough to betray me.

The rest of the day was devoted to lofty discourse and exaggerated phrases, which I pronounced with all the gravity I could command; and I had the pleasure of seeing his fanatical excitement grow greater and greater. I took care to enhance the effect of my mystical preaching by a copious exhibition of wine, of which I gave him large draughts from time to time;

and I never left him in peace till I saw him dropping with drunkenness and torpor.

Although he had no notion of metaphysical speculation, and had never exercised his wits for any purpose but to devise some spy's tricks, the brute embarrassed me for an instant by saying that he could not imagine how an angel could need make so much work of opening our prison.

But I, raising my eyes to heaven – or rather to the ceiling of my dismal cell – replied:

"The ways of God are inscrutable to mortals; besides, the messenger of Heaven does not work as an angel, for then a mere breath would suffice; he labours as a man, having no doubt taken the form of a man, since we are unworthy to endure the glorious presence of a celestial being. But indeed," I added, like a true Jesuit, able to take advantage of every trifle, "I foresee that to punish you for your evil thought, which is an offence to the blessed Virgin, the angel will not come to-day. Wretched man! your thoughts are not those of an honest, pious soul, but of a vile sinner who is always dealing with Messer Grande and his servants."

I had hoped to make him miserable, and I had succeeded. He began to cry violently, and was choked with sobs when the clock had struck nineteen and he did not hear the angel. Far from soothing him, I tried to add to his despair by my own bitter lamentations. Next morning he was still obedient, for Lorenzo having inquired after his health, he replied without looking round. He behaved equally well next day, and at length I saw Lorenzo for the last time on the morning of the 31st of October. I gave him a book for Balbi, and desired the monk to come at about noon to pierce the ceiling. This time I feared no disaster, having learnt from Lorenzo that the Secretary and Inquisitors had already gone into the country. I had no reason to fear the advent of a new messmate, and I need no longer try to hoodwink my rascally companion.

When Lorenzo had left us I told Soradaci that the angel would come to make the opening in the ceiling of our cell at about eleven o'clock.

"He will bring a pair of scissors," said I, "and you must trim my beard and his."

"An angel with a beard!"

"Yes. You will see. When that is done, we will get out and force our way through the roof of the palace; then we will get down into the Piazza of St. Mark, and from thence make our way to Germany."

He made no reply. He ate by himself, for my heart and mind were too full to allow of my eating. I had not even slept.

The hour strikes. Hark! the angel!

Soradaci was about to fall on his face, but I assured him that this was superfluous. In three minutes the hole was pierced through; the board fell at my feet, and Father Balbi slid into my arms.

"Your task is done," said I, "and now mine begins."

We embraced, and he gave me my crowbar and a pair of scissors. I desired Soradaci to trim our beards, but I could not help laughing as I saw the creature, open-mouthed, staring at this strange angel, who looked more like a demon. Though utterly bewildered, he cut our beards to perfection.

Being impatient to survey the locality, I desired the monk to remain with Soradaci, for I would not leave him alone, and I went out. I found the hole rather narrow; however, I got through. I got above the cell in which the Count lay; I went down and cordially embraced the venerable gentleman. I saw a man of a figure ill-suited to surmount the difficulties of such an escape over a steep roof covered with sheet lead. He asked me what my plan was, and told me that he thought I had been rather heedless in my action.

"I only want to go on," said I, "step by step to liberty or death."

"If you imagine," said he, "that you can pierce the roof and find a way along the leads – from which, too, you must get down – I do not see how you can possibly succeed unless you have wings. I have not courage enough to accompany you. I shall stay where I am and pray to God for you."

I left him, to inspect the outer roof, getting as close as I could to the outer side of the loft. Having succeeded in touching the inside of the rafters at the part where it was lowest, I perched myself on a beam, such are to be found under the roof of every large palace. I poked at the rafters with the end of my bar, and, to my joy, found them half-rotten; at each touch the wood fell in dust. Being sure, therefore, that I could make a large enough opening in less than an hour, I returned to my cell, and spent the next four hours in cutting up sheets, counterpanes, and mattress-covers, to make ropes of. I took care to tie all the knots myself, to be sure of their firmness, for a single knot badly tied would have cost us our life. When all was done I found we had about a hundred yards of rope. There are certain things in every great enterprise which are of the highest importance, and for which a leader worthy of the name trusts no one.

* * * * *

When the rope was finished, I made a bundle of my coat, my silk cloak, some shirts, stockings, and handkerchiefs, and we all three went into the Count's cell. This worthy man first congratulated Soradaci on having been so lucky as to be put in the same room with me, and being so soon enabled to recover his freedom. The man's stupid amazement almost made me laugh. I no longer attempted any concealment, for I had thrown off the mask of Tartuffe, which I had found most inconvenient while this villain had compelled me to wear it. I saw that he was convinced I had deceived him, but he could not understand how; for he could not imagine how I had communicated with the sham angel so as to make him come and go at fixed hours. He was listening eagerly to the Count, who declared we were rushing on our fate; and, coward that he was, he was revolving in his mind a scheme for avoiding the perilous attempt. I told the monk to collect his things while I went to make the hole in the roof of the loft.

At two hours after sunset the hole was finished; I had worked the rafters to powder, and the opening was twice as large as was needful. I could touch the sheet of lead outside. I could not raise it single-handed because it was riveted; the friar helped me, and by pushing the crowbar between the gutter and the sheet of lead I detached it, then, raising it on our shoulders, we bent it up high enough to allow of our squeezing through the opening. Putting my head out to reconnoitre, I saw with dismay how bright the moon was, now in the first quarter. It was a check which we must endure with patience, and wait till midnight to escape, when the moon would have gone to light up the Antipodes. On such a glorious night all Venice would be out on the Piazza below, and we dared not venture out on the roof; our shadows cast on the ground would have attracted attention; our extraordinary appearance up there would excite general curiosity, and above all, that of Messer Grande and his spies, the sole guards of Venice. Our fine scheme would soon have been disturbed by their odious interference. I therefore decided positively that we were not to creep out till the moon had set. I invoked the aid of God, and I asked for no miracle. Exposed as we were to the caprice of Fortune, I was bound to give her as few chances as possible, and if my enterprise was to fail, at any rate I would not have to reproach myself with having made a false move. The moon would go down by about five o'clock,[1] and the sun would not rise till half-past thirteen; we should have seven hours of total darkness in which to act, and though we had a hard struggle before us, in seven hours we ought to get through it.

I said to Father Balbi that we might spend three hours in conversation with Count Asquino, and that he was to go to him first and ask him to lend me thirty sequins, which might be quite as necessary to me to do what remained to be done as my crowbar had been to bring me so far as this. He undertook the commission, but came back in five minutes to bid

[1] Soon after ten.

me go myself, as the old man wished to speak with me alone. The poor old man began by saying gently that I needed no money to make my escape; that he had none; that he had a large family; that if I perished in the attempt, any money he might give me would be lost; in short, endless futile excuses to disguise his avarice or the aversion he felt to parting with his coin. My reply lasted half an hour. Excellent reasons I gave him; but such as, since the creation of the world, never had the smallest effect, because all the forms of eloquence fall dead against the iron face of the most tenacious of passions. This was a case for *Nolenti baculus* (a stick for the obdurate), but I was not so cruel as to use violence against an unhappy old man. I ended by telling him that if he would escape with me I would carry him on my shoulders as Eneas had carried Anchises; but that if he decided on remaining and beseeching God for our success, I warned him that his prayers would be unavailing, since he would be asking God to grant success to an enterprise which he would not help by the most obvious means.

He replied by shedding tears, which moved me deeply. He asked me whether two sequins would be enough; and I told him that I must make it enough. He gave them to me, begging me to return them if, after walking round the roof, I saw that the wiser plan would be to return to my cell. This I promised, somewhat surprised that he should suppose I would ever make up my mind to retrace my steps. He did not know me; I felt I would certainly die rather than go back to a prison I should never afterwards quit alive.

I called my companion, and we placed all our parcels close to the opening. I divided the hundred yards of cord into two bundles, and we then spent two hours in talk, reviewing, not without pleasure, the vicissitudes of our enterprise. The first evidence Balbi gave me of his noble soul was that he told me again and again that I had broken faith with him, since I had asserted that my scheme was complete, while it was not so. He had the insolence to tell me that if he had known it he would never have helped me out of my cell. The Count, with the gravity of seventy years, assured me that my better plan was not to pursue so rash an enterprise, which could not possibly succeed, while the risk of killing myself was evident. Being a lawyer, this was his statement of the case, but I could easily guess that what really prompted him was the thought of the two sequins I should have had to return to him if he had persuaded me to remain.

"The slope of the roof," said he, "being of lead, you cannot walk on it; at most, can you stand upright? That roof has indeed seven or eight dormer windows, but they are all barred with iron, and inaccessible in any way which would enable you to stand in front of them, since they all project beyond the edge. Your ropes will be useless, since you will find nothing to which to fasten them; and even if you should, a man descending from such a height can neither hold on nor guide himself to the ground. One of you three will therefore be obliged to tie the two others firmly round the body, one at a time, and let you down like a pail or a log; and the one who does it must return to his cell. Which of you three feels moved to do this charitable and dangerous deed? And even if one of you is so heroic, on which side of the palace will you attempt it, if you please? Not on the side where the columns are, on the Piazza, for there you would be seen; not by the church, for it is impossible – you would find yourself shut in; on the side by the courtyard it is vain to think of it – you would fall into the hands of the *Arsenalotti*, who constantly make their rounds. So you can only descend on the side of the canal. And have you a gondola or a boat waiting for you? No. So you will be obliged to plunge into the water and swim to St. Apollonia, where you will arrive in a miserable condition, not knowing which way to turn to get any further. Remember that the leads are slippery, and that if you fell into the canal, even if you could swim like sharks, you would not escape death, seeing what the height is and the shallowness of the water. You would be dashed to pieces, for three or four feet of water are not a sufficient body of fluid to neutralize the momentum of a body falling from such a height. In short, the least disaster you can anticipate is to find yourself at the bottom with all your limbs broken."

This speech made my blood boil, imprudent as it was under the circumstances; however, I had enough fortitude to listen with a patience very unlike me. The friar's reproaches, of which he was not sparing, enraged me; I longed to retort on him severely, but I felt that my position was delicate, and I might ruin my undertaking; for I had to deal with a coward quite capable of telling me that he was not so desperate as to risk being killed, and that if I pleased I might go alone; but, alone, I could not flatter myself that I should succeed. So I controlled myself, and, taking a gentle tone, I told him that I was sure of success, though I could not inform them of all the details.

"Your wise advice," said I to Count Asquino, "will make me proceed with the greater caution; but my confidence in God and in my own strength will enable me to overcome every difficulty."

Now and then I put out my hand to assure myself that Soradaci was there, for he never uttered a sound. I laughed to think what he might be revolving in his brain now that he knew I had cheated him. At about half-past four I told him to go to see in what part of the sky the moon stood; he obeyed, and returned to say that in an hour and a half it would have disappeared, and that a very thick fog was making the leads most dangerous.

"All I care for is that the fog should not be of oil," said I. "Make a bundle of your cloak and part of the ropes, which we must divide between us."

At these words, to my astonishment, I felt the man on his knees to me, taking my hands and kissing them as he wept, beseeching me not to lead him to his death.

"I am certain," he said, "to fall into the canal. I cannot be of the smallest use to you. Leave me here, and I will spend the whole night entreating Saint Francis for you. You are master; you may kill me here; but I am determined not to go with you."

The idiot had no idea how he was anticipating my desires.

"You are right," said I. "Stay; but on condition of your praying to Saint Francis. And first of all go and fetch all my books, which I will leave to the Count."

He obeyed me, gladly I have no doubt. My books were worth at least a hundred crowns. The Count told me he would return them to me when I came back.

"You will see me no more," replied I; "you may rely on that. The books will cover the loss of the two sequins. As to this rascal, I am delighted that he is not brave enough to accompany us. He would be in the way; and, besides, such a wretch is not worthy to share with Father Balbi and myself the honours of such a splendid escape."

"Very true," said the Count; "unless he has reason to-morrow to congratulate himself."

I begged the Count to furnish me with pen, ink, and paper, with which he was supplied in spite of the rules; for prohibitions were as nothing to Lorenzo, who would have sold St. Mark himself for a crown-piece. I then wrote the following letter, which I entrusted to Soradaci, and which I could not read through, having written it in the dark. I began with a lofty motto, which I wrote in Latin, to this effect:

" 'I shall not die, but live, and sing the praises of the Lord.' "

"Their Highnesses the State Inquisitors have a right to do their utmost to keep the guilty by force under the Leads; the prisoner, glad not to be on parole, has a right to do his utmost to obtain his liberty. Their right is founded on justice; that of the prisoner on nature; and just as they do not ask his consent before shutting him up, he does not wait for theirs to recover his freedom.

"Jacques Casanova, who writes this in the bitterness of his heart, knows that it may be his misfortune to be recaptured before he can get out of the States of the Republic and find safety in a hospitable land, and that then he will be under the sword of those he hopes to escape from; but if such a misfortune befalls him, he invokes the humanity of his judges not to make his lot a worse one than he is endeavouring to flee from, by punishing him for yielding to the instincts of nature.

"He implores you if he is recaptured to return him all the things belonging to him which he had left in his cell; but if he is so happy as to succeed in his purpose, he makes it all a present to Francesco Soradaci, who remains in prison because he had not courage enough to run the risk. He does not, as I do, prefer liberty to life. Casanova beseeches your Excellencies not to deny him this gift.

"Written in the dark, one hour after midnight, in the Count Asquino's cell, October 31, 1756."

I desired Soradaci not to entrust this letter to Lorenzo, but to give it to the Secretary in person; for there could be no doubt that he would send for him, if he did not come up to the cells, which was even more likely. The Count said that there could be no doubt my letter would have the desired result, but that everything must be restored to me if I should re-appear, and the simpleton said that he hoped he might see me again to prove how gladly he would do so.

But it was time to be off. The moon had set. I hung half the rope round Balbi's neck on one side and his bundle of clothes on the other shoulder. I did the same for myself; and both, in our waistcoats, with our hats on, went to the opening in the roof.

*   *   *   *   *

I crept out first; Balbi followed me. Soradaci, who had accompanied us to the roof, was ordered to pull the sheet of lead down again and then to go and pray to his saint. Crawling on my knees on all fours, I clutched my crowbar firmly, and, stretching as far as I could, I slipped it obliquely between the points of the sheets; then, grasping the edge of the sheet I had turned up, I dragged myself up to the ridge of the roof. The friar, to follow me, inserted the fingers of his right hand into the belt of my breeches. Thus I had the double task of a beast which drags and carries both at once, and that on a steep roof, made slippery by a dense fog. Half-way up this dreadful climb Balbi bid me stop, for one of his parcels had fallen, and he hoped it might not have gone further than the gutter. My first impulse was to give him a kick and send him after his bundle; but, God be praised, I had enough self-command not to do this, for the punishment would have been too severe for both of us, since I alone could never have escaped. I asked him whether it was the packet of ropes, but as he replied that it was only his bundle, in which he had a manuscript he had found in the loft, and which he had hoped would make his fortune, I told him he must take patience, for that a step backwards would be fatal. The poor monk sighed, and, clinging still to my waistband, we climbed on again.

After having got over fifteen or sixteen sheets of lead with immense difficulty, we reached the ridge, on which I perched myself astride, and Balbi did the same. We had our backs to the island of San Giorgio Maggiore, and two hundred yards in front of us we saw the numerous cupolas of the church of Saint Mark, which is in fact part of the Ducal Palace; for the church of Saint Mark is, properly speaking, no more than the Doge's chapel, and certainly no sovereign can boast of a finer one. I began by relieving myself of my load, and desired my companion to follow my example. He tucked his bundle of ropes under him as best he might, but, wanting to take off his hat which inconvenienced him, he managed so badly that it rolled from ledge to ledge, and went to join the bundle of clothes in the canal. My poor comrade was in despair.

"A bad omen!" he exclaimed. "Here I am at once without a shirt, without a hat, and bereft of a precious manuscript containing a most curious and unknown history of the festivals at the Ducal Palace."

I, less disposed to be fierce than I had been when I was climbing, calmly assured him that these two little accidents had nothing so extraordinary about them as that a superstitious spirit should regard them as ominous; that I did not think them so, and that they did not in the least discourage me.

"They should serve you, my good fellow," said I, "as a warning to be prudent and wise, and to suggest to you that God certainly protects us; for if your hat, instead of tumbling to the right, had slipped off to the left, we should have been lost. It would have fallen into the courtyard, where the guards must have found it, and it would of course have told them that there must be someone on the roof. We should have been recaptured at once."

After sitting for some minutes looking about me, I desired the monk to remain motionless till I should return, and I made my way forward, shuffling along astride on the roof without any difficulty, my bolt in my hand. I spent above an hour going about the roof, examining and observing every corner, but in vain; nowhere did I see anything to which I could attach a cord. I was in the greatest perplexity. I could not for a moment think of the canal, nor of the palace courtyard, and among the many cupolas of the church I saw nothing but precipitous walls leading to no open space. To get beyond the church to the *Canonica* I should have had to surmount such steep slopes that I had no hope of achieving it, and it was natural that I should reject as impossible everything that did not seem feasible. The situation in which I found myself required daring, but absolutely no rashness. It was such a dilemma as I imagine can have no parallel for difficulty in any moral question.

However, I had to come to some conclusion; I must either get away or return to my cell, never probably to leave it again; or, again, throw myself into the canal. In this predicament a great deal must be left to chance, and I must begin somewhere. I fixed my eyes on a dormer window on the side towards the canal, and about two-thirds of the way down. It was far enough from the spot we had started from to make me think that the loft it lighted was not connected with the prison I had broken out of. It could light only an attic, inhabited or vacant, over some room in the palace, where, when day should dawn, the doors no doubt would be opened. I was morally certain that the attendants in the palace, even those of the Doge himself, who should happen to see us, would be eager to favour our escape rather than place us in the hands of justice, even if they had recognized us as the greatest of state criminals, so horrible was the Inquisition in their eyes.

With this idea I decided on inspecting that window, so, letting myself slip gently down, I soon was astride on the little roof. Then, resting my hands on the edge, I stretched my head out and succeeded in seeing and touching a little barred grating, behind which there was a window glazed with small panes set in lead. The window did not trouble me, but the grating, slight as it was, seemed to me an insurmountable difficulty, for without a file I could not get through the bars, and I only had my crowbar. I was checked, and began to lose heart, when a perfectly simple and natural incident revived my spirit.

Philosophical reader, if you will for an instant imagine yourself in my place, and picture to yourself the misery I had endured for fifteen months; if you will consider the perils to which I was exposed on a leaden roof where the least rash movement would have cost me my life; if, again, you reflect that I had but a few hours in which to surmount all the difficulties which might multiply at every step, and that in case of failure I might rely on double severity on the part of an iniquitous tribunal, the confession I am about to make with the candour of truth will not lower me in your eyes; above all, if you remember that the nature of man when in anxiety and distress is not to be half so cool as when he is at ease and calm.

It was the clock of Saint Mark's at this moment striking midnight which roused my spirit, and by a sudden shock brought me out of the perplexed frame of mind in which I found myself. That clock reminded me that the morning about to dawn was that of All Saints' Day; that, consequently of my saint's day – if indeed I had a patron saint – and my Jesuit confessor's prohecy recurred to my mind. But I own that what tended most to restore my courage, and really increased my physical powers, was the profaner oracle of my beloved Ariosto:

"*Fra il fin d'Ottobre e il capo di Novembre.*"

If a great misfortune sometimes makes a small mind devout, it is almost impossible that superstition should not have some share in the matter. The sound of the clock seemed to me a spoken charm which bid me act and promised me success. Lying flat on the roof, with my head over the edge, I pushed my bar in above the frame which held the grating, determined to dislodge it bodily. In a quarter of an hour I had succeeded; the grating was in my hands unbroken, and having laid it by the side of the dormer I had no difficulty in breaking in the window, though the blood was flowing from a wound I had made in my left hand.

By the help of my bar I got back to the ridge of the roof in the same way as before, and made my way back to where I had left my companion. I found him desperate and raging; he abused me foully for having left him there so long. He declared he was only waiting for seven to strike to go back to prison.

"What did you think had become of me?"

"I thought you had fallen down some roof or wall."

"And you have no better way of expressing your joy at my return than by abusing me?"

"What have you been doing all this time?"

"Come with me and you will see."

Having gathered up my bundles, I made my way back to the window. When we were just over it I explained to Balbi exactly what I had done, and consulted him as to how we were to get into the loft through the window. The thing was quite easy for one of us; the other could let him down. But I did not see how the second man was to follow him, as there was no way of fixing the rope above the window. By going in and letting myself drop I might break my legs and arms, for I did not know the height of the window above the floor. To this wise argument, spoken with perfect friendliness, the brute replied in these words:

"Let me down, at any rate, and when I am in there you will have plenty of time to find out how you can follow me."

I confess that in my first impulse of indignation I was ready to stab him with my crowbar. A good genius saved me from doing so, and I did not even utter one word of reproach for his selfishness and baseness. On the contrary, I at once unrolled my bundle of rope, and fastening it firmly under his armpits I made him lie flat on his face, his feet outwards, and then let him down on to the roof of the dormer. When he was there, I made him go over the edge and into the window as far as his hips, leaving his arms on the sill. I next slipped down to the little roof, as I had done before, lay down on my stomach, and holding the rope firmly, told the monk to let himself go without fear. When he had landed on the floor of the attic he undid the rope, and I, pulling it up, found that the height was above fifty feet. To jump this was too great a risk. As for the monk, now he was safe, after nearly two hours of anguish on a roof, where, I must own, his situation was far from comfortable, he called out to me to throw in the ropes, and he would take care of them. I, as may be supposed, took good care not to follow this absurd injunction.

Not knowing what to do, and awaiting some inspiration. I clambered once more to the ridge, and my eye falling on a spot near a cupola, which I had not yet examined, I made my way thither. I saw a little terrace or platform covered with lead, close to a large window closed with shutters. There was here a tub full of wet mortar with a trowel, and by the side a ladder, which I thought would be long enough to enable me to get down into the attic where my comrade was. This settled the question. I slipped my rope through the top rung, and dragged this awkward load as far as the window. I then had to get the clumsy mass into the window; it was above twelve yards long. The difficulty I had in doing it made me repent of having deprived myself of Balbi's assistance. I pushed the ladder along till one end was on the level of the dormer and the other projected by a third beyond the gutter. Then I slid down on to the dormer roof; I drew the ladder close to my side and fastened the rope to the eighth rung, after which I again allowed it to slip till it was parallel with the window. Then I did all I could to make it slip into the window, but I could not get it beyond the fifth rung because the end caught against the inner roof of the dormer, and no power on earth could get it any further without breaking either the ladder or the roof. There was nothing for it but to tilt the outer end, then the slope would allow it to slide in by its own weight. I might have placed the ladder across the window and have fastened the rope to it to let myself down, without any risk; but the ladder would have remained there, and next morning would have guided the archers and Lorenzo to the spot where we might still be hiding.

I would not run the risk of losing by such an act of imprudence the fruit of so much labour and peril, and to conceal all our traces the ladder must be got entirely into the window. Having no one to help me, I decided on getting down to the gutter to tilt it, and attain my end. This in fact I did, but at so great a risk that but for a sort of miracle I should have paid for my daring with my life. I ventured to leave go of the cord that was attached to the ladder without any fear of its falling into the canal, because it was caught on the gutter by the third rung. Then, with my crowbar in my hand, I cautiously let myself slide down to the gutter by the side of the ladder; the marble ledge was against my toes, for I let myself down with my face to the roof. In this attitude I found strength enough to lift the ladder a few inches, and I had the satisfaction of seeing it go a foot further in. As the reader will understand, this diminished its weight very perceptibly. What I now wanted was to get it two feet further in, by lifting it enough; for after that I felt sure that, by climbing up to the roof of the dormer once more, I could, with the help of the rope, get it all the way in. To achieve this, I raised myself from my knees; but the force I was obliged to use to succeed made me slip, so that I suddenly found myself over the edge of the roof as far as my chest, supported only by my elbows.

It was an awful moment, which to this day I shudder to think of, and which it is perhaps impossible to conceive of in all its horror. The natural instinct of self-preservation made me almost unconsciously lean with all my might, supporting myself on my ribs, and I succeeded – miraculously, I felt inclined to say. Taking care not to relax my hold, I managed to raise myself with all the strength of my wrists, leaning at the same time on my stomach. Happily there was nothing to fear for the ladder, for the lucky – or rather the unlucky push which had cost me so dear, had sent it in more than three feet, which fixed it firmly.

*   *   *   *   *

Finding myself resting on the gutter literally on my wrists and my groin, I found that by moving my right side I could raise first one knee and then the other on to the parapet. Then I should be safe. However, my troubles were not yet over, for the strain I was obliged to exert in order to succeed gave me such a nervous spasm that a violent attack of painful cramp seemed to cripple me completely. I did not lose my head, and remained perfectly still till the spasm was over, knowing that perfect stillness is the best cure for nervous cramps – I had often found it so. It was a frightful moment. A few minutes after, I gradually renewed my efforts. I succeeded in getting my knees against the gutter, and as soon as I had recovered my breath I carefully raised the ladder, and at last got it to the angle where it was parallel with the window. Knowing enough of the laws of equilibrium and the lever, I now picked up my crowbar, and climbing in my old fashion, I hauled myself up to the roof and easily succeeded in tilting in the ladder, which the monk below received in his arms. I then flung in my clothes, the ropes and the broken pieces, and got down into the attic, where Balbi received me very heartily and took care to remove the ladder.

Arm in arm, we surveyed the dark room in which we found ourselves; it was thirty paces long by about twenty wide.

At one end we felt a double door formed of iron bars. This was unpromising, but laying my hand on the latch in the middle it yielded to pressure, and the door opened. We first felt our way round this fresh room, and then, trying to cross it, ran up against a table with armchairs and stools round it. We returned to the side where we had felt windows, and having opened one, by the dim starlight we could see nothing but steep roofs between domes. I did not for an instant think of escaping by the window; I must know where I was going, and I did not recognize the spot where we were. So I closed the window, and we went back to the first room, where we had left our baggage. Quite worn out, I let myself drop on to the floor, and putting a bundle of rope under my head, utterly bereft of all power of body or of mind, I fell into a sweet sleep. I gave myself up to it so passively, that even if I had known that death must be the end of it I could not have resisted it; and I remember distinctly that the pleasure of that sleep was perfectly delicious.

I slept for three hours and a half. The monk's shouting and shaking could scarcely rouse me. He told me that it was past twelve (five in the morning), and that my sleeping was to him quite inconceivable in such a situation as ours.

It was inconceivable to him, but not to me. My sleeping was quite involuntary. I had only succumbed to natural exhaustion – nature at bay, as I may say. Nor was my exhaustion surprising; for two days my agitation had prevented my taking any food or rest; and the efforts I had just made were almost superhuman, and enough to exhaust the strength of any man. However, this blessed sleep had restored my original energy, and I was delighted to see that the darkness had so far diminished as to enable me to act with more decision and promptitude.

As soon as I had glanced round me, I cried: "This is not a prison! There must be some way out quite easy to discover."

We examined the wall opposite to the iron gate, and in a very small recess I fancied I discerned a door. I felt about, and at last my fingers fell on a keyhole. I put in the end of my crowbar, and with two or three wrenches I opened it, and we found ourselves in a small room, where, on a table, there lay a key. I tried it in a door facing me, and, on turning it, saw that I had unlocked the door. I desired the monk to go to fetch our bundles, and after replacing the key on the table from which I had taken it, we went out and found ourselves in a corridor fitted with pigeon-holes full of papers. These were archives. I discovered a little stone staircase; down I went, and came to another. This, too, I descended, and found at the end a glass door, which I opened, and found myself in a room I knew. We were in the Doge's chancery office. I opened a window; it would have been easy to get out of it; but I should have got down into the labyrinth of little courts round the church of Saint Mark. Heaven preserve me from such folly!

On a desk I espied an iron punch, with a round point and a wooden handle, such as the clerks use for piercing parchment to attach the leaden seal with a string; of this I took possession. I opened the desk; in it was the copy of a letter announcing to the Commandant of Corfu a grant of three thousand sequins for the restoration of the old fortress. I looked for the sequins; but they were not there. God knows how gladly I would have taken possession of them; and how I should have laughed at the friar if he had accused me of theft! I should have regarded such a windfall as a gift from heaven! Frankly, I should have considered them my own by right of conquest.

*   *   *   *   *

I went to the door of the room, and put my bolt into the lock, but perceiving instantly that I could not force it, I decided at once to break through one of the panels. I took care to choose the one where there were fewest knots in the wood, and, setting to work with my crowbar, I split and rent it as best I might. The monk did his best to help me with the punch I had found on the desk, trembling all the time at the echoing noise each time I tried to drive my tool into the wood. The noise must, indeed, have been audible at a considerable distance; I was well aware of the danger, but was compelled to run the risk.

In half an hour the hole was large enough; and that was fortunate, for I should have had great difficulty in making it larger without a saw. The edges of this gap were horrible to behold; they were set with teeth and jags to tear our clothes and our flesh. And it was five feet up. Having placed two stools side by side, we stood on these; the monk, crossing his arms, put his body through head foremost; I took him by the buttocks, and then by the legs, and succeeded in pushing him through. Although it was still dark I was not now uneasy, because I knew where we were. When my companion was outside I passed him out our bundles, excepting the ropes, which I left behind. I now placed a third stool on the top of the other two, and on this I mounted; the hole was now on the level of my thighs, and I put my body through as far as it would go, though with great difficulty, as the gap was very narrow; and as I had no hold to which to cling with my hands, and no one to push me as I had pushed Balbi, I desired him to put his arms round me and simply pull, even if he brought me through in fragments. He did so, and I had the fortitude to endure the horrible pain of my legs being frightfully torn; the blood streamed down them.

As soon as I had the joy of finding myself outside, I hastened to pick up my bundle, and after going down two flights of steps, I easily opened the door leading to the corridor in which are the great doors of the main staircase, and that to the office of the *Savio alla Scrittura*. This great door was closed, as that of the hall of archives had been, and one look assured me that without a catapult to break it down, or a train of gunpowder to blow it up, it would be impossible to move it. My bolt in my hand seemed to say to me: "*Hic fines possuit*. You have done with me – you may leave me to my fate!" It was the instrument of my freedom, and I treasured it; it was worthy to hang as an *ex voto* on the altar of release and liberty.

Calmly resigned, and perfectly cool, I sat down, and desired my companion to do the same. "My part of the work is done," said I; "now God or good fortune must do the rest. I do not know whether the cleaners will think of coming to the palace to-day – All Saints' Day, or to-morrow – the Day of the Dead. If anyone comes, the instant the door is opened I fly. You must follow at my heels; but if no one comes, here I stay. And if I die of hunger I cannot help it."

On hearing this the poor wretch flew into a rage. He called me a madman, a liar, desperate, deceitful, treacherous. I let him rave; I was immovable. Meanwhile the clock struck thirteen. Since the moment when I awoke in the attic only one hour had elapsed.

The first point of any importance was to change everything I had on. Father Balbi looked like a peasant, but he was not scratched; he was neither in rags nor covered with blood. His red flannel waistcoat and violet leather breeches were not torn; while I could only be an object of horror or pity, for I was bleeding and in tatters. Having turned my stockings down from my knees, the blood was streaming from two deep grazes I had got from the gutter; the hole in the door had torn my waistcoat, shirt, and breeches, my hips and legs. I had fearful scratches all over me. Tearing up some handkerchiefs, I bandaged myself as well as I could; I put on my fine coat, which on a winter's day must have had a comical effect; I tucked my hair into the bag as well as I could, put on a pair of clean stockings, a laced shirt – for want of a plain one – with two more over it, and I stuffed my pockets with stockings and handkerchiefs. Everything else I tossed into a corner. My silk cloak I threw over the monk's shoulders, and the poor devil looked as if he had stolen it. I must have had very much the appearance of a man who, after leaving a ball, had fallen into very bad company. The bandages about my knees alone mis-matched with my inopportune finery.

Thus dressed, with my fine hat trimmed with Spanish gold point and a white feather, I opened a window. My face was at once observed by some idlers in the palace courtyard, who, puzzled to imagine how such a person could be at that window so early in the morning, went to inform the keeper of the key. The door-keeper, fancying that he must have locked someone in the day before, went to fetch his keys, and came to open. I was vexed at having shown myself at the window, not knowing that in this fortune had befriended me; and I was sitting by the monk, who was talking nonsense, when the rattle of keys fell on my ear. Greatly excited, I rose, and putting my eye to a crack which happily divided the hinges of the door, I saw one man only, slowly coming up the steps with a bunch of large keys in his hand. I desired Balbi very earnestly not to say a word, to keep behind me, and follow me closely. I took my crowbar, holding it in my right hand hidden in my coat, and I placed myself in such a position with regard to the door as that I could fly the instant it was opened, and rush down the steps. I prayed heaven that the man might not show fight, for if he had I must have struck him down, and I was fully determined to do so.

The door was opened, and on seeing me the poor man stood petrified. Taking advantage of his amazement, without pausing, without speaking a word, I quickly went down the steps, the monk following me. Without looking as if I were running away, but walking at a good pace, I went by the magnificent Giant's Staircase, not listening to Balbi, who kept calling to me: "Come into the church!"

The door of the church is not twenty yards from the great stairs; but the churches of Venice were no longer, even then, a sanctuary for criminals, and no one took refuge there. This Balbi knew, but in his terror he had lost his memory. He told me afterwards that what urged him to press me to go into the church was a religious impulse which drew him to the altar.

"Why did you not go alone then?"

"I would not forsake you."

He ought to have said: "I would not lose sight of you."

The refuge I hoped for was beyond the frontiers of the Most Serene Republic, and I began to make my way thither; I was there already in spirit, and I must take the body there. I went straight to the royal entrance of the Doges' Palace; and looking at no one, so as to attract less attention, I crossed the little square, went straight to the quay, and stepped into the first gondola I came to, saying aloud to the gondolier: "Take me to

Fusina; call another man to help you." He was at hand, and while they cast off the rope I flung myself on the centre cushion, while Balbi seated himself on a bench. His grotesque appearance, without a hat, and wearing a handsome cloak, and my unseasonable finery, must have made them take me for a charlatan or an astrologer.

As soon as we were round the corner by the custom-house, the men set to work to row vigorously through the canal of the Giudecca, along which we must go to reach Fusina, or rather Mestre, which was where I meant to go. Half-way down the canal I put out my head and said to the boatman in the stern: "Do you suppose we shall reach Mestre before nightfall?"

"But, signor, you bid me go to Fusina."

"You are a fool; I told you Mestre."

The other gondolier assured me that I was mistaken, and the gaby of a friar, a zealous Christian and a friend of truth, must need insist that I was in the wrong. I longed to give him a kick to punish him for his idiocy; but reflecting that a man can only have common sense by the Grace of God, I went into fits of laughter, admitting that I might be mistaken, but adding that I certainly intended to go to Mestre. No one replied till, presently, the master boatman said he was ready to take me to England if I liked.

"Bravo!" said I; "then go to Mestre."

"We shall be there in three-quarters of an hour; wind and tide are with us."

Very well content, I looked behind me at the canal, which seemed to me more beautiful than I had ever seen it, above all because there was not a single boat coming our way. The morning was delicious, the air pure, the first sunbeams glorious; my two young gondoliers rowed with as much ease as vigour. And reflecting on the dreadful night I had gone through, on the dangers I had escaped, on the freedom I was just beginning to taste and had in certain prospect, everything so moved my soul that, filled with gratitude to God, I was choked with emotion and melted into tears.

My adorable companion, who till now had not opened his lips but to take the part of the gondoliers, thought it his business now to console me, and the way he set to work made me, in fact, forget my delicious emotion and burst out laughing in so strange a way, that he fell into the contrary error and thought I had gone mad. The poor monk, as I have said, was an ass, and his malice was only the outcome of his stupidity. I had been under the painful necessity of making use of him; but, without meaning it, he was now near being my ruin. He was not to be convinced that while I had ordered the boatman to go to Fusina, I had intended to go to Mestre: the idea, he said must have entered my head on the Grand Canal.

* * * * *

We reached Mestre. I could find no post-horses, but there were several *vetturini*, who drive quite as well, and I agreed with one to carry me to Treviso in an hour and a quarter. In three minutes the horses were harnessed, and supposing that Balbi was just behind me, I turned round to say, "Get in." But he was not to be seen. I told a stable-lad to go and find him, quite determined to give him a rating, for in such a predicament no delay was permissible. He came back to say that my companion was not to be found. I was furious. I thought of leaving him to his fate; but a sentiment of humanity checked me. I got out, I made enquiries; everyone had seen him, but no one knew where he was or could be. I hunted the arcades of the High Street, and instinct prompting me to put my head into a café, I found the wretch at the counter, drinking chocolate and flirting with the barmaid. He saw me, pointed out that the girl was a pretty girl, and desired me to take a cup of chocolate and pay for his, for that he had not a sou. Suppressing my indignation, "I will have none," said I. "Make haste!" and I gripped his arm so tight that he turned pale with the pain. I paid, and we went out, I trembling with rage. We got into the chaise, but hardly had we gone ten yards when I met a native of the town named Balbi Tomasi, a good fellow, but reputed to be one of the familiars of the Holy Office. He recognized me, and coming up to me he exclaimed:

"You, signore! – you here! I am delighted to see you. You have escaped then? How did you manage it?"

"I did not escape; I was released."

"That is impossible; for only last evening I was with Messer Grimani, and I should have heard of it."

Reader, you can more easily imagine my feelings at this moment than I can describe them. I was discovered, and by a man whom I believed to be paid to arrest me, and who to do so had only to wink at the first officer of the police – and Mestre was full of them. I told him to speak low, and getting out of the chaise, I begged him to come aside with me. I led him behind a house, and seeing that there was no one to watch me, and that I was close to a ditch beyond which lay the open fields, I drew out my crowbar and collared him. Perceiving my purpose he wrenched himself free, and jumped the ditch. Instantly, without looking back, he ran as fast as he could go in a straight line. As soon as he was some way off he relaxed his pace, and kissed his hand to me to wish me good luck. When I had lost sight of him, I thanked God that this man's agility had preserved me from committing a crime, for I was about to make an end of him, and it seemed that he meant no harm after all.

My position was terrible to contemplate. I was alone, and at open war with the Republic. I must sacrifice everything to my own immediate safety, and must reject no means which might conduce to that end.

Dejected as a man must be who has escaped such peril, I glanced contemptuously at the monk by whose delay we had been exposed to it, and got into the chaise again. I was thinking how I could be quit of this blunderer, who now dared not open his lips. We reached Treviso without further adventure, and I desired the post-master to have horses in readiness by seventeen o'clock.[1] It was not, however, my intention to pursue my journey by post; in the first place I could not afford it, and in the second I was afraid of being tracked. The innkeeper asked me if I would not breakfast. I needed food to keep me alive, for I was almost dead of inanition; but I dared not accept. A quarter of an hour lost might be fatal. I was afraid of being overtaken, and blushing for it as long as I should live: for a wise man in the open country ought to be able to defy four hundred thousand; if he cannot hide himself he is a fool.

I went out of the Saint Thomas's gate as if I were going for a walk, and after following the high-road for about a mile, I cut across the fields, intending to keep to them till I should be out of the Republican territory. The shortest way was by Bassano; but I took the longest, for it was not impossible that they might be on the look-out for me at the nearest frontier; while it was hardly probable that they should imagine that I could take the road by Feltre, which was the longest way to get into the domain of the Bishop of Trent.

After walking for three hours, I dropped on the ground quite incapable of further exertion. I required some nourishment, or I must make up my mind to die where I lay. I told the monk to lay the cloak by me and go to a farmhouse I saw, to get something to eat, paying for it of course, and to bring it to me. I gave him the necessary money. He went off, saying he thought I had more courage.

This creature did not know what was meant by courage, but he was more strongly constituted than I; and no doubt had taken care before leaving his cell to line his stomach well. Beside, he had had some chocolate; and he was thin, and a monk, and his mind was not tortured by considerations of prudence and honour at the expense of his body.

Though the house was not an inn, the good farmer's wife sent me out an ample dinner, by a peasant girl, which cost me but thirty sous of Venice. After having satisfied my appetite, feeling that I could hardly keep

[1] About ten in the morning.

awake I made haste to set out again, knowing pretty well where I was. After walking for four hours, I paused outside a hamlet, and found that I was twenty-four miles from Treviso. I was quite worn out; my ankles were swelled, and my shoes torn and cut. There was but an hour of daylight. Lying down in the midst of a clump of trees, I made Father Balbi sit down by me, and spoke to this effect:

"We must try to get to Borgo di Valsugnano. It is the first town beyond the frontier of the Republic. There we shall be as safe as we should be in London, and we may then rest; but to get there we must take many precautions, and the first is to separate. You must go by the woods of Mantello, I will go by the hills; you by the easiest and shortest way, I by the longest and most difficult; you shall have some money, and I not a sou. I will make you a present of the cloak, which you can exchange for a peasant's cape and hat, and everyone will take you for a peasant, for you fortunately have the face of one. Here is all the money I have left of Count Asquino's two sequins – twenty-seven lire; take them. You will reach Borgo to-morrow evening; I about twenty-four hours later. Wait for me at the first inn on the left, and you may rely on my coming. For to-night, I must sleep somewhere in a good bed, and Providence will enable me to find one; but I must be perfectly at ease in my mind, and in your company that is impossible. I am certain that by this time they are hunting for us in every direction, and that our description has been so accurately given, that we should be arrested in any inn which we ventured into together. You see the miserable condition I am in, and that ten hours' rest is really indispensable to me. So farewell; go your way, and leave me to go mine. I shall find a night's lodging somewhere in the neighbourhood."

"I expected this," said Balbi. "But the only answer I can give you is to remind you of what you promised me when you induced me to break into your cell. You promised that we should never separate, so do not hope that I shall leave you. Your fate is mine, and mine yours. We shall find a good lodging for our money, and go to no inns. We shall not be arrested."

"Then you are determined not to follow the good advice I have offered you out of prudence?"

"Yes, quite determined."

"We shall see."

I rose, not without an effort. I measured his height, and laid it out on the ground; then, taking out my crowbar, I lay down, reclining on my left side, and with the utmost coolness I began to dig out the earth, making no reply to his further questions. After working for about a quarter of an hour I looked up at him sadly, and I told him that as a good Christian,

3

I must bid him commend his soul to God, "for I am going to bury you here, alive or dead; or, if you are the stronger, you must bury me. This is the extremity to which your stupid obstinacy reduces me. However, you may run away—I shall not run after you."

As he made no reply I continued digging; but I confess I was beginning to be afraid that this brute would drive me to extremities, and I was determined to be rid of him.

At last, out of fear, or thinking better of it, he threw himself on his knees by my side. Not knowing his purpose, I turned my iron bar against him; but I had nothing to fear. "I will do whatever you please," said he.

So I embraced him, and having given him all the money I had, I repeated my promise to join him at Borgo. Though left without a sou, and obliged to cross two rivers, I congratulated myself on being rid of the company of a man of his quality; for, alone, I felt sure of escaping beyond the frontier of my beloved Republic.

The Napoleonic War, 1805-1814

CHAPTER FOUR

BOTH JOHN GERARD and Casanova were able to bribe their gaolers to help, however unknowingly, in their escapes; but from now on the escapers are prisoners of war and the patriotism of the guard must be taken into account. In the following stories the guards may indeed be corruptible in small matters, but not usually to the extent of taking any action that would help the enemy to win the war.

With Seacome Ellison in the Napoleonic Wars we come to a new sort of captivity. Except for those who have given their parole, the barriers are still stone walls, there are still chains, moats and subterranean dungeons. But there is also comradeship. Here there are many men imprisoned together; men with a common cause who are held by an enemy of their country and who, if they succeed in their escape, are not outlaws but are welcomed at their journey's end. These men are not convicted, even of political crimes. Their imprisonment is without shame, unless it be the private shame of having surrendered, and there is more lightness of heart in their escapes.

Seacome Ellison was master of the brig *Rachel*, which was taken by the French frigate *Vaillant* in 1803. He was sent to the internment camp at Verdun where he lived on parole in the town with the other master mariners, "men of his cloth" as he calls them.

The comfort of the prisoners of war on parole in Verdun depended very largely on the length of their purses. In addition to his military prisoners, Napoleon had rounded up most of the English civilians (about ten thousand in all) who were on French soil at the outbreak of war. Midshipman Boys says in his *Narrative* that there were four hundred British in Verdun at the time of his arrival, and Seacome Ellison was shocked at the profligate way in which the *détenus* lived. On the other hand, as in modern p.o.w. camps, there were great opportunities for study, and two schools were opened for the English in Verdun.

The prisoners on parole were allowed to roam at will about the countryside within a six-mile limit of the city walls, leaving their passports at the city gates and collecting them again on their return.

Seacome Ellison

IN THE summer of 1807, Cecil, a bold, open-hearted, generous, friendly fellow, who had been my chief companion, became unhappy at losing so much of his time. Disease and disappointment sensibly affected his disposition, which was naturally irritable, though at the same time engaging; for, if ever he gave offence by an unguarded word, he was always ready to acknowledge his fault. He carried himself high to those who he thought assumed an unbecoming consequence; and, on the other hand, was kind and condescending to those who met him in a friendly manner; and he had a ready way of conciliating all around him. Often, while musing, he would regret his descent (for he was of a noble family), as giving rise, occasionally, to expectations that he was never likely to realise. His father had been improvident; and his last words to him were, "Remember, Tom, thou wast born a gentleman." Poor Cecil never forgot this; and it was all his patrimony. Once he said to me, "Ellison, bad as we are off here, very likely it may be the happiest part of our lives"; and, as it regarded himself, he spoke prophetically: "still I am determined," said he, "to remain here no longer than I can, with credit to myself, forfeit my parole"; and immediately he began to devise means to get unsuspectedly into close confinement; when, as far as his honour was concerned, he would be a free man. My principal reason for not joining him, was the fear of our being separated, if the plan did not succeed; because, from Wirion's known hatred to my cloth, I was likely to receive the greatest share of punishment: besides, my mind was not quite made up for the enterprise, and Boys was not prepared; therefore he determined to go alone, an undertaking which none but a first-rate spirit would have had the courage to attempt. However, we both promised to render him all the aid in our power; and forthwith commenced smuggling every thing that was necessary into a wood about two leagues from the *Porte de Paris*, ready for his journey, provided he should be so fortunate as to escape from the citadel. His plan was, by some little misdemeanour to get confined there for a few days – the common punishment for trifling irregularities. By some accident, his original plan proved abortive; and his next went rather beyond the mark; for, instead of the citadel, he was ordered off, the following morning, to Bitche, in company with Gordon, Maxwell, and others, who had been previously in confinement, and under that sentence. Boys and I, hearing of the order, waited at the gate, and walked with him to the extent of our limit. On bidding him a melancholy adieu, he said, "Never fear; if anything like a favourable chance occurs, these fellows shall not take me to Bitche." There we left him, and hastened back to the

Appel. Early next day the news arrived of their escape, and the *gendarmerie* and peasants were all on the *qui vive* to stop their progress. Boys and I, naturally presuming that he would make the best of his way back to the wood where his stores were deposited, set out thither as soon as the gates opened on the following morning. Judge our pleasing surprise, to find Cecil, Gordon, and Maxwell had gained the rendezvous about half an hour before us. It appeared that at the first house of correspondence, by some fortunate occurrence, only one *gendarme* met them, and he, the better to secure his charge, put them all upon the baggage cart. When ascending a steep hill, with a wood at a short distance, the three that escaped told the other two that they would get off, on a pretence of lightening the horse, and would have a run for it; and they might follow their example, if they chose. At a given point they started, and gained the wood. The *gendarme* fired his pistols, but did not chase them; his horse could not have entered the wood, and, if he had left the cart, he might have lost all the five. He was not like an Englishman in London, who hired two fellows to carry his luggage, whom he could not keep together; at length one bolted into a narrow passage, and he ran after him; but losing sight of the chase, he returned to look for the other, who had decamped also.

Having had plenty of time to select a good hiding-place before the *gendarme* reached the next village to raise the peasantry, and send them in pursuit, they lay still, and remained undiscovered till dark, when they shaped their way back to Verdun in the best manner they could, avoiding the main road; but made very little direct progress. At day-light, there being no wood in view, they concealed themselves among the standing corn, where their sufferings were indescribable from heat and thirst; Maxwell was nearly sinking under it. About four in the afternoon, they were discovered by a peasant; he said he knew who they were, and told them not to be afraid, for he would not betray them. They begged for water. "Lie still," said he, "until it is dark, and then I will bring you both meat and drink." He kept his word, and brought them some bread and wine, which soon revived them. "Now then," said he, "get up, and I will direct you in any way that you choose to go." He accompanied them into the fair track, and observing Maxwell had only one shoe, he gave him one of his own, and bid them adieu. At two, they reached the suburbs of Verdun, forded the river a little below the town, and had scarcely lain down in their hiding-place, when we joined them.

After much congratulation and hearty shaking of hands, we wrote a list of all they wanted, and hastened back to the *Appel*. Then going round to our friends in whom we could place confidence, we related their adventures, and collected for them about twenty louis. I went to my shoe-maker's with the measure of Maxwell's foot, chose a pair of shoes, and told the man to put plenty of nails in them. "O," says he, with a knowing look, "I suppose to run away in." "You have nothing to do with that," I replied, "obey your orders, and I will return in an hour." At the time appointed they were ready, I gave him his price, and nothing more passed. Having obtained all they were in want of, and having provided a stock of eatables and plenty of wine, we hired a vehicle, and, accompanied by four others, rejoined our emancipated countrymen early in the afternoon, the remainder of which was spent in high glee. When the wine began to operate, a proposal was made to drink a bumper to the peasant's health out of his shoe. This was unanimously adopted, and he who drank first did him the greatest honour, tasting the richest flavour of the worthy foot it had once covered. We left them about seven in high spirits, expecting soon to be in the land of liberty; and we by no means depressed, though return-ing to our place of confinement. We were scarcely out of the wood, when we met Wirion and his wife, but being within the limits, and having sufficient time to enter our prison-house before the shutting of the gates, we had nothing to fear; all that passed was a mutual salute. Some of the party afterwards blabbed, and the adventure was whispered about, but, fortunately for the parties, it did not reach headquarters.

We were all anxiety for the fugitives, dreading to hear of their recap-ture, but every day, as it passed without any report of them, strengthened our hopes. In about a month I had the pleasure of hearing from Cecil, at Saltzburg, giving me the leading particulars of his journey. A few days after their departure, he and Gordon differed; they were both high spirited, but the latter had not the noble mind of the former. He was of singular habits, very neat in his person, and very consequential; so that he generally went by the name of Lord George. They were by no means of kindred dispositions, and as they could not agree, they separated; but in the act of parting one of them recollected that he owed the other a louis, which he tendered; but the lender, though poor, supposed the borrower still poorer, and thought it dishonourable to accept payment under the then circumstances, and therefore refused it. What was to be done? The one was too lofty to take it back, the other too proud to be under an ob-ligation. The borrower put it upon a stone in the middle of the road, and thus their proud spirits left it; although they had to accomplish a march of hundreds of miles, a great part through an enemy's country, with the dreary prospect of wanting even the common necessaries of life – a fair specimen of the folly and weakness of man. Gordon and Maxwell bent their course through Prussia to the Baltic. Cecil continued in the route he first determined on, to Trieste, but by keeping to the north made a great angle. He passed the Rhine about Worms; then entering the town of Wurtsburgh, he had the good fortune to obtain a passport to Saltzburg, which passport he enclosed to me, thinking it might be serviceable if ever I followed his track. Both parties arrived safe in the November following, and met accidentally in London.

The success attending Cecil's attempt was a reproach to my supineness, and an excitation to dare all obstacles. Early the following year, being the fifth of my captivity, K—— told me that he was authorised by a mutual friend to communicate a secret to me; which was, that a plan of escape had been devised for this friend, but that he was in want of some little assistance. As his name has not yet appeared in this narrative, I shall here introduce to the reader Mr. Archibald Barklimore, surgeon, now very comfortably settled in the metropolis. This gentleman was captured early in the war: he was of a cheerful, jocose disposition, and had a talent for learning the language, and imitating the manners of the French. He had all their grimace, their shrugs, their grins, their every motion; in fact, he was to all outward appearance a genuine Frenchman. He was upon a friendly footing with all the officers of the regiment, whose *depôt* was Verdun, as well as with their families, and had the privilege of the *entrée* into the citadel whenever he pleased, night or day. He was their surgeon-in-chief; they preferred his advice to that of their own countrymen. Fortunately, the gentleman that had been responsible for him was gone home, and by an unaccountable oversight another bondsman was never required: so that he had no restraint further than waiting a feasible opportunity of being off. These officers had fitted him with a complete uniform, sword, etc., obtained for him a *feuille de route* (military passport), and one of them actually went down to the sea coast to prepare his way, but found it next to impossible to engage a boat owing to the extreme watchfulness of the coast guard. On his return, Barklimore taking into consideration the risk he ran of being sent to the gallies, if taken when presenting a false passport, gave up the scheme.

* * * * *

It was at this time that K—— and myself volunteered to accompany Barklimore in some way less hazardous, for which we began to make preparations. At the first, I viewed the undertaking with a good deal of dread, particularly when, in a morning, I looked out at the window and the weather happened to be wet and cold. This, said I to myself, is a pretty sort of a day for a man to take up his lodging in a wood; and then I would contrast it with my comfortable room, warm fireside, and good bed.

there was the risk of ill health, the chance of being shot by a sentinel, or cut down by a *gendarme*; but all these fears vanished as the plan matured, and I found that in this, as in every other case, the anticipation of evil is always much worse to bear than the reality.

Our intention was to make for Trieste. Barklimore made many attempts to extract by acids the endorsement on Cecil's passport, and succeeded in all but one, and that one rendered it useless; still this did not induce us to change our plan. We bought maps for our direction, and marked out our intended route. We also purchased gimlets, and small lock saws, together with one fine one, made out of a watch spring, and nicely set in a steel frame, for the purpose of cutting iron bars: these we sewed in the crowns of our hats. After making small knapsacks of strong linen, we covered them with fine oil-cloth, of which we also made capes to cover our shoulders. These, with a spare shirt and provisions for our journey, we deposited in the spot whence Cecil had taken his departure.

And now I shall introduce John Innis, late purser of H.M.S. *Ranger*; a man who, for sterling worth, unbounded generosity according to his means, and staunchness of friendship, could not be surpassed in the *depôt*; a man who would pinch himself to serve his neighbour; who actually gave half of his goods to the poor; a general favourite with all parties, and whose advice was sought by most who knew him, and they were not a few: careful of everybody's interest but his own; would not run away himself, but would aid and abet anyone that was disposed to move off in an honourable manner. If my memory is not at fault, he secreted a midshipman in his lodgings for three months, who threw himself upon his generosity, although he did not stand high in his esteem. He was remarkable for the plainness of his dress, and wore a hat that had the appearance of having weathered all the storms that the ship he was taken in had encountered. In the lodging of this worthy fellow we deposited all our things, leaving only empty trunks in the lodgings we purposed to evacuate. I have now on my table a snuff-box, a parting present from poor Cecil, which Innis (whose remains are now mouldering in the churchyard of Festiniog, North Wales) delivered into my hands seven years after I bade him adieu in Verdun.

He was the last man we called upon to bid farewell, late on the night that we intended to commence operations in the morning; he had previously begged so hard that we would take a fellow lodger of his (named Robert Alison, a purser in the India service) with us, that we could not say nay, although it was sadly against our inclination, three being a sufficient number. It was then fixed that in the morning Alison should go out of the *Porte de Paris* to avoid suspicion, and K—— and I out of the *Porte Chaussée*, and to remain outside an hour after the time for the *Appel*, calculating that for the offence we should be shut up in the Citadel, by which means our fellow-bondsmen would be exonerated.

In the morning K—— came to my lodgings and we lapped the rope that we have previously prepared round our bodies; it was about the thickness of a log-line, or, what will be better understood by landsmen and the fair sex, the thickness of window-blind cord; this we doubled, and marled together, that is, tied it round and round. Thus equipped, with our marching clothes on, with saws and gimlets in our hats, we sallied out, breakfasted at one of the villages, and waited until the time we supposed our guardians would be looking after us. We went carelessly up to the *bureau* and asked for our passports, when, to our great surprise and morti-fication, instead of being told there was an order to conduct us to the citadel, the *gendarme* put them into our hands without asking a question. We then hastened to our lodging, and inquired had the *gendarmes* been looking after us; "Yes," was the reply, "but we told them you had not been gone out long, and they went away satisfied." Here for once we found the disadvantage of having a good character, for hitherto we had never transgressed, and therefore our staying out excited no suspicion. "What's to be done now?" we asked each other. "We cannot repeat the same thing with safety." After consulting a few minutes, we determined to go to Demanget's *bureau*, and see if we could not outwit him. He hap-pened to be at home, and, as usual, not in a good humour. We pretended to be very penitent, and put on long faces, telling him we had imprudently exceeded our time and had missed the *appel*; he began to storm, and we were fearful of over-acting our parts; however, he swallowed the bait and ordered us off to the citadel, and away we went very cheerfully, enjoying the deception. But we had no sooner reached the street than it struck us we could not gain admittance without either a *gendarme* or an order; I therefore returned, and said, "You have ordered us into the citadel, and when we get there they will not let us in." "Won't they?" said he; and calling a *gendarme*, he gave us in charge.

This was about twelve o'clock, and we had been but a short time in the prison, when a friendly *gendarme*, thinking to give us pleasure, told us to make ourselves easy, for we were to be set at liberty next morning. Our time being short we began to reconnoitre, and found everything favour-able to our plan. There were but a few prisoners then in confinement, and these K—— was to divert, and keep as far from the place of operation as possible. About five I descended the stairs leading from the prison into the adjoining church, and bored holes with the gimlet close together round one of the panels of the door, and then, with my knife, cut from one to the other, leaving only one space uncut: I then filled the nicks with tallow, and sprinkled ashes over it; the panel was not thicker than a common door, so that I was not more than half an hour doing the business. One or other of us kept near the top of the stairs the rest of the evening to prevent any stragglers going down. Eight was the set time for going to bed, when we pulled off our coats and waistcoats and lay down, anxiously looking for the hour of ten, for the *gendarmes* to make their appearance, having orders to visit the rooms every two hours: ten came, but no *gendarmes*. In a little while we saw a light glide past the door, which we took for them, and soon after K—— and I crept out to call Alison, who lay in another part of the prison. Then, proceeding softly through the long corridors and down the stairs, I put my hand against the loose panel, thinking the small part of it which I left uncut would break gently off, but to my surprise it made a crack which sounded through the empty buildings like the report of a pistol, but it caused no alarm. I and K—— were through in a moment; but Alison, being a big man, stuck fast in the hole, and cried out lustily as loud as he dare, "Pull, pull!" which we did to the utmost of our strength, and pulled him through. Then, crossing the church, we climbed up one of the windows by the help of the iron bars, expecting to get through the tracery, but to our disappointment there was not sufficient room. Then, groping about in search of a place of exit, we upset a horse upon which a number of things were piled (the church having been converted into a store-house). This made a thundering noise: the dogs barked, the guard was turned out, all seemed to be in confusion outside, and we remained motionless, expecting every minute to hear the church door open; but, fortunately for us, the *gendarmes* neither entered the church, nor went round into the bedrooms to see if all were safe.

Soon after all was quiet; we were again on the move, feeling our way with more caution. At last we came to an altar, on the left side of the choir, which, when we had mounted, discovered unto us a ready way of escape, through a partition of the window undefended by bars, and divested of glass; not being more than from six to seven feet above the ground. From this we dropped quietly into the garden of the convent; we had then a wall to surmount, rather higher than the window sill, which was tiled upon the top; by the help of a rail, which made us a good standing, one end being let into the wall, we unroofed it; but, in spite of all our care, being near a sentinel, we made now and then a clink; but he, being set on the other side of the choir, was out of sight, and, as it happened, out of hearing.

As the church clocks were striking one, the last of us was descending into the open citadel, where we found Barklimore laid snugly his whole length along the bottom of the wall. We walked quietly across the green in the direction of the general's house, which was unoccupied, he then living in town, and consequently we did not expect to find a sentinel posted there, but to our astonishment we ran almost against him; he challenged us, but as he gave no alarm, we supposed him to be a green conscript, quite as frightened of us as we were of him. We darted into the general's garden, K—— foremost; he leaped over a wall about three feet high, expecting it to be the same height on the other side, but he found he had to descend about twenty before he reached the bottom. He called as loud as he dare, told us to ease ourselves down, and he would endeavour to break our fall; we did so, but the nails in my shoe heels came in contact with his nose; fortunately they did no other injury than making it bleed (which caused the report of one of us being seriously hurt); with this exception we escaped uninjured. We soon came in sight of a sentry-box, with the sentinel leaning against it, apparently asleep. Having passed him, I, being then foremost, got over the rampart, presuming it was a breastwork inside, and was standing upon the cordon, when K——, who had better eyes than I, seeing my situation, said, very collectedly, Ellison wait until I come to you – give me your hand, said he – he pulled me up, and then pointed out the danger. Had he not arrested my progress, I should most likely in one moment have been dashed to pieces. The night was dark, and being turned out of our road by the first sentinel, and seeing another where we did not expect one, we became rather confused, and unable to find the spot where we had intended to descend, which was but about thirty-five feet high, but where we did descend was at least sixty-five.

Coming to a place where the breastwork was broken down, we agreed to run no further risk, but stripped, and unwound the rope off our bodies, and tied one end to a stone that stood out beyond the others. We had previously cast lots which was to be the last, which K—— drew. Alison being the most fortunate, went first; then Barklimore – both of whom, though landsmen, descended safely; then came my turn, but K—— begged for the preference, to which I conceded. When I began to descend, I found the cord so stretched – by the three who had preceded me all being heavy men, and so smoothed down and slimy that I could not support my weight, and that I must either have my hands cut through or let go my hold – which latter I did, when I supposed I had descended fifteen to twenty feet. I fell flat upon my back among the rubbish, and heard K—— cry out, "Ellison is killed!" but I soon undeceived him by jumping on my feet.

Finding not much difficulty in getting out of the *fossé*, which was dry, we made the best of our way to our storehouse, K—— and myself walking in much pain. We had not gone far, before I felt something inside my pantaloons, just above and behind the knee, which I could not account for. I said nothing, but felt very uncomfortable, having heard, or read, that people have been severely wounded without knowing it, until the excitement had passed; and, therefore, fancied that the fleshy part of my thigh had been cut off by the fall, and lodged in the place mentioned. I was some time before I could muster courage to feel what it was – arguing the matter *pro* and *con* with myself; till at last, thinking that I must eventually know the cause of my fear, and that whether it was for good or for evil, a few minutes sooner or later would make little difference, down went my hand, and to my inexpressible joy, discovered that it was my neck-kerchief and stiffener, which I had put into my bosom in the hurry of dressing, instead of putting them round my neck.

Being arrived at our hiding-place, in the act of stooping to uncover my knapsack, I fainted; but soon recovered. After having eaten and drank, we took a little repose; and, as soon as it was daylight, we penetrated farther into the wood. About five, we heard the gun – a signal for the peasantry to beat the bushes. About ten, we heard voices, and a rustling among the leaves; but no one came very near us. After all was quiet, and the excitement passed, K—— found both his ancles so strained, that he could scarcely stand – for he also had let go the rope long before he reached the bottom. Instead of leeches, Barklimore applied his lancet, and bled them in different places: he then examined my back, and found the lower part much discoloured; it gave me considerable pain, especially when I stooped or straightened myself.

Here we lay four days – the first two fine, the last two almost continual rain. The third night, I was better; and accompanied Barklimore to a rivulet about two miles off, to lay in a fresh stock of water. What we had, being in bladders, had become so offensive, that we could not drink it; therefore we threw them away, and trusted to our canteens, which held about three quarts. On the fifth night, K——'s ancles being something stronger, we left the wood, and about twelve arrived at the Meuse, in the middle of which was a small island, connected by bridges to a village on each side. We had passed through the one next us, and found all apparently asleep, for we saw no one stirring; but when we reached the first bridge, the church bell began to toll an alarm. We ran to gain the other, and on drawing nearer it, were met with three or four pistol shots. By this time all the villagers were up, sounding their horns. What was to be done? we had run into the toil – the enemy was before and behind – the river on each side – and none of us swimmers. We turned off the road, ran along the bank, and, at the extremity of the island, to our great joy, found a boat: we jumped into it, were across in a moment, and very soon out of hearing of our pursuers. At daylight, we found ourselves near a wood, which we entered; but all the brushwood having been cut down, there was not a hiding-place left, but behind the trunks of the trees. This we were obliged to put up with; for we durst not go in search of better quarters. It was a trying day for us; but we kept a good look out, ready to manoeuvre according to circumstances.

Having remained undisturbed, we set out again at dark, and were progressing tolerably well, marching by night and lying in the woods by day, suffering most from want of water: it was rarely that we could fill our canteens with any that was clear and refreshing; and had to take up our quarters in the woods several times with a very small stock. When we had plenty, we shaved, and made ourselves as decent as circumstances would admit of. We brought with us provisions for eighteen days – allowing ourselves one inch and a half of thick Boulogne sausage, a quarter of a pound of bread, and two mouthsful of brandy, per diem; the latter was measured in a shaving-brush case, being the only utensil we had, in addition to the canteens. We found the time, from three in the morning to nine at night, tedious and irksome; after our first nap, we felt cold and shivery, in which state we remained until the burning rays of the sun dispelled the cold, and we became overheated.

By the help of our maps, we kept in a pretty direct course, never entering a house, nor having any communication, save with two individuals. One directed us round the town of Toul, without asking a question; the other overtook us going through a valley between two woods. He accosted us civilly, and asked where we were going? We told him, to the *depot*, to join our regiment; but he soon gave us to understand, that he thought we were conscripts who had deserted. We did not undeceive him, knowing that the peasantry, to a man, hated the conscription. He told us not to be afraid of him; that he was only a poor labourer; that if we would go to his cottage, we should have the best that it afforded. We told him that we were in a great hurry, and could not stop. He pressed us in every way; and at last the poor fellow said, "O do come, *et je vous mettrez dans ma chemise.*" When he found he could not prevail, he said, "Well, I will not leave you until I have set you in the right road, for there are a number of turnings and windings in this valley, and you may lose your way." He went with us about three miles; we gave him a drink of brandy; he shook hands with us all round, wished us well out of the country, and bid us good-night.

The eleventh day, our hiding-place was a wood on the side of a hill, which was so steep that we durst not lay down, being only a few yards from the edge of a precipice, over which K—— had nearly fallen, it being hidden by brambles. Indeed, if we could have lain down, we should have had an uncomfortable bed, for it rained incessantly all the day. We sat against the roots of the trees, wet, cold, and hungry. The previous night we had passed over very little ground, K——'s ancles failing him; and he was worn as thin as a whipping post. Very unwisely, we had entered into an engagement to sink or swim together. Having passed such a miserable day, we started sooner than usual, though not until it was nearly dark. About half-past ten, we came to the small town of Charmes, and, presuming that the bad weather would keep the small portion of inhabitants that might not happen to be in their beds (for the French retire early) within doors, we ventured to enter, and soon discovered that we had miscalculated: for we found a number of people stirring; still we thought it more prudent to advance than retreat. On passing a corner, we were hailed by a *gendarme* (our knapsacks, no doubt, excited his suspicion). "Where are you going, *Messieurs*?" "To look for a lodging." "Where are your passports?" "In our pockets," we replied, "but you cannot see them in the dark." We were soon in the midst of a crowd, the *gendarme* insisting on our passports. We requested he would shew us a lodging, and then he should see them. According to our desire, he took us into a house, where Barklimore began to joke with him; but it was useless – the man would see the passports. Then you shall see them, said Barklimore, with all the *sang froid* imaginable; and taking out of his pocket-book some testimonials that he had received from Messrs. Munro, Gregory & Co., he put them into the *gendarme's* hands. He turned the papers in all directions, and said he had never seen such passports. "You have never seen such passports!" said B——, "and you are a *gendarme*?" "Yes." "And you dare stop gentlemen in the street, without being able to read their passports; and are, moreover, so ignorant as not to know that of late all passports have been issued at Paris in a new form?" The man stared with astonishment, and we were beginning to flatter ourselves that Barklimore would out-general the *gendarme*; when in came a *brigadier*, and very good-humouredly said, "Ah, gentlemen, I am glad to see you; I have been expecting you for above a week"; and then pulling out a paper, he read our names and descriptions. Finding ourselves caught, we made the best of it – ordered something to eat, and invited the *brigadier* and *gendarme* to share with us; which they did. The latter told us that he had been in bed; but his wife being poorly, she had requested him to go to the apothecary's; and that, returning, he met with some acquaintances, who kept him in conversation until we came up.

After supper, the officer asked how much money we had? We told him, "Very little." "Well," says he, "although it is a breach of my duty, I shall not deprive you of it; neither shall I search you: you will find the need of it. But my orders are very severe, and I must act in accordance with them; and, for my own safety, lodge you in the town prison. I am extremely sorry to be the instrument; but you know the nature of the service; and will not think I treat you more harshly than my duty requires."

Early next morning, we began to retrace our steps towards Verdun, under a strong escort of *gendarmerie*. At St. Mihiel we rested a day, in the most comfortable prison I ever abode in; and had the whole range of it – even the privilege of sitting with the jailer and jaileress – two very good sort of people. Here we met with a pretty, interesting-looking female, formerly of respectability, waiting her trial for poisoning her husband, the proof of which was clear against her, and for which she suffered a short time afterwards. The wanness of her face depicted her inward pangs: not so her conversation, which was still *a la Française*, light, frivolous, and indelicate – telling us what she had heard of the English and their *amours*, and what a poor opinion she had of their taste; shewing the ruling passion. Her voice was sweet, but lost its effect in the words she uttered; and whether she was more an object of pity or contempt, it was hard to say. If all the prisons lying in the way of the English had been as comfortable as that of St. Mihiel's, much of the dread of running away would have been removed.

On entering the town of Verdun, we found all our friends waiting to receive us; but not a word was permitted to be exchanged. We made, as may readily be imagined, a sorry appearance; our clothes bearing evident signs of what had been the nature of our lodgings, and our linen shewing that it had not lately been in the hands of the laundress. We were paraded through the streets into the citadel, and lodged in the *Tour d'Angouleme*, a small round building with only two apartments, one above the other, with a circular stair outside, leading to the upper one. Barklimore was put into the lower one, the rest above.

A little while after we had been shut up, an officer and three *gendarmes* came to search us. They commenced with Barklimore; then coming up-stairs, told Alison to strip to his shirt; twisted his hat and shoes in every direction; then his neck-kerchief, coat, waistcoat, pantaloons, and stock-ings; but found nothing. K—— was next in turn. While his clothes were undergoing a similar examination, I contrived to place myself between Alison and the *gendarmes*, when, putting my hand behind me, I slipped into his hand four louis, which I had had loose in my pocket. When they came to K——'s pantaloons, one of them observed a button above the common size, and, thinking it looked suspicious, he cut into it, and out dropped a double louis – which brought a grin upon all their countenances, and a few *sacrés* from their tongues. All their knives were instantly in requisition, and the poor buttons were disembowelled in the most cruel and wanton manner: coat buttons, waistcoat buttons, pantaloon buttons – all were ripped up; their hard hearts spared none, neither large nor small. After supposing they had found all the golden eggs upstairs, they went down to commit the same acts of cruelty upon Barklimore's. But they had not left me so bare as they imagined: I had five double louis sewed inside my flannel waistcoat, and one under the arm of my coat. Still the booty amounted to about sixty louis. They even took our knives, razors (which we begged hard for), pocket handkerchiefs, in short, every-thing out of our pockets. A three livre piece dropped out of one of mine, while they were examining them, which I picked up. "Let him keep that," said one of the men, "it is but a trifle." "No," said the officer, "my orders are to take every farthing."

Immediately afterwards we saw Barklimore led out. We were all con-jecture what they were going to do with him; but seeing him return in a short time, we supposed Demanget had been lecturing him. The sentinel that was placed over us, would not allow any communication. Before dark, the gaoler brought us a loaf of black bread each, and a pitcher of water, saying, he had strict orders not to give us anything else, not even straw; but that was no great deprivation, as we had been accustomed to much worse lodgings.

The next morning two *gendarmes* came for us; and as we were going down the steps which went in front of Barklimore's window, he called out, "Say you know nothing of me! say you know nothing of me!" We took the hint. We were led to Demanget's office; he went with us to that part of the rampart whence we had descended, and asked us, was that the spot? We said, "Yes"; though we had no means of knowing it, but by the breast-work having fallen. He knew it well enough, the rope having been found there. It was frightful to look down, after having fallen nearly from the top; it was the very highest part on that side of the citadel, and ap-peared double the height of the spot where we had intended to descend. We then returned with him, when he took our depositions separately, only one being in the room at a time. When I was called, I met K—— in the lobby, who told me, in a few words, what he had said. Demanget addressed me in a mild, insinuating manner, and the words from his oily mouth flowed so smoothly as almost to throw anyone, ignorant of the lieutenant's character, off his guard. The following dialogue then ensued :

"Which of the four, first made the proposal to the others to desert?"

"It had been the theme of our conversation for many months past, and it would be very difficult to tell who it was that first mentioned it."

"But some one of you must have made the first proposal?"

"Very likely; but it has so long passed that I have forgotten the circumstances."

"Where did you get your gimlets, saws, and maps?"

"At different shops, under various pretexts."

"Who cut through the door?"

"I did."

"And then you got into the church, and thence into the garden?"

"Yes."

"And then you untiled the wall and got over it?"

"Yes."

"And then, you found the Doctor?"

"*Non, Monsieur*, we did not find the Doctor until we gained the wood."

Then Demanget was himself again; and jumping up in a terrible passion, his eyes flaming with rage, said, "Ah, f——, I'll teach you to lie with impunity! Here, *gendarme*, take away this fellow, and put him in irons, hand and foot." In going from him, I met Alison, and told him what I had said of Barklimore.

The examination concluded, we were put into the lower apartment with Barklimore, who was, and had been all night, in irons. He was in a most distressing plight, being scarcely able to express how he had been tortured by fleas – so much so, that he hardly expected to survive until morning. He could not defend nor scratch himself, his hands being fettered; and what made it still worse, he had put them lengthwise into the irons, instead of crosswise. Having heard his pitiable tale, we prevailed upon the gaoler (who was an old acquaintance, through selling us wine when we had been previously shut up in the citadel, and who was a tolerably decent fellow) to sell us a besom, and lend us a spade and two or three buckets. We all, save Barklimore, set to work, and carried out all the litter, which had been straw some eight or ten years past. Having swept the place clean, the sentinel accompanied us backwards and forwards to the well, and we gave the floor, guard-bed, and walls a good rinsing, which quieted the enemy for the time we remained there. Then, by dint of large promises – for it was presumed we had no money – we prevailed upon him to bring us some straw; and thus we had a pretty fair lodging-house; a little damp, or so, but that did not affect us.

In the afternoon a guard came to execute Demanget's threat. The officer made a number of apologies for putting me to so much inconvenience, but he must obey orders. A little while afterwards came the jailer to tell us that the General, out of his wondrous clemency, had ordered him to give us everything that we chose to eat, and were willing to pay for, but on no account whatever to allow us more than a bottle of small wine each per day, not one drop of brandy, lest we should be riotous – a very unnecessary precaution; for, had we been so inclined, we could have done no harm; the wall of the prison was six feet thick, with only one window secured with strong iron bars, and a sentinel placed before it.

A guard always attended the jailer when he brought our victuals, and he favoured us by setting our hands and feet at liberty, in order that we might eat with more comfort, and exercise our limbs. My hand irons were in the shape of the letter U, with the letter T standing in the centre of it, one wrist being put on each side the T; then the cross of the T, being something shorter than the width of the U, screwed down until the wrists were confined between the bottom of the U and the cross of the T, and when sufficiently low it was locked. The jailer had some feeling, and whenever he was turning the screw he would say, "Now, *Monsieur* E——, do not let me hurt you; tell me when the screw is low enough." I was not backward in taking his advice, and took care to cry out in time: my coat sleeves were long, and he did not take the precaution to turn them up. I, by raising my thumbs, made my wrists thicker; thus I deceived him, and he was no sooner gone than my hands were at liberty. Not so with poor Barklimore; his irons were of a different description – no manoeuvring could get them off. He told us the General was present at his examination, and abused him with all the gross expressions that a low-bred Frenchman's voluble tongue can with so much facility utter.

He was more enraged against Barklimore than any of us, because he was liable to censure for having a prisoner under his charge without any security either by parole or by bondsman. The reason we were so strictly examined was, to obtain proof that he was the *chef de complot* (ringleader), in order that the General might with some show of pretence visit him with a greater degree of punishment; but that was all moonshine, for he punished him first and tried him afterwards; and perhaps his lieutenant felt a little extra soreness on my account, for the prominent part I took in the trick played upon him. The irons Barklimore and I had upon our legs were about eight pounds weight; we could shuffle about a little, advancing two or three inches at a step, which enabled us to get at the window to breathe the fresh air, on the sill of which we could lay our whole length. Occasionally we saw our friends at a distance, but the sentinel would not allow us to speak, and pen, ink, and paper were forbidden.

In the middle of the eighth night we heard voices and the noise of cart wheels; "What's this?" was the simultaneous cry. By-and-by the doors were unlocked, and in marched four *gendarmes* with a lantern; I had scarcely time to put on my irons. "*Allons, Messieurs, en route*" ("Come along, Gentlemen"), was the only salute. "Where to?" we asked; "What are you going to do with us?" "Ask no questions, but come along directly." "Are you not first going to take off these *bêtise*?" I asked, looking at the irons. "*Bêtise*, do you call them? We will inquire about that." Having obtained permission, they set our limbs at liberty. We were then ready, having no toilette to make, at least Barklimore and I. They led us out and placed us in a covered wagon, having four seats, a prisoner and a *gendarme* on each, with the irons dangling *in terrorem* at our sides. In mounting, we saw Demanget skulking on the off side, but he never spoke. We were all conjecture what was to be our fate; we could not tell by what gate we left the town, and the *gendarmes* would not answer a question, but when the day broke they were more communicative, and told us our destination was Bitche. "Our orders," said they, "are to show you no lenity, but to lodge you in prison wherever we stop; but if you will promise not to take advantage of the kindness we are inclined to shew you, we will give you any liberty you can reasonably require." We accepted their conditions and gave our word that they should have no cause of complaint; they believed us, and we travelled like gentlemen, parading the towns where we stopped, and seeing all the lions, each of us with a liveried servant at his heels. On our way we met fourteen of our countrymen chained together, among whom were some old acquaintances, Messrs. Tuthil, Ashworth, and Brine, marching jovially along, hallooing and singing, with as much apparent joy as if they were on their way homewards. "Where are you going?" we asked. "To Metz." "What for?" "To be tried for setting the *souterrain* on fire, and attempting to blow up the magazine." In fact they had been attempting to escape by a passage that led from the *souterrain* outside the fort; they had cut through one wooden door, undermined an iron one, and trying to force a third, the noise alarmed a sentinel, and put an end to their career. They underwent a long trial, and were all condemned, some to ten years and others to seven in the gallies. Then the president of the court-martial rose and addressed them as follows: "Gentlemen, for your sakes and that of your countrymen I have given you a fair trial, in order to show you that you stand legally condemned; but, as a portion of you are British officers, I, to show the respect I have for your honourable profession, shall not put the law in force: you are all pardoned, and I trust you will never again be guilty of the same offence; if you are, you must not expect the same lenity."

CHAPTER FIVE

SEACOME ELLISON failed in his first attempt to escape but he had made his start and, like most escapers, did not rest content in captivity again. He escaped twice more, each time with his friend K——, before he finally managed to reach Trieste and thence Malta, Gibraltar and England.

The fortress of Bitche where Ellison and K—— were sent as a punishment was, I think, the first "naughty boys' camp" in the history of captivity, and takes its place alongside Ingolstadt in World War I and Colditz in World War II as a collecting place for inveterate escapers. In his book Seacome Ellison says of the prison:

"The fortress of Bitche is situated ten leagues north of Strasburg in the midst of a valley, upon a rock about one thousand feet above the level. It is ascended on one side by a zigzag footpath and on the other by a carriage road, winding round and ascending gradually, till both meet at a draw-bridge that communicates with an inclined plain raised upon arches, leading to the gate at the entrance to the fort, the approaches to which are exposed to a battery of ten pieces of heavy artillery. The entrance is by a tunnel cut through the rock, a hundred and twenty feet long, having a massy gate at each end and one in the centre. The rock has been cut through in two places, as low as the ditch; one extremity called the *grosse tête*, the other the *petite tête*; both connected to the body of the fort by draw-bridges. The whole is capable of mounting about forty pieces of cannon. On the west side, forty or fifty feet lower than the upper part, is a mortar battery; this I traversed in making my escape, but from the darkness of the night did not observe it. In the centre of the fort stand two large barracks, and at the two ends storehouses and magazines. The rock is excavated to a considerable extent, sufficient to contain the whole garrison, provisions, etc.; and divided into compartments connected by narrow passages and secured by doors, some of iron and some of wood. There is also a subterraneous passage which communicates with the town. Although this fort is formed of solid rock, cut down perpendicularly ninety to one hundred and fifty feet deep, yet it is faced all round with masonry, except a small portion that juts out and runs along, about the centre. The expense of constructing it was so great that it is said when Louis XIV was applied to for money to complete it, he enquired if they were building it of louis."

* * * * *

While Ellison and K—— were still in the punishment cells at Bitche, Lieutenant Donat Henchy O'Brien, R.N., made his final and successful escape. O'Brien was an Irishman, and judging by his portrait a man not to be trifled with. He was nineteen years of age when he was captured with his crew off the coast of Brittany in 1804. After a forced march of seven hundred miles the prisoners were held in Givet, but they were later transferred to Verdun where O'Brien was allowed to live in the town on parole. But he soon tired of this pacific life and with three other naval officers, Essel, Ashworth and Tuthill, he decided to escape.

Being on parole, they had first to commit the minor breach of the regulations. They, also, had some difficulty in inveigling the guards into placing them under arrest. Once imprisoned, however, they were free to escape, and this they did by descending the eighty-foot walls of the prison by means of a rope. Travelling on foot and feeding off the country as they went, the four escapers set out for Etaples where they hoped to steal a boat. They walked for three weeks and were arrested right on the coast by customs officers – not as escaped prisoners but for being without the proper papers. Discovery of their true identity was the inevitable result. The captain of *gendarmes* congratulated them on their escape and expressed his sympathy with it. Nevertheless the recaptured prisoners were returned to Verdun in chains. After several interrogations they too were sent to Bitche.

During the journey to Bitche the escapers jumped from the wagons in which they were travelling and got away again. O'Brien, separated from the others, hid in a swamp. It was November, raining, and he had no food nor adequate clothing. In spite of this he walked for nine nights, hiding in the daytime and sleeping in woods and caves. It rained constantly throughout his journey, and his feet became so swollen that he was forced to walk without his shoes. His only food was turnips and cabbage stumps, yet this amazing man forced himself along to Strasburg where he crossed the Rhine into Germany. From here he wandered into the Schaffhausen salient where so many prisoners have since come to grief. He was arrested as a spy and was compelled to disclose his true identity to save his life. After eleven days in gaol he was taken in chains to Bitche, from which fortress he made the successful break which he describes here.

Donat Henchy O'Brien

AT ABOUT noon, on the 21st of December 1807, the high turrets and massive towers of the gloomy fortress in which I was going to be incarcerated presented themselves to my sight. Their very appearance was sufficient to strike the mind with horror; and I cannot but believe that the engineer had this object in view when he gave such outward forms to his structure. The prospect of being shut up in that detestable fortress, perhaps for the remainder of my days, could only be relieved by the probability that my length of life would be shortened by the nature of my imprisonment. Death itself was preferable to protracted persecution, and I sometimes devoutly wished to be at rest. In this train of thought and feeling I proceeded; and so absorbed was I by my affliction, that I was almost unconscious of any objects or circumstances around me, until I was roughly awakened from my stupor and found myself in the centre of the fortress of Bitche.

*   *   *   *   *

As soon as I could collect my scattered senses and compose my distracted mind, I found that I was stared at from all sides by my unhappy countrymen, who at that moment happened to be out of their *souterrains*, on their permission to take those few gasps of fresh air that were essential to their being able to exist for the rest of the day in their noxious dungeons. I could hear some of these poor fellows questioning whether I was a British subject. "He must have been at the head of some banditti!" said one. "He looks like it," observed another. "Perhaps," remarked a third, "he is the captain of the soldiers he is chained to." "Very likely," rejoined another. "At all events," said a fifth, "whether he is an Englishman or a foreigner, it is clear he is not a prisoner of war, for they never would load a prisoner of war of any nation so heavily with chains." In this opinion, and in this alone, did they all agree; and I was set down by universal consent as some daring criminal that had committed one, or even a host of atrocious crimes. At length some of my old friends saw and recognised me. "Good heavens!" exclaimed one, "it is our old friend O'Brien." "But why such chains, and with such a gang?" was the reply. None dared approach to ask a question; and, as I afterwards found, the general inference was, that, in my attempt to escape, I had killed some officer or soldier who had opposed me, and that I was led here thus secured preparatory to my trial and execution for murder.

86

But it was not many minutes before my old friends and companions, Ashworth and Tuthill, found means to get at me.

I was never more thunderstruck in my life, for I had flattered myself, that they had effected their escape, and had been happy in the thought which had worked itself into my mind as a fact, that they had arrived safely in England. Mr. Baker, of the merchant service, and in a short time all my old companions, surrounded me, except poor Lieutenant Essel; and on my anxiously inquiring for him, to my great grief was I informed that he had been dashed to pieces in endeavouring to get over the walls, in a fresh attempt to escape. Mr. Ashworth and Tuthill told me that they had been arrested or recaptured about two hours after they had parted from me in the wood. It had, in fact, been so suddenly surrounded by soldiers and peasantry that it was impossible to escape from it. They added that they never had been able to account for my getting clear. The other prisoners had not taken advantage of the diversion we had made in their favour, but had remained in the waggon.

The melancholy intelligence of my poor fellow-sufferer Essel's violent death was an additional pang to my misfortunes and anguish. I was anxiously asking the particulars, when the guard came up, and angrily drove my friends to their respective dungeons for daring to communicate with me. I, with the Corsicans, was most unceremoniously conducted to a different part of the fortress, called *La Grosse Tête*.

I shall not attempt to describe the fortress of Bitche. To give a minute detail of its strength, *souterrains*, etc., would fill a volume. At this moment it is sufficient for me to say that it is reckoned one of the strongest fortifications of France, and is built on the summit of an immensely high rock, out of which all its subterranean caves are hollowed. It has, on one side, three ramparts. The first is from ninety to one hundred feet high; the second, from forty to fifty; and the third, from twenty-five to thirty, with redoubts, entrenchments, and all contrivances of military engineering, almost innumerable. As I surveyed these stupendous heights and depths, it appeared to me a physical impossibility to escape from it, and I was filled with despair. Nothing but madness could entertain a thought of attempting to escape. Being now arrived at the wretched dungeon I was to inhabit, my handcuffs and chains were taken off, and the Corsican deserters were conducted to the condemned cells. They were, I believe, soon afterwards shot. A dismal dungeon was unlocked, in which it seemed that I was doomed to be entombed alive. Solitude appeared to me dreadful, and I looked upon a "living death" as my final lot; but I found in the dungeon Mr. Worth, midshipman, and a Captain Brine of the merchant service. The latter was one of those who came from Verdun with me.

They were on a door, which they had managed to unhinge, and which lay as a platform to keep them out of the excrement and wet, that were more than ankle deep: they had a little straw and a blanket. They informed me, they had been companions of the unfortunate Essel in the late attempt to get over the ramparts. Six of them had broken out of their cave, had got a rope made of sheets, and were on the point of lowering themselves down, when they were discovered and the alarm given, which made four of them clap on the rope together, though only strong enough to lower one at a time, or two at most; the rope, in consequence, broke. One was dashed to pieces, and the three others – I think their names were Nason, Potts, and Adams – so severely mangled and bruised that little hopes were at first entertained of their recovery; Worth and Brine were soon seized by the guards on the embrasure. The others were then improving fast, and they expected them in the dungeon in a few days, as soon as the surgeon had reported them well enough; after which they would have to remain in this receptacle of filth for thirty-one days, which was the usual time of being buried alive in the first and most horrible gradation of our captivity. It was fifty deep stone steps under ground, for I have often counted them, and the most dark and intricate passages led from it to the gaoler's house, who had the watching and superintending of the prisoners, in conjunction with a guard.

I had not been more than half-an-hour in this dismal and filthy abode, when a *gendarme* came, and desired *le nouveau arrivé* to follow him. I imagined it was to liberate me (that is to say, from this dungeon), and to place me with my companions, Messrs. Ashworth and Tuthill, in one of the caves, which was deemed a kind of indulgence, they having a bed and fire allowed in the latter; but I was greatly in error.

I followed my guide through all the before-mentioned passages, and at last arrived at the gaoler's house; where I was accosted, in the following words, by a man who wore a leathern cap and frock-coat:

"You, sir, are the person who has given us so much trouble, and been the cause of the *gendarmes* having been transported to the galleys."

"Not to my knowledge."

"You are, sir, and merit the greatest severity that can be inflicted."

This induced me to request to be informed what he meant.

"I mean, sir," revociferated he, "that you deserve the severest punishment, for not resting quietly with your guards, and for being accessory to the punishment of them."

I replied, "I was conscious that I had only done my duty in endeavouring to escape from slavery, tyranny, and oppression, and every other cruelty that could be invented."

I showed him the marks I then had on my wrists and different parts of my body, expressing very warmly at the same time my detestation of a country that could countenance such treatment.

"Pray," said he, "do you know who you are thus accosting?"

"I really do not."

"Then, sir, I would have you to know, that I am commandant over all the prisoners confined in this fort; that I have very great power invested in me, and could place you, in a moment, where you would never be seen or heard of."

I replied, "That I was not aware he was commandant – I had not the smallest doubt with regard to his power – was far from having a wish to give him the least offence – that I was entirely in his power – he could therefore act by me as he thought proper."

He listened with great attention; became quite soft and mild; was extremely sorry, but could not avoid punishing me. He accordingly ordered me to be conducted back to the dungeon I had just left. My companions procured me something to eat; and I absolutely felt happy, although in so miserable a place, at being with my own countrymen: I had nothing now to fear but the guillotine, or slavery in the galleys.

Thus, my mind being a little at ease, and my spirits somewhat recruited, I gathered together a few of the scattered straws, laid myself down on the platform that had been contrived by my comrades in adversity, and fell fast asleep. When I awoke, the night was far advanced. My companions, by some means or other, had procured a flint, tinder-box, and candle, and we struck a light. They were anxious to have an account of my adventures, with which I indulged them, and they in return narrated to me their misfortunes and sufferings. In this manner did I pass my first night in this horrible dungeon.

There were three, and but three, livres of my money still remaining, and with this, by dint of bribery, we procured some brandy from the gaoler. This stimulus we found very necessary, for the effluvium from this noxious and pestiferous place was as strong, and almost as offensive, as that of the last dungeon at Niederbronn, in which I had been confined with the Corsican soldiers. We had recourse also to smoking tobacco, which to a great degree mitigated the effects of the fetidity of this revolting place, although it made me very sick. I now received secret intelligence, that a Madame B—l—a—d, in the little town of Bitche, had lately received, through the medium of my worthy friend, the Rev. Launcelot C. Lee, an order to supply my pecuniary wants to a certain extent; and I need not say how much this considerate and humane act of generosity and kindness had exhilarated my drooping spirits.

I could not help expressing to my comrades my astonishment at the immense strength and security of our dungeons. They surpassed anything I had ever seen, or anything I had ever formed an idea of; and it seemed to me wonderful how men could ever imagine and construct such places for the torment and slow destruction of their fellow-creatures.

It was some time the next day before we could obtain anything whatever to recruit exhausted nature, although our cries on the gaoler's name, La Roche, had been re-echoed a thousand times from the bottom of our cell. We had taken it by turns to call out, but all of us were nearly worn out, when the fellow came to the bars of the small hole that admitted air; and after soliciting and praying, flattering and appealing, to all his good qualities (Heaven forgive us for our hypocrisy!), the rogue agreed to give us some refreshment. This he passed through the triple bars of the hole, as he was not entrusted with the keys of the door, and whatever he brought we eagerly devoured.

I inquired of my companions if they were never permitted to breathe fresh air; and, to my sorrow, they replied that as yet they had never enjoyed that indulgence. It appeared to me an impossibility to exist many days in such a place without it. I told my fellow-sufferers that I thought it would be advisable to solicit the indulgence by a joint letter to the commandant, stating our situation – at the same time requesting immediate death, if it were his intention to deprive us of health, and so cause us to linger away, and terminate a miserable existence by degrees.

This application had the desired effect, and we were allowed to breathe the air every day, between the hours of eleven and one. On this the first day, whilst respiring the air, which proved to us a relief beyond expression, I was informed by one of the *gendarmes*, that on the day after I had escaped, their commanding officer had issued strict orders to the men of his corps, who had been despatched to scour the woods and the country in search of me, that, in the event of their *finding* me, they were to scar and disfigure me with their sabres *au front et au visage*, and to mutilate me in such a manner as would prove an example to deter, in future, any British prisoner of war from attempting to escape. This circumstance I heard frequently repeated afterwards by others of the same corps.

Upon my putting the question to them, whether, in the event of falling in with me, they would have actually put in execution those injunctions, some made an evasive reply and hesitated; while others, more candid, acknowledged that they would have been obliged to obey their orders *à la lettre* – and that, of course, they would have been directed to state, in justification of such conduct, that they had no alternative, as I would not surrender, but resisted most desperately.

No entreaty whatever could procure us any more cleanliness. We were literally worse off than pigs or dogs.

We now again began to devise and meditate upon plans for escaping. One proposed undermining the dungeon. I saw no prospect whatever of succeeding in this point. I, however, was willing to try every means to regain my liberty. Hammers and chisels with great difficulty were procured, and we carried them always about us, as the dungeon was ransacked every day in our absence. We hung an old coat up against that part of the rock which we intended to begin upon. Rope was necessary to descend the ramparts after we had got out of the dungeon; we accordingly, through some friends, who had obtained permission to come and see us, contrived to purchase some stout linen for shirts (which we really much wanted), and from the shoemakers amongst the prisoners we got, now and then, a ball of twine. We procured needles, bees'-wax, etc., by degrees, and made a rope of four or five fathoms for each, which we *marled* with the remainder of the twine, and passed tight round our bodies underneath the shirt. Our working time commenced immediately on being locked up after breathing the fresh air. Night would not do, as it would be necessary to have candle-light, and we might have been seen through the bars by our sentinels.

The undermining business was found impracticable, and was consequently dropped. Having a rope, we flattered ourselves we might, some day whilst allowed to breathe the fresh air, be able to elude the vigilance of the sentinels and scale the walls. However, this proved to be a plan so difficult to accomplish that it was abandoned, and our only hope was that we might have an opportunity of using the rope when we should be liberated from our present dungeon and placed in another *souterrain* or apartment of the fortress.

Christmas night came, but without either Christmas cheer, etc., or cheerfulness. We were reflecting upon our miseries without anything to soothe them. The tune of "Oh, the roast beef of Old England!" would occur to us, and visionary plum-puddings and rich sirloins would torment the imagination. All the hospitality, mirth, and good-heartedness that are displayed in our native isles on this festivity were vividly before us in recollections. "*Nessun maggior dolor che ricordarsi del tempo felice nella miseria*," was now fully verified. Intense thought and intense feelings overcame the frame, and I at length fell into a profound sleep. In a short time I was suddenly roused by my friends and violently dragged into a corner of my cell. Upon my inquiring what this meant, I was informed that the sentinel had burnt priming through the bars at Mr. Worth, and had snapped his musket again before I was apprised of it; if it had gone off, the ball must have passed through my body, as I was point-blank opposite the bars. The fellow had desired Mr. Worth to put his candle out, and he had refused, upon which the unfeeling wretch (perhaps intoxicated), without saying a word more, had twice snapped his piece at him – a summary method of enforcing orders. We soon placed ourselves where he could not hit us, even if his musket should go off. The candle was still burning, and this fiery though non-firing sentinel was obliged to turn suppliant, and to beg us to put it out. All the time of his supplication he kept his piece levelled at the candle. We had had an abundance of experience with reference to the character of such rascals, and carefully kept out of his way. At midnight he was relieved, and we made known his conduct to the corporal of the guard, who rebuked him severely, and gave us permission to keep our candle burning. What was the harm? We could hatch no treasons, and contrive no stratagems, by a rushlight; nor were we in danger of setting fire to a damp, vaulted, stone dungeon.

This fellow's conduct, however, had been so outrageous that we determined to report him to the commandant the next day, and we endeavoured to compose ourselves for the remainder of the night, thanking Providence that, by his musket missing fire, we had escaped his murderous intentions.

Accordingly, during the time we were out, I made what had happened known to the *maréchal de logis*, Monsieur Mitchell, who was second in command. I pointed out to him the inhumanity of this wretch, in endeavouring to deprive poor prisoners of war of their lives, who had been placed already in the most horrible state imaginable, for having an inch of candle burning on Christmas night. He replied with a vast deal of *sang froid*, "But his piece did not go off; none of you were hurt; and where is the use of taking any more notice of it?"

23rd January 1808. – We were, at length, conducted from the dungeon to a miserable hole under ground, to which I descended by thirty steep stone steps, where Messrs. Tuthill and Ashworth, with fifty of our countrymen, were already buried alive. Here I remained, planning and scheming everything possible to effect my escape, but in vain. I, however, wore the rope constantly round me; yet the guards were so watchful that I had very little hopes of ever being able to make the intended use of it.

This continued during the months of February, March, April, May and June; at the expiration of which the commandant had the kindness to allow me to go up into a small room, where there were already twelve more. This indulgence, he had the courtesy to say, was in consequence of my good conduct. Messrs. Tuthill, Ashworth, and Brine were of the number. The latter wore his rope as I did, and was the only person of the party, then in the room, who knew I had one. We became daily more intimate from this confidence in each other; and after a vast number of fruitless endeavours, on the 17th of July 1808 the term of our slavery appeared to be drawing to a conclusion: I was on that day told in confidence by one of the seamen – a young Irishman, whose name I forget – that a party had thoughts of breaking out that night from the *souterrain*; that he was one of them; and he informed me who the rest were. I began to regret having ever left the cave. However, I imagined there was a probability of getting down to them for the night. I accordingly waited upon the heads of this party during their time for breathing the air, and, without intimating my motives, I requested that they would allow me to visit them in the cave, or *souterrain*, that evening. They stared, and the oddness of the request made them suspect that I had a knowledge of their designs. Knowing their complete confidence in me, I did not hesitate to tell them the truth. With everything complimentary in their opinions of me, they still refused to comply with my request; for they assured me that they could not deviate from their fixed plan, and that was, that none of those upstairs were to be admitted below. The motive of this was a dread to excite suspicion, for it was necessary to obtain permission from the *maréchal de logis* for us to go to the lower cell, and even asking it might put the authorities on the *qui vive*. Greatly did I feel mortified at my exclusion from the enterprise. At the usual hour, six in the evening, they were made to descend, in order to be locked up, but as they went below I told them that I did not despair of joining them that evening. After their doors had been locked, I had observed that it was the habit of the *maréchal de logis* to quit the fortress for some time, and this night I anxiously watched his departure. At about half-past six I saw him go out; at seven it was our turn to be locked up. The interval was to me momentous – no time was to be lost. Never was I in a greater state of anxiety. At last I went boldly up to the *gendarme* on guard, whose name was Buché, and told him that I had been invited to celebrate the anniversary of an old friend's birth-night in the *souterrain*, and that he would oblige me greatly by allowing me to descend. He hesitated. "Nay, my kind Monsieur Buché," I said most civilly, "what apprehensions can you possibly be under? Am I not by far more secure in the *souterrain* than in the cell upstairs?" This well-timed observation satisfied him, and I received his permission to descend.

I immediately apprised Messrs. Tuthill, Brine, and Ashworth, of my success, when they also persuaded the guard to let them join in celebrating the birth-night. I was afraid that their application would create suspicion, and prevent even my joining the party; but I was glad to find that the very reverse was the case. My celebrity for stratagems in effecting escapes was unhappily so great that any request I might make immediately conjured up a host of confused suspicions; but when poor Monsieur Buché found so many wishing to celebrate the birth-night, he concluded that there really was a birth-night to celebrate, although it might have struck a more sapient brain that it was rather an absurdity for men to celebrate anything who had scarcely sufficient food to put in their mouths.

However, it was not our business to be too curious, and I descended with my companions. As we approached the cave, my ears were struck with the din of merriment, which was artfully assumed in order to prevent the sentinels hearing the noise of chisels, saws, and other tools, that I concluded were hard at work. Some were singing or shouting, others dancing, others were making their dogs howl and bark, and by no gentle means; and the deception was so admirably kept up that the gaoler and guards might have supposed that there was a boisterous saturnalia celebrating amongst their prisoners. Before seven we were in the midst of these "merry fellows", and our guard locked us all in together, laughing that we English could make ourselves so happy upon little or nothing. We had taken a few necessaries with us for the night, which could not be observed, in our pockets.

Our friends received us with open arms, and admired our perseverance. I found they were getting on rapidly; the miners were very active. One door was already forced. The second door was an immense iron one; it was impossible to break through it; the miners had therefore worked away the earth and rock under it. It was half-past ten before we got a hole large enough for a small man to creep through, which enabled him to force the bolts and bars at the opposite side and to open the door. This man, whose name was Daly, was afterwards a navy agent, and lived at Greenwich: he escaped from Verdun with, I believe, Dr. Clarke, and landed safely in England. The principal obstacles were now removed in everyone's opinion, and there remained but two slight doors more to impede our advancing to a subterraneous passage that led out of the fort. This was a very intricate communication, and we had to feel our way to those slight doors, as it was dangerous to have candle-light.

Some unfortunate English prisoners, owing to treachery amongst themselves, had been sabred in the same passage years before, in a vain attempt to escape during the night. How valuable would a dark-lanthorn have been now! Everybody, except the few that were appointed to force the doors, were preparing for their escape. It was nearly midnight. Our over-eagerness in forcing the third door shot the bolt back, which caused a noise that was overheard by the sentinels outside. This occasioned a general alarm to be instantly beat – all hopes were at an end. "What unfortunate wretches!" were the only words that could be heard, everybody endeavouring to get to his respective place before the guards entered. Those who were all over dirt tried to strip and hide their clothes; the confusion was great in all parts of the cave; the running against one another, mistaking each other's beds, and clothes, etc., was quite ludicrous. The visitors were, of all others, worst off; their friends, whom they came to spend the evening with, had no beds to offer them. The doors were now opening, the guards entering, and I, who was all over dirt, was rambling about without being able to find any place to creep into. By accident I stumbled over a bed, and I instantly crawled under the blankets, with my boots and all my clothes on. The guards passed close by me, even before I had settled myself; but they were too intent upon reaching the spot from whence they imagined they had heard the noise. In our cave, at this time, everything was silent. You might have heard a pin drop. Every prisoner seemed fast asleep, and one or two were even snoring. By the guard's light, as they passed, I found that I had got into the bed of a servant, an American named Clarke. He was so intolerably intoxicated (they managed that night to get some *snique*, or brandy, smuggled in) that I was a long time before I could rouse him; and when he was awake, I had as much difficulty in making him understand who I was, and why I had got into his bed. I dreaded lest the stupefied fellow might utter some ejaculation that might expose everything. Fortunately, however, as soon as he was able to understand what I said, he desired me to cover my face, and assisted me to conceal myself as well as he could. It afterwards appeared that he had gone to bed fully aware of the part he was to play the next morning, and that he had got a little drunk to give him courage for his enterprise; and as in drunkenness a little always leads to more, he had at last got very drunk, under the delusion that he would recover himself before the time of decamping arrived. This is the common self-deception, I believe, of all incipient drunkards.

On discovering that the first door had been opened, the commanding officer of the searching party said, with a sneer, "That he would give us weeks to get through the next"; meaning the ponderous, massive iron door which I have already described. On advancing a few paces, one of the guards proclaimed, with a horrid oath, that even the iron door had been forced. This put the officer in a furious passion, and he swore outrageously against the "*sacrés coquins, les Anglais*", uttering a tirade of oaths upon his resolution to discover the chiefs of such a horrible conspiracy. "Where are the visitors?" cried he, in a furious voice. "Where are those who, I understand, prevailed on the *gendarmes* to be admitted to the cell? They must be the authors of this horrible business, or complot."

Passion is never rational, or it would have taught this officer that those who had been admitted as visitors for only one evening could not have been the authors of a plot that must have been in active operation for many days, or weeks, or even months.

The infuriated officer called over the muster-roll of the visitors, and Tuthill, Ashworth, and O'Brien resounded from his angry lungs. I was too old a sailor to notice the first call. The first two officers were so indiscreet as to answer. They thought that as they were stripped and in bed they could escape suspicion. But far different was the result. They were ordered to get up, put on their clothes, and, under very rough usage, they were about to be conducted to what had been my former habitation – the dungeon. Again did the enraged officer repeat my name – O'Brien. Poor Mr. Brine answered to the call; and he was, without ceremony, ordered to dress, and compelled to join the other two. Again did the name of O'Brien resound from the lips of the enraged officer; but Mr. O'Brien had no more inclination to answer to the call than he had had at first. The drunken servant had sufficiently recovered himself to understand the whole scene, and he played his part with great tact. I remained under the bed-clothes, whilst he sat up with his knees so raised as to prevent the possibility of discovering me. He protested that he was alone in bed; and appearances favouring his assertion, the guards did not trouble him, but passed on to the next bed. For my part, I saw no prospect of escaping, as the searchers were well aware of my being below, and I was frequently on the point of jumping up and joining my comrades, who were now put on march for the dungeon. The intoxicated servant shrewdly observed, "That it would be time enough to join that party when I was discovered, and that I ought to wait patiently the result." I found a good deal of reason in what he said, and remained quiet. There were three or four more ringleaders (as they called them) discovered by the clay and soil found about their garments, and the whole were escorted to the direful dungeon. The doors were then locked, sentinels being placed on those that had been broken open. I expected that the guards would return to search for another set of ringleaders, and I remained full of anxiety waiting their arrival. In the meantime, I was of opinion that it would be as well to take my boots and clothes off. I accordingly stripped, and concealed those that were full of earth and dirt in different parts of the *souterrain*. Some time elapsed, yet no return of the guards disturbed me. I composed myself as well as I could: my bedfellow left me in full possession, and I fell into a profound sleep.

When I awoke it was daylight. The usual hour for allowing the prisoners to breathe the fresh air had arrived; but the doors were not opened as before: and they were soon informed that they would be kept locked down, until they thought proper to deliver up the names of all those who had intended to escape on the preceding night. The prisoners laughed at such a proposition, since there was nothing more certain than that all who had been capable of walking would have embraced so excellent an opportunity of regaining their liberty. On second consideration, it was agreed to give only the names of those already in the dungeon, they being certain of punishment. The commandant would not credit the assertion of so small a number of names, and the *souterrain* was kept locked. At all events, I was sure of being missed from my room, as there was no possibility of getting back to it. At eleven o'clock they generally mustered us – the *gendarme* who gave us permission to go down was in confinement, and it appeared that he had not given the correct names in the beginning, and had not been interrogated particularly afterwards, which accounted for the mistake between my name and Mr. Brine's. However, the moment which left me no hope or possibility of avoiding detection was quickly approaching.

At nine o'clock, the commandant, Monsieur Clement, and all the other officers of the garrison, descended in order to ascertain the havoc that the English prisoners had made in the engineering of the fortification.

They found, of our tools, only an old piece of a saw, one solitary hammer, and a few chisels, and they all expressed their astonishment at our having made such great progress through such massive obstructions in so short a time, and with such few and bad implements. During this investigation I had a great deal of difficulty to conceal myself; and, although I succeeded, I knew that eventually it could not be of any use, for that when eleven o'clock arrived my fate would be decided.

At about ten o'clock, a load of wood came for the prisoners. Permission was then asked to have the doors opened, that they might come up and fetch it. This was denied, and the prisoners in the rooms above were ordered to throw the wood down to those in the dungeon, through the air holes, but, fortunately for me, the billets were too large to pass through the gratings. Our guards were therefore obliged to open the *souterrain*, and allow a certain number of prisoners to ascend, in order to fetch the wood down. A strict guard was placed at the door.

I contrived to get some clean clothes down, which were conveyed to me through the bars, and I concerted a plan with one of my fellow-prisoners that were bringing the wood down, a very respectable and well-conducted man, a serjeant of marines of H.M.S. *Magnificent*. He was to make a particular sign, by putting his hand on the back part of his head, when the guard's eyes were off the door; which he did, and at that instant I glided, or rather jumped out.

4

The sentinels seized me, and desired me to descend again instantly. I asked why they did not allow me to come up, since they had just now permitted me to go down? I told them that I did not belong to the *souterrain*, and that I had descended merely out of curiosity to see what the prisoners had been about the last night. I reminded those who had been in the habit of mustering the room to which I belonged, of their mistake, and asked them how they could possibly suppose that I belonged to the *souterrain*? They looked at me, appeared convinced, and seemed surprised that they could not recollect my having passed them in my descent, begged my pardon, and allowed me to pursue my way. I reached my own apartment, where, in a few seconds, I was indisposed, and snug in bed. Thus did I avoid being sent to the galleys: for, after my reiterated attempts to escape, one more detection would have consigned me to that horrible fate.

There was no danger of my being now discovered, until the *gendarme*, who granted me the permission, should be liberated. In the afternoon I obtained leave to go to the dungeon, to see my poor comrades and condole with them. They were much rejoiced at my good fortune, but feared my trick would soon be found out. Eight days passed on: I frequently paid those poor fellows a visit during the time. The *gendarme* Buché was then released, and I was obliged to keep constantly in the room when he was on duty; and, when he came to muster us, I was covered over in bed. They never called the names: to count heads was their method, which suited me admirably. Five more days had passed away in a similar manner, when we received orders to prepare for a general review, which usually takes place once a month.

4th August. – On this day we were all placed in ranks and minutely inspected. It appeared to my friends and myself that I could not avoid discovery on this occasion, as all the *gendarmes* attended. There was no exception or excuse of sickness to be made; if a prisoner was able to crawl he must attend, and frequently they were carried. I took my station in the ranks, expecting in a few minutes to be lodged with my old companions in limbo.

The *gendarme*, whom I had so long avoided, riveted his eyes upon me. I had received information that he was going to make known to the commandant Clement, or to General Maisonneuve, that I had importuned him more than the rest, and was the person who prevailed on him to let any down. He was astonished at seeing me, having been informed that I was in the dungeon with the others. Shortly afterwards he passed me, and I saw him go and speak to both the above-mentioned officers: I was then confident he had completed the business. The review took place; everyone was inspected, and some were asked several questions. I was passed over with very little notice. I could not account for it, yet was of opinion that they would have said something on the subject had they been made acquainted with it. Glad was I when we were all dismissed and the officers allowed to retire. My escape was to me unaccountable, but not on that score the less welcome; I was, however, so confounded at my good fortune that I had forebodings that some latent mischief was held in reserve.

Whilst I was pacing to and fro, in an awkward dilemma, the *gendarme* Buché approached me and accosted me in these words:

"By what miracle have you escaped from the dungeon? How, in the name of all wonders, have you got up from the *souterrain*? I have seen you walking about some days, although perhaps you did not see me."

There was no mistaking his meaning, but, full of apprehensions as I was, I resolved to put on a face of wonder at his thus presuming to address me, and to persevere in an assertion of my ignorance of all he alluded to.

"Pray, sir," I replied, "and why should I be put in the dungeon?"

"My God!" he exclaimed, astonished at my effrontery, "were you not the very person that was chiefly the occasion of my letting you and your three companions down to visit your friends, and to celebrate the anniversary of a birth-day, as you called it?"

"You must certainly, sir, have made a mistake; it was not me," I rejoined with an air of offended innocence.

The man was not to be browbeaten or imposed upon in this way. He stuck to his text, and insisted that I was the culprit; but, to my great relief, he added that he had no desire to see me punished, for, as his punishment was over, mine could afford him no alleviation. I was glad to find one human being so devoid of the spirit of revenge; and yet the fellow added that he would have told the general and commandant of me, had not his wife persuaded him – *Anglicè*, ordered and compelled him – not to do it. Perhaps the lady might have had some peccadilloes on the part of her husband to resent, and was not over-grieved at the punishment into which I had betrayed him.

I still preserved my dignified composure, and assured him that he should lose nothing by his indulgence, and for what he had suffered in consequence of it, for I knew the generosity of the *gentleman* on whose account he had been put into confinement.

At this he could retain his countenance no longer, and he burst out into a horse-laugh in my face. I was obliged to throw off the mask. He shook me by the hand, and we became such good friends that he even took me to the dungeon that afternoon, to see my unfortunate companions. Nothing could astonish them more than my appearing with this man, whom they imagined it morally impossible to appease, as his indulgence to me had led to his disgrace and punishment. I gave them an account of all that had happened, and of the dialogue that had that day taken place between him and me, upon which they all congratulated me, and styled me the most fortunate prisoner of the fortress.

*   *   *   *   *

It was the next day (5th August, 1808) that my unfortunate companions received orders to prepare for a march to Metz, to which place they were sent under a strong escort, in order to take their trial as conspirators. How the simple attempt of prisoners of war at gaol-breaking could come under such a class of crime was to me inexplicable. Buché, the *gendarme*, was ordered to repair to Metz, to act in the double capacity of prosecutor and chief witness. I was now entirely in this man's power. A single word from him would have included me in the number of the proscribed and condemned; for to be tried and condemned before such a tribunal were tantamount to the same thing. Fortunate did I consider myself that Buché did not denounce me.

I had the mortification to see my poor companions heavily ironed and bound in chains. After being closely confined in their filthy and pestiferous den for many days, they were to be marched twenty-five leagues, in order to be put upon their fictitious trials. We parted as affectionately as possible, and I could almost voluntarily have shared their fate – "Our crime was common," in the words of the poet, and I could not help repeating the end of the line, "and common be the pain".

In a few days I received a letter from my friend Mr. Ashworth, giving me a melancholy narration of the trial; and he concluded by stating that himself and several of our friends, were sentenced "*as slaves to the galleys for fifteen years. Mr. Tuthill was sentenced to only nine*".

I was so shocked with this part of the intelligence that I dropped the letter, and proceeded no further, and I hurried to relate the afflicting news to my brother-prisoners. The feelings of indignation it excited were extreme, and though under the absolute power of the enemy, we loudly exclaimed against the barbarity and tyranny of a nation that called itself civilised, and could suffer such a judicial sentence to be passed or executed.

After the first ebullitions of rage and indignation had subsided, one of my friends picked up the letter, and the whole scene was quickly changed; for, on reading further, he found that the sentence of the court had been reversed. Great as was this consolation, it did not alter my feelings towards the chief of the French nation.

The letter went on to inform me that two of our seamen were condemned to the galleys for six years, and that they had actually been sent off to their destination. This I thought was horrible.

I knew both of these unhappy victims. One was an Italian by birth, and the other an Englishman. The former, John Gardner, *alias* Italian John, I found had been condemned for making out a false passport for the other, one Henry Hudsell, *alias* Quiz. Hudsell escaped from Bitche, and travelled several leagues with this fictitious passport, before the imposition was discovered. If the reader will only consider the treatment which our prisoners had endured, with no prospect of having an exchange during the war, and that although this said crime may be termed forgery, it was not done to molest or injure any person whatever, but was simply planned to liberate the bearer, I have not the smallest doubt but that he will agree with me in opinion, that it falls very short of deserving a punishment equal to six years, with all denominations of malefactors, in the galleys.

There was an Englishman lately arrived from the galleys, who had served in our army on the Continent, under His Royal Highness the Duke of York; his name, to the best of my recollection, was Barnes. He stated that he, with some others, had been made prisoners by the French, and, by some accident, one of their guards was killed. The whole of the prisoners were accused, and sentenced to twelve or thirteen years' slavery – I am not confident which; however, he was the only survivor. His time being up, they conducted him to the depot of punishment, still to be considered as a prisoner of war. It surely behoved our government, at the peace of 1814, to direct strict inquiry to be made whether any of our countrymen were still suffering in the galleys!

September, 1808. – I had by this time another plan of escaping in contemplation, and with every hope of success. The arrival of a Mr. Hewson and a Mr. Butterfield, midshipmen (who, in March last, had escaped from Verdun, and had got down to the Gulf of Lyons, in the Mediterranean, where they had been arrested and brought back to Bitche), favoured my plan very much. Mr. Hewson being an intimate friend and very old acquaintance, I communicated to him my plan, and he rejoiced exceedingly at an opportunity so soon offering for another attempt to be off. However, it was necessary to wait some time, as he was placed in the *souterrain*. In a few days he contrived, owing to real indisposition, to be moved upstairs into a room appointed for the sick. I now only waited for the worthy Hewson; it was necessary to endeavour to get him up into my room – no other prospect was left. He made application by letter to the commandant; and on the 11th of September succeeded. We wanted nothing now but a favourable moment. The next day, Mr. Barklimore, a mutual friend of ours, also received permission to reside in our apartment. This gentleman is at present a surgeon of reputation in Charlotte Street, Bloomsbury. We were, fortunately, only seven in number, in consequence of the other poor fellows being at Metz; and of these seven, three were confined to their beds. The fourth was a Mr. Batley, a dragoon officer of the East India Company's service, who had been captured in the *Bell* packet, bound to India. He had been a long time in the room, and informed me that he had conjectured what we were about, and requested to be allowed to join and partake of our danger, which we agreed to. No opportunity of getting past the sentinels yet presented itself. Our friends arrived from Metz, but were put below. I communicated the business to them: they thought it a very dangerous and hazardous plan; however, they would have willingly run the same risk with us, if they could: but that was impossible. On the 12th of September, and the very evening before our meditated attempt to escape from the fortress, the commandant, M. Clement, in passing through the yard in which we were allowed to respire the air, very condescendingly stopped a few minutes to converse with me; when he addressed me by saying, "Well, Monsieur O'Brien, I think now that the Emperor of Austria has joined us, you must relinquish all hopes of escaping, for there is no chance whatever for an Englishman to get off from the Continent." I replied, "That is very true, Monsieur le Commandant; but if that had not been the case, Monsieur le Commandant, where is the possibility of getting out of this strong fortress, and so well guarded too?" "True," said he, smiling; "but the attempt has been made more than once, though it has invariably proved unsuccessful, and frequently fatal to some of the party." He continued by saying, "My opinion is, that if prisoners of war, I mean English, could manage to get out of confinement, their only course would be that towards Flushing or Rotterdam, where they are always pretty certain of finding English smugglers ready to embark them." I assured Monsieur le Commandant that his remarks were quite correct, and that if I thought there was the slightest chance of escaping from the fort, I would not hesitate to try and do so to-morrow, or as soon as possible. "I believe you truly, Monsieur O'Brien, and I give you credit for your candour," was his reply; "had you spoken otherwise, I would not have believed you"; and he added with a smile, as he bade me adieu, "you may try and get away if you can, and we shall take care and do all in our power to prevent you." I could not help thinking this conversation at so critical a moment very extraordinary. However, this opinion of his did not make us alter our intended course for Austria.

It was now the 13th of September, and the third day since my friend Hewson had joined us. The night was very boisterous and inclement, and this we thought proved much in our favour. Everything was got ready.

Our rope was tightly wound into a ball and concealed in a pocket hand-kerchief. Every moment was anxiously watched and counted. At length darkness set in. It rained in torrents, blew almost a hurricane, the thunder rolled with a tremendous sound, and I scarcely ever witnessed in any part of the globe a more desperate night. All this was so far, we considered, propitious; but, unfortunately, the flashes of lightning were vivid and incessant, and this was a serious source of danger.

We now unlocked our door, and remained at the bottom of the flight of stairs, waiting to see the sentinels go into their boxes. This was about eight o'clock, and four hours did we watch, until midnight, and not a single soul of them left his post. This was the more provoking, for as it poured a deluge of rain, and they were without their greatcoats, we had calculated with certainty upon their requiring and seeking shelter. The reverse was the case, and during the whole time they were as vigilant as if they had suspected our designs.

We at last agreed to return to our apartments until the ensuing night, and to deposit all our apparatus in places we had previously fixed upon for concealment; but, upon second thoughts, we considered that, in all pro-bability, the sentinels that came to relieve the watch at midnight would not be so very hardy or watchful as their predecessors, and that we might yet have an opportunity of putting our scheme into execution. In this expectation or hope we waited, in a state of intense anxiety, until two in the morning; but, to our discomfiture, we found that the sentinels defied the elements, and kept their posts in the strictest sense of duty. Chagrined and vexed, we returned to our apartments, locked the door and went to bed.

The *souterrain* was opened at the usual hour, and our friends came running up, imagining, from the inclemency of the night, that we must have succeeded in effecting our escape; and greatly were they disappointed at finding us all snug in our beds. I related all the circumstances to them: they shrugged up their shoulders, and expressed their fears that, if we could not get off in such a night as the last, there was little hope of our escaping in fair weather.

On the 14th of September we dined early, that we might have the pleasure of our friends' company to a farewell dinner during the time allowed them for breathing the fresh air. We were determined to lay in a good foundation for our journey, and got a very large piece of beef, had it roasted, and procured plenty of bread, beer, and vegetables. This, for our circumstances, was more than an alderman's feast: we all enjoyed it, earnestly hoping that it might be the last that we should ever eat within the walls of a French prison. Our friends pointed out to us the number of difficulties we should have to surmount in passing the guards – the danger that would attend it – and expressed the anxiety they were under for us. We, however, were determined not to relinquish our undertaking, and to be ready every night until an opportunity offered. We parted as we had done the night before. They did not suppose we should have any chance that night, as the weather was moderate and fair. At our usual hour of six (the winter regulations having commenced) we were locked up, and immediately recommenced our preparations. We thought, perhaps, the sentinels might be more careless early in the evening; that is to say, before eight, which was the usual time to set the night-watch and give the necessary orders.

We were now again all ready. Our door was opened; and we could see the sentinel, whom we had most to fear, walk up and down before our windows. His box was in front of the door, in the yard through which we had to go; but, as our guards lived underneath our apartments, we thought he would take anybody moving about so early for one of them: and it was unusual to challenge anyone before eight o'clock.

At about seven, the soldier, to our infinite joy, entered his box. I instantly descended the stairs that led into the yard. It was just dusk; and I was to take six minutes on the forlorn hope, as it might justly be termed, to fix our rope to a palisade, and to descend the first rampart, before Mr. Hewson followed, who was next on the list. I passed the sentinel quite close, and could see him leaning over his musket. He never moved, though I met his eye, probably taking me for one of the guards; and I arrived, providentially, at the spot fixed upon to make fast the rope, which I very soon accomplished, and was just in the act of descending when my friend Hewson arrived. In a few minutes, to my inexpressible satisfaction, we were all four at the bottom of the first wall. Our principal object being now accomplished, we congratulated each other. We had two walls yet to descend; the heights, as I have already mentioned, being respectively from ninety to one hundred, from forty to fifty, and the third from twenty-five to thirty feet. We all clapped on to the rope, and crawled up with our feet against the wall, until we got a good height. We then swung off together, when the rope broke, and we fell upon one another, leaving in our hands enough to enable us to descend the next rampart. We made this piece fast to one of the upper stones of the embrasure, and again descended. We had now to repeat our haul upon the rope, and it again broke, leaving a piece of sufficient length for our future purpose, the descent of the third and last rampart.

We had taken the precaution of providing two long boot-hooks to stick in the wall, to make our rope fast to, in case we should find no other means of securing it. These proved of the greatest use in getting down the third rampart. In fact, had we not had them with us, we must have surrendered ourselves, for not one single means could we find of fastening the rope to anything, and to drop from a height of thirty feet might have been destruction. The boot-hooks served our purpose: we were at the bottom of the third wall; and all that we had now to do was to pass the outer sentinels, who were few in number, and rather slack in vigilance, perhaps from the supposed impossibility of any prisoner effecting an escape in this direction. We had, in fact, let ourselves down by this frail rope a total height of from about 180 to 200 feet.

At the bottom of the third rampart we remained in the *fosse* or ditch; and we had to watch the turn of the sentinel that was pacing immediately before us. As soon as his back was fairly turned, we ascended the scarp of the ditch, and gently rolled ourselves down the slope or glacis. In a few minutes, with our hearts rebounding with joyous emotions, we were on the road to Strasbourg, on which we continued running as fast as we possibly could for nearly an hour. We then halted to put on our shoes, which we had hung round our necks as we rolled down the glacis, as we had found it more secure to descend the walls without shoes than with them, the feet being much more pliable.

We now turned round to take, as we hoped, a final view of the Mansion of Tears, the name that had been so long given to this detestable fortress by the unfortunate prisoners, many of whom had shed an abundance, or showers of them, within its horrid cells and dungeons. We spontaneously returned our thanks to Almighty God for our deliverance, and shook each other cordially by the hand, overwhelmed with exultation at our almost miraculous success. When we looked at the stupendous heights of the rock and fortress, it seemed as if a miracle alone could have enabled us to descend them, suspended by so slight and ill-made a cord as that which we had been able to construct out of our shirt-linen and a little cobbler's twine.

CHAPTER SIX

NAPOLEON, LIKE Hitler in modern times, was forced to make some provision for his British captives by reason of the many thousands of his soldiers and sailors who were held in British prisons, some of them for as long as twenty-three years. (The Austrian, Prussian, Spanish and Russian prisoners in his hands were, according to contemporary accounts, treated in much the same way as the Russian and Polish prisoners of Nazi Germany in World War II.) Some six thousand of these French prisoners were held at Norman Cross in Huntingdonshire, and according to George Borrow their conditions were far from ideal. He says in *Lavengro*:

"And a strange place it was, this Norman Cross, and, at the time of which I am speaking, a sad cross to many a Norman, being what was then styled a French prison, that is, a receptacle for captives made in the French war. It consisted, if I remember right, of some five or six casernes, very long, and immensely high; each standing isolated from the rest, upon a spot of ground which might average ten acres, and which was fenced round with lofty palisades, the whole being compassed about by a towering wall, beneath which, at intervals, on both sides, sentinels were stationed, whilst outside, upon the field, stood commodious wooden barracks, capable of containing two regiments of infantry, intended to serve as guards upon the captives. Such was the station or prison at Norman Cross, where some six thousand French and other foreigners, followers of the grand Corsican, were now immured.

"What a strange appearance had those mighty casernes, with their blank blind walls, without windows or grating, and their slanting roofs, out of which, through orifices where the tiles had been removed, would be protruded dozens of grim heads, feasting their prison-sick eyes on the wide expanse of country unfolded from that airy height. Ah! there was misery in those casernes; and from those roofs, doubtless, many a wistful look was turned in the direction of lovely France. Much had the poor inmates to endure, and much to complain of, to the disgrace of England be it said – of England, in general so kind and bountiful.

Rations of carrion meat, and bread from which I have seen the very hounds occasionally turn away, were unworthy entertainment even for the most ruffian enemy, when helpless and a captive; and such, alas! was the fare in those casernes."

There are several accounts of the escape of French prisoners in England at this time, but the next one, from Norman Cross, is I think the most exciting, although unfortunately I do not know the escaper's name. His story is similar in many details to that of another Frenchman, Felix Durand, who got away from the Tower of Liverpool in 1759.[1] Like Durand, the unknown French sailor chose a stormy night for his attempt, and was helped on his way on several occasions because of his attraction for the opposite sex. Like Durand, he used the subterfuge of appearing deaf and dumb to disguise his ignorance of the English language.

The same pretext was used by Grinnell-Milne[2] when at large in Germany in 1915, while another great escaper of the First World War, J. L. Hardy[3] – "that maniac Hardy" as the Germans called him – used to travel as a congenital idiot. He escaped five times in all, and got away with it in the end. Some modern escapers employed a pronounced stammer to cover their language difficulty, but here one was faced with the possibility of being offered pencil and paper. Acting deaf and dumb was not considered a good proposition in rigidly controlled Nazi Germany, as it was thought that such unfortunates would not be granted permits to make long journeys in time of war.

An Unknown Frenchman

ON THE 1st of August 1809, a day I shall ever have cause to remember, I went on a pleasure excursion, in a small vessel belonging to my father, from Marseille to Nice. At this time the coast of France was strictly watched by English cruisers; and to elude these, we kept as much as possible close inshore. This precaution was, unfortunately, useless. When off the isles of Hyères, we were observed, and chased by an English cutter, which soon came up with us. Resistance was of course useless, and foreseeing the result, we at the first shot yielded ourselves prisoners. Before going on board the enemy's vessel, I concealed about my person as much money and other valuables as I could; and of this property I was not afterwards deprived.

[1] *Recollections of Old Liverpool by a Nonagenarian.*
[2] *An Escaper's Log.*
[3] *I Escape.*

We were indeed treated with less severity that we had reason to expect. On the day after our capture, we were removed, with many other prisoners, into another vessel, with orders to make the best of our way to England. What my sensations were on being thus torn from my beloved country, my friends, and relations, may be easily conceived.

In a few days we arrived on the coast of England, and were immediately ordered round to an eastern port – Lynn, in Norfolk – whence we were forwarded, to the number of some hundreds, in lighters and small craft, to the depot of prisoners of war at Norman Cross – I think about fifty miles inland. Arriving at Peterborough – a respectable-looking town with a handsome cathedral – we were marched to our destination. On reaching Norman Cross, we all underwent the usual scrutiny by the inspecting officers; and an exact description was taken of each individual as to his age, size, colour of hair and eyes, etc., which was entered in a book kept for that purpose. All these preparations gave a fearful presentiment of what we were afterwards to expect, and raised emotions in my breast of a nature I cannot define, but which several times, whilst the examination was going on, made me shudder with a kind of convulsive horror, not at all lessened on our admittance into, and review of our prison. The English had here upwards of seven thousand prisoners of war, of one nation or other, but chiefly Frenchmen. I will endeavour to describe a few particulars of the place, as well as I can recollect, which may at the same time also serve to illustrate my escape from it.

The whole of the buildings, including the prison and the barracks for the soldiers who guarded us, were situated on an eminence, and were certainly airy enough, commanding a full and extensive view over the surrounding country, which appeared well cultivated in some parts; but in front of the prison, to the south-east, the prospect terminated in fens and marshes, in the centre of which was Whittlesea Mere, a large lake, of some miles in circumference. The high-road from London to Scotland ran close by the prison, and we could, at all hours of the day, see the stage-coaches and other carriages bounding along the beautiful roads of the country with a rapidity unknown elsewhere; and the contrast afforded by contemplating these scenes of liberty continually before our eyes only served to render the comparison more harrowing to our feelings.

There was no apparent show about the place of military strength, formed by turreted castles or by embrasured battlements; in fact it was little better than an enclosed camp. The security of the prisoners was effected by the unceasing watch of ever-wakeful sentinels, constantly passing and repassing, who were continually changing; and I have no doubt this mode of security was more effectual than if surrounded by

moated walls or by fortified towers. Very few, in comparison of the numbers who attempted it, succeeded in escaping the boundaries, though
many ingenious devices were put in practice to accomplish it. However, if
once clear of the place, final success was not so difficult.

The space appointed for the reception of the prisoners consisted of four
equal divisions or quadrangles; and these again were divided into four
parts, each of which was surrounded by a high palisade of wood, and
paved for walking on; but the small ground it occupied scarcely left us
sufficient room to exercise for our health, and this was a very great privation. In each of these subdivisions was a large wooden building, covered
with red tiles, in which we ate our meals and dwelt; these also served for
our dormitories or sleeping-places, where we were nightly piled in ham-
mocks, tier upon tier, in most horrible regularity. One of these quadrangles was entirely occupied by the hospital and medical department. A
division of another quadrangle was allotted to the officers, who were
allowed a few trifling indulgences not granted to the common men,
amongst whom I unfortunately was included. In another division was a
school, the master of which was duly paid for his attendance. It was conducted with great regularity and decorum, and there you might sometimes
see several respectable Englishmen, particularly those attached to the duties
of the prison, taking their seats with the boys to learn the French language.
Another small part was appropriated as a place of closer confinement or
punishment to those who broke the rules appointed for our government,
or wantonly defaced any part of the buildings, or pawned or lost their
clothes; these last were put, I think, upon two-thirds allowance of provisions, till the loss occasioned thereby was made good; and I must confess
this part was seldom without its due proportion of inhabitants. The centre
of the prison was surrounded by a high brick wall, beyond which were the
barracks for the English soldiers, several guard-houses, and some handsome buildings for both the civil and military officers; whilst a circular
blockhouse, mounted with swivels or small cannon, pointing to the
different divisions, frowned terrifically over us, and completed the *outside*
of the picture.

*   *   *   *   *

With respect to the interior economy of the prison, we were not treated
with any particular degree of harshness or of unnecessary privation,
further than the security of so large a number of men required. On Sunday, Monday, Tuesday, Thursday, and Saturday, we had one pound and a
half of bread, half a pound of beef, with a proportionate quantity of salt
and vegetables; or, if no vegetables could be procured, we had in lieu

pearl-barley or oatmeal. On Wednesdays and Fridays we had the usual quantity of bread, one pound of cod-fish or herrings, and one pound of potatoes. No ale or beer was served out to us, but we were allowed to purchase it at the canteen in the prison.

To insure to us no fraud or embezzlement, each department or division sent two deputies to inspect the weight and quantity of the provisions, which, if not approved by them and the agent to the prison, were invariably rejected and returned; and if any difference of opinion existed between the agent and the deputies, a reference was made to the officers on guard at the time, and their decision was final. A regular daily market was held in the prison, where the country-people brought a variety of articles for sale, and where every luxury could be purchased by those who had money. Our cooks were appointed from amongst ourselves, and paid by the English government, so that, in regard to diet, we had not much to complain of. The hospital or medical department, I have heard – for I was never an inmate of it, except to visit a sick comrade – was amply supplied with every necessary and attendance; the nurses being generally selected from the friends of the sick.

For our amusement, amongst other things, we had several excellent billiard-tables, very neatly made by the prisoners themselves, which were attended by many English officers, and others off duty; but, unfortunately, these were the sources of frequent quarrels and duels, two of which terminated fatally, whilst I was there, both between Frenchmen. Having no arms, they affixed the blades of knives, properly sharpened and shaped, to sticks formed with handles and hilts, with which they fought as with small-swords. I was a witness to one of these conflicts, and it sank deep in my memory for many months. It appeared, in some instances, as if confinement had deprived us of the usual humanity of our nature, and hardened our hearts; for some shocking scenes of depravity and cruelty would occasionally take place, which even the counsel and presence of the good and venerable Bishop of Moulins, who voluntarily attended to the religious duties of the prison, could not restrain.

I had been confined about a year and a half, when, seeing no other prospect of release, I determined to attempt an escape; for death itself was to be preferred to the misery of delayed hope which I daily endured. The execution was difficult in the extreme. The high-paled enclosures of wood which I have before mentioned were of no great strength, and easily passed; but on the outside of these was a belt of sentinels, at only a few yards distance from each other; beyond these was the outer fence, or wall of brick, very high, which was to be surmounted by a ladder or rope, close to which was another belt of sentinels as before. The fences and wall were not the greatest difficulties to contend with: it was the sentinels, close to each other, who, perpetually on the alert, scarcely left a chance for escape unperceived.

Before anything, however, could be attempted, it was necessary to make a few preparations, and that, too, without giving any room for suspicion, even to my fellow-prisoners. With some difficulty, and by degrees, I exchanged part of my French gold for English money with those of my comrades who, by making toys and fancy-work in straw, which they were allowed to dispose of for their own benefit, had got a little together. Many of our men made large sums of money that way, and, had they been provident, might have returned home with more wealth than they could have gained in the same space of time had they been at large in their own country. One of them, a most ingenious fellow, had absolutely, during the many years of his imprisonment, accumulated the sum of £300 of English money. Of this man I procured, for a *louis-d'or*, a good and correct map of England of his own drawing, on which was pointed out a line of travelling as offering the best route for escape. The names of the towns, and of many of the villages, with their distances, together with other useful remarks, were all written at length, and I found them exceedingly accurate. He sold several of these maps to many who never attempted their escape, but who, nevertheless, had that hope often in their breasts. For some time after I had the map in my possession, I endeavoured to learn to pronounce the names of the places I was to pass through; but finding all in vain, I gave up the attempt as hopeless, for Russian itself is easy to this unpronounceable language. Well assured, if ever I endeavoured to speak English, I should betray myself, I determined, if once I got clear of the place, *never to speak at all*.

The route pointed out as most preferable was to the eastern coast, a part of Norfolk, and there to bribe some fisherman or smuggler to carry me over to Holland. The name of one of these latter was given me, with ample instructions how to find him out, and to make myself known to him. One thing I was well aware of, and which, in fact, was almost everything in my favour; namely, that in the land of liberty, as they call it – and in this instance deservedly so – no passport was wanted; nor, as I was well informed, had anyone a right to inquire whither I was going, or what was my business. To say the truth, they do not seem to require such safeguards in England. The ocean which girds it round acts far more effectually for security than passports or gendarmes.

I got together, I think, about five pounds of English money in silver and a little copper; I had also between twenty and thirty *louis-d'ors* and other gold coin, and a few guineas, which I concealed in different parts of my clothing. I also procured a small pocket tinder-box, which I hid in the crown of my cap. I do not know how I came to think of this last article, as I had never made any use of it. I also concealed, in different parts of my dress, several other things which I thought might be of service to me, particularly a French and English Dictionary; and being thus provided, I only waited for a favourable opportunity to make the attempt.

After waiting day after day and week after week with emotions and impatience indescribable, the moment of liberation at length arrived in a dark and dismal night in the month of February. The rain had poured down in torrents all that day, accompanied with a heavy fall of snow, and the wind blew a most violent storm. Nothing could better answer my purpose, as in darkness lay the only chance I could possibly have of eluding the keen and vigilant eyes of my ever-watchful guards. Being now determined to make the attempt, I took from their places of concealment, where I had arranged all ready for the occasion, a strong knife to cut the wood paling, and a rope, which I had made out of wool, with a hook at the end, to surmount the wall. I also put a biscuit or two in my pocket, with a shirt and pair of stockings (which last I found exceedingly comfortable and refreshing to me), to put on dry when my others were wet and dirty. I had no room for anything else; in short, what I had, filled my pockets, as my dress was only a sailor's jacket and trousers, both of coarse blue cloth, but sound and warm. I had also a good strong pair of shoes on, another great comfort, and which ought always to be particularly attended to by every adventurous wanderer.

                    *   *   *   *   *

My fellow-prisoner of whom I bought the map was the only one I acquainted with my purpose; not that he might accompany me, for he had given up all thoughts of escape himself, but that he might answer to my name if called over, which sometimes was the case, or otherwise assist me as far as lay in his power, without rendering himself liable to suspicion. It was a regular custom in the prison to count us out of our lodging-places in the morning, and in again at night, so that, if any were missing, it was immediately discovered, and the alarm given. This rendered it necessary that the first attempt should be made from within, after we were shut up. As soon, therefore, as it was dark, I began my operations – my friend standing before me as I lay on the ground, and screening me from observation as well as he could by several artful manoeuvres, which were much assisted by a long bench and table near us, on which he was apparently very deeply engaged at work. My object was to cut out one of the boards from the bottom of the building, which I had previously prepared for removal. In this I succeeded better than I could possibly have expected; and, creeping out on my hands and knees, silently replaced the board, and, unperceived by anyone, concealed myself among a heap of fagots in the yard, which had been brought there during the day for firing. The rain and wind seemed, if possible, to increase as the night approached, and soon shrouded all around me in pitchy darkness. There were here and there, at long intervals, and at a great distance from me, regular rows of lamps; but they only served to make the outer darkness more intense.

As I crouched up in my hiding-place, wet and almost benumbed with cold – which nothing but the hope of ultimate escape could have enabled me to bear – I could occasionally hear the clang of the arms of the sentinels at their post, notwithstanding the pattering of rain and the howling of the wind, which had now increased to a perfect hurricane; nay, I could now and then even distinguish their voices. I continued in this horrid state of suspense till the clock struck eleven, which I had chosen as the most favourable point of time, the sentinels being then, as I thought, more likely to be tired, and not so much on their guard, being changed at nine and twelve. Commending my soul to God, I left my hiding-place, but was at first so stiff and cramped with being so long confined in one posture, that I could scarcely stand; however, this soon went off, and I found my courage rise as my blood circulated more freely.

The wood paling could scarcely be called an impediment; and listening attentively for a moment, and hearing nothing to alarm, I silently cut a part out, and crept through on my hands and knees as far and as quick as I could. I was interrupted by no one, and the sentinels were undoubtedly sheltered in their boxes. My success so far inspired me with great confidence. I knew that I had passed the first line of the guards, and that there were no more obstacles on the inside of the wall. If anything at this moment, the hurricane blew with tenfold violence; and justly thinking that no soldier would face it, but seek shelter, I jerked the hook, with the line attached, on the top of the wall, which, fortunately for me, caught the first time, and with but little noise to alarm. I, however, listened for a moment in great agitation; but all appeared quiet. I then tried the rope with all my strength, and it proving safe, I made the desperate venture; and desperate indeed it was; but what will not a man attempt for his liberty?

With great difficulty I got to the top, and gently and by degrees peeped my head over. I listened most attentively, but could hear nothing; and had just got my knee upon the wall in the attitude of ascent, when a door opened close by me, and a soldier passed along. In a moment I threw myself flat upon my face on the wall, and very plainly heard his footsteps directly beneath me. I continued in this posture for some minutes, and had almost given myself up to despair, when, after passing and repassing several times – for I could hear him, though not see him – he again retired to his box, and I heard the door close after him. I seized the favourable moment, and pulling up the rope, descended in safety on the other side. I then took off my shoes, and softly walked on tiptoe across the beat of the sentinel, till I had got to some distance, when I threw myself on the wet grass, and stopped to take breath. My greatest difficulties were now surmounted; but as no time was to be lost, I soon started off again, and had nearly approached some of the lamps, which I was obliged to pass, when I plainly saw a picket or patrol of five or six men across my very path. It was astonishing they did not see me; but my good star predominated, and I remained unnoticed. The lamps were now, indeed, in my favour, as they shewed me what to avoid, whilst I was myself shrouded in darkness. Choosing the most obscure places, and proceeding step by step with the utmost precaution, I at last reached, unmolested, the boundary ditch, which I soon cleared; and in a moment after found myself free of the prison and on a high-road, with nothing further to obstruct my progress.

Scarcely crediting my good fortune in succeeding thus far, I put on my shoes, and set off in a northerly direction, running with all my speed, notwithstanding the wind and rain continued for about an hour, when I came to a house situated at a point where four roads meet (Kate's Cabin). Lights were in the windows, and a stage-coach with lamps, and the words "London and York", which I well remember, painted on it, was standing at the door. Shunning observation by keeping under the hedge, I took the left-hand road, though totally ignorant to what part I was going. Continuing my flight, I proceeded for two hours more, when my apprehensions of immediate pursuit being somewhat abated, and also beginning to feel fatigued, I slackened my pace. I had passed through two or three villages, but had met with nothing to interrupt me, or indeed to notice. I kept on thus some short time longer, when I came to a toll-gate, situated at the foot of an extraordinary long bridge, which led to Oundle, a town of considerable size. The chimes of the church clock were just playing the hour of three as I seated myself for a moment on the steps of the foot-gate. I was at first in doubt whether or not I should proceed straight on, or seek a by-road, one of which adjoined the bridge on the left hand. I determined, however, on the former, and continued my journey through dark, long, and dirty streets, without stopping or seeing anyone, when I came to another bridge, at the farther extremity of the place, almost as long as the one I had before passed, so that the town appeared to be situated on an island. The moon had now got up a little, and afforded me light enough to discern, in a field just beyond the bridge, on the left hand, a small shed or hovel. I was now exceedingly fatigued, and I determined to rest here a short time at least, till I could collect my scattered senses, which had been so long in continual agitation.

The door of the hovel was luckily open, and it afforded me an excellent shelter. I cannot express my mingled feelings of fear and joy, hope and thankfulness, as I now stretched myself on the straw with which the ground was covered. No longer cooped up in what I may call a dungeon, where life itself almost ceased to be worth caring for, I now had before me a fair prospect of succeeding in my enterprise; and my energies being thus brought into action, I became a new man, and felt renovated accordingly: my mind, as it were, expanding and adapting itself to the occasion, called forth all its powers.

In the hovel, tied to a manger, was a cow, and her calf was placed in a pen just by her. At first the cow gave tokens of alarm and uneasiness; but humouring her by degrees, and treating her gently, she suffered me to approach her more familiarly, which I took advantage of, by milking her in the crown of my cap. The milk, with part of a biscuit, afforded me a delicious meal. I had taken off my shoes and wet stockings; and putting on the dry ones which I had in my pocket, I felt inexpressibly refreshed, though my wet clothes and fear of pursuit prevented my sleeping. Indeed it would not have been prudent to have slept, for it was evident the owner of the cow would be there in the morning to milk her; so, contenting myself with the good berth I had obtained, for it still continued raining, I waited very patiently for the first dawn of day, when I intended to start again. Of course I had not yet been able to examine my map, which, being enclosed in a case, was quite dry; but I thought that of little consequence, as, whether the road I had taken was right or not, a few hours would make up the difference.

As the day broke, the weather cleared up a little, so far as to cease raining, but the road was very wet and dirty; however, there was no alternative, and leaving with regret the hovel which had so kindly sheltered me for the night, I continued my journey. My wet clothes made me feel extremely cold and uncomfortable at first, and I kept up a pretty good pace for some time, in order to warm me. It was not my intention to go far, and seeing a haystack in a retired part of a field some distance off on my left, I quitted the high-road, and proceeded to it. It was farther than I expected; but it appeared to be the very spot I should have chosen for concealment, there being no public path or road leading to it. Part of the stack had been cut, so that I easily gathered enough of the hay to make me a soft and dry bed; and here I determined to stop and examine my map, and devise a plan for my future proceedings.

After I had rested some time, the sun, to my infinite delight, suddenly broke forth, and gave every sign of a fine day; and though February sun in England is very different from a February sun in the south of France, yet the warmth I derived from it gave me great comfort, and refreshed me exceedingly; so much so, that, after several vain attempts to keep my eyes open, I sank into a sound sleep, which must have lasted for some hours, as the height of the sun on my awakening shewed it to be past noon. Having risen and looked around, and finding nothing to interrupt me, I took out my map to see whereabout I was. This I accomplished with great ease; for the names of the places I had passed being painted on the mile-stones and direction-posts, as I observed when I started in the morning, and corresponding with those on my map, I soon found out that I had come diametrically opposite to the road I had intended to have taken. But this was of no great moment; and I now determined to pursue a direct easterly course, in as straight a line as I could, and to make for the coast in that direction. I may as well mention here, that, through the whole of my route afterwards, I could at any time find out the exact spot I was in by observing the names of the towns or villages painted on the mile-stones and direction-posts. This I found of great service to me, as I seldom wandered far from my way, and never had occasion to ask the road, even had I been able or inclined to do so. But to proceed. The clock of a neighbouring church was just striking one when I started again, in high spirits, my clothes being now quite dry, eating my last piece of biscuit as I went. How I was to get a fresh supply of provisions did certainly now and then strike me; but it made no very deep impression, my chief object being to get on as fast and as far as I could, not doubting but I should make the coast in two or three days more at farthest; but in that I was woefully out of my reckoning.

*   *   *   *   *

The day continued fine, and I walked on at a pretty round pace, in as straight a line as I could, over hedge and ditch, carefully avoiding any house or person passing, for about two or three hours; and I was congratulating myself on the progress I had made, when, suddenly casting up my eyes, and looking around me, to my utter horror and dismay I saw, but a few fields off, and in the exact path I was taking, the very prison I had left!

I could not be mistaken; its red tiles and striking appearance, with the numerous holes cut in its wooden walls for air by its unfortunate inmates, were too deeply imprinted on my memory to be forgotten. In short, not having any guide across the open fields, and there being no mile-stones to direct me, I had wandered back again to within half a mile or less of my former prison. I cannot express what I felt at that moment; I seemed to have lost the very power of perception; and, instead of turning back immediately, I absolutely continued for a little time walking on in the same direction – like the squirrel fascinated to its own destruction by the eyes of the rattlesnake.

Fortunately for me, going thus without heed, I tripped and fell, which brought me suddenly to myself, when, turning round, I took to my heels, as if pursued by a whole legion of devils, and never stopped till I once more found myself in the very hovel, near the long bridge I have spoken of at Oundle, where I had before found shelter, and which remained in the same state as I had left it, with the exception that the cow and calf had been removed.

Though nearly dark for the last mile or two, I found my way back without much difficulty; but I was nearly exhausted by fatigue, and had nothing to refresh myself with; however, I did not as yet feel so much from hunger as from the disappointment I had experienced in being obliged to retrace so many weary steps. On the other hand, I had much to congratulate myself upon, independent of the lucky avoidance of running my head again into the very bars of my prison, which I was certainly in a fair way of doing; for in a few minutes after my arrival in my old quarters it began to rain, and it continued throughout the night in torrents. Having a good roof over my head, I considered the rain in my favour, as it would doubtless prevent anyone from interrupting me in my resting-place. The human mind, particularly in youth, soon reconciles itself to circumstances; so, making the best of the matter, I nestled myself snugly in the straw, and slept comfortably and undisturbed till morning.

It still continued raining, and the floods had come down in the night with great rapidity, inundating the meadows around me till they looked like a sea. A few qualms at breakfast-time flitted over unheeded, when of a sudden it struck me that my situation was too exposed for the day, as, should anyone come into the hovel merely by accident, which was not at all improbable, I must inevitably be discovered; and I appeared too like what I really was to be passed by unquestioned. I by no means wished to leave till I had laid out some definite plan to act upon, and some other route to follow. Looking, therefore, about me, I found a hurdle or two and an old gate thrown over the beams or rafters which supported the roof. On these I climbed, and with little trouble succeeded in making, in the most obscure corner, a sort of floor or landing-place. On this I carried some straw to lie upon, and was glad to perceive that, when looked up to from below, it by no means appeared calculated to excite suspicion of concealment; and here I spent the remainder of the day. It was well I took this precaution.

I had constructed a small hole in the roof, through which I could see everything passing on the high-road, which was not more than a few yards from me. I could also see the town, and the country round me on all sides.

The church clock had just chimed the hour of noon, when, looking through the opening I had made, I plainly saw three soldiers coming over the bridge within a hundred yards of me. They had their bayonets fixed, and I knew, at the first glance of their uniform, that it was the same as that of one of the regiments on duty at the prison. My heart now sank within me, and I gave myself up for lost. They came exactly opposite to the place, as if they had intelligence I was there. I held my breath almost to bursting as they got over the gate which led to the hovel. Two of them came in and looked around; but seeing it an open stable, and not much like a hiding-place, they walked out again without stopping, but not till one of them had thrust his bayonet twice or thrice through the hurdles and straw upon which I lay; they then, to my inexpressible relief, slowly rejoined their comrade, and continued their journey.

[The escaper was disturbed no more after this, but determined to leave so dangerous a situation as soon as possible. Travelling by night, he passed through Oundle again, and lingered at a shop where some loaves of bread seemed to invite a purchaser, but discretion overcame hunger. He went on to Peterborough "whose noble cathedral, in its dark mass of shade, rose full before me just as the clock struck three". He was by now famished, having been forty-eight hours without food; and had found nothing, even a turnip, to appease his hunger. During the next night, on his way to Wisbeach, he chewed straw. At Wisbeach he stopped on Saturday evening to look longingly into the last shop of the little town, where candles, bread, cheese, and other articles were displayed. He would willingly have given a *louis d'or* for a loaf of bread.]

Whilst I was deliberating with myself how to act, a waterman, as I judged from his dress, passed by me in at the door, and throwing himself on a chair, made a sign to the person within, by drawing his hand across his face and chin, as if he wanted shaving. He never spoke a word; but the shopkeeper appeared perfectly to understand his meaning, and placing a cloth, which was none of the cleanest, over the fellow's shoulders, made preparations for performing that very necessary operation. By this I understood that the shopkeeper was a barber also; and as I had a very suspicious beard myself, which I was particularly anxious to be rid of, I viewed all their actions with great interest.

The barber was a little, thin, spare bodkin of a man – I think I see him now standing before me – about seventy years of age, with a most antique cast of countenance, and a face, when taken in profile, exactly like a half-moon, his nose and chin forming the horns. There could not possibly be a finer specimen of the taciturnity of the English nation than in the scene before me, exemplified as it was both in the operator and him operated upon. As to the former, he took no more notice of the automaton whom he was shaving than if he had been scraping a marble block; and for the latter, he was as immovable as the marble block under the chisel of the statuary, and with much about the same degree of feeling. I kept my eyes upon them both, with the hope of profiting by what I saw, and carefully noted that, after being shaved, the man threw two copper coins upon the counter. He then walked to the window, took down a loaf of bread and two or three red herrings, then drawing a mark with his fingers across a piece of cheese, it was cut off, and weighed out to him. For these he threw down a silver coin, a half-crown, receiving some small change in return; and, tying up his purchase in an old handkerchief, departed in the same silent surly mood he entered.

I thought I could never have a better opportunity; for I certainly was more than a match for the shopkeeper, should he give any alarm; and I determined also to make good use of my heels if necessary. Summoning, therefore, all my resolution to my aid, I marched boldly into the shop, threw myself into the same chair, and made the same signs as my predecessor had done; and, as I anticipated, the same silent scene followed exactly. The same cloth was put round my neck, I was lathered the same, and shaved the same, and the same sum of two copper coins was thrown by me upon the counter.

I now began to feel very courageous, and went up to the window to lay in a stock of provisions, which I intended should last me the whole of my journey. Bread alone would not now serve me, and I looked about for a few minutes to see what I should take – spreading, however, some silver ostentatiously before me, that the good man might not be alarmed. At the same time I found out that my friend was not dumb, which I had seriously begun to suspect; for, on my taking down some different articles from a shelf, he did speak, or rather made an attempt to speak. What he said, I know not; but on my continuing whistling, which I had been doing for some time – and which I did not from any want of respect to the old gentleman, but truly because I was unable to give him an answer – he withdrew his eyes from my face, and very resignedly turned back to the counter, holding the loaf I had reached down to him with both hands across his chest.

Imagine my ecstasy on leaving the shop, which I did completely un-suspected, with two loaves of beautiful white bread, some excellent cheese, and three or four herrings – for in this last I had the same taste as the waterman; and, to crown all, some tobacco and a pipe! I do not exactly recollect what I paid, but I had some change out of two half-crowns, which I threw down. No mother ever hugged her first-born to her bosom with more exquisite delight than I did the handkerchief which held all these good things. I kept eating as I walked; but that was no father than to the first shelter I could find, which was, as usual, a barn or stable, where I made amends for my long fasting in a supper in which nearly one whole loaf, two of my herrings, and a proportionate quantity of cheese dis-appeared.

It was Saturday night when I thus provided myself, and I determined to stop where I had been so fortunate the whole of the next day, Sunday, and rest my legs. The building in which I was being, however, as I thought, too near the bank, after I had eaten my supper I sought out another lodg-ing, in a hovel which stood a little distance off, more in the fields, and which, having neither hay nor straw, nor anything else of the kind liable to occasion interruption, appeared admirably adapted for the purpose – it being about a quarter of a mile from the bank or road, and a mile at least from any house. Here, then, I removed with all my stores, and scraping together what little straw and rushes I could find, made myself a couch or bed. But I had another luxury yet to enjoy in my pipe and tobacco.

My sleep this night was indeed invigorating and refreshing, and I awoke the next morning a completely new man, with the additional happy prospect of a good breakfast before me. The day was remarkably fine for the season, and the bells from the different churches, some of which I could hear a most astonishing distance, were quite in unison with my feelings. It might be called the first fine day of spring, as the sun had really much warmth, and the birds, such as the pewit or lapwing, and others of the same kind, were dashing in playful evolutions about me. I took more notice of these things, perhaps, from being so long deprived of the enjoyment of them; but, though trivial in themselves, they diffused a kindly feeling through my whole frame, and cheered my spirits wonderfully. Nor could I help contrasting my present situation with that of the preceding Sunday, when, at the same hour, I was breathing the tainted and noxious atmosphere of an over-peopled prison-house; and now inhaling the pure and animating breezes of a fine spring morning in the fields. A man must be confined as many months as I was, in the space of only a few square yards, to enjoy in an adequate degree the happiness I felt.

I took the opportunity, during the day, of washing a pair of stockings, which I hung in the sun to dry, and of cleaning myself, and making myself comfortable; indeed, having a clean-shaved face, clean shirt, shoes, and stockings, and brushing myself up a little, which every Frenchman knows how to do, I by no means looked the suspicious character I otherwise should have done; and this was now particularly to be attended to as I drew near the end of my journey. My map pointed out two routes to the coast, after arriving at Downham, a town which was situated at the end of the bank on which I was travelling – one by way of Lynn, which was re-presented as a considerable seaport town, which was by all means to be avoided, if possible; and the other more in the interior of the country, through some smaller towns, Swaffham and Fakenham. Of course I selected the latter – with what success, the reader will learn.

Having passed the day with much comfort and satisfaction, I resumed my journey about nine o'clock, and, without any interruption worth mentioning, arrived at Downham about midnight. The weather turned out bad at this time, and it began to rain as I got to the bridge. I neverthe-less continued on through the town, although so dark that I was obliged to grope my way, taking the different windings as correctly as I could remember from my map; which instructed me, on getting through the place, to turn to my left, and afterwards to my right, and then to take the first road, and continue straight on. All this I did, as I presumed, very exactly, and prosecuted my journey with great spirit; and was rewarded for it, on the day breaking, by finding myself within a little distance of what appeared to me a fortified town. In short, I had taken the wrong turn of the road at Downham, and had got to the very place I was particularly cautioned to avoid – Lynn in Norfolk.

From the success I had hitherto met with – although, it must be owned, checkered with trifling disappointments – I had become over-confident; and so far from feeling this wandering from my direct road of any con-sequence, I rather rejoiced at it, and foolishly resolved to endeavour to get a passage to Holland at this place, without going any farther. Perhaps I was encouraged in this resolution by the sight of the harbour and shipping, now gilded by the rays of the morning sun, and the knowledge that it was the port we were brought prisoners to on our first arrival in England; nay, the very smell of the pitch and tar, which was wafted to me by the wind, contributed, I think, not a little to confirm me in my purpose. Leaving the direct road I was on, after crossing several fields, I took up my abode for the day – for I still had sense enough not to think of doing anything till night – in a haystack which stood on a bank about a mile from the place.

    *   *   *   *   *

I passed the time rather impatiently till the hour of action arrived. What infatuation led me on this night I know not, but I wandered to the quay adjoining the square, in the centre of the town, though several people were walking about, and seated myself on a bench affixed to a building overlooking the harbour. By degrees the people dropped away, and left me to myself.

I had not, however, enjoyed my own reflections many minutes in solitude, when six or seven men in sailors' dresses, with large sticks in their hands, headed by an officer in naval uniform and sword, passed close by me. They looked very earnestly in my face, and went on. The next minute they returned; and one of them, tapping me on the shoulder, said something, of which I could make out no more but that I must follow them; for I understood a little English, though I could not speak it. My heart sank within me at the sound of their voices. I knew all was over.

Seeing me hesitate to accompany them, one of the most ruffianly looking of the set seized me by the collar of my jacket to pull me along, which so irritated me, that, regardless of consequences and the disparity between us, I struck right and left with a stout stick I had in my hand, and sent two of them on their knees; at the same time receiving a blow myself on my hand, which twirled my stick into the air, and another on my head, which felled me to the ground. Seeing, therefore, resistance of no avail, I sullenly submitted to my fate, and suffered myself to be raised on my feet, the whole party abusing me all the way we went.

Whether these men were police-officers, appointed for the apprehension of runaway prisoners of war, as I suspected, or whatever other description of guards they might be, they were the most brutal set of fellows I ever met with—the officer who commanded being little better than his men. All the time this scene passed I never opened my lips, which seemed to enrage the officer much, as he several times, on not receiving any answer from me, flourished his cutlass over my head, as if he would cut me down. However, I will do him the credit to say that he never struck me with it.

After we had passed through two or three streets, we came to a small inn, when the officer said something to one of the men, who beckoned me to follow him into the house, which I very quietly did, whilst the officer and the other men set off in another direction. I was rather surprised at being taken to a decent inn instead of a jail; but I thought that part of the tragedy was yet to come. As far as I could judge from the manner and behaviour of the fellow who was with me, he took my silence for a fit of the sullens, as he several times addressed me with the words: "Cheer up, my lad! Cheer up, my hearty!" words I had often heard aboard ship, and which I knew the meaning of. I also very well understood I was his prisoner; and, seeing no alternative, I sat myself down, though in a very melancholy mood, by the fire, in a little room he took me into, he seating himself on the opposite side.

My companion, after several ineffectual efforts to draw me into conversation, at last gave up the attempt, and left me to my own thoughts, at the same time ordering some grog and a pipe to comfort himself with. Occasionally he would deign me a sour look, and now and then, eyeing me at the same time very contemptuously from head to foot, would mutter something between his teeth, of which I could make out nothing.

I leant my elbow on the table, and rested my cheek on my hand, absorbed in the most bitter recollections. My head ached dreadfully from the blow I had received, and I felt my heart, as it were, almost bursting with vexation and disappointment. After being so near the accomplishment of my wishes, to be thus in a moment again doomed to imprisonment and sorrow, and perhaps punishment, almost drove me mad.

The room in which we were had no other furniture but the two chairs on which we were seated, and a large oak table, with leaves reaching to the ground. In observing this I also saw that the window – which was a sashed one, and which opened into the street – was not fastened. The idea of escape had never left me, and I thought, could I but get to that window, something might be attempted. My heart sprang to my lips at the bare suggestion, and hope, when I imagined it most distant, suddenly reappeared.

I watched my companion for some time after this, with the expectation of his going to sleep; but he knew his duty too well for that; when a loud noise and quarrelling in an adjoining room gave me the opportunity I wished. There appeared to be a violent scuffle going on; and my guard, after being repeatedly called upon by name, looking round to see that all was safe, and saying something to me, snatched up his stick and rushed out of the door, taking care, however, to shut it after him. Now was the time to venture, or never.

I flew to the window, and threw up the sash, which offered no impediment, and was just on the point of getting out, when I heard him returning. It was of no use attempting any farther, and I immediately, and with a heavy heart, drew back; but, fearful of the first vent of his anger, before he entered, and unperceived by him, I crept under the table, the large leaves of which concealed me from his view.

He shut the door after him, and looked round for me; when, finding the window open, and I nowhere to be seen, he jumped out of the window, and set off in the imaginary pursuit of me. I could scarcely credit this wonderful instance of good fortune in my behalf, and hastening from my hiding-place to the window, kept my eyes on him till I saw him turn the corner of the street, when I leaped out also, running with all my speed in a contrary direction.

*   *   *   *   *

I had continued thus for some time through several streets, without in the least knowing where I was going, but with the hope of somehow or other finding my way to the gates of the town, and once more taking refuge in the haystack which I had so unfortunately left, when, turning the corner of a lane, I of a sudden, and most unexpectedly, came in sight of my guards again, all of whom were together. They at once discovered me, and, inflamed with rage and revenge, immediately gave chase. I must inevitably have been retaken, for I could have run but little further, if, providentially for me, I had not observed, as I was running along, the door of a small house standing a little open. Unperceived by anyone, I entered the house, and safely closed the door, holding, with breathless suspense, the latch in my hand. In a few minutes I heard my pursuers passing in full cry after me, clattering and shouting most terrifically. It was the last time I either saw or heard them; and happily it proved for me that it was the last time; for I verily believe, had I then been taken, it would have broken my heart: as it was, I sank exhausted upon my knees, almost fainting with agitation and terror.

An aged female, of most prepossessing appearance, with a cat in her lap, was sitting at work by the fire when I entered. At first she seemed rather frightened at my intrusion, and had her hand on the wire of a bell which communicated with the adjoining house to give the alarm; but the next moment, from my action and manner, she appeared in part to comprehend my situation, particularly when she heard my pursuers after me; for she held up her forefinger in the attitude of listening, and said very softly: "Hush – hush!" two or three times. After waiting thus a little while, till she was convinced they were gone by, she came closer to me, and looked in my face. I was pale as death, and so spent with running that I could scarcely draw my breath. She spoke to me in the most soothing accents of kindness and compassion, and made signs for me to rise and take a chair, for I was still on my knees.

The voice of compassion, let it be spoken in what language it will, is intelligible to all men and to all nations. I comprehended her accordingly, and looked thanks, for I could not speak them. However, she made amends for my want of tongue by running on with great volubility, doubling her little withered fists in the direction my pursuers had taken, as if she spoke of them, as she doubtless did, and repeating the word "pressgang" several times with great emphasis and anger.

As she seemed waiting to hear me speak, and not knowing what else to say, I faintly answered: "Press-gang, madame; press-gang!" as well as I could, without in the least understanding what it meant. But this was quite enough for the old lady, who continued venting her anger against them for some minutes longer. It appeared afterwards that my kind protector took me for a sailor, who had escaped from a set of men denominated a "press-gang," who are employed by the British Government to procure seamen for their navy, in which service many cruel and oppressive measures are resorted to.

I was, as I have said, quite exhausted with the variety of sufferings I had undergone for the last few hours. The benevolent woman on whose protection I had been so unaccountably thrown soon saw this, and poured me out a glass of brandy; but ere I could receive it from her hand, a film came over my eyes, the room appeared to swim round me, and I thought myself dying. I had only time to take off my cap and point to my wounded head, which she had not before perceived, when I fainted away.

I know not how long I remained in this state, but when I came to myself, my head was reclining on a pillow placed by her on the table for me, and she was bathing the contusion in the tenderest manner with some sweet-scented embrocation. Seeing me revive, she gave me the brandy, which I had scarcely strength to hold to my lips, so much was I reduced by pain and fatigue; but after I had swallowed it, I felt immediately relieved, and heaving a deep sigh, lifted up my head. She appeared greatly rejoiced at my recovery, which was, however, very transient and fleeting; for, unable to hold myself up, my head sank again upon the pillow, when, as considerate as she was good, she made signs for me to keep my head down and hold my tongue. I found no difficulty in complying with this, and in a few minutes was fast asleep upon the table.

*   *   *   *   *

I never awoke till next morning, when for some minutes my head was so confused, I neither knew where I was nor what had happened; but my recollection soon returned, and with it came a train of hopes and fears. Although much revived, I was still in great pain from the blow on my head, and otherwise feverish and unwell. My guardian angel, as I must always call the excellent creature who thus sheltered and nursed me, was at my side as soon as she saw that I was awake. She had sat up all night to watch me, and the Bible, which she had been reading to beguile the time, was still lying on the table. She did not appear by any means fatigued, but busied herself in getting breakfast ready, for it was past eight o'clock; and in a few minutes more placed before me a basin of excellent tea, and some bread and butter. At these repeated instances of kindness and benevolence from a stranger, and at such a time, I could no longer restrain myself, but burst into a passionate flood of tears, which seemed to have a sympathetic effect upon the good woman's heart, for she wiped her eyes with the corner of her apron several times. I now found it to be both proper and prudent to say something, as she seemed surprised at my continued silence, which she expressed by several intelligent signs; and as I felt myself too ill to continue my journey, it was necessary for me to endeavour to raise an interest in her feelings, that she might not withdraw her protection from me.

I therefore, after many struggles between hope and apprehension, summoned up resolution to throw myself entirely upon her compassion; and I had no reason to repent my determination. In the best English I was master of, I told her I was "un foreigner, un stranger. Ah, madame, good madame," I said with tears in my eyes, "a-ve pitie on me!" At the first word I spoke, she discovered I was not an Englishman, but took me to be a foreign sailor from one of the vessels in the harbour, who, she supposed, from what had happened on the preceding night, had escaped from a "press-gang", as I have already mentioned. She had seen much and heard a great deal of the cruelty of these men; and that it was which made her so inveterate against them, and prompted her so readily to conceal me. But when I told her that I was "un pauvre Frenchman – un prisonnier François", she started, and her countenance fell; but it was but for a moment, the natural benevolence of her disposition getting the better of that national antipathy which even existed in this good woman's breast.

I took my dictionary from my pocket, and with its aid, and partly by signs, soon made her comprehend my situation and hopes. I also emptied my money on the table, and made signs for her to take it; and, throwing myself on my knees, concluded by begging her not to betray me. The worthy creature caught my meaning much more readily than I could have expected, and at the same time, weeping as she spoke, made me understand that she had a grandson, an only child left of many, now a prisoner of war in France; she likewise told me, with great emotion, that she would not betray me. "God forbid that I should!" she said; and added, that if I got away safe, all the return she asked was, that I would assist the escape of her grandson, who, the last time she had heard from him, was at Verdun. As to my money, she insisted upon my taking it back again, and would by no means receive it.

An intercourse being now established between us, I felt as if a mountain had been removed from my breast; and as there was some danger to be apprehended to my kind hostess should it be known that she had assisted in the escape of a French prisoner, I was removed into a little back parlour, which opened into a small garden or yard about twelve feet square, surrounded by high walls, and where none could oversee me. For the time I was concealed there, I was nursed with the same care and attention that a mother would pay to an only son. My health and strength returned but slowly, the blow on my head having deranged my whole system, and it was some days before I could call myself completely restored; but she managed everything with so much discretion, that none, not even her nearest neighbours, had any suspicion of her having an inmate. I always kept the door of the room locked, and could often hear her talking with her acquaintance, whom she made a rule of getting rid of as soon as possible. It would have amused anyone to have witnessed our conversation of an evening. After she had made the doors and windows of the house fast for the night, which she generally did about six o'clock, she would come and sit with me, bringing her work, and make the tea and toast – which, I perfectly agree with the English people, is certainly a most refreshing meal, or *comfortable*, as they call it. If she said anything which I did not understand, I would write it down, and translate it, word for word; and the same by what I said to her; and it is surprising with what readiness we comprehended each other's meanings. Often have the tears run down the good creature's eyes as I told her of my sufferings in the prison; and as often would she rejoice with me in the anticipation of my once more seeing my parents.

My kind hostess – whose name, for prudential reasons, I shall omit – was, as she told me, in her seventieth year. She was the widow of a captain or master of one of the vessels which sailed from Lynn, I think she said in the Baltic trade. Her husband had been dead some years; and she told me, with some pride, that he had left her a comfortable competency, the fruits of his industry and economy, to maintain her in her old age. All her children and grandchildren, she said, were dead but one, who, as I have before mentioned, was a prisoner in France; having been captured in a voyage to St. Petersburg in a ship in which he was mate, and from whom she had received no account for upwards of two years, which afflicted the old lady grievously. I promised her, should I succeed in reaching France, I would use all the interest of my family, which I assured her was not small, in effecting his exchange; and if I did not succeed in that, I would make him as comfortable as money could make him.

We also talked, as you may suppose, of my future proceedings; and as a first step towards their successful termination, she provided me with a complete dress of coloured clothes which had belonged to her deceased son; and also with two fine linen shirts – my own being checked cotton, such as seamen wear – and a hat, and stockings, and other useful articles; nor would she receive any payment whatever for them, but bade me place them to the account of "her dear grandson, and do the same for him". The next morning, according to her wish, having discarded my old clothes, I put on my new ones, which fitted me exceedingly well; and I felt the change, as it were, through my whole frame. I appeared to myself at once, and most unexpectedly, restored to that station in life to which I had been so long a stranger, and to which I at one time thought I should never return. I had also the satisfaction of knowing that I might now pass from one end of the kingdom to the other without being suspected or interrupted – no small comfort to a man in my situation. My kind hostess, at first seeing me in my new dress, was visibly affected; the remembrance of her son rose in her bosom, and she sank on a chair overwhelmed with her feelings. After a few minutes given to silent sorrow, in which I felt for her as if she had been my own mother, she wiped away her tears, and taking my hand very affectionately, prayed God "to restore me to my family again, and not leave my parents childless". I recollect her words well; for the tone and manner in which they were delivered made an impression upon me I shall never forget.

Being now perfectly recovered, and well aware of the inconvenience I must be putting my inestimable friend to, I prepared for my departure. I had been her guest a week; and having told her my determination to start next morning, once more requested her to allow me at least to repay her the expenses she had been put to on my account. But I could by no means prevail upon her to take a single farthing; her constant reply to everything I advanced upon that subject was "to give it to her grandson one way or other". All I could induce her to accept was a ring of little value, but esteemed by me as given me by my mother, and having my name, age, and place of birth engraven on it. I had concealed it about my person on being first captured by the English vessel, and had worn it round my neck by a ribbon ever since. I thought I could not do better than to present it to this, as I called her, my second mother; and she received it with great pleasure, and promised always to wear it in remembrance of me. This, with four small Spanish coins as counters for whist, which I had seen her admire, was all I could get her to accept.

The next morning, after partaking of a good breakfast, about eight o'clock I rose to depart; when, with tears in her eyes, which she in vain attempted to conceal, she gave me a letter for her grandson, enclosing a bill of exchange. I endeavoured to smile, and told her "I trusted we should yet meet again in happier circumstances, her grandson with us". But she shook her head, and said, "No, no; not in this world; never, never!"

I then took her hand, and kissed it with great devotion several times, and thanked her repeatedly for the kind protection she had afforded me. But the good creature had not yet done. She brought me some provisions of bread and meat, neatly done up, to put in my pocket, with a small bottle of brandy; and once more bidding me not forget "her poor boy", we parted – and for ever!

The very mention, even after a lapse of so many years, of all this kindness and unexampled liberality, brings tears of grateful recollection to my eyes; and think not, reader (and I may as well mention it here), that her goodness was forgotten by me. Immediately on the restoration of peace, I commissioned a friend to go to England to seek out this excellent woman, bearing letters from my mother and myself, saying all that grateful hearts could say; and offering her, if she chose to accept it, an asylum with us in France for life; or should she, as was more natural, prefer staying in her native country, we remitted the necessary funds for securing to her the payment of an annuity of £50. We also sent several presents, such as we thought might be acceptable to her. But alas! to our unspeakable sorrow, on our correspondent's arrival at Lynn, he found she had been dead some years – an event, I have no doubt, hastened by the melancholy end of her grandson; of whom I was obliged to write her the distressing account – which I did immediately after I had ascertained the fact – that he had been wounded in an attempt, with many others, to escape, and that he had died of his wounds.

I had been fully instructed by my kind hostess how to get out of the town, and the route I was afterwards to take. It being market-day, the streets were full of people, whom I passed with much apparent unconcern; and it gave me great confidence to see myself so unnoticed, as it more fully convinced me of my personal security. Having walked across the great square or market-place, beset with numbers of busy faces, I discovered I had come a little out of my way, but it was of no consequence; and in a few more turns I found myself in the street I had been directed to, leading to the eastern entrance of the town. In a few minutes more I was clear of the place, and on an excellent road in the direct line to the coast. Everything conspired to make this part of my journey pleasant. The day was very fine, the sun shining bright, and the birds whistling around me in all directions; nor was it the least pleasing part of my reflections that I was travelling by day instead of night; in short, I was in great spirits, which, though they had been for the moment damped by the parting with my kind old friend, revived at the scene around me, and the animating thought of my approaching deliverance, to which every step I took drew me nearer.

5

[Passing through Gaywood and Fakenham, the French prisoner arrived at last at Langham, "a well-built, interesting village, the houses of which, from the neatness, not to say elegance, of their structure, gave a flattering picture of the condition of English farmers as contrasted with those of other nations". It was near here that he was to find his smuggler accomplice (the actual place is no doubt purposely left uncertain) living in a house with a pre-arranged mark upon the door and three oyster shells over the window. Finding these signs, he walked boldly in, as he had been instructed.]

A man in sailor's dress, with a hair cap on his head, and huge boots turned over his knees, was sitting at a small round table smoking his pipe, with a can of grog before him. A woman, apparently superannuated by age and infirmity, was spinning flax with a spindle by the fire; and close by her, on a stool, half-asleep, sat an arch-looking boy, about twelve years of age, also in a sailor's jacket and trousers and cap.

I threw a hasty glance over them all, and, fixing my eyes on the man, was convinced all right as to him; for he had a scar, as I had been previously informed, reaching from right to left, deeply imprinted on his forehead; and he also wore a silver ring on this thumb, through some superstitious notion prevalent among seafaring people. As to the other inmates, I was not quite so certain.

On my entrance, he eyed me very suspiciously from head to foot. I approached the table, and holding up two fingers of my left hand over my head, made a sign, clearly seen and understood by him to whom it was addressed, though unperceived by his companions. He immediately gave me the countersign, and said: "All's right." I replied boldly in words I had been taught, and which I had conned over so often as to have completely by rote. He understood me perfectly well, and told me in French, which he spoke very fluently, to sit down and make myself easy. He then went to the door and window, which he bolted with strong bars of iron.

"There now," says he; "we are safe from all disturbance; yet it's as well to be secure. Cant that into your hold," continued he, pouring me out a glass of excellent hollands as he spoke, "whilst I get something for the bread-room. – Ah," he added, with a knowing wink, as I took his advice, and drank off the very acceptable gift, "it's genuine, I warrant it".

He then placed on the table some beef and bread and other eatables, and seating himself by me, filled a fresh pipe, and bade me tell him all about it. I told him, in as few words as I could, the heads of my story, and that I would reward him with any sum to furnish me with the means, as I was well aware he had done for others, of escaping to Holland.

He heard me very patiently to the end – during which time I think he

smoked half-a-dozen pipes of tobacco, and drank as many glasses of
grog – never speaking or interrupting me the whole time; but evinced the
interest he took in my tale by sending forth from his mouth a denser
column of smoke, according as the various incidents excited his feelings.
After I had concluded, he shook me heartily by the hand, and told me
again all was right. He would do what he could; but that we must act with
caution, as "hawks were abroad".

*　　　*　　　*　　　*　　　*

My host, whom I shall call Jack, a name he was usually designated by
among his comrades, was about forty-five years of age; and, notwithstanding the scar across his forehead – which, by-the-bye, he told me he
had received from one of my own countrymen – might be called a fine-
looking fellow. His complexion was deeply embrowned by the service he
had seen, and the winds and weathers he had encountered, as he had been,
he said, a sailor from the time he was no higher than a marline-spike. I
need not say he was a smuggler; but he carried on the "free-trade", as he
called it, in a manner peculiar to himself, and never ran a cargo within a
certain distance of his home.

He was, he informed me, the sole agent of a house in Holland, connected with certain people in England, who placed implicit trust in him.
While telling me this, he was tossing off glasses of grog one after another.
The dose was repeated so often that I began to find it was high time to go
to rest. With some demur, on account of my refusing to take "just
another drop", Jack shewed me to my apartment – a curious concealed
place, which had defied discovery on divers occasions. Pointing out a
strong iron bar, he directed me how to place it across the door, and which,
for my further security, he told me not to open without a password. At
the same time he shewed me a small and almost imperceptible hole in the
wall, by which I could reconnoitre every comer.

Next morning he was with me betimes, and we entered into conversation about our future proceedings. He bade me remain in my room
all day, and not show myself at the window, which faced the ocean, lest
I should be seen from the beach; and to be sure to close the shutter as soon
as evening fell, so that no light might be seen from without. At night, if
I wished it, I might join them below, but I was not by any means to go out
of the house. He assured me that these precautions were all necessary, both
for his and my own security. The old woman, he said, was always on the
watch to give notice of the least alarm; and that, under the appearance of
being half-crazed and superannuated, she concealed the greatest cunning
and vigour of mind. At the same time he shewed me another small

aperture, through which I could see whatever passed in the room below.

"For the last assurance of your safety," said he, "see this"; and, as he spoke, he discovered to me a recess in the wall, so artfully contrived as to elude the closest inspection. "If need be," continued he, "conceal yourself there. One of your generals knows its dimensions well, for he was in it when every house in the hamlet was filled with red-coats in search of him. They were within two inches of him," added he, laughing heartily as he spoke, "and the old woman held the candle; but they might as well have been on the top of Cromer light-house." He then left me.

I remained in my hiding-place several days. Notwithstanding every attention was paid to my wants, and even wishes, by the whole household, my time passed very heavily. I had no books, nor anything to divert my thoughts by day, and I would sit for hours contemplating that ocean on which all my hopes were now centred. At night, indeed, I generally joined the party below, or my friends would come and spend it with me. During these times he would amuse me by relating several tales of daring hardi-hood and of extraordinary escapes in which he had been a party; and of the incredible subtlety and invention with which he and his companions had circumvented the officers of the English customs. These last stories he always told with great glee, as if the very remembrance of them diverted him.

At length the period of departure arrived. It was about twelve o'clock on a fine starlight night that, looking out of my window previously to undressing and going to bed, I saw a boat approaching the shore. I knew it in a moment to be the coble usually moored at the creek. Two men and a boy were in it. The boy, whose face was towards me, was steering, and I immediately knew him, notwithstanding the distance, to be my host's son. They approached with great precaution and silence, and I scarcely breathed with hope and expectation; but in a few minutes all was lulled into certainty by the appearance of Jack himself, who, without allowing me time to speak a word, which I much wished, to the old woman, hurried me to the boat and jumping in after me, pulled away with all his strength, seconded by the other man, as if life depended on it.

In about two hours or more we arrived on board a small sloop, which had lain-to for us; and the skipper, a Dutchman, who spoke good French, received me with much civility, bidding me, however, be quick. Jack accompanied me into the cabin, and in a few words – for no time was to be lost – acquainted me the vessel was one in which he was concerned, and had run a valuable cargo not far off; that the skipper readily consented to receive me on board, and had watched a favourable moment – com-municated by signals from the shore – to run in and take me off.

The master of the vessel having several times called to us to make haste, I satisfied the faithful fellow for his services to the utmost of his wishes, to which I added a guinea for the old woman, and another for his son; and going upon deck, shook him heartily by the hand, and bade him farewell – he and his boy waving their caps several times to me as they pulled away to the shore. We immediately put the vessel about; and having the advantage of a favourable breeze, we soon lost sight of the cliffs and coast of Norfolk – the last object in England which struck my sight being the fluttering and revolving blaze of Cromer lighthouse; and this, too, having faded in the distance, I retired to the cabin, where the skipper was sitting with his mate over a good and capacious can of grog, of which they invited me to partake.

On the evening of the second day we arrived in safety in the *Texel*, when I paid my friend the skipper ten *louis d'or* for my passage, and gave five more to be divided amongst the crew.

Little more now remains for me to say. Immediately on landing, I wrote home the news of my escape; and the next morning started for Paris, where I was detained a day by the commands of the Minister of the Marine, to whom I rendered all the information in my power; and without losing another moment, took my place in the diligence for Marseille, where I arrived in safety, and the next minute was in the embraces of my dear and beloved parents.

The American Civil War, 1861-1865

CHAPTER SEVEN

SO FAR all the escapers in this book have gained their freedom by climbing, but I would say that the prisoner's favourite method of escape is through a tunnel. There is something fascinating about the slow, relentless forward creep of the column of foul air that you yourself are carving under the hated barrier that has held you for so long. Tunnels are slow to dig, and all that time the escaper is savouring the satisfaction and excitement of his work. He has something to do and something to lose. His life is so much the richer because of a dank, slimy hole in the ground, in which he toils and of which he dreams. Nothing else matters to him while the tunnel is in operation, and from the moment the first load of spoil is hauled to the surface he has, in fact, escaped.

An even more personal reason for the prisoner's fondness for tunnelling is that down there in his narrow burrow he is alone. It is his only chance of enjoying solitude during his captivity except in the cells – and solitary confinement is usually treated by the escaper as a "rest-cure" in preparation for his next attempt.

A tunnel seems to catch at the imagination of the reader as well as at that of the escaper, and is remembered because of this. There are several successful tunnel breaks in the history of escape, but not so many as one would expect. Few of the tunnels dug are ever finished; the length of time required for their construction makes them particularly vulnerable, the spoil is difficult to disperse, and the tunnel entrance, used constantly as it must be, hard to camouflage.

Recently I had the opportunity to talk with a German who had been one of our guards at *Stalag-Luft III*, and I was able to learn the answers to a number of questions which had always puzzled me. One was, "Why were so many tunnels discovered just before the break was due?" Time and again the escape party, fully briefed and equipped for their journey, would be disappointed on the very eve of departure. How did the Germans know?

"Oh, we usually knew when a tunnel was started," I was told. "We found out through the hiding-place of the sand, the seismographs or the dogs. Once we knew where the tunnel was we did not disturb you, because we knew that you were happy and busy down there and out of mischief. We only uncovered the tunnel when it was becoming dangerous."

I accepted the reply with due allowance for professional pride, but nevertheless it is a disconcerting thought.

Apart from the time taken in its construction and the resulting vulnerability to searches, the tunnel has many advantages as a means of escape. The escaper can leave in his own good time and carry with him far more in the way of luggage than is usually possible. The hue and cry can be delayed, for if he is careful no evidence is left behind to shout his absence to the skies. Perhaps its greatest attraction is the fact that many men can escape together through it. In 1864, one hundred and nine prisoners of the American Civil War left Libby prison through the tunnel which James M. Wells describes in the next account. The famous Holzminden tunnel of the 1914 War afforded the passage of twenty-nine, while the number of escapers who used the ill-fated tunnel from *Stalag-Luft III* was ninety-eight.

Personally I think that such large-scale breaks as these are bad policy. The enemy is so upset by the magnitude of the break that a widespread military operation is launched to recover the escapers. Police checks more stringent and far-reaching than those following a small-scale break are organised, and although many men may be at large their chances of getting away are greatly diminished. Of course, I am considering this from the point of view of the escaper who wants to get away. There is no doubt that the large-scale break, necessitating as it does the employment of so much enemy manpower, is valuable as a military operation in itself.

Only forty-eight of the hundred and nine prisoners who escaped through the tunnel from Libby prison remained at large. Among Holzminden's twenty-nine, ten got clean away; while but three of the ninety-eight who crawled from the Sagan tunnel had the good fortune to reach England. Fifty of those recaptured were murdered by the Gestapo on Hitler's orders.

The Civil War tunnel was elementary by present-day standards, which demand electric light, air pumps and railways to carry the spoil from the working face to the vertical shaft. The big tunnel at Sagan, which was about forty feet deep, even had bunks for the shift who were resting, and a workshop for repairs to the shoring and railway lines. James Wells' tunnel was very small, a mere sixteen inches wide, but it fulfilled its purpose magnificently and set an example which has been followed by generations of eager "molers".

James M. Wells

FROM THE village of Calhoun on the Hiawassee River, the morning of the 26th September 1863, our little troop of cavalry began the retreat northward, hotly pursued throughout the day by the enemy under General Forrest until just at daylight of the following morning when near a small station called Mouse Creek, a number of our soldiers riding in the rear were cut off and captured, myself and two other officers being among the number. But the Confederates soon after halted, for they were now in the vicinity of Loudon, where a large force of Federal infantry was stationed, a territory upon which it was unpleasant, if not dangerous, for any small or detached command of Confederates to venture at that time.

At this point, by an officer with a couple of men who seemed to be exercising special jurisdiction over me, I was taken into a house which was known to me in raids made through that country previously as a house occupied by Union people. The male members of the family had retreated with our troops during the night, two ladies being its only occupants.

While my escort was preoccupied in looking the place over, it occurred to me to give my money and watch (which I had previously taken the precaution to secrete in the leg of my boot) to one of these ladies, believing they were in sympathy with me, and much preferring them to the Confederates as heirs to my little personal effects.

Accordingly, when an opportunity presented, I quietly removed my watch and money – some thirty-odd dollars – from the place of their temporary concealment, and without saying a word or even giving her a look handed them both to the lady who chanced to stand nearest and a little behind me.

She took them in silence, as they were offered, and without being observed by my captors, as I have always believed. Shortly after, we were taken up the road a mile or two where the Confederate troops had halted in a wood. Stretching myself out on the ground for a little rest, I was presently accosted by a Confederate soldier who seemed to take a fancy to my boots, they being of excellent quality with high tops. I was finally persuaded to take them off, when my curious friend gave me his shoes in return – "just as a keepsake," he said. They were so ragged that in order to keep them on I was compelled to tie them together with cotton strings. More soldiers gathered round and in compliance with oft-repeated demands article after article of my wardrobe disappeared in exchange for others mis-shapen and curious enough. After this transformation the picture I presented must have been amusing; with a pair of trousers made out of green baize (the material generally in use for covering billiard-tables), six inches short in the leg and large enough in the seat for Barnum's Fat Boy. Sharp search was made for money about my person and they seemed to think it strange that an officer in the "Yankee" army carried no watch or other valuables.

That afternoon all the prisoners, about one hundred and twenty-five in number, were started south, destined we knew not whither, nor into what fate the fortunes of war would eventually plunge us. All the remainder of that day and the following night we were hurried on foot, with mounted guards on either side, over the same ground that marked the course of our retreat the day and night before, reaching Calhoun and the Hiawassee River (the scene of our first conflict with the enemy forty-eight hours before) some time the next day. Having ourselves burned the bridge at this point, we could not well complain at being compelled to ford the stream, in water reaching above our waists.

The march on foot extended to Dalton, Georgia, a distance of about one hundred miles.

Reaching that place, footsore and weary, we were shipped in open cars to Atlanta, and there turned into a pen, or stockade, in company with twelve or fifteen hundred other prisoners, mostly captured at Chickamauga and many of them wounded. After remaining in Atlanta two weeks all who were able to be removed – some ten hundred, I suppose – were shipped by way of Augusta, Columbia, and Salisbury to Richmond, Virginia. This trip, generally in box- or open freight-cars, occupied fourteen days more. On this journey promises were made (as we afterwards found, for the purpose of keeping our men quiet and in order) to the effect that an exchange of prisoners would take place as soon as we reached Richmond.

Coming up from Petersburg we crossed the long bridge just below Belle Isle and were disembarked on the Richmond side of the James River, and in a body marched down Cary Street to what most of us then believed was some convenient place where an exchange of prisoners would soon be made. Visions of faraway homes which we hoped soon to see in reality were uppermost in our minds; but alas! these hopes proved a chimera, and all too many of our poor fellows never saw their homes again. For my own part I remember to have read all the signs along the way, but of the great number thus observed only one fixed itself indelibly upon my memory. Halting under the shadow of a dark and frowning wall of brick and mortar, on casting my eye upward, there, over a broad entrance, in large black letters painted on a board, I read the words: "A. Libby & Son, Ship Chandlers & Grocers," and then for the first time it flashed upon my mind that we had reached our destination, and that the building in front of us was Libby Prison, and instinctively the familiar quotation from Dante came to my mind: "All hope abandon, ye who enter here." At the windows, which were heavily barred, and standing a little back, could be seen the wan faces of our friends who had preceded us.

The officers of our number (I was at the time a second-lieutenant in the 8th Michigan Cavalry) were singled out and shown the way to the office, situated on the first floor of the "Hotel de Libby", while the enlisted men were sent to the Smith Building, Castle Thunder, Belle Isle and other places.

At the office, after registering our names, rank and regiment, we were relieved of the few valuables we chanced to have left. We were then conducted to the floor above and put through a door which was immediately closed and bolted on the outside.

Our group, on entering, was quickly surrounded by the old prisoners, all anxious to learn something of the progress of the war and of their friends in the various commands to which they belonged, as the information the Confederates furnished was always meager and exceedingly unreliable. For the first three months many of the prisoners lay on the bare floor without a thing in the world either over or under them, with nothing but their boots on which to lay their heads at night. Among the twelve hundred men confined there at the time, all officers in our service, of greater or less rank, were represented by almost every trade and profession. Many were the masters of science, art, and literature whose names were not unknown to fame. There were preachers, painters, sculptors, orators and poets. Many were the curious and beautiful designs wrought from beef bones saved up for the purpose after the bones had first been picked to the very marrow by our hungry men.

The pencil and pen sketches, drawn on whatever even surface might be found, often showed evidences of genius and a cultivated hand. Among those more or less famous in music I remember one of the Lumbard family of Chicago, at that time celebrated singers of the Northwest. General Neal Dow, the father and founder of the Maine Liquor Law, treated us now and then to temperance lectures which, in a practical view, seemed to be quite unnecessary as food was very scarce and intoxicating drinks absolutely out of the question. Religious services were held quite frequently, but in an evil hour a minstrel troupe was organised, which came near swamping religion and all else for the time being.

We were constantly hungry, and our dreams by night were filled with visions of home and loved ones, and tables spread with every conceivable luxury known to the culinary art, and on waking in the morning the old sensation of hunger came back with renewed force. In my more contrite and submissive moments I remember to have agreed with myself that, if spared to get out of that place, I would never ask nor require anything more or better to eat than bread and butter. Many a time I have wakened in the night, gone down to the kitchen and scraped the burned rice from the bottom of the kettles left soaking in water that they might readily be cleaned for the next meal.

Libby Prison, at the time of which I write, was situated between Cary and Canal Streets, in the city of Richmond, Virginia, the width of the building extending one hundred and ten feet from one street to the other, its sides running along either street one hundred and forty feet east and west. It was three stories high on Cary Street, with a basement cellar under the center of the building, making it four stories high on Canal Street.

Across the width of the building, extending from the basement to the roof, were two partition walls, dividing each floor into three rooms, or apartments, of equal size. Our prisoners at this time occupied the two upper floors, or the six upper rooms. The rooms were designated as the upper and lower east rooms, the upper and lower middle rooms, and the upper and lower west rooms. The middle room on the first floor below was used for cooking purposes and was known as the "kitchen". It had three fireplaces in its east partition wall. This kitchen was the only place in the building the prisoners had free access to, save the six rooms spoken of above. The fireplaces were not utilised, but in front of each one of them were three stoves, the pipes of which went into the chimney flues running upward above the fireplaces. The flues did not extend below this floor, so the partition wall from here down was solid. The east room on the first floor was used for hospital purposes; the west room was the office where the prison officials were quartered, and the basement beneath was divided up into dungeons for the confinement and punishment of unruly prisoners. The doors and windows of the prison were barred like those of a jail.

Aside from the effects of hunger, there was a feeling of unrest among many of the prisoners which, if yielded to, often led to serious despondency and even insanity. Plan after plan was devised for escape, only to be proved impracticable. In the dead hours of the night men could be seen prowling around the prison, in the hope that some means of escape might offer. Often on dark, stormy nights the guards would come up for temporary shelter, under cover of the prison walls where, unobserved by anyone from the outside, they would enter into conversation with the prisoners, often giving expressions of sympathy. Among them frequently was found a man of Northern birth who had been conscripted into the Confederate army and was at heart a Unionist. Bribes were sometimes

offered by the prisoners and taken by the guards; but attempts to escape
by that means generally resulted in the prisoner being handed over to the
authorities, after he had gotten outside and given up his valuables.

At one time a plan was laid for a general escape of all the prisoners then
in Richmond. There were then fifteen or twenty thousand confined in the
various prisons in different parts of the city. At a preconcerted signal these
were to break out, overpower the guards, take their arms, seize the
Tredagar Iron Works, where, it had been learned from the daily papers
which reached the prison occasionally, there were enough small arms and
ammunition stored to put a loaded gun into the hands of every prisoner.
Successful thus far, the design was to take possession of the city and the
Confederate Congress then in session (including President Davis), and
hold them until aid could come from our forces in Virginia. The signal for
the outbreak was fixed; every prison had its special duty assigned, and the
day of the night on which the attempt was to be made came, when lo!
the secret had been revealed by some traitor in the prison.

After this misadventure it was then resolved that any new plan should
include only men whose sagacity and fidelity could be implicitly relied
upon. By their continued movements at night the prisoners most desirous
of escape gradually came to know each other and to take counsel together,
and in this way a compact association consisting of only fifteen men was
formed in Libby, and tunneling was decided upon. An effort to go out
through a large sewer was abandoned as impracticable after considerable
time and labor had been lost.

It was finally determined to begin in the basement under the east end of
the building, a place familiarly known among the prisoners as "rat hell",
and tunnel eastward, coming out under a carriage-shed attached to a large
building on the opposite side of the street, where the escaping prisoners
could lie screened from the observation of the guards around the prison
behind a high board fence, extending from the ground to the roof of the
shed, until they found it safe to emerge. The tunnel was to run under a
short cross street reaching from Canal to Cary Street, at the east end of the
prison.

But how was this cellar, which was to form the base of all operations, to
be reached? The prisoners could not go into the hospital room and thence
through the floor into the cellar, for in this room were nurses and guards
who would at once discover the plan. They could not go into the basement, under the cook-room, and then through the partition wall into the
east basement for there were guards on duty there all the time. Every step
taken had to be kept a profound secret, not only from the Confederate
authorities but from the majority of the prisoners also; and until

secure access to the cellar could be obtained nothing could be done.

It was finally determined to go behind the stoves in one of the fireplaces just described and, taking out the bricks in the center, follow the partition wall down below the floor on which the cook and hospital rooms were located, a distance of three or four feet, and then go through the wall into the cellar, thus escaping observation from every quarter. This was successfully accomplished. Major A. J. Hamilton, of the Eleventh Kentucky Cavalry, was the author of this plan, while Thomas E. Rose, later of the Sixteenth U.S. Infantry, then colonel of the Seventy-seventh Pennsylvania Volunteers, was the chief engineer of all tunneling operations and the leading spirit of the entire enterprise.

Beginning in the fireplace, then, the bricks were removed from the center of the wall, so as to make an opening wide enough to admit a man's body. From fifty to seventy-five bricks were taken out. The work was all accomplished secretly and at night. After "lights out" or nine o'clock, at which time everybody in the prison was supposed to be lying down, two men, having first quietly removed the bricks, would go down and take turns with each other in digging throughout the night. In the meantime two or three others, detailed for that purpose, would remain on watch in different parts of the prison and be ready to give the signal and help the two workmen up on the first approach of day. The night's work done, the bricks were carefully replaced, covered over with soot and dirt which was always plentiful behind the stoves, and in this condition the place was left secure from observation until night came on again. This operation was repeated nearly every night for about seven weeks.

The authorities made regular tours of inspection through the prison every day, while hundreds of prisoners were in this room and about these stoves, engaged in cooking from early morning till nine o'clock at night, and yet not more than twenty or twenty-five men ever knew of the work until it was nearly all accomplished. From the bottom of the cellar an opening was first made through the stone wall, some four or five feet thick, and then the work of excavating began. Clam shells and case-knives were the principal tools used, and with these simple instruments a tunnel sixteen inches in diameter, eight or nine feet below the surface of the ground and about sixty feet long, was dug.

As the work progressed, difficulty in removing the dirt from the tunnel was experienced. To overcome this, a spittoon from one of the rooms above – a box about eight inches square and five inches deep – was taken down into the cellar; and the man digging inside would pull the box in by means of a cord attached to one side and, after filling it with dirt, give a signal, when the man in the cellar, by another string, would pull it out and empty it. By this slow and wearisome process the whole mass of dirt was removed.

The back end of the cellar or basement was not used by the authorities and was seldom invaded by any person or thing except rats; but it was filled several feet deep with straw which had been placed there for hospital purposes, though not in use at that time. As the dirt from the tunnel came out it was spread evenly over the bottom of the cellar and covered with this straw, thus concealing it from observation through the day. The front part of the cellar was used as a store-room, and attachés of the prison were in and out by day, but seldom if ever at night.

When the tunnel had reached a distance of twenty feet the air became so foul that one man had to fan at the open mouth while the other man dug. So foul was it at times that a candle would not burn; yet to dig successfully light was found to be a necessity as well as air. Lights were obtained by stealthily taking a portion of the candles furnished the various rooms each night.

Those who had been let into the secret of the tunnel now began to put themselves in readiness for the exodus, which they foresaw would mark the beginning of their greatest trials. To harden our limbs and muscles persistent and continued walking and other physical exercises were resorted to. My comrade and myself once walked a distance of twenty-two miles around the room in a single day. I was nearly barefooted and for a long time had my eye on a pair of boots belonging to one Lieutenant Mead of a Union Kentucky Regiment. I had received a box from home and had offered Mead many of my choicest things for his boots, for boots I must have before making the escape. But Mead, who knew nothing of the tunnel or the special purpose for which the boots were wanted, was inexorable. I had often tried them on to show how well they fitted me – even better, I thought, than they fitted Mead – but to no effect; it was no go. When the night came for the escape I lay down by Mead's side according to my custom and as if for the usual night's rest. An hour had not passed before Mead was wrapped in profound slumber, when I pulled on his boots and, like the Arab, folded my tent and silently stole away. I still lacked a hat; but in passing out among my sleeping comrades I stumbled upon one belonging to Lieutenant Thomas McKee of the First West Virginia Regiment, who nightly shared the luxuries of the floor with me in that immediate neighborhood, and, without compunction or further ceremony, I hurriedly placed it where, in my own judgment at least, it would do the most good.

There was no way of judging the distance across the street under which the tunnel ran, save as it was measured by the eye from the windows above. So, when the tunnel had been carried far enough, as was believed, to reach the carriage-shed, it was thought best by those in charge of the digging to prospect by means of a small hole dug upward for the purpose. The men engaged below that night commenced running up at an angle of forty-five degrees. A short time before this some workmen had been employed in the prison, making repairs and strengthening the doors and windows. It was their custom to leave their tools in the prison overnight and these, used by them for fastening our chains, were now made use of by the tunneling party in cutting them loose; for, one night, from the carpenter's outfit, our fellows stole an augur and chisel and carried them down into the cellar for use in that quarter, and they were for ever lost to the Confederacy though they did good service in forwarding our escape. I believe the chisel was the principal tool in use the night the prospecting hole was made. The man engaged in digging was reaching ahead into the small opening, letting the dirt rattle back down the inclined plane, when suddenly the chisel went through the surface at a point full in the glare of a street lamp, and not more than ten or twelve paces from where a sentinel walked. The noise made by the chisel as it went through was heard by a guard who asked another nearby if he had heard the noise. He replied, "Yes," but that it was "nothing but rats", and both walked on. Their conservation was plainly overheard by the real "rat" under the ground. The hole was at once stopped up with little stones and whatever material could be utilised for the purpose, and the main tunnel went on some ten or fifteen feet further.

The plan was, when the tunnel should be completed, to let as many prisoners into the secret as could well get out in a single night, and then, leaving it to someone behind to cover up the excavations in the wall and so preventing the discovery of the tunnel by the Confederates, let as many more escape at another time.

On the night of the 9th of February 1864, everything being in readiness, about two hundred men who at this time had been let into the secret were assembled in the cook-room after nine o'clock, ready to take the desperate chances of escape. It was a trying moment. The digging of the tunnel had been a gigantic undertaking, accompanied with the greatest anxiety, hardship and privation; and now, completed at last, it only opened the way to dangers no man of us could forecast.

About a dozen or fifteen men had gone down through the hole in the wall into the cellar and my turn had just come, when a noise at the outside door caused a report to be circulated that those who had gone out had been recaptured and that the guards were coming in to take us all under arrest. This was made the signal for a general stampede across the room, a distance of one hundred and ten feet, to the stairway in the corner leading up to the rooms where the prisoners belonged. My partner, who was equipped with a haversack containing a scant supply of rations saved for the occasion and a map of the country which we had drawn up with a pencil, ran back with the crowd. I remained behind the stoves and reflected a minute. Listening at the door, I could hear no one coming in. "And if they do," said I to myself, "they know nothing of this hole and nothing of the tunnel, and anyhow I may just as well go down and out; it can be no worse for me." Accordingly down through the hole in the wall I went.

On reaching the tunnel I found a young man by the name of White, a lieutenant from Erie, Pennsylvania, just going in. He said, "Wells, I will wait for you at the shed". I waited until he had made his way through, for, on account of the foul air, it was dangerous for more than one to enter the tunnel at once. I was soon through, dragging my overcoat on my legs behind me. I found on emerging that White had gone and that I was alone. I stretched myself up at full length and breathed the fresh air for the first time in six long months. I felt the soft ground under my feet, and looked over and about me as if to assure myself that it was not all a dream. I never felt a greater determination to accomplish a purpose in my life, and resolved to push on and by continued efforts realise the benefits of the labors already performed, or perish in the attempt. My nerves were strung to the highest tension. All fear had vanished, and my senses were as alert and quick as those of a wild animal.

From the shed we had to pass through a gate which opened on Canal Street. Along this street, to within twenty steps of the gate, a sentinel walked, who on reaching a certain point would face about and go a distance of forty or sixty paces the other way. Taking advantage of the time when his back was turned, the prisoners opened the gate and, stepping out on Canal Street, passed out of sight. In this manner all emerged from the gate, one by one, or sometimes in parties of two or three. The alarm causing the prisoners to stampede from the cook-room proved to be a false one, and that night one hundred and nine men got out. Among the number was my partner, but after five days he was recaptured. Of the whole number who went through the tunnel only forty-eight got entirely away.

Watching my opportunity, I slipped out in the manner just described and walked two squares down Canal Street. I had no fixed plan for getting out of the city but was guided wholly by impulse and by circumstances as they were presented, though my general purpose was, by some means, if possible, to place the Chickahominy River, which to the northward was not more than six miles distant, between myself and Richmond that night. My especial object in this was to baffle any pursuit that might be made with dogs.

The Federal uniform which I wore was rather an advantage to me than otherwise, for the Confederate soldiers had appropriated clothing sent by our Government, and were then commonly wearing our uniforms on the streets. After reaching the borders of the city, out of reach of the street lamps, I took the center of the road and made my way as quietly and rapidly as possible. But soon I discovered a light immediately in front. I dropped upon the ground and, watching closely, saw a sentinel pass the light with a musket at right shoulder. The place I took to be a guard-house or perhaps a hospital. I then crept on my hands and knees some distance around, thus flanking the light and the sentinel, and, soon after, came to the fortifications around the city, where I apprehended great danger and difficulty in eluding detection and arrest. On these fortifications were large siege guns in position, and sentinels mounted on the parapets. For more than an hour I felt my way along, never standing up at full height, and most of the time on my hands and knees. My caution and perseverance finally brought me safe out upon an open plain far beyond the city's limits and defenses.

Presently I came into a dense thicket on low bottom-land, covered here and there with water. I believed myself near the Chickahominy. Coming to some flood wood on the edge of a considerable body of water as black as midnight, I broke off a large piece of the light-coloured bark and threw it into the water, deeming that if it floated off the water was that of the river. It did float off, and immediately I proceeded to place the stream between myself and Richmond. In doing this, however, I had to wade in water and mud waist deep.

I had barely reached the uplands on the north side when daylight came on, and I at once sought a hiding-place for the day. This I found a little further on, by crawling inside an old inclosure which had grown up to a dense thicket of laurel and other brush. As the day approached, I could hear the voices of the Confederate soldiers encamped near the river a half-mile away. About nine or ten o'clock I heard a body of cavalry coming up the road from the direction of Richmond and, standing up, could just see their heads as they passed on the gallop, not more than two hundred yards distant.

These men, as I readily divined, were in pursuit of escaped prisoners, for that morning at the accustomed roll-call one hundred and nine men had failed to put in their appearance, and dogs were at once brought into requisition to hunt down the fugitives. A rigorous search was also instituted to discover, if possible, the means of our escape; but some of our men, by previous arrangement, took the precaution to stop up the places of egress, at the same time prying off a bar from the window and hanging out a rope made by tying together strips of blankets. This ruse led the authorities to suppose we had escaped through the window, having first bribed the guards. This deceived them for a while, and the guards and officers on duty were arrested and sent to the guard-house, all the while protesting their innocence. Search was then made throughout the day, and it was not until nearly nightfall that a colored boy,' chancing to go into the shed, discovered the hole where we had emerged; but for many days thereafter they did not learn how we went into the cellar from the cook-room.

My hiding-place was on a gentle slope of land at the lower end of which was a spring, where some colored women came that day to do their washing. I could hear their conversation, and about the time the cavalry passed up the road I heard them say something about "de Yankee prisoners". Chickens and hogs came about me through the day, all seeming to view me suspiciously, the hogs especially; these would dash away with a boo-a-boo, after looking at me intently for a moment. This, I feared, greatly increased the chances of my discovery and capture.

When night came, after first taking an observation, I moved on and presently came into a road which I ventured to follow for a short distance before turning into the brush again. In passing, I noticed some saw logs, and it occurred to me that there must be a mill not far off. Soon, at a point where the road forked, I saw a man coming toward me and, believing that the country must now be all up in arms about our escape, this gave me great anxiety. But I decided that it would not do for me to show signs of fear or hesitation, and I accosted the unwelcome stranger with: "Good evening, sir; can you tell me which of these roads will take me to the mill?" He said, "To Gaines's mill?" and I said, "Yes"; and then told him I had an uncle living down there somewhere by the name of Jackson, and asked if he knew of any of the Jackson family. He said he thought there was a man, not far from the mill, by the name of Henry Jackson, and I assured him that Henry Jackson was the very man I was looking for, and told him that I belonged to the First Virginia and had just obtained a furlough for a few days for the purpose of paying my relatives a visit. I then hurried on my way.

Towards morning I came to a crossroads where there was a mile-post and finger-board. I climbed the post and, holding on by one hand, with the other struck a match which I had carried in my pocket for a long time. On the board was an index finger pointing nearly in the direction I had been traveling for the past two hours, and beneath it the words "Twelve miles to Richmond". I had then traveled the greater part of two nights and made but twelve miles. By this time hunger and fatigue and loss of sleep were closing in upon me with a deathlike grip. I pushed on however, though from sheer exhaustion often stumbling and falling to the ground. In going through an open woodland I suddenly came upon an encampment of Confederate teamsters, doubtless a quartermaster's train carrying provisions to the army about Richmond. Some of the men were up knocking about among the mules and wagons. It was very dark. Assuming the rôle of a driver and bursting out in the vernacular common to the class, I walked up to a mule and gave him a kick in the ribs, and in a gruff voice commanded him to "Stand around". Repeating this and similar operations two or three times, I soon, without interruption, made my way through the encampment.

When morning came I again sought a hiding-place. Shivering and hungry throughout that day, and unable to move for fear of detection, I had a good opportunity to reflect upon the mutability of human affairs and the vicissitudes of a soldier's life. Night coming on, I again took my bearings and was about to start out when I overheard footsteps in the brush not far distant and, crouching down like a frightened rabbit, awaited developments. Nearer and nearer the steps came. I thought I had been discovered and that my time had come, for now I could distinguish the steps of two persons. Soon into plain sight, almost on tiptoe, walked two escaped prisoners, McCain, of the Twenty-first Illinois, and Randall, of the Second Ohio Regiment. I recognised them at once and I hailed them in a whisper. They shared with me from their scant rations of corn bread, and then, for the first time in thirty-six hours, I tasted food. We here traveled on together; and once or twice during the remainder of the week we obtained provisions of colored men, who were true to the escaped prisoners in every instance.

We had been traveling four nights, all the time in the woods, and Sunday morning found us well-nigh exhausted. We came to the conclusion that it would be impossible to travel in that way any longer and so, after lying down for an hour or more for a little rest, we started out for the first time by daylight. Following up a ravine, we soon came out into an open field inside of which was a schoolhouse or church, and people, evidently attending service, had already begun to assemble. Beyond ran a road which forked near the schoolhouse, and not more than one hundred and fifty yards from our hiding-place in the brush. Two or three little dogs came uncomfortably near and, while we were debating what course to pursue, about seventy-five cavalrymen rode by and halted at the fork of the road. Randall volunteered to crawl around to the road below the school, to see if it were possible for us to cross in that direction unobserved. He disappeared in the brush and we never saw him again, but the report of three or four guns fired down the road in the direction he had taken led us to suppose he had been shot and killed. One of the dogs now discovered McCain and myself, and commenced barking furiously. We started back down the ravine, keeping as far as possible under cover of the brush. The firing below and the barking of the dog had set the soldiers and everybody else on the *qui vive*. We were discovered in our flight and pursued by cavalrymen, but finally eluded them. Through the rest of the day we remained in the swamp, closely secreted, being fully satisfied with our experience in trying to travel by daylight. When night came on the weary march was resumed.

Coming to an opening, we discovered, some distance off, a man standing in the doorway of a cabin. Believing him to be colored we had little hesitancy in approaching him; but on coming to within a few paces, we found him to be a white man. It was then too late to back out, and putting on a bold front we walked up and asked him for something to eat, telling him at the same time that we were Yankee prisoners recently escaped from Libby Prison, and that we were likely to perish for want of food. He told us that he had already heard of the escape, that he had been a Confederate soldier, and that he knew something of the life of a soldier. "But," said he, "I never turned a hungry man away from my door yet, and do not propose to do so now". Whereupon, by his invitation, we followed him into the house. He gave us three or four dry biscuits, stating that they constituted his whole store of provisions. He appeared friendly and kind from the start, but we followed him into the house, fearing he might possibly bring out a musket instead of meat. He even directed us which way to go to avoid detection and capture, and told us that we were only a short distance from the York River, where a gunboat flying the American flag had passed down not more than an hour before.

Our objective point now was Yorktown, or Williamsburg, the nearest point where our troops were stationed. We had gone a long distance out of the way and must now travel south. I had lost my hat, our clothing hung about us in rags, and all the time we were getting weaker. On the night of the seventh day out, there came a terrible storm of sleet and rain and, raking up a quantity of dry leaves by the side of a large log and covering them with boughs, we crawled under, lying closely together for shelter and warmth and rest. How long we had lain there I do not know, but presently I was awakened by McCain who said we must get up and go on or we would surely perish. I agreed with him but neither of us made an effort to rise. While lying in this state of half-stupor, I found my memory was failing me and that I could not recall my only brother's name. Suddenly, as by a concert of thought as well as action, we sprang to our feet, and soon found ourselves in an open field near a road which proved to be the Williamsburg Pike, though at the time we were in doubt as to the fact. We concluded to follow it in the direction of Williamsburg, as we believed; but, for safety, we kept back a little distance in the field. Presently we heard cavalry coming ahead of us. We had already had a little experience with Confederate cavalry and were not anxious to repeat it. But these might be our friends. We were on neutral ground, at least, and very near our own lines. It was a great risk to hail them, and a great risk to let them pass by unchallenged, for it was becoming apparent that we could not stand the pressure much longer. Approaching within a few paces of the road, we secreted ourselves in the weeds and brush. By the clatter of the iron scabbards I knew the cavalrymen were armed with sabers (it was too dark to see), and I told McCain this was to me an evidence that they belonged to our side, for the Confederate cavalry as a rule were not armed with sabers. They came up and passed on, but nothing occurred and no word was spoken to give us any clue to their identity. The situation was terrible. The cold, freezing rain was now coming down in sheets and our bones were chilled to the very marrow. The main column had got by and the rear guard, about twenty in number, were in front of us. We could endure it no longer, and resolved to hail them. Accordingly, we both stood up, and I cried out, "What regiment is that?"

As quick as thought, wheeling their horses into line along the fence, and at the same time drawing their pistols, they demanded our immediate and unconditional surrender. The click of the hammers, which we could plainly hear as they came into position, added to the horror of the moment. My hair actually stood on end. I said to McCain: "We are gone up." With this he seemed to agree, and replied that we had better surrender, as our lives depended upon it, and that no time was to be lost. Accordingly, we threw up our hands and together cried out, "We will surrender". On going to the fence we discovered that we were in the hands of a detachment of the Eleventh Pennsylvania Cavalry, which had been sent out as a rescuing party and had made every provision for our further comfort and safety.

The Boer War, 1899-1902

CHAPTER EIGHT

O N October 6th, 1899, Mr. Winston S. Churchill, as he then was, twenty-four years of age and newly appointed war correspondent to the *Morning Post*, sailed from Southampton for the Cape to report the progress of the Boer War. He landed at Durban, and on hearing that Ladysmith was besieged he hurried to Estcourt, the nearest British post to the beleaguered garrison. From there he sent despatches to his paper, and accompanied military reconnaissance parties in an inadequately armoured train known as "Wilson's Death Trap", which they drove up and down the line as near as they dared to the Boer positions.

Three weeks after Mr. Churchill had left England, the train was ambushed and de-railed. A brisk fight followed which lasted for an hour and a half. Most of this time Mr. Churchill, under heavy fire, was busy organizing the clearing of the line. After much effort the working party cleared the débris sufficiently for the engine to get through, and the wounded were put aboard the engine and tender, which pulled away to safety. The rest of the party, under the command of Captain Haldane, remained behind to cover the retreat.

Mr. Churchill, who was then directing operations from the driver's cab, stopped the engine some distance away and walked back along the line to guide the rearguard to where the engine was, so that they could make their retreat under its cover. He says:

". . . I had not retraced my steps two hundred yards when, instead of Haldane and his company, two figures in plain clothes appeared upon the line. 'Platelayers!' I said to myself, and then with a surge of realization, 'Boers!' My mind retains its impression of these tall figures, full of energy, clad in dark, flapping clothes, with slouch, storm-driven hats, poising on their levelled rifles hardly a hundred yards away. I turned again and ran back towards the engine, the two Boers firing as I ran between the metals. Their bullets, sucking to right and left, seemed to miss only by inches. We were in a small cutting with banks about six feet high on either side. I flung myself against the bank of the cutting. It gave no cover. Another glance at the two figures; one was now kneeling to aim. Movement seemed the only chance. Again I darted forward: again two soft kisses sucked in the air; but nothing struck me. This could not endure. I must get out of the cutting – that damnable corridor! I jigged to the left, and scrambled up the bank. The earth sprang up beside me. I got through the wire fence unhurt. Outside the cutting was a tiny depression. I crouched in this, struggling to get my breath again.

"Fifty yards away was a small platelayers' cabin of masonry; there was cover there. About two hundred yards away was the rocky gorge of the Blue Krantz River; there was plenty of cover there. I determined to make a dash for the river. I rose to my feet. Suddenly on the other side of the railway, separated from me by the rails and two uncut wire fences, I saw a horseman galloping furiously, a tall, dark figure, holding his rifle in his right hand. He pulled up his horse almost in its own length and shaking the rifle at me shouted a loud command. We were forty yards apart. That morning I had taken with me, Correspondent-status notwithstanding, my Mauser pistol. I thought I could kill this man, and after the treatment I had received I earnestly desired to do so. I put my hand to my belt, the pistol was not there. When engaged in clearing the line, getting in and out of the engine, etc., I had taken it off. It came safely home on the engine. I have it now! But at this moment I was quite unarmed. Meanwhile, I suppose in about the time this takes to tell, the Boer horseman, still seated on his horse, had covered me with his rifle. The animal stood stock still, so did he, and so did I. I looked towards the river, I looked towards the platelayers' hut. The Boer continued to look along his sights. I thought there was absolutely no chance of escape, if he fired he would surely hit me, so I held up my hands and surrendered myself a prisoner of war."

Mr. Churchill did not long remain a prisoner. Once in the State Model Schools, Pretoria, he spent his first three weeks of captivity trying to persuade his captors that as a non-combatant he should be repatriated; but his behaviour during the ambush had hardly been that of a looker-on, and as soon as it appeared clear that his plea would be of no avail he decided to escape.

The first plan was an organized mutiny of the prisoners – an overpowering of the guards, a seizing of arms and a fight for freedom – the pipe-dream that every prisoner indulges in. Fortunately the plan was abandoned. It is always unwise for an escaper to use violence unless his freedom is in sight. As Mr. Churchill himself says, "You are in the power of your enemy. You owe your life to his humanity and your daily bread to his compassion."

Mr. Churchill's next plan was to climb the wall surrounding the

Schools, with Captain Aylmer Haldane and Sergeant-Major A. Brockie. They had discovered that by hiding in a circular lavatory near the perimeter they could watch the sentries patrolling the *inside* of the wall and, choosing their moment, they would be able to dash the short distance separating the lavatory from the wall and haul themselves to the top. There were no sentries on the outside.

An abortive attempt was made on December 11th, but the sentries were too observant. On the following day Mr. Churchill made his dash, and reached the wall.

Winston S. Churchill

Now or never! I stood on a ledge, seized the top of the wall with my hands, and drew myself up. Twice I let myself down again in sickly hesitation, and then with a third resolve scrambled up and over. My waistcoat got entangled with the ornamental metal-work on the top. I had to pause for an appreciable moment to extricate myself. In this posture I had one parting glimpse of the sentries still talking with their backs turned fifteen yards away. One of them was lighting his cigarette, and I remember the glow on the inside of his hands as a distinct impression which my mind recorded. Then I lowered myself lightly down into the adjoining garden and crouched among the shrubs. I was free! The first step had been taken, and it was irrevocable. It now remained to await the arrival of my comrades. The bushes in the garden gave a good deal of cover, and in the moonlight their shadows fell dark on the ground. I lay here for an hour in great impatience and anxiety. People were continually moving about in the garden, and once a man came and apparently looked straight at me only a few yards away. Where were the others? Why did they not make the attempt?

Suddenly I heard a voice from within the quadrangle say, quite loud, "All up". I crawled back to the wall. Two officers were walking up and down inside, jabbering Latin words, laughing and talking all manner of nonsense – amid which I caught my name. I risked a cough. One of the officers immediately began to chatter alone. The other said, slowly and clearly, "They cannot get out. The sentry suspects. It's all up. Can you get back again?" But now all my fears fell from me at once. To go back was impossible. I could not hope to climb the wall unnoticed. There was no helpful ledge on the outside. Fate pointed onwards. Besides, I said to myself, "Of course, I shall be recaptured, but I will at least have a run for my money." I said to the officers, "I shall go on alone."

Now I was in the right mood for these undertakings – failure being almost certain, no odds against success affected me. All risks were less than the certainty. A glance at the plan will show that the gate which led into the road was only a few yards from another sentry. I said to myself, "*Toujours de l'audace*," put my hat on my head, strode into the middle of the garden, walked past the windows of the house without any attempt at concealment, and so went through the gate and turned to the left. I passed the sentry at less than five yards. Most of them knew me by sight. Whether he looked at me or not I do not know, for I never turned my head. I restrained with the utmost difficulty an impulse to run. But after walking a

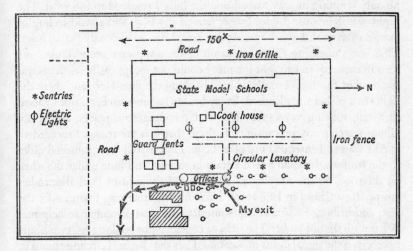

hundred yards and hearing no challenge, I knew that the second obstacle had been surmounted. I was at large in Pretoria.

I walked on leisurely through the night, humming a tune and choosing the middle of the road. The streets were full of burghers, but they paid no attention to me. Gradually I reached the suburbs, and on a little bridge I sat down to reflect and consider. I was in the heart of the enemy's country. I knew no one to whom I could apply for succour. Nearly three hundred miles stretched between me and Delagoa Bay. My escape must be known at dawn. Pursuit would be immediate. Yet all exits were barred. The town was picketed, the country was patrolled, the trains were searched, the line was guarded. I wore a civilian brown flannel suit. I had seventy-five pounds in my pocket and four slabs of chocolate, but the compass and the map which might have guided me, the opium tablets and meat lozenges which should have sustained me, were in my friends' pockets in the State Model Schools. Worst of all, I could not speak a word of Dutch or Kaffir, and how was I to get food or direction?

But when hope had departed, fear had gone as well. I formed a plan. I would find the Delagoa Bay Railway. Without map or compass, I must follow that in spite of the pickets. I looked at the stars. Orion shone brightly. Scarcely a year before he had guided me when lost in the desert to the banks of the Nile. He had given me water. Now he should lead to freedom. I could not endure the want of either.

After walking south for half a mile I struck the railway. Was it the line to Delagoa Bay or the Pietersburg branch? If it were the former, it should run east. But, so far as I could see, this line ran northwards. Still, it might be only winding its way out among the hills. I resolved to follow it. The night was delicious. A cool breeze fanned my face, and a wild feeling of exhilaration took hold of me. At any rate, I was free, if only for an hour. That was something. The fascination of the adventure grew. Unless the stars in their courses fought for me, I could not escape. Where, then, was the need of caution? I marched briskly along the line. Here and there the lights of a picket fire gleamed. Every bridge had its watchers. But I passed them all, making very short *détours* at the dangerous places, and really taking scarcely any precautions. Perhaps that was the reason I succeeded.

As I walked I extended my plan. I could not march three hundred miles to the frontier. I would board a train in motion and hide under the seats, on the roof, on the couplings – anywhere. I thought of Paul Bultitude's escape from school in *Vice Versa*. I saw myself emerging from under the seat, and bribing or persuading some fat first-class passenger to help me. What train should I take? The first, of course. After walking for two hours I perceived the signal lights of a station. I left the line, and circling round it, hid in the ditch by the track about two hundred yards beyond the platform. I argued that the train would stop at the station and that it would not have got up too much speed by the time it reached me. An hour passed. I began to grow impatient. Suddenly I heard the whistle and the approaching rattle. Then the great yellow head-lights of the engine flashed into view. The train waited five minutes at the station, and started again with much noise and steaming. I crouched by the track. I rehearsed the act in my mind. I must wait until the engine had passed, otherwise I should be seen. Then I must make a dash for the carriages.

The train started slowly, but gathered speed sooner than I had expected. The flaring lights drew swiftly near. The rattle became a roar. The dark mass hung for a second above me. The engine-driver silhouetted against his furnace glow, the black profile of the engine, the clouds of steam rushed past. Then I hurled myself on the trucks, clutched at something, missed, clutched again, missed again, grasped some sort of hand-hold, was swung off my feet – my toes bumping on the line, and with a struggle seated myself on the couplings of the fifth truck from the front of the train. It was a goods train, and the trucks were full of sacks, soft sacks covered with coal-dust. They were in fact bags filled with empty coal-bags going back to their colliery. I crawled on top and burrowed in among them. In five minutes I was completely buried. The sacks were warm and comfortable. Perhaps the engine-driver had seen me rush up to the train and would give the alarm at the next station; on the other hand, perhaps not. Where was the train going to? Where would it be unloaded? Would it be searched? Was it on the Delagoa Bay line? What should I do in the morning? Ah, never mind that. Sufficient for the night was the luck thereof. Fresh plans for fresh contingencies. I resolved to sleep, nor can I imagine a more pleasing lullaby than the clatter of the train that carries an escaping prisoner at twenty miles an hour away from the enemy's capital.

How long I slept I do not know, but I woke up suddenly with all feelings of exhilaration gone, and only the consciousness of oppressive difficulties heavy on me. I must leave the train before daybreak, so that I could drink at a pool and find some hiding-place while it was still dark. I would not run the risk of being unloaded with the coal-bags. Another night I would board another train. I crawled from my cosy hiding-place among the sacks and sat again on the couplings. The train was running at a fair speed, but I felt it was time to leave it. I took hold of the iron handle at the back of the truck, pulled strongly with my left hand, and sprang. My feet struck the ground in two gigantic strides, and the next instant I was sprawling in the ditch considerably shaken but unhurt. The train, my faithful ally of the night, hurried on its journey.

It was still dark. I was in the middle of a wide valley, surrounded by low hills, and carpeted with high grass drenched in dew. I searched for water in the nearest gully, and soon found a clear pool. I was very thirsty, but long after I had quenched my thirst I continued to drink, that I might have sufficient for the whole day.

Presently the dawn began to break, and the sky to the east grew yellow and red, slashed across with heavy black clouds. I saw with relief that the railway ran steadily towards the sunrise. I had taken the right line, after all.

Having drunk my fill, I set out for the hills, among which I hoped to find some hiding-place, and as it became broad daylight I entered a small grove of trees which grew on the side of a deep ravine. Here I resolved to wait till dusk. I had one consolation: no one in the world knew where I was – I did not know myself. It was now four o'clock. Fourteen hours lay between me and the night. My impatience to proceed while I was still strong doubled their length. At first it was terribly cold, but by degrees the sun gained power, and by ten o'clock the heat was oppressive. My sole companion was a gigantic vulture, who manifested an extravagant interest in my condition, and made hideous and ominous gurglings from time to time. From my lofty position I commanded a view of the whole valley. A little tin-roofed town lay three miles to the westward. Scattered farmsteads, each with a clump of trees, relieved the monotony of the undulating ground. At the foot of the hill stood a Kaffir kraal, and the figures of its inhabitants dotted the patches of cultivation or surrounded the droves of goats and cows which fed on the pasture. . . . During the day I ate one slab of chocolate, which, with the heat, produced a violent thirst. The pool was hardly half a mile away, but I dared not leave the shelter of the little wood, for I could see the figures of white men riding or walking occasionally across the valley, and once a Boer came and fired two shots at birds close to my hiding-place. But no one discovered me.

The elation and the excitement of the previous night had burnt away, and a chilling reaction followed. I was very hungry, for I had had no dinner before starting, and chocolate, though it sustains, does not satisfy. I had scarcely slept, but yet my heart beat so fiercely and I was so nervous and perplexed about the future that I could not rest. I thought of all the chances that lay against me; I dreaded and detested more than words can express the prospect of being caught and dragged back to Pretoria. I found no comfort in any of the philosophical ideas which some men parade in their hours of ease and strength and safety. They seemed only fair-weather friends. I realized with awful force that no exercise of my own feeble wit and strength could save me from my enemies, and that without the assistance of that High Power which interferes in the eternal sequence of causes and effects more often than we are always prone to admit, I could never succeed. I prayed long and earnestly for help and guidance. My prayer, as it seems to me, was swiftly and wonderfully answered.

During the day I watched the railway with attention. I saw two or three trains pass along it each way. I argued that the same number would pass at night. I resolved to board one of these. I thought I could improve on my procedure of the previous evening. I had observed how slowly the trains, particularly long goods-trains, climbed some of the steep gradients. Sometimes they were hardly going at a foot's pace. It would probably be easy to choose a point where the line was not only on an up grade but also on a curve. Thus I could board some truck on the convex side of the train when both the engine and the guard's van were bent away, and when consequently neither the engine-driver nor the guard would see me. This plan seemed to me in every respect sound. I saw myself leaving the train again before dawn, having been carried forward another sixty or seventy miles during the night. That would be scarcely one hundred and fifty miles from the frontier. And why should not the process be repeated? Where was the flaw? I could not see it. With three long bounds on three successive nights I could be in Portuguese territory. Meanwhile I still had two or three slabs of chocolate and a pocketful of crumbled biscuit – enough, that is to say, to keep body and soul together at a pinch without running the awful risk of recapture entailed by accosting a single human being. In this mood I watched with increasing impatience the arrival of darkness.

The long day reached its close at last. The western clouds flushed into fire; the shadows of the hills stretched out across the valley; a ponderous Boer wagon with its long team crawled slowly along the track towards the township, the Kaffirs collected their herds and drew them round their kraal; the daylight died, and soon it was quite dark. Then, and not until then, I set forth. I hurried to the railway line, scrambling along through the boulders and high grass and pausing on my way to drink at a stream of sweet cold water. I made my way to the place where I had seen the trains crawling so slowly up the slope, and soon found a point where the curve of the track fulfilled all the conditions of my plan. Here, behind a little bush, I sat down and waited hopefully. An hour passed; two hours passed; three hours – and yet no train. Six hours had now elapsed since the last, whose time I had carefully noted, had gone by. Surely one was due. Another hour slipped away. Still no train! My plan began to crumble and my hopes to ooze out of me. After all, was it not quite possible that no trains ran on this part of the line during the dark hours? This was in fact the case, and I might well have continued to wait in vain till daylight. However, between twelve and one in the morning I lost patience and started along the track, resolved to cover at any rate ten or fifteen miles of my journey. I did not make much progress. Every bridge was guarded by armed men; every few miles were huts. At intervals there were stations with tin-roofed villages clustering around them. All the veldt was bathed in the bright rays of the full moon, and to avoid these dangerous places I had to make wide circuits and even to creep along the ground. Leaving the railroad I fell into bogs and swamps, brushed through high grass dripping with dew, and waded across the streams over which the bridges carried the railway. I was soon drenched to the waist. I had been able to take very little exercise during my month's imprisonment, and I was quickly tired with walking and with want of food and sleep. Presently I approached a station. It was a mere platform in the veldt, with two or three buildings and huts around it. But laid up on the sidings, obviously for the night, were three long goods-trains. Evidently the flow of traffic over the railway was uneven. These three trains, motionless in the moonlight, confirmed my fears that traffic was not maintained by night on this part of the line. Where, then, was my plan which in the afternoon had looked so fine and sure?

It now occurred to me that I might board one of these stationary trains immediately, and hiding amid its freight be carried forward during the next day – and night too if all were well. On the other hand, where were they going to? Where would they stop? Where would they be unloaded? Once I entered a wagon my lot would be cast. I might find myself igno-miniously unloaded and recaptured at Witbank or Middelburg, or at any station in the long two hundred miles which separated me from the frontier. It was necessary at all costs before taking such a step to find out where these trains were going. To do this I must penetrate the station, examine the labels on the trucks or on the merchandise, and see if I could extract any certain guidance from them. I crept up to the platform and got between two of the long trains on the siding. I was proceeding to examine the markings on the trucks when loud voices rapidly approaching on the outside of the trains filled me with fear. Several Kaffirs were laughing and shouting in their unmodulated tones, and I heard, as I thought, a European voice arguing or ordering. At any rate, it was enough for me. I retreated between the two trains to the extreme end of the siding, and slipped stealthily but rapidly into the grass of the illimitable plain.

There was nothing for it but to plod on – but in an increasingly pur-poseless and hopeless manner. I felt very miserable when I looked around and saw here and there the lights of houses and thought of the warmth and comfort within them, but knew that they meant only danger to me. Far off on the moonlit horizon there presently began to shine the row of six or eight big lights which marked either Witbank or Middelburg station. Out in the darkness to my left gleamed two or three fires. I was sure they were not the lights of houses, but how far off they were or what they were I could not be certain. The idea formed in my mind that they were the fires of a Kaffir kraal. Then I began to think that the best use I could make of my remaining strength would be to go to these Kaffirs. I had heard that they hated the Boers and were friendly to the British. At any rate, they would probably not arrest me. They might give me food and a dry corner to sleep in. Although I could not speak a word of their language, yet I thought perhaps they might understand the value of a British banknote. They might even be induced to help me. A guide, a pony – but, above all, rest, warmth, and food – such were the promptings which dominated my mind. So I set out towards the fires.

I must have walked a mile or so in this resolve before a realization of its weakness and imprudence took possession of me. Then I turned back again to the railway line and retraced my steps perhaps half the distance. Then I stopped and sat down, completely baffled, destitute of any idea what to do or where to turn. Suddenly without the slightest reason all my doubts disappeared. It was certainly by no process of logic that they were dispelled. I just felt quite clear that I would go to the Kaffir kraal. I had sometimes in former years held a "Planchette" pencil and written while others had touched my wrist or hand. I acted in exactly the same unconscious or subconscious manner now.

I walked on rapidly towards the fires, which I had in the first instance thought were not more than a couple of miles from the railway line. I soon found they were much farther away than that. After about an hour or an hour and a half, they still seemed almost as far off as ever. But I persevered, and presently between two and three o'clock in the morning I perceived that they were not the fires of a Kaffir kraal. The angular outline of buildings began to draw out against them, and soon I saw that I was approaching a group of houses around the mouth of a coal-mine. The wheel which worked the winding gear was plainly visible, and I could see that the fires which had led me so far were from the furnaces of the engines. Hard by, surrounded by one or two slighter structures, stood a small but substantial stone house two storeys high.

I halted in the wilderness to survey this scene and to revolve my action. It was still possible to turn back. But in that direction I saw nothing but the prospect of further futile wanderings terminated by hunger, fever, discovery, or surrender. On the other hand, here in front was a chance. I had heard it said before I escaped that in the mining district of Witbank and Middelburg there were a certain number of English residents who had been suffered to remain in the country in order to keep the mines working. Had I been led to one of these? What did this house which frowned dark and inscrutable upon me contain? A Briton or a Boer; a friend or a foe? Nor did this exhaust the possibilities. I had my seventy-five pounds in English notes in my pocket. If I revealed my identity, I thought that I could give reasonable assurance of a thousand. I might find some indifferent neutral-minded person who out of good-nature or for a large sum of money would aid me in my bitter and desperate need. Certainly I would try to make what bargain I could now – now while I still had the strength to plead my cause and perhaps to extricate myself if the results were adverse. Still the odds were heavy against me, and it was with faltering and reluctant steps that I walked out of the shimmering gloom of the veldt into the light of the furnace fires, advanced towards the silent house, and struck with my fist upon the door.

There was a pause. Then I knocked again. And almost immediately a light sprang up above and an upper window opened.

"*Wer ist da?*" cried a man's voice.

I felt the shock of disappointment and consternation to my fingers.

"I want help; I have had an accident," I replied.

Some muttering followed. Then I heard steps descending the stairs, the bolt of the door was drawn, the lock was turned. It was opened abruptly, and in the darkness of the passage a tall man hastily attired, with a pale face and dark moustache, stood before me.

"What do you want?" he said, this time in English.

I had now to think of something to say. I wanted above all to get into parley with this man, to get matters in such a state that instead of raising an alarm and summoning others he would discuss things quietly.

"I am a burgher," I began. "I have had an accident. I was going to join my commando at Komati Poort. I have fallen off the train. We were sky-larking. I have been unconscious for hours. I think I have dislocated my shoulder."

It is astonishing how one thinks of these things. This story leapt out as if I had learnt it by heart. Yet I had not the slightest idea what I was going to say or what the next sentence would be.

The stranger regarded me intently, and after some hesitation said at length, "Well, come in." He retreated a little into the darkness of the passage, threw open a door on one side of it, and pointed with his left hand into a dark room. I walked past him and entered, wondering if it was to be my prison. He followed, struck a light, lit a lamp, and set it on the table at the far side of which I stood. I was in a small room, evidently a dining-room and office in one. I noticed besides the large table, a roll desk, two or three chairs, and one of those machines for making soda-water, consisting of two glass globes set one above the other and encased in thin wire-netting. On his end of the table my host had laid a revolver, which he had hitherto presumably been holding in his right hand.

"I think I'd like to know a little more about this railway accident of yours," he said, after a considerable pause.

"I think," I replied, "I had better tell you the truth."

"I think you had," he said, slowly.

So I took the plunge and threw all I had upon the board.

"I am Winston Churchill, war-correspondent of the *Morning Post*. I escaped last night from Pretoria. I am making my way to the frontier." (Making my way!) "I have plenty of money. Will you help me?"

There was another long pause. My companion rose from the table slowly and locked the door. After this act, which struck me as unpromising, and was certainly ambiguous, he advanced upon me and suddenly held out his hand.

"Thank God you have come here! It is the only house for twenty miles where you would not have been handed over. But we are all British here, and we will see you through."

It is easier to recall across the gulf of years the spasm of relief which swept over me, than it is to describe it. A moment before I had thought myself trapped; and now friends, food, resources aid were all at my disposal. I felt like a drowning man pulled out of the water and informed he has won the Derby!

My host now introduced himself as Mr. John Howard, manager of the Transvaal Collieries. He had become a naturalized burgher of the Transvaal some years before the war. But out of consideration for his British race and some inducements which he had offered to the local Field Cornet he had not been called up to fight against the British. Instead he had been allowed to remain with one or two others on the mine, keeping it pumped out and in good order until coal-cutting could be resumed. He had with him at the mine-head, besides his secretary, who was British, an engineman from Lancashire and two Scottish miners. All these four were British subjects and had been allowed to remain only upon giving their parole to observe strict neutrality. He himself as burgher of the Transvaal Republic would be guilty of treason in harbouring me, and liable to be shot if caught at the time or found out later on.

"Never mind," he said, "we will fix it up somehow." And added, "The Field Cornet was round here this afternoon asking about you. They have got the hue and cry out all along the line and all over the district."

I said that I did not wish to compromise him.

Let him give me food, a pistol, a guide, and if possible a pony, and I would make my own way to the sea, marching by night across country far away from the railway line or any habitation.

He would not hear of it. He would fix up something. But he enjoined the utmost caution. Spies were everywhere. He had two Dutch servant-maids actually sleeping in the house. There were many Kaffirs employed about the mine premises and on the pumping-machinery of the mine. Surveying these dangers, he became very thoughtful.

Then: "But you are famishing."

I did not contradict him. In a moment he had bustled off into the kitchen, telling me meanwhile to help myself from a whisky bottle and the soda-water machine which I had already mentioned. He returned after an interval with the best part of a cold leg of mutton and various other delectable commodities, and, leaving me to do full justice to these, quitted the room and let himself out of the house by a back door.

Nearly an hour passed before Mr. Howard returned. In this period my physical well-being had been brought into harmony with the improvement in my prospects. I felt confident of success and equal to anything.

"It's all right," said Mr. Howard. "I have seen the men, and they are all for it. We must put you down the pit to-night, and there you will have to stay till we can see how to get you out of the country. One difficulty," he said, "will be the *skoff* (food). The Dutch girl sees every mouthful I eat. The cook will want to know what has happened to her leg of mutton. I shall have to think it all out during the night. You must get down the pit at once. We'll make you comfortable enough."

Accordingly, just as the dawn was breaking, I followed my host across a little yard into the enclosure in which stood the winding-wheel of the mine. Here a stout man, introduced as Mr. Dewsnap, of Oldham, locked my hand in a grip of crushing vigour.

"They'll all vote for you next time," he whispered.

A door was opened and I entered the cage. Down we shot into the bowels of the earth. At the bottom of the mine were the two Scottish miners with lanterns and a big bundle which afterwards proved to be a mattress and blankets. We walked for some time through the pitchy labyrinth, with frequent turns, twists, and alterations of level, and finally stopped in a sort of chamber where the air was cool and fresh. Here my guide set down his bundle, and Mr. Howard handed me a couple of candles, a bottle of whisky, and a box of cigars.

"There's no difficulty about these," he said. "I keep them under lock and key. Now we must plan how to feed you to-morrow."

"Don't you move from here, whatever happens," was the parting injunction. "There will be Kaffirs about the mine after daylight, but we shall be on the look-out that none of them wanders this way. None of them has seen anything so far."

My four friends trooped off with their lanterns, and I was left alone. Viewed from the velvety darkness of the pit, life seemed bathed in rosy light. After the perplexity and even despair through which I had passed I counted upon freedom as certain. Instead of a humiliating recapture and long months of monotonous imprisonment, probably in the common jail, I saw myself once more rejoining the Army with a real exploit to my credit, and in that full enjoyment of freedom and keen pursuit of adventure dear to the heart of youth. In this comfortable mood, and speeded by intense fatigue, I soon slept the sleep of the weary – but of the triumphant.

CHAPTER NINE

CAPTAIN AYLMER HALDANE, D.S.O., was the officer in command of "Wilson's Death Trap", the armoured train in which Sir Winston Churchill was ambushed in 1899; and in his book *How We Escaped From Pretoria* he, like so many prisoners, regrets his neglected opportunities to make an early escape. The first hours of captivity offer many chances which the confused and shocked prisoner is unprepared to take. Very few men are on their toes from the moment of capture and these, like Sir Basil Embry and Spencer Chapman, nearly always reap the reward of their resilience.

Not only did Haldane's party persuade themselves that they would stand a better chance of escape once they reached a permanent camp, but they were treated so humanely by the Boers that they felt that an escape would be an act of ingratitude. M. C. C. Harrison of World War I also confesses to this sense of obligation in *Within Four Walls*. This desire not to seem churlish, combined with the knowledge that an escape attempt, successful or not, will probably completely reverse the captors' attitude to their prisoners has a very strong inhibiting effect on early escape, and great strength of mind – or lack of imagination – is required to overcome it.

From the moment Haldane arrived in his permanent camp he began to plan his escape. First, together with Churchill, he tried bribing the guards, but as Sir Winston says in his account they could not afford "to insult them heavily enough".

Haldane and Churchill then teamed up with Sergeant-Major A. Brockie in an attempt to climb the wall surrounding the camp. It was on this attempt that Churchill got away, the other two being unable to follow him. After this escape the defences of the camp were strengthened, day and night sentries were posted and extra roll-calls were ordered; in fact, the remaining prisoners suffered the usual reprisals which follow a successful break.

In spite of the extra sentries, reinforced lighting and other special precautions, Aylmer Haldane lost no time in preparing another escape. In his book he acknowledges the inspiration he got from reading of the escapes of Latude, Jack Sheppard and the fictitious Edmond Dantes. It was the last of these which gave him the idea for his next attempt which was, in spite of his claustrophobia, a tunnel. Digging was started under the floor of the room he shared with four other officers, but the tunnellers soon struck water and work was abandoned.

Haldane spent the next few weeks waiting for further inspiration, trying to learn the native language and making maps of the surrounding countryside. Inspiration came; this time to fuse the boundary lights and under cover of darkness climb the now heavily guarded fence. The attempt was made, but a hitch occurred and this scheme too was abandoned.

Then came the news that the prisoners were to be moved to another camp, and Haldane had his final inspiration. The plan was that he, together with Lieutenant Le Mesurier of the Dublin Fusiliers and Sergeant-Major Brockie, should be sealed under the floor of their room in the hope that the guards could be led to believe that the three of them had escaped. After the move was completed they would emerge into what they hoped would be an empty camp. This scheme required from Haldane, because of his claustrophobia, a very special kind of bravery.

The plan succeeded in so far that the Boers thought that the three prisoners had escaped, but Haldane had anticipated the date of the move and the escapers were forced to spend three weeks in their confined quarters. Of those three weeks Aylmer Haldane writes, "it makes one shudder to recall them".

At last, unwashed, ill and weak from inanition, the three escapers heard the welcome sounds of the evacuation fade away to the silence of a deserted camp.

Aylmer Haldane

THE MOMENT for our "moonlight flitting" had arrived. All above seemed still and deserted, but lest we might be mistaken we listened intently for some minutes. Sergeant-Major Brockie, who was deputed to reconnoitre the building, to make sure that no caretaker had been left in charge, now pushed up the trap-door; but so firmly had it been fastened down the previous night, that despite the greatest care he was unable to prevent it from making a loud noise, which echoed in the deathlike stillness. Creeping into the room above, he made his way out through the doorway into the passage, and shortly returned to say that all was clear.

Le Mesurier and I followed, carefully shutting the trap-door after us.

We were astonished to find how weak the confinement and cramped position had made us. Le Mesurier's legs gave way and he fell down; and all of us, when we tried to walk, reeled like drunken men. Several minutes passed before we dared leave the room, and it was not till we were some distance from Pretoria that our limbs regained their wonted strength.

Leaving the room which we had lived in and under for four months, and threading our way with care along the passage, which was blocked with forms, we reached the back-door which opens on the yard. It was locked, but the absence of a large pane of glass, which had been broken and completely removed, provided an easy exit. Strange to say, after my long incarceration I felt almost reluctant to go forth into unknown dangers and difficulties; but such a feeling was of brief duration, and this no time to moralise. We now put on our boots, which we had been carrying, and passing through this opening gained the verandah. Pausing for a moment to see that no one was in the yard, we crossed over to the low buildings on the other side. The moon was full, and the electric lights not being turned off, as we had anticipated they would be, we felt unpleasantly conspicuous. The dog's kennel was in its usual place, but fortunately the occupant was gone.

We had intended to leave the yard by climbing over the iron paling into the next garden; but the moon was far too bright for this, and the windows of a house which looked on to the garden were open and some people were looking out. We therefore made our way to the railings, near which the police tents had been, and climbing over reached the street on the south side of the school. A couple happened to pass, just after we had got into the street, but they took no notice of us, and Le Mesurier told me afterwards that a special policeman slowly turned the corner of the Model School at that very moment.

Crossing the road, we went up the street which leads towards the fort guarding the southern entrance to Pretoria. Of the town itself we had a small scale plan, which many months before we had removed from a biography of President Kruger, a book belonging to the Staats library. I stopped to light my pipe, and Brockie, keeping in the shadow of some trees, donned a white sling in which to place an arm, and this pious fraud, supported by his wearing the Dutch colours round his hat, gave him the appearance of a wounded Boer. We next bore to our left, then to the right, and finally struck a road which, from the plan, we conjectured would cross the Delagoa Bay Railway.

Brockie had warned us both that if we wanted to escape notice we must slouch along with knees bent and backs rounded, as is the manner of the Boer. This to me was somewhat difficult, for the exquisite sense of exhilaration which I was experiencing made me feel much more inclined to run, jump, or indeed do anything but walk soberly along.

So far, although we had passed a few special policemen, our appearance had seemed to attract no particular notice. In the Transvaal, as in many other parts of the world, the country bumpkin, when he honours his county town with a visit, puts off his workaday garments and comes in his Sunday best. Our garb could scarcely be said to come under the latter heading: we looked more like three moon-lighters than anything else I can think of. Fortunately for us, the town had been depleted of many of its inhabitants, most of whom were at the front, and in consequence the streets presented a very deserted appearance; and although we knew that the Dutchman is abominably inquisitive, yet we hoped to evade his notice. Le Mesurier and Brockie kept to the middle of the road. I followed them on the pathway, a little behind. In this fashion we were tramping along towards the outskirts of the town, with the villas in gardens on our right and left, when we met a special constable. This one, instead of passing us as the rest had done, stopped, and turning round scanned us with suspicion. I expected every minute that he would ask us in Dutch who we were and whither we were bound. But Brockie, having noticed that we were running the risk of being challenged, turned half round, exposing to view his quasi-wounded arm. This seemed to partly satisfy the guardian of the peace, for he turned up a side street, stopped to have a good look at us, and ultimately moved off, unaware perhaps that

> "*Them as is watched out of sight*
> *Bide away for many a night,*" –

which proved to be the case. Perhaps he thought discretion the better part of valour, for we were three desperate men, and he was alone, with no help near. Whatever may have been his motives, his action was fortunate, for we were prepared to go to any length to avoid a hue and cry. Brockie had vowed that nothing would induce him to be captured a second time, and had armed himself with a sausage-shaped bag of cloth filled and jammed tightly with earth. He was burning to use it on someone, and must have lamented this lost chance.

The road along which we were travelling now began to leave the town, and the gates of a level-crossing, betokening the presence of the railway, were plainly to be seen. We halted for a moment to consider whether it would not be wiser to turn aside and avoid a spot where a patrol might possibly be met; but our anxiety to get clear of Pretoria without delay overcame the inclination to make a detour, and pressing on, we found that nothing barred our way. Crossing the railway-line, we sat down in some long damp grass to decide whether we should follow road or railway. I had a small medicine-bottle full of whisky, presented by a fellow-prisoner as a parting gift. The occasion was not one to be overlooked, and we proceeded to drink success to our venture; then, having decided to take the railway as our guide, we set off again, and found we were clear of Pretoria and its suburbs.

I inwardly congratulated myself that now no officer or man who wore the Gordon tartan was a prisoner in the hands of the Boers. But we were not yet out of the wood.

Straight before us, high up in the eastern sky, shone the moon, dimming the brilliancy of the evening star which followed closely in her wake; to the right the Southern Cross, and low down in the north-east Orion's Belt. With guides like these, to lose ourselves would not be easy. Reaching the railway, we walked along in single file, halting now and then to listen and make sure that all was clear in front. A coal-train from Balmoral, going westward, passed us, and soon after we had to throw ourselves down in a ditch beside the line to conceal ourselves from a Dutchman going home off bridge-guard – for every bridge and every culvert from Pretoria to Komati Poort had its guard by day and night. These guards (we were afterwards told) had orders to fire on anyone walking on the track at night.

When we had gone about three miles, and were covering the ground at a good rate, we almost walked into the arms of a sentry who was sitting on the parapet of a bridge which carried the railway over the road. We came upon him suddenly, as he was sitting partly hidden by a bush, and walked to within a few paces from him; and that he did not see us, unless he was asleep, is a miracle. We dropped like stones beside the rails, lay absolutely still for some moments, then softly crept back down the slope of the embankment in the direction whence we had come. Then along a muddy ditch until we had lost sight of him, climbed a barbed-wire fence beside the railway, which shook and rattled, after which, making a wide detour, and creeping through a mealie-field to avoid a Kaffir kraal, we passed along the face of a hill and found ourselves close to a telegraph-wire. This wire, we discovered later, ran like a Roman road over hill and dale to Komati Poort, and had we followed it we should have made our journey many miles shorter, and escaped the annoyance of losing our way in the dark. All around us dogs in the neighbouring farms were baying loudly at the moon, and this, and occasional shouts from afar, made us hasten on our way. We now followed the wire for a couple of miles, but thinking we were going out of our way, we left it and climbed a rocky ridge not far from Koodoespoort, where Churchill had caught the train when he escaped. Below us we heard the sound of running water. Hastily making our way to it, for we were growing thirsty, we came upon a muddy stream evidently used for irrigating the fields on the hillside, down which it flowed.

Unfortunately at this juncture Le Mesurier, who had got off the path among some rocks, twisted his ankle. Painful as it was, to walk on, however slowly, was better than to rest, and so allow it to grow stiff. Pluckily recognising this, he kept moving forward, and we made some progress, though slow. Our way led us over the open veldt, where the grass was long and wet. Brockie was growing tired, and insisted that he saw Boers under every tree and bush, and for some time we moved with great caution. We again struck the railway, crossed it, and a black patch in the distance told us we were approaching the first station, thirteen miles from Pretoria, and decided to halt there till next evening. I felt a good deal disappointed at covering so short a distance the first night; but it was no one's fault, and it was as well, perhaps, not to walk too far at first, for we were not in the best of training just then.

Reaching Eerste Fabriken, our farther progress was barred by a ditch some fifteen feet deep, with just beyond it a sluggish muddy river. Hunting up and down the ditch, we at length found a spot where, hidden by the thick bushes, it gradually sloped up to the ground-level. The bottom was damp, but that was soon remedied by covering it over with straw, which we found lying about. We had, however, got into a veritable hotbed of mosquitoes, for they attacked us with the greatest fury, and to sleep was impossible. The arrival of morning and dispersal of these greedy bloodsuckers was a great relief. At 6.30 a.m. the steam-horn of the Hatherly Distillery hard by sounded, bidding the workmen rise for another day of toil. At this establishment I am told, strong waters of every variety, from Hennessey's three-star brandy to Long John of Ben Nevis fame, can be procured. It is merely a matter of labels, and they are not so hard to copy as bank-notes. Our hiding-place proved to be admirable for though it was uncomfortable it was improbable that anything but a dog would find it and we were well sheltered from the sun. This was the first day for nearly three weeks that we had seen the sun and we were not sorry to be protected from his burning rays by the thick foliage. During the day we ate a little chocolate and some meat lozenges; but as regards water we were as badly off as Tantalus for the river a few yards distant could not safely be approached. Someone seemed to be fishing it in close to us – an Englishman we thought for he whistled one after another many tunes that were familiar to us. His *repertoire* was somewhat antiquated and included amongst others "Oh what a surprise!" and "After the ball is over". Except for the occasional song of a Kaffir, the noise of cows busily cropping the grass and the buzzing of many insects, all else was silent. The ubiquitous fly had of course marked us down and did not spare us his objectionable attentions, and to drive him off by smoking was not considered safe. Even here, and indeed throughout all our travels, we never raised our voices above a whisper lest some passer-by might hear and discover us. Our determination was if possible neither to see anyone nor to be seen by anyone till we reached the frontier. This would free us from incriminating explanations, if any were demanded.

Time passes slowly when one has nothing to do all day but brush off flies, and we regretted that a pack of cards had not been included among our baggage for then we might have called the "demon" to our aid. A few trains passed up and down: these and the occasional sound of the distillery horn alone served to break the monotony. At half-past four Sergeant-Major Brockie, armed with Le Mesurier's field-glasses which he had managed to secrete when taken prisoner, was despatched to do a little scouting in order to find out whether there was a drift over the river near where we lay hidden. After a short time he returned, bringing the satisfactory news that the ford lay between us and the station, and across it several waggons were outspanned. There had been a heavy fall of rain during the afternoon but we hoped insufficient to flood the river.

When darkness at length came, we sallied forth from our retreat, crossed the river, then the railway, and reached the road. By the small scale map we possessed, the railway appeared to make a considerable bend to the south-east, and as the road seemed to form the chord of the arc, it would be shorter to follow it. But Transvaal roads are not as other roads, and are as unlike their counterpart in England as a lane in Devonshire is unlike the turnpike to Bath. Looking at a map of the Transvaal, you are tempted to believe that once on the road, so clearly defined on paper, you have only to shut your eyes and go ahead. Try it, and you will find a close resemblance between yourself and the blind led by the blind. The highways in the South African Republic are innocent of metal – Macadam is a name unknown: they consist of nothing but deeply indented wheel-tracks left by the clumsy, ponderous transport of the country – the ox-waggon. As a Dutchman in wet weather leaves the main track where it has become swampy and marks out a line for himself, the natural consequence is that in time the vicinity of a road becomes a maze of tracks, and to find your way in the dark and in an unknown district is nigh impossible.

To-night we were to experience this. Sergeant-Major Brockie, who posed as a fairly good "pathfinder", took the lead, and we pushed boldly along; for our lame comrade was a little better, and had secured a bough as a walking-stick. We noticed that the track we were following went due south, but thought that doubtless it would soon change its course. A waggon coming towards us on the road, we had to turn off and wait until it had gone by. Not long after we had crossed the railway we came upon a large white wooden gate. Passing through it, we found we were on an avenue, both sides of which were lined with firs – a most unusual luxury for a Dutchman; for the Boers have done almost nothing for their country in the way of wood-growing, and except for a few trees round a farmstead, you may travel miles without seeing a leaf or finding shade. A little farther on we noticed the lights of a cottage, which we took for the lodge of some larger building. Passing by as quietly as we could, we soon came to four crossroads, but we were beginning to lose faith in our conductor, and we turned north-east. Our route now led along what appeared to be a deer-park, for in the moonlight several of these animals could be seen to fly at our approach. We must have diverged considerably, for it seemed a long time ere we again met the railway, and both my companions were footsore and tired. Before us lay a range of hills in which was a *poort*, or gap, through which the railway passed, and on the name-board of the deserted station we read Pienaars Poort. As we drew nearer to the hills we heard the noise of rushing water, and once inside the *poort* we sat down by the river to refresh. The spot looked singularly picturesque. Road, railway, river – all were crowded together into the gap, which at its narrowest point was about two hundred yards wide; and on either side the hills, tenanted by chattering baboons, rose steep and bare. The ground ascended before us towards the farther entrance of this defile, and the gradient of the railway was steep. One felt instinctively that this would be a bad place in which to encounter a patrol, for the only way out of it seemed forwards or backwards.

Brand's essence and whisky worked wonders on my tired companions, and, reinvigorated, we started off full of the intention of reaching Elands River station, twenty-nine miles from Pretoria. I led the way along the railway-line. On our left, a stone's-throw distant, flowed the river, its surface shining like a mirror under the rising moon. Before me ran the double rails, looking like bars of silver; and beyond them, on the right, the road. As we trod softly and looked ahead as far as one could distinctly see, some tents appeared on the right of the railway, pitched close under the hill; one of them seemed larger than the rest. I turned to Brockie, who followed me, and asked his opinion. "Only a Kaffir kraal," he replied, so on we pressed. A few paces farther, and the stillness of the night was broken by the angry barking of a dog. Immediate action was imperative. Down we dropped into the long rushy grass which filled the space betwixt the river and the railway. The dog continued barking – he had evidently seen us. Presently voices became audible, one of them bidding the cur be silent. But he did not cease, and another followed suit. After lying in the grass about twenty minutes, for we did not care to move so long as the dogs remained on the alert, we heard voices coming in our direction, and the barking of the dogs became more distinct. A patrol was on its way to clear up the situation. A whispered conference was held, when it was decided to retreat, and then we dragged ourselves like snakes diagonally back towards the river. Fortunately the rushes had been beaten down by a recent flood, and our tracks were barely visible. Reaching a broad ditch full of water, Le Mesurier, who was following me, came alongside and asked me if I had seen Brockie, who had been following him. Being in front I had not, so we waited a few moments; but seeing nothing of him, and the enemy drawing near, we crossed the obstacle and found ourselves at the edge of the stream. Again we paused, this time for several minutes, and the searchers came in view, following our track. One of them, who was walking along almost bent double, we thought was Brockie, but looking through the rushes we quickly found our mistake.

At this moment many things rushed through my mind, and more especially one. Shortly before leaving Pretoria I had been reading again a very ancient friend, *Tales of a Grandfather*, and now I instinctively remembered how the Bruce, when hunted by John of Lorne's bloodhound had waded down a river and so destroyed the scent. My mind was quickly made up.

The crisis had come: to stay where we were meant probably recapture. I whispered to Le Mesurier to follow me silently and not to splash. Transferring my manuscript map from my pocket to the lining of my hat, the next minute I was in the river, which was out of my depth, and Le Mesurier dropped in beside me. Holding on to the roots of the reeds which lined the bank, we paused and watched the searchers, then carefully pulled ourselves some distance downstream, and paused again. The Boers and their dogs were evidently now at fault, and showed no signs of coming our way, so we continued our downward course, and ultimately swam across and into a ditch on the other side.

We had been a good half-hour in the stream, which seemed to us intensely cold, and our teeth were chattering so that we could scarcely speak. My wrist-watch had stopped; but Le Mesurier's – a Waterbury – was still going, for it had been provided by his care with a waterproof case. We now crept along the ditch up-stream again, and then turned off towards the hillside, which was dotted with large boulders. Coming round the corner of one of these, we found a tent in front of us, in which a light was burning, and not caring to pass it, we tried to climb up the steep face

of the hill. Failing at one point, we found a kind of "chimney", up which
we climbed, pulling and pushing each other till the top was gained. A few
minutes' rest was necessary, for our clothes were heavy with water and
the climb had made us breathless. Le Mesurier had done wonders with his
ankle – the cold water had been most efficacious. Next we walked along
the rocky face of the hill, parallel to the direction we had followed below,
and gradually descended to the level and struck a path. While on the hillside we had looked down into the valley below, where all seemed quiet
and nothing moved. Brockie was irretrievably lost, and it was useless to
attempt to find him. He had with him a water-bottle and sufficient food,
and knew both the Dutch and the Kaffir language. Following the path, we
passed several clumps of bracken, one of which we selected as a suitable
hiding-place. To have walked farther in our wet and clinging garments
might have been wiser, but we decided that we had had sufficient excitement for one night without trying to add to it.

Carefully avoiding breaking down the fern, we took our way into the
centre of the clump, and made ourselves as comfortable as was possible.
I took as a prophylactic ten grains of quinine and four of opium, all that
was not reduced to pulp by our recent immersion. The dose of opium, I
have since been told, was a large if not indeed a lethal one, but it did not
make me sleep. The night was bitterly cold – for where we lay was nearly
five thousand feet above the sea-level – and, soaked as we were, we shook
and shivered. Of course the mosquitoes did not spare us, and we spent the
remainder of the night in fighting this useless scourge.

When day broke I found I was so stiff and rheumatic that I could not
move, and Le Mesurier was not much better. However, when the sun rose
and penetrated our wooden bodies we soon found movement possible,
and by noon we were dry and ready for any more adventures that might
come. We had suffered some loss by that unavoidable dip in the river.
Le Mesurier had lost a pocket-book[1] and I the contents of the whisky-
bottle, the cork of which had come out when we were crawling along in
the grass – by accident, not design. I had also lost a triangular file, a
memento of the Model School. Further, our food-supply was water-
logged, our tobacco spoilt, and likewise our matches. We managed to eat
some pulpy chocolate, which was becoming nauseous to us, besides
creating a thirst we had no means of quenching. We had trusted to finding
plenty of mealies growing; but the harvest was just gathered in, and this
source of supply was lacking.

[1]Rather more than a year after Le Mesurier lost his pocket-book, it was found at the spot
where he dropped it by a corporal of an infantry regiment stationed at Pienaars Poort. This
man, ascertaining from the contents to whom it belonged, sent it to the owner, and except
that the cover had been eaten by insects it was in wonderful preservation.

Our hiding-place, although overlooked by the hills, was a good one. Only a few Dutchmen and Kaffirs passed by along the paths, and they saw no sign of us. The want of proximity to water was its greatest fault, and we mutually agreed that howsoever uncomfortable a swamp might be as a sleeping-place, it was the only place in which to pass a day under the broiling sun, unless a shady nook were forthcoming. Few trains passed, as it was Sunday. One could not help carrying one's thoughts back to Pretoria, and wondering where our accomplices would think we had reached, and what they would think we were doing. Only too well we knew, at any hour of the day, how they were passing their time, and how unhappy many of them were. How light-hearted we felt at being free again! All that was necessary for us now was care and caution, and these we had been accustomed to when below the floor, and we were now determined not to leave anything to chance, or what people term luck, or to spare any trouble which might help to ensure our ultimate freedom.

In addition to the ordinary risks of being captured or shot – for being in plain clothes we ran the risk of treatment as spies – there were two others which now presented themselves. My fear was lest the trap-door, which we could not shut down very neatly, might have been noticed; and also that Sergeant-Major Brockie should get ahead of us, reach Lorenço Marques, and, forgetting that we were still behind him, talk. That the latter supposition was not devoid of foundation will appear later. On the whole, however, I felt exceedingly confident that our enterprise would prove successful: if we should have the misfortune to be recaptured, at least we would feel satisfied for ever after that we had made a determined bid for freedom.

The hour had now come round when it was time to continue our journey. It was decided to leave the railway and use the moon as a guide till near dawn, when by turning north we could regain the railway with certainty and reach Elands River station. The distant roll of thunder and the lightning-flashes gave every sign of a coming storm. The moon was not yet up; but the flashes which from time to time shot forth from the inky clouds made the bare veldt look as bright as day, and we felt that we were very conspicuous. Dropping down into the valley, we crossed at a narrow spot the same river whose water we had encountered the night before. Soon we came to the railway, which we had decided not to follow, crossed it, and proceeded up a long steep hill. After we had covered between two or three miles, to my dismay I discovered that I had left my money-belt, containing some £18, and a compass, at our last hiding-place. The risk of returning to look for them was too great, for on quitting our hiding-place we had noticed many lights in the neighbourhood, and the probability of finding the clump of ferns in the pitchy darkness was remote. Besides which, both Le Mesurier and I were even now not entirely devoid of money, and it was doubtful if we should require what we still had. We therefore pushed on till by the light of the moon we saw in front of us a Kaffir kraal, and found that we were walking past a field of water-melons. The opportunity was too good to be lost. Since we left our hiding-place we had had no water save that which a shower had left in the hoof-marks of some cattle. We now sat down and simply gorged this thirst-quenching pulp. I have often eaten Afghan melons, which the caravans bring on their camels to Peshawur, and these more resembled them than any others that I have tasted. But we had been heard or scented, for the kraal dogs near by began to bark. I hastily tied up a melon in my handkerchief, and we walked silently away. Treading our way softly through some mealie-fields, we came to a deep donga at the bottom of which was a muddy rushing stream. We followed this for some time, till, thinking that our destination must be near, we crossed over and mounted a hill. Half-way up its side we heard a sound of galloping. The place was very open and the grass burnt short, but after a few moments of suspense nothing worse than a frightened horse appeared.

It seemed as if we were never going to strike the railway; but in this particular locality, where the ground is hilly and the gradients steep, I believe its windings are extraordinary. As with all the railways in South Africa, the contour of the ground was followed, cuttings and embankments being rare. Suddenly the glint of the moonlight reflected from the rails caught our eyes, then the black telegraph poles like spectres, and the wires, through which the chilly breeze was softly moaning. We had reached it at last.

But our last two nights' experiences with railway guards had had their effect, and we foolishly left the line and wandered far from our course. After some miles we saw in front of us a small wood, close to which some waggons were outspanned, and soon after passing them I had what cannot have been anything but a hallucination. Brockie was in my thoughts, and I was wondering where he was and if by any chance we should meet him to-night at Elands River, for we had talked with him of making for that place. On the ground a little to my left I saw what seemed to be a man lying at full length, his elbows resting on the ground, his head between his hands. Telling Le Mesurier what I saw, we went nearer, but the vision of my fancy had gone; yet it was so clear that I can recall it and the spot where it occurred with the utmost distinctness.

Not far from here we came to a ridge of grey rocks, where we sat down. I was tired out, principally from having slept badly when below ground and from not having slept at all since we left Pretoria, and was prepared to lie down on the veldt and take my chance of discovery. But dawn was near, and before us we saw a signal-post and a little farther off a wayside station. Crossing the railway, we made for a clump of trees which rose prominently before us on the sky-line. No river was to be seen, although the name of the place betokened one: there was nothing in a liquid form visible save a tiny trickling stream. This, however, is a little way of their own that South African rivers have – at one time a roaring torrent, at another a microscopic stream.

Hard by a cock was shrilly crowing, betokening the presence of some inhabited dwelling, but, tired as I was, that was of no concern to me.

Nearing the trees, we walked into a barbed-wire fence, and crossing it, selected a small clump of blue-gum or eucalyptus trees for our lair. These were only saplings, six to eight feet high, interspersed with larger trees of a kind unknown to me. Behind us we had left two alarming tracks in the dew-sodden grass – but the sun would soon rectify that. Throwing ourselves down, we endeavoured to get some sleep before the mosquitoes found us and made repose impossible. We were far from comfortable, for the place was strewn with roots and stones; but my melon made such an excellent pillow that I was soon in the land of Nod, and awoke startled at seven to hear Le Mesurier whispering, "I think we are discovered!" I could get no more from him just then, so lay thinking what was to be done, and hoping that he was mistaken.

He told me afterwards that someone had passed close by, and, he thought, had seen us. A heavy shower of rain now fell, perhaps hiding our footprints in the grass. Two hours later the sound of advancing footsteps became audible. It was a young Dutchman coming along a path not six feet from where our heads lay on the ground. He stopped when he came opposite to us, and a dog which accompanied him growled. How this animal did not immediately discover us will always remain a mystery to me, but perhaps the same shower which hid our tracks also spoilt the scent. Visions of bloodthirsty *vrouws* arose in one's mind; for now there were few men on their farms, and it was said on all hands that the women were more than Spartan in their severity. The lad now began shouting loudly what I supposed to be some Kaffir name, and after a brief interval was joined by someone with whom he talked for a space. It seemed to us as if he must have seen us, and, not daring himself to disturb the intruders, had called for help. But it is marvellous how, if one remains absolutely still, one may pass unnoticed, and our imaginations here had led us astray. Nothing happened, they moved away, and the incident only increased our confidence; for we felt that having had two such close shaves, we must eventually escape altogether.

All day long the Kaffirs worked near us, busy cutting wood and drawing water, and the Dutch lad passed more than once again. The Kaffir is more like an animal than a human being in the way he will detect a spoor and traces that would not catch a white man's notice; but we were completely unnoticed that day by black or white.

Of course, by now we knew that we had walked right into the middle of a Boer farm; but I had been too tired the night before to care where I went. The difficulty now was to leave it so quietly at night that even the dogs might not hear us. At seven o'clock we quitted the gum-tree thicket and made our way through mealie-fields and hedges till we were quite clear of our dangerous surroundings. This took a long time, for each sun-dried mealie-stalk in our path had to be held aside, lest the rustling noise which they would have made if we had attempted to pass quickly through should rouse the watch-dogs. I eagerly scanned each plant as we made our way between them, but not one single corn-spike remained.

It might almost seem as if we had departed from our original plan of trying to catch a night train; but on the three preceding evenings we had wandered far from the railway, and had thought that during our absence from its vicinity the eastward-going train might well have passed. To-night, however, though some doubts had certainly arisen in our minds as to whether the train ran or not, it was our intention to lie in wait for it and board an empty truck as it moved slowly up a gradient. Should we be successful, it would bring us to near Balmoral by daybreak. But we were destined to pass that night and the two next on the veldt. We now made direct for the railway, which was near, and shortly after found a gradient of 1 in 57 for some hundred metres. Lying down close to it, and shielding our faces from the mosquitoes with our coats, we remained till 2 a.m., but no train passed. It now seemed certain that the night-service no longer ran, and there was nothing left but to go on walking. Our experiences of the previous evening decided us as to our route, and for a couple of hours we followed the line, and then began to look for water and a place to hide in. As there was a ganger's house close to the railway-line, it seemed probable that we should find water of some sort near. In this we proved to be right, for we nearly walked into a circular pit, at the bottom of which were some inches of the precious liquid. Quenching our thirst and filling the bottle, we looked everywhere for some place that would hide us. There was nothing for it but to lie down by an ant-bear hole upon which we fortunately stumbled. The dwelling of this animal is a hole like a badger's, with a trench about two feet deep, and as broad, leading to the entrance. Here we lay down and prepared, when the sun rose, to be grilled for nine or ten hours, for there was no shade, and we had no means of making it without attracting notice; and our ten-ounce water-bottle would not go very far. In two more marches we should reach Balmoral, and once there, we had a very good hope of hiding ourselves in a coal-truck bound for Portuguese territory.

* * * * *

We had prepared ourselves for a warm day, but this one far exceeded our anticipations: however, so long as we remained well hidden and knew that at nightfall we should be cool and able to procure water, we had no great cause for complaint. The main road and the telegraph-wire were only a few yards distant, but very few Kaffirs passed our way and not a Dutchman, for except the house which stood close to the railway, no other human habitation was near. As usual, we had got soaked to the waist in going through the long grass; but the hot sun soon remedied such a trifle, and before the day came to an end we would have given something to have been in a condition similar to that in which we had first invaded the ant-bear hole.

I have often since thought that in our wanderings on the veldt we were fortunate to escape a grass fire, an everyday occurrence in these regions. Had it happened that one had come our way – and the tell-tale smoke we sometimes saw afar off showed how possible that was – nothing would have remained but to seek safety in flight, a course which would inevitably have led to discovery.

We calculated by the kilometres marked on the white boards at various points along the line that we had only covered thirty-six miles in four days – a poor record – and had still twenty-one to compass before we should reach the neighbourhood of the collieries at Balmoral. Short commons, lack of sleep, and want of water were beginning to have their effect upon us, and we thought we had done well when we had walked ten miles. It was scarcely dark when, our thirst having got beyond endurance, we hurried to the pool which we had enjoyed the night before.

Except an army emergency ration which Le Mesurier had carefully preserved ever since he was captured at Dundee, and a scrap of biltong, we had nothing left to eat. Seating ourselves by this pool we broke into our last reserve, and seldom have I enjoyed a meal (if such it can be called) so much. This ration is intended to last the soldier for thirty-six hours, and it is divided into two parts, each in a small tin which is enclosed in a larger one. One tin contains what I cannot clearly describe, but it is a species of powder, or pemmican, greyish in colour, caked hard, and tasting slightly of "Bombay duck". The other tin is full of cocoa in a highly concentrated form with a pleasant acid taste. They are both to be cooked or not, as circumstances will allow. Cooking-pots were not included in our kit, and means to light a fire, had we desired to do so, did not exist. We therefore dined off our delicacy in its raw state, but only ate about one-third of it, for it had to last two hungry men for seventy-two hours, not one soldier for thirty-six. Our supper at an end, we proceeded on our way, and avoiding the ganger's house, from which the sound of laughter could be heard, gained the railway. From constant listening and peering through the darkness, eyes and ears had grown far more sensitive, and the least sound of voices, or dogs barking, or the faint glimmer of a light in a bridge-guard's tent, did not escape our senses. I cannot but think that the use of dogs in war by us British, a dog-loving nation, has been unaccountably overlooked. I believe certain nations – the Germans and French – use them; but we, who have our kennel-clubs, and every encouragement to breed the best and purest of the canine species, do not include these faithful friends among our war-material. In India, where one suffers so much from rifle-thieves, without his dog there would be many a court-martial on the owner of a stolen rifle. There the dogs are chained to the arm-racks, sentries with whose vigilance no human being can compete. Often in Tirah the wily Afridi would bring his dog with him when bent on disturbing our rest by firing into camp. He knew right well that if the plucky little Ghoorka was engaged in stalking him, his four-footed friend would give him timely warning.

Le Mesurier and I know what a curse were the dogs within whose hearing we came on our way to Lorenço Marques; and I think that if we employed them on outpost duty, and trained them to growl softly when some stranger was approaching, the possibility of surprise would be greatly lessened, and the soldier on his lonely post, where he has to depend on the acuteness of his sight and hearing, would feel the value of this assistant.

The night was wet and windy, which made both hearing and seeing doubly difficult. Keeping along the railway, we passed through a long but shallow cutting, and after going for a few miles saw in front of us a tent in which was a light, and heard the low murmur of voices. As usual, we left the line and made a detour, which brought us to the well-known Bronkhurst Spruit – a fact we ascertained by stealthily creeping along the station platform and reading the name-board. I may be pardoned for recalling to my readers the episode which befell the 94th Regiment under Colonel Anstruther near here, on the 20th December 1880. It was the opening scene of the war of 1881, which terminated with Amajuba. A detachment of that corps was marching to Pretoria, before any declaration of hostilities had been made, when they were ambushed by the Boers, and out of 250 persons all but one officer and 120 men fell within a few minutes. The Boers boast of this brutal massacre as a victory; and in spite of this, and their abuse of the white flag and use of expanding bullets during the present campaign, there are men who call themselves Englishmen who are ready to extend to them the hand of friendship and of sympathy.

Hurrying past this place of mournful memory, we soon came to the village of the same name. The dogs here seemed strangely restless, and as the moon was shining brightly and the rain had ceased, another wide detour on hands and knees was essential. Then we came to a river, and crossing it we regained the railway. A few miles farther on, with no incident worth recording – except that Le Mesurier had the misfortune to tumble full-length into a marsh – we began to think it was time to make our nightly search for a hiding-place. I had been told by a colonial that the grass when at its longest would hide a man from view, and had expected when we left Pretoria to experience no difficulty with regard to hiding-places. But like many tales from South Africa, this one proved untrue. After a good deal of hunting up and down, backwards and forwards, we agreed to lie down in a swamp where the grass and reeds were fairly tall, and near which no human habitation could be seen. It was very wet, probably full of fever-germs; but no matter, we should have the wherewithal at hand with which to fight the sun when he rose.

Next day passed peacefully; we were evidently "far from the madding crowd", for all day long we did not see a soul except some Kaffirs, who were working on the railway-line some way off. By the side of a tiny stream we sat, paddling our feet in its cooling waters, talking over the adventures we had met, anticipating those which were to come, and longing fervently for anything, no matter what, of an edible nature – for the pangs of hunger absolutely declined to be postponed by copious libations of water. Refreshed by a few hours' sleep, we made our way to the railway as twilight turned to night, and, avoiding one or two bridge-guards, reached some running water. The night was very dark, so much so that two Dutchmen passed close by us while we lay down, and crossing rivers by faith and not by sight is not pleasant work.

The river we had reached is called the Wilge river, and being at that season in flood, was broken into several branches. After negotiating four, we thought no more remained; but a girder railway-bridge was dimly visible on our right, a gentle hint that all were not yet passed. The Boer who guarded this bridge must have heard us, for he came out of his tent with a lantern, and, while we lay hidden in the wet grass, listened for some time. Of course at the very moment he appeared the moon began to rise over the crest of a hill in front of us; but as the lantern soon disappeared, we got up and continued our travels.

A few paces brought us to the edge of a most uninviting-looking river – one of those sluggish, stagnant streams such as one meets in Belgium. Neither of us was in the mood for a swim – it was too early in the evening for that; and on trying its depth I found it reached to my waist, and its bottom was composed of soft mud. Along the bank we walked, and were soon rewarded by hearing the sound of running water, and a little farther brought us to a shallow ford: overlooking it on the opposite bank was a cottage, which seemed to be deserted. We crossed over, and found ourselves on a hillside covered with loose stones – an ideal spot for spraining an ankle, and a place which caused my lame companion some distress. The moon came to our rescue, and we again struck the railway without mishap. We now thought that Balmoral could not be far off, and the hope of reaching there before dawn made us push along quickly – so quickly that we failed to bear in mind the maxim, *festina lente*. In consequence we nearly walked into a tent, and had to hide beside the railway till, after reconnoitring, I ascertained that we had not been seen. Before us on either side of the railway, and close to it, were farms, easily recognisable by the clumps of trees around the buildings. To follow the railway, which bent sharply to the left, was inadvisable, so we turned aside and made a flank march round the outskirts of a farm. In front was a line of hills which seemed to block the way, but on approaching we found a rocky gap down which a stream of water ran. Following this to its source, we traversed a tract of marshy ground, and after another mile or two rejoined the railway.

Suddenly we were aware of an odour familiar to us both, the smell of burning coal. We had not expected to find a colliery so close, nor was there one, for the wind brought from a distance what our nasal organs had at once detected. However, we very soon came upon a siding full of coal-trucks. I now made a systematic examination of every truck, to see by the ticket on it where its contents were bound for. It is not the custom to put the full name of a place on these labels, and had I seen L.M., I should have known that it meant Lorenço Marques. But nearly all these trucks were labelled N.C. or J.K. There was no mistaking the first two letters – they must stand for Newcastle in Natal; but as for J.K.,[1] it was Greek to us. Standing at one end of the siding as wan engine, and close by the trucks a small Kaffir hut, outside which were some embers where the occupants had cooked their evening meal.

[1] Johannesburg.

We were tempted to try to clear up the situation, and find out if any trucks were bound for our destination; but it was 2 a.m., the Kaffirs were probably asleep, so we returned to the swampy spot which we had passed before. On our way back I found a large-sized mushroom, one-half of which I ate forthwith, while the other served for breakfast next morning. Cutting down some rushes, we spread them in the swamp, and lay down to snatch a few hours' sleep, which the mosquitoes were determined we should not have. The night, as usual, was very cold, and as I had had rheumatism in my knees ever since the night we took to the river, I was right glad when the sun rose. The day was very warm; but there was more than enough of water, and our hopes were high, for we were determined to secure a truck at one or other of the colliery sidings, and get the rest of our journey over. All day long the noise of the shunting at the siding, where we had been so early in the morning, could be heard, and more than one train seemed to leave it. We hoped that there might be some trucks for Delagoa Bay, where many ships must surely stop to coal.

Towards evening a middle-aged Boer, accompanied by a boy and armed with a sporting rifle, passed us not far off. As luck would have it, a bird, not unlike a curlew, rose from the swamp close to us and flew behind him; but he neither heard nor saw it, and soon they disappeared from view.

The weather, which all day had been very sultry, now began to look most threatening. From every quarter black clouds seemed to roll towards that part of the sky which overhung our swamp. There was no mistaking these signs – we were in for a very heavy storm. Half-past five passed and still it did not come, but by six the rain had begun to fall, and a few minutes later we left the swamp drenched to the skin. Amid flashes of lightning which caused the veldt to look bright as day, and the thunder's sullen roar, we made our way to the Kaffir hut at the siding.

Before leaving our hiding-place we had finished every scrap of food we possessed, yet I have no recollection of feeling anxious as to the future. Not even an inch of biltong remained. This succulent and sustaining stuff is always carried by the Boers when travelling or compaigning. It is made from the flesh of the buck or ox, cut from the choicest parts. Strips of this meat are steeped in vinegar and pepper for two hours, then covered with salt, which it sucks in all night. Next day the strips are hung up in a shady place until their exterior is dry, when they are put in the sun, which soon makes them as hard as wood. This is now fit for eating, and as much as is required for a meal can be cut from it as one slices a cucumber.

Miserable objects, indeed, were we when we came opposite the coal-siding. Not a stitch of dry clothing on us, starving and weak; but shelter and perhaps food were to be found inside the hut, and Le Mesurier had impressed on me from previous experience that Kaffirs were absolutely to be trusted. He had some years before served in Zululand, and had the utmost confidence that no Kaffir we met would betray us, more especially so now that we were at some distance from Pretoria.

The door was open and a light burned within. We entered, and saluting the occupants with the Kaffir greeting "*Sacabona?*" (How do you do?) sat down. There were five thick-lipped, ebony-coloured negroes seated round a cauldron, which, turned on its side, displayed its half-eaten contents – thick dry mealie-meal porridge. Without another word we joined the circle, those nearest us drawing aside their mats, for the rain water was running off us on to the hard mud floor. Indicating our desire to share their meal, the vessel was tilted towards us, and stretching out a hand we drew forth a lump of the coagulated mess. We were both so hungry that the desire for food left us when it was within our grasp; but after a short time the craving returned, and we did justice to the simple fare, realising keenly what it was to eat to live.

The Kaffirs exhibited no vestige of a sign of surprise at our sudden inroad, behaving in the same phlegmatic, dignified manner that one meets with in the East. They must have wondered too who we were, for had we been Dutchmen we should have known their language.

Meantime we had tried the few Kaffir words and sentences we knew upon our black friends, one of whom took pride in repeating his very few words of English. The conversation was not long sustained, and having satisfied our hunger we left the hut. It was pouring still, and the prospect of finding other coal-sidings and examining trucks without the aid of a light – for, as I have said before, we had no matches – was not a pleasing one. We therefore entered the hut again, having decided that we would disclose who we were and try to enlist the help of its occupants. It was easily explained that we were Englishmen from Pretoria running away from the Boers and making for Delagoa Bay. We at once had the sympathy of all, who showed their hatred of the Dutch by signs and gestures, drawing their fingers across their throats, clenching and shaking their fists. So thoroughly did they grasp the situation that the conversation was now conducted in whispers, for outside, not far off, was an engine the driver of which was a Hollander. It was now necessary to try and explain what we wanted them to do. I happened on the previous evening, for no particular reason, to have taken the label off a truck and put it in my pocket; producing it, no word of explanation was required. Two of the Kaffirs left the hut and did not return for some minutes, but when they did they brought with them several other labels. Looking at them, we found that none of them bore the mystic letters L.M. Again they went out. We now gave five sovereigns to the elderly Kaffir who seemed to be the *doyen* of them all, and made him understand that they were his if he could get us a truck for Delagoa Bay. It may be remembered that before we left Pretoria, Sergeant-Major Brockie had given me some slight instruction in the Kaffir tongue, and having some suitable sentences written down, I read them out, much to the curiosity of the listeners, who wanted to see the paper on which they were inscribed. After several more visits had been paid to the coal-trucks, it seemed certain that none was bound for the coast. The old Kaffir then handed back the gold, and giving him a trifle in return for the food, we again left the hut.

Outside everything looked so black and unpromising that we agreed to put our fate entirely in the hands of the five Kaffirs. For the third and last time we entered the hut and asked them point-blank who their *baas* was. Was he an Englishman or a Dutchman? The reply came from all that he was the former and lived not far away, and we thereupon decided to go and ask his help. It might be that we should find that he was a man on parole to take no part in the war, and to remain neutral; but it could do no harm to see him and obtain some food and information. We therefore indicated that we wanted one of them to conduct us to his house; whereupon the youngest Kaffir rose, put on an ancient overcoat, and we went forth again into the night. The rain had ceased, and, following our guide, we crossed the siding, feeling that our difficulties were coming to an end.

In the distance a burning slack-heap of a coal-mine could be seen against the sable background of the sky. It looked nearer than it was, for almost an hour passed before we got into close proximity to it; but the walk seemed to dry our clothes, and we stumbled along in the dark, anxious to know what was in store for us. Passing some sheds, we came to the pit's mouth, and then climbing over some rubbish-heaps, found ourselves facing a row of one-storeyed dwellings. Our cicerone indicated that he had performed his part of the undertaking, and that the manager's habitation lay before us. Knocking on his door, a voice bade us enter. We did so, and found ourselves in the presence of a tall fair man, who later told us that he thought we were Boers. I asked him if he were an Englishman. He replied that he was, but from his accent and appearance he looked more like a Swede. Eventually he informed us that he was a native of Denmark, whereupon I told him my name was of Danish origin. I then inquired if he were on parole, as we wanted his help. As he replied in the negative, I added that we wanted to travel to Delagoa Bay concealed in a coal-truck, and asked how far he could help us. He remained lost in thought for several minutes, and then said that it would be difficult; that his mine was sending no coal to the sea-coast, but that three trucks were to be loaded for Lorenço

Marques at a small mine close by on the following morning, and that he
would try to have the loading postponed till night, so that we could reach
our hiding-place unseen. This meant taking another man into our confidence, but as he was a Scotsman there was no objection. He said that he
would arrange the matter at once, but the question was where to put us
for the night. On my suggesting the coal-mine, he said that there were
several Hollanders on duty there, none of whom could be trusted to
keep their counsel.

Le Mesurier and I then said that the veldt was good enough for us, and
that if he could get us some food, we would lie out all night and come to
some appointed place next evening. He answered he would bring the
storekeeper to us, and, leaving the room, shortly returned with that, to us,
most welcome individual.

Mr. Moore, the manager of the Douglas Colliery store, now took complete charge of us. He led us to his house, which stood in a garden quite
apart from any others, and soon we were seated at his hospitable table
eating as if our lives depended on it. Our first civilised meal for over three
weeks consisted of tinned salmon, cocoa, and the usual adjuncts. I think we
horrified our host by our indecent rapacity, but it gave him a good idea of
what we should require on the morrow. Mr. Moore told us that he was
the son of a late Indian general who had served in the 13th Madras Native
Infantry, and that his brother, in the Imperial Light Horse, had fought at
Elandslaagte side by side with my regiment.

It was a great relief no longer to talk in whispers, and our voices
sounded strange to us. Our host occupied himself in considering where to
lodge us for the night, and decided to put us in a forage-shed next the
store, which was generally occupied by his Kaffir boys, who need not
know who we were. The moon was up, and we made our way to the
shed. In the next house was an Irishman who was in sympathy with the
Boers and had some grievance against Moore, so we were cautioned to
keep very quiet. With apologies for putting us in such a place – a palace to
what we had been accustomed to of late – Moore left us for the night.

A deep sense of contentment and satisfaction now came over us, partly
engendered by the feeling of repletion, and of being able to look forward
to a much-wanted night's rest without mosquitoes. A slight arrangement
of the forage bundles was necessary, and this made, we were soon fast
asleep, despite numbers of mice whose dwellings we had invaded. At a
quarter-past six next morning we were startled by hearing someone
knocking at the small window, which was partly covered by a sack to
hide our presence within. Whoever it was next came round to the door,
which was bolted inside. Cautiously opening it a few inches, a black face

peered in at me, and the owner thereof having apparently satisfied his
curiosity gave a loud guffaw and went off. Shortly after this a man's face,
of somewhat forbidding aspect, appeared at the window and shouted
something in Dutch. Receiving no answer, he tried us in English, saying,
"Hulloo! who told you to doss down there?" Le Mesurier said by mistake,
"Mr. Jansen," which was the name of the Dane who had passed us on to
Moore. This seemed to excite the inquirer's ire, probably because this
store was Moore's, and saying, "Damn his cheek!" he went off. It left with
us a most uncomfortable feeling that, even if he were friendly, of which
I felt some doubts, not knowing who the strangers were, he might reveal
what he had seen to someone better kept in ignorance. Our fears were dispelled when at nine o'clock Moore appeared, bringing with him our
recent visitor, who turned out to be the butcher of the mine, and lived
next door. He told us that his name was Smith, and that he was a Natal-
born Englishman, and had been compelled by the Boers, being a burgher,
to fight at Elandslaagte and Spion Kop; but that he had made a rapid
strategical move to the rear at the former fight and escaped the lancers.
He said he had avoided pointing his rifle so as to inflict damage on his
fellow-counrtymen.

A door which led from the store into the forage-shed was now opened,
and throughout this day a liberal supply of meat and drink was passed in
to us. At ten o'clock we were told that the medical man who had charge
of the miners, and happened to be making one of his occasional visits, was
coming in to see us. Dr. Gillespie, one of those fortunate beings whose
voice and manner at once inspire confidence, now entered the shed. He
told us that, purely on chance of hearing some news at the mine, he had
driven over from Brug Spruit on the previous day, and stopping the night
had chanced to hear in the morning that the escaped prisoners, of whom
everyone knew, had at length arrived.

The extraordinary chain of circumstances which had brought us to the
mine, exactly at the right time, was now made evident to us. Had not Le
Mesurier delayed us owing to his sprained ankle, had not the thunderstorm driven us to the Kaffirs' hut, we should probably never have heard
of Dr. Gillespie. It was not his usual day for visiting the mine. He now
told us his plans for getting us safely over the border. To my amazement
he said that he and some others had managed it for Churchill, and they
would do the same for us. He told us to say nothing to anyone of the fact
that they had helped Churchill, and that when it grew dark he would
drive us to another mine, where plans for the future would be matured.
He added that we might now consider ourselves out of the country, our
further movements would be so devoid of risk.

The First World War, 1914-1918

CHAPTER TEN

WITH THE beginning of the First World War the Germans were quick to realise that "stone walls do not a prison make, nor iron bars a cage". Barbed wire, invented in America in 1874, proved a much more effective barrier. One of its greatest advantages from the guard's point of view was that it was transparent; and the plain barbed wire fence, with a trip-wire inset a few feet to provide a border of "no man's land", and machine guns mounted on towers, confronted the would-be escaper with a new set of problems. Escaping from now on had perforce to become a science, and the prisoner began to rely more and more on disguise or tunnelling as a means of passing this flimsy but strongly guarded barrier to his freedom.

A popular method of defeating the new obstacle was to pass through it dressed as a German officer. The rank-consciousness and blind obedience to orders of the German soldier of World War I was a great help to the disguised escaper who, if he could bluff loudly enough, could often shout even a suspicious sentry into unlocking the gate. The advance of popular education has made this deception increasingly difficult, and in World War II even the German officers were made to show their passes to the guards. In 1942 however Airey Neave[1] walked out of Colditz castle disguised as *Oberleutnant Schwartz* and got clean away.

There are many other amusing stories of such masquerades in my library, and I have chosen the one by H. A. Cartwright from *Within Four Walls* to represent World War I.

H. A. Cartwright

THE BURG camp was bounded all round by a fence of solid boarding about eight feet high with six strands of overhung barbed wire on the top. Outside this was a twenty-strand barbed wire fence about ten feet high – in all about thirty-one miles of wire were used for a perimeter of six hundred

[1] *They Have Their Exits.* Hodder & Stoughton.

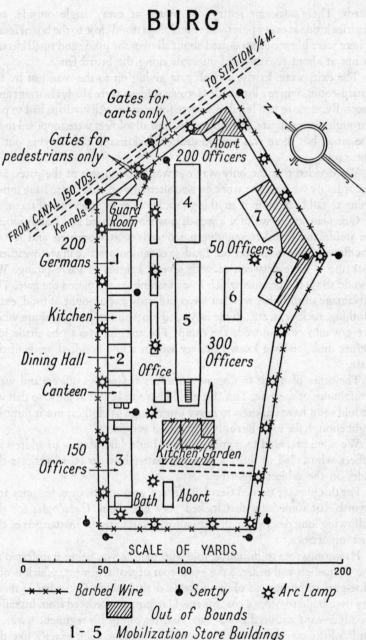

BURG

TO STATION ¼ M.

N

Gates for
carts only

Gates for
pedestrians only

FROM CANAL 150 YDS.

Abort

200 Officers

Kennels

Guard
Room

4

7

50 Officers

8

6

200
Germans

1

Kitchen

5

Dining Hall

2

300
Officers

Office

Canteen

Kitchen Garden

150
Officers

3

Bath

Abort

SCALE OF YARDS

0   50   100   200

×—×—× Barbed Wire   Sentry   Arc Lamp

Out of Bounds

1 - 5 Mobilization Store Buildings
6 - 8 Wooden Huts

yards. There was one sentry – or more – at every angle outside, and sentries inside at every point where buildings stood close to the board fence. There were big arc lights dotted about all over the inside and small electric lamps at about twenty-yard intervals along the board fence.

The exits were, firstly, a small gate giving on to the road just by the guard-room, where a lot of idle German soldiers were always loafing; and, secondly, close to it, a big double gate for wagons. All civilians had to pass through the small gate, showing a pass, and all soldiers were supposed to do the same, but there was a good deal of slackness in the carrying out of these rules.

We decided that the only way out was through one of the gates, and accordingly we began to work on two alternative plans so as to have something to fall back upon if anything should occur to upset one of them.

One plan was to wait for a wet day, when the guard and loafers would be inside the guard-room, disguise ourselves as workmen and try to shuffle out with sacks over our heads (a common practice in wet weather), carrying a stove between us with several lengths of stove-piping. We should show the permits which I was making, as we passed the gate. The advantage of this plan was that we could stow any amount of food, extra clothing, rucksacks, etc., in the stove and pipes and re-pack at leisure when we got into cover outside the camp. The attempt was to be made just before dusk, and we knew of cover within a few hundred yards of the gate.

The other plan was to disguise ourselves as German officers and walk straight out of the gate. This also would have to be just at dusk, so that we should soon have darkness to cover our change of clothes; but it must be light enough for us to be easily recognized as officers.

We were prepared to gamble on no Hun soldier daring to address an officer who failed to show a pass, no matter how strict or intricate the rules on the subject might be.

For this plan we needed German officers' great-coats, caps, leggings and swords – or something that looked very like them. I apologise for the following long description of our uniform, but to us the matter was of the first importance.

Harrison wrote to his tailor, told him that he was being transferred to the Grenadiers and ordered the great-coat of that regiment, which is of a blue-grey colour instead of the universal drab. I asked a Grenadier of about my own build to order a coat for me. Harrison also ordered from his tailor two blue caps with red bands – the undress cap of his regiment – which, with a little card-board stuffing, could be made to look exactly like the German home-service cap. The German wears two small badges on his cap; they consist of, in Prussia, small silver rings with, in the top one, a red spot in the middle, and, in the bottom one, a silver Maltese cross on a black ground. Each is mounted on a rosette of patent leather. With buttons and silver paper I made badges which would have passed any inspection, notwithstanding the fact that the red spots were really minute Union Jacks and the Maltese crosses were spread-eagle angels of peace. We made this little variation because we were not too happy as to how the Germans might view the wearing of their uniform by enemies in the event of our recapture, and preferred to be able to deny that what we were wearing was their uniform at all; but we have since often wondered what the infuriated Germans would have thought had they caught us wearing what appeared to be German uniform with a Union Jack on the cap!

The shoulder-straps were more difficult. They consist each of two pieces of silver braid, curled round a button and mounted on cloth of various colours, according to the corps, regiment, etc. They carry badges of rank, numerals and sometimes regimental badges. I made the braid by weaving blue, grey and white silk on a kind of Heath Robinson loom, and the effect was a good enough imitation of silver. Later the German took to making his shoulder-straps, for active service, of silk instead of silver, so ours were not only effective but correct. We bought stars (they were much like our own pattern) and numerals and plain gilt buttons (as worn by all ranks) at the camp canteen. On a show of worn-out boots – borrowed without leave from a Belgian private – we were allowed to buy new yellow boots, and we bought yellow leggings from the merchant who came to supply them. Harrison carved the swords very artistically out of bits of packing-case. The German service-dress scabbard is of black metal, so we blackened the last eighteen inches of them, which was as much as would show below our great-coats, and polished them with boot-blacking.

While waiting for our great-coats we began to work out a route. The Swiss frontier was ruled out by distance.

At this time nothing was known of the Dutch frontier by anyone in the camp, but we imagined that it was very closely guarded, and possibly wired, and we thought it probable that the whole frontier district would be very carefully supervised and controlled.

We knew, from watching the comic "alarms" which the Commandant was in the habit of staging, that cyclist patrols would be sent out on all likely roads as soon as any prisoner was missed, and we thought it likely that towns and villages lying west of the camp would be on the look-out. For these reasons, and on account of many other difficulties, possibly quite imaginary, which our complete ignorance of conditions in Germany may have made us exaggerate, we decided to go north to the Baltic.

Not till daylight on the morning after we were missed was the "alarm" given a genuine trial. Then with all the prisoners craning from the windows of their rooms, the Commandant himself dispatched his patrols, giving them suitable advice in a loud harangue. Police dogs, the things now called Alsatians, were produced, our bedding was brought out, and they were invited to take up the trail from it. They were interested in the bedding neither more nor less than they would have been in a lamp-post.

We decided to go first to Rostock, whence we believed there was a daily service of ferry-boats into Denmark. As a matter of fact we were wrong; the ferries ran from Warnemünde, at the mouth of the Warne, fifteen kilometres north of Rostock.

We thought it might be possible to board a ferry at night, stow ourselves away and so cross into Denmark. Failing this, rumour had it that there were many small sailing-boats about the Baltic coast engaged in smuggling cheese, butter, etc., into Germany. We thought we might find one of these and persuade the skipper to take us across. If we found a Dane all would probably go smoothly; if a German, ten months in the Fatherland had shown us that the conscience-price of the average working-class German was very dear at fifty marks, and we had about two hundred between us. Thirdly, there was always the possibility of finding a boat on the beach and rowing or sailing it across. We were neither of us experienced sailors, but the distance was not much over twenty miles, and we had only to steer approximately northwards and we could not fail to hit Denmark somewhere. We gathered that, owing to the shortage of food, which was beginning to be seriously felt, and the consequent desirability of getting as much Danish produce as possible into the country, the customs' officers did not unnecessarily worry the masters of fishing or small trading vessels, and were not too severe in their visits to the ferries and other small steamers, though they kept, of course, a very strict watch for spies on the docks and in the town.

Apropos the question of bribery, a few words on the German soldier as I found him may not be out of place here. After nearly twelve years I have come to the conclusion that he was not, on the average, a bad fellow. The swine among them were such incredibly swinish swine that for some years it was difficult to realize that the swine were a small minority.

More often than not the camp guards and escorts tried to do their job, and to do it without being unnecessarily offensive. I do not include the sergeant-majors or other senior N.C.O.'s or the office staffs, which were composed principally of ex-waiters, shopkeepers and commercial travellers, and were about ninety-nine per cent swine; nearly all those who were not swine found pleasanter, if more dangerous jobs, than looking after prisoners.

Most of the swinish acts of soldiers which I saw, both in Germany and in Belgium in 1914, were done under the direct orders or incitement of officers.

The rank and file were corrupt in a small way, but only in accordance with the custom of the country, and I doubt if many of them would have accepted money to help a prisoner to escape. Probably most of them would have taken the money and reported the prisoner or sought kudos and promotion by waiting for him and shooting him in the act – as was actually done on at least one occasion. Anyhow, it wasn't a game worth risking. They couldn't resist food, but when, by accepting it, they were assisting the plans of a prisoner they did so, probably, from sheer stupidity. Their stupidity was incredible.

There were of course revolutionary socialists who were given jobs in camps because they could not be trusted anywhere else, and their kind would do anything for money; but no prisoner ever risked trusting them in an actual attempt to escape.

Rostock was due north of us and distant a little more than two hundred kilometres (a hundred and twenty-five miles) as the crow flies – to which must be added about twenty-five per cent to get the distance as the prisoner treks. The road, as far as we could tell from Baedeker, was nearly straight, and one of the Baedeker maps covered a little more than half the distance. We got the names of a couple of small towns which lay on our line, beyond the limits of the map, from a small-scale map of Europe which was sold as a war map. We stole a compass from a brother officer, who, by some oversight, had not been deprived of it on his capture. We must give him a new one some day.

We hoped to start about the last week in September, when the nights would be fairly long and the weather not too cold. We did not reckon, however, on the imbecility of tailors.

Since June we had been walking ten or twelve miles a day, very fast, round and round the exercise ground.

Early in September our "workmen" scheme was knocked on the head by the Germans so wiring off the small gate that no one could approach it without passing through the guard-room (see plan on page 187). This was more than we could face. At the same time the rule that no civilian might pass out by the wagon gate was strictly enforced.

These precautions were due to the escape of a Belgian, who walked out of the camp during a thunderstorm disguised as a female Hun cook. His line of departure had been a complete mystery to the camp authorities, but on re-capture the next day he had told them how it was done, so the net result of his efforts was to queer our pitch.

There remained the "officer" scheme.

The first hitch in this took the shape of a post-card from Harrison's tailor saying that he was sending off the great-coat, but suggesting that Harrison had made a mistake in asking for the caps of his old regiment when he must have meant the Grenadiers' cap.

Harrison, however, managed to bluff the censors into allowing him to send off a postcard immediately – without the usual fourteen days' delay which was the rule in all the camps – asking his tailor not to try to think but to do what he was told. The delay in the censor's office was intended to ensure that any secret information sent by prisoners' post should arrive stale. It also gave the censors time to test at leisure for all kinds of invisible ink. Harrison was allowed to dispatch this card at once, as the camp rule was: "Prisoners must always wear headgear so as to be able to salute German officers." He always went about bare-headed, claiming he had no head-dress, and had been ordered to write home for a uniform cap. The reply from the tailor was sufficient to justify an extra card to expedite dispatch.

Then the Grenadier who had ordered a coat for me was transferred to another camp, and although he tried to arrange for me to have the opening of the parcel containing the coat when it came to Burg, the censors somehow muddled things and I never got it.

I therefore began to negotiate with an old Russian colonel for a cape which he had had made by a German tailor, and which, while it was, presumably, something like the cape of his regiment, was exactly the cut and colour of the German article in all respects, except that it had no red-lined collar. After weeks of haggling I persuaded the old man to part with the garment in exchange for a "British Warm", a large sum of money and a promise that, if I were caught and the cape traced to him, I would swear that I had stolen it. He was a confirmed drunkard, and we hated his knowing anything about the scheme, but I had to have his cape.

Harrison's great-coat and the caps arrived together on 5th November. Everything else had been ready for some weeks.

Having had no sample in the camp from which to judge, we had rather banked on the Grenadier great-coat bearing a strong resemblance to the German article, but we found to our horror that it was entirely different both in cut and colour. The former is a thoroughly serviceable, comfortable garment of a dark slatey-blue grey, while the latter is almost as tight as a frock-coat, of a lightish blue colour, and is covered with flaps and buttons. We had been quite prepared to add the flaps and buttons, and we had hoped that the difference in colour would be so slight as hardly to matter in a bad light, but we had not contemplated any dyeing or extensive and complicated tailoring. However, there was nothing for it but to start in on the job.

The tailoring which we had to do could not be done with any sort of secrecy in the crowded room in which Harrison and I lived, but Elliot of Harrison's regiment, who had a small room to himself in a hut barrack (Block 7 on plan), very kindly allowed us to use it as a workshop, and here for a time we worked undisturbed. But, just as the coat and cape began to look unmistakably German, the room was suddenly raided by a gang of under-officers, who arrested Elliot, on some trumped-up charge of bribery, and proceeded to search the room. We managed to shuffle our gear out of the window, which was fortunately open, and, not being ourselves "wanted", got clear of the room in the general mess-up and retrieved everything unharmed. Elliot's arrest was the work of the Belgian informer, mentioned earlier in the note on his kind, who had been hanging around the room for some days without, however, being able to discover what was going on. He had been assisted by a Polish Jew, in the uniform of a Russian Red Cross orderly, who had offered to supply Elliot with anything from brandy to machine-guns, and had been very unkindly rebuffed.

We went on with the work in another small room in a similar hut.

Three or four days after the arrival of the coat the tailoring was complete. We then laid it on the floor and poured over it about a pound of boracic powder, the only white powder available, which we beat into the cloth with brushes. This rather crude treatment had the desired effect of raising the shade of the coat to a much lighter blue – a bit patchy, but good enough in a bad light.

We first dressed for the attempt on the 10th November. We wore double or treble the usual allowance of underclothes and numerous sweaters, cardigans, etc. I had an old Norfolk jacket, acquired in hospital by a British officer who had lost his uniform. Harrison had a uniform jacket, dipped in ink, from which the pockets, flaps, shoulder-straps, etc., had been removed. We both wore corduroy trousers with thin red stripes down the seams, this being the only kind of nether garment which we were allowed to buy to replace our worn-out uniforms. We painted out the stripes with water-colour.

Our food, which consisted of chocolate, biscuits, potted meat, "Bivouac" cocoa, beef tabloids, malted milk, oxo, etc., with a "Tommy's cooker" and supply of solid spirit (all from home parcels) was packed all over our bodies. Some was in pockets and some down trouser legs, some in rucksacks hung over our stomachs and some in sacks hung on our backsides. The latter two loads gave the correct Prussian figure.

I had for months past worn a long, straggling moustache; I hogged this closely and mounted a pair of enormous round gold-rimmed spectacles. Harrison is very fair, so his moustache, eyebrows and back hair were blacked with grease-paint (the kindly Hun provided this for a purely imaginary dramatic club) and his face was washed in a strong solution of coffee. These alterations changed our appearance enough to make recognition unlikely in a bad light, but they were, as things turned out, quite wasted.

Our outer garments consisted of the uniform caps, the great-coat in Harrison's case, the cape in mine, yellow boots and leggings and the correct brown leather gloves. We wore our wooden swords. Since I should have to discard my cape when we were safely out of the camp, I wore beneath it a Belgian army great-coat (dark blue) deprived of its frills and with civilian buttons. I had to pin up the skirts to prevent them from showing beneath the cape.

Harrison's German overcoat could be hastily converted into a seedy-looking civilian garment – most of the powder would soon wear out of it and we did not intend to be seen, as civilians, by daylight.

We intended to loiter in the darkness of a doorway near the wagon gate, until the departure of a kitchen refuse wagon which went out nearly every evening at about the right time. Then, when the gate was opened we hoped to be able to strut through it without attracting undue attention. Strange German officers often visited the camp on mysterious missions to the Russians, so that, if they accepted us at all as officers, the guard were not likely to pay much attention to us.

The German officer's collar, when turned up, shows a deep lining of scarlet cloth. This splash of red marks out the officer very clearly at any distance at which the colour can be seen, and the German soldier who sees it coming either bolts for cover or, if too late, shakes himself together for a terrific salute.

Lieutenant Terlinden, a Belgian officer of Guides, who afterwards brought off a particularly neat escape and sent me a lot of valuable information and material from Holland, sacrificed his breeches to provide our red collars.

We reached our doorway (in Block 4 – see plan on page 187) safely, wearing English great-coats on top of all the rest. One British officer

carried our caps while another lounged outside reporting German movements and watching for the wagon.

Just as the wagon hove in sight and our quick change was being effected,
two German under-officers elected to loaf into our particular doorway,
where they stood, talking about food, but not for the moment taking any
great interest in us. This was not on the programme. Our group broke up
in some disorder, but, after dodging all over the camp and meeting an
unexpected German (all of them, fortunately, stone-blind) at every turn,
we eventually reached our rooms with the loss of only one cap-badge.

After this fiasco we had to change our tactics. Secrecy was no longer
possible, since half the officers in the camp knew now what we were at,
and any unusual movement of Britishers attracted a mob of chattering
allies. We decided to wait in my room (in Block 5 – see plan on page 187),
which I shared with five other British officers until the wagon was
signalled, when we would walk out of it, along a corridor, down a staircase and across about a hundred yards of exercise ground to the gate.
We hoped to time our start so as to reach the gate just as it was being
opened. We took the precaution of smashing the electric lamps in the
corridor and on the stairs, in case we should meet a German on our way
down.

A little diversion, in the shape of a fire-alarm, was arranged for the guard
in case any of them should think too much, after our departure, of the
two strange officers who had walked out by the wagon gate. This was
to be the burning of a large range of wooden latrines, and Bevan, of the
Intelligence Corps, very kindly undertook to be the incendiary.

Large quantities of paper were thrown into the pit, and half a dozen
large bottles of methylated spirit, which we could at that time buy in
unlimited quantities for cooking purposes, were poured on to it. Bevan
was to carelessly drop a match as soon as we were safely past the last
sentry, and we felt sure that the subject of fire would crowd all other
thoughts from the minds of the camp staff and guard for some hours at
least.

We dressed for an attempt on 11th November, but it was dark before
the wagon appeared. The same thing happened on 12th and 13th. On 13th
a German officer came into the room while we were waiting, and we had
to dive into very insufficient cover under a bed and a table while he stood
within a few inches of Harrison asking silly questions about Irish politics.
This sort of thing was more than I had bargained for, and, although
Harrison was quite willing to dress up every night until our chance
came, the thing was getting on my nerves, and I was afraid of doing something idiotic and spoiling the whole business. We therefore decided not to

dress again until there was reason to expect a wagon to be going out at exactly the right time. We had smashed the lamps on the stairs on 11th, 12th, and 13th – the German was very keen on light and always replaced them – but for some reason which we never discovered he posted no sentry to watch them and took no apparent notice of the damage. He must have been playing some very deep game, but, since the lamp-smashing stopped after our departure and he could not connect us with it it was never played out.

On the afternoon of 18th November a small party of British soldiers was told off to gather up the paper, straw, etc., from the room in which our parcels were unpacked and censored. They were to have it baled up and ready for loading on to a wagon at 5.30 p.m. This was just what we were waiting for. The oldest soldier was let into the conspiracy and asked to arrange for the loading to be completed at exactly 5.30 – and he carried out his instructions almost to the second.

We had a big feed, with exactly the right quantity of German brandy, and were dressed and ready a few minutes before the hour.

On the stroke of the half-hour the wagon was signalled. We left our room and the building and walked down the yard towards the gate, accompanied by an English officer – dressed as a Russian to make the party look more commonplace – who was talking bad German to us at the top of his voice. We were very much encouraged by meeting some French and Russian officers, who, in all innocence, gave us the grudging salute on which the German always insisted. We carried in our hands the bunches of papers which seemed to be part of the dress of the German staff officer, and each smoked the customary foul cigar.

While the gate was being unlocked we stopped and exchanged the customary series of salutes and bows with our imitation Russian, and, that over, turned and walked out by the side of the wagon. The gate sentry jerked himself to attention, the Sergeant of the guard dropped his keys and saluted, and the worst was over. We politely returned the salutes and walked ahead of the wagon towards the gate in the outer fence. Here the sentry, whose job it was to unlock it, remained at ease, staring with open mouth at the two strange officers and apparently trying to screw himself up to draw their attention to the regulations by which no pedestrian might pass through his gate. Possibly he was expecting an order from us, but this was something we were quite unable to give him.

We were brought up short by the gate, and were both of us silently wondering what on earth to do next, the situation for a moment looking desperate, when, in despair, I raised a finger as if returning the salute which he had so far forgotten himself as to omit. He must have realized that he, a private soldier, was standing at ease within a yard of two officers – than which, in Prussia, it would be hard to imagine a more appalling situation. Seized with remorse he hurled himself at the gate, threw it open, clicked his heels and froze to attention. We walked out, acknowledged some jerks from the sentry on the fence and strolled down the road towards the town. We had to walk down some hundreds of yards of main road – Harrison going dead lame and rattling like a cheap-jack, a tin of biscuits having come adrift in his trousers – before we came to the turning down which we hoped to get into cover. I had made several visits, under escort, to a dentist, for the purpose of reconnoitring the surroundings of the camp, and knew of cover close by if we could only get into it unobserved. We were lucky, and within five minutes of leaving my room we were hidden between a couple of green-houses in a large garden.

We hastily peeled off our caps, coats, leggings, etc., and stuffed them, with the rucksacks and food, into the sacks, put on civilian caps and emerged as heavily laden workmen.

Harrison wore a service-dress cap, deprived of its stuffing and dyed in ink. I wore one which had been given to a British soldier in a soldiers' camp. The playful Hun had decorated it with an identification patch of yellow paint, but this was easily removed.

It was only when we emerged from the garden that Harrison, who is a complete non-smoker, discovered that he had smoked his cigar right through and that it was singeing his moustache.

We passed the camp again at a little distance, and were rather disappointed not to see the fire-works which had been planned. I forget exactly what had occurred to spoil the show, but we were not unduly worried since, if there was no great conflagration, there was certainly no other sort of commotion, as there would surely be had any suggestion of an escape reached the sergeant of the guard.

"According to plan" we made our first night's march due east along a canal bank – the direction in which we least wanted to go but also the one in which the Germans were least likely to look for us. After going at top speed for five or six miles we stopped, got rid of most of the traces of our disguise, and removed the surplus clothing, which was only needed for the daily hide. The caps, Harrison's red collar, his shoulder-straps, patches, buttons and other frills were done up in my cape, which was weighted with stones and sunk in the canal. We had broken up and thrown away the swords at our first quick change.

After this we got on much more comfortably, with our baggage properly stowed in rucksacks. A good deal of rain and sleet was falling and we only met two or three men, with whom we exchanged the customary "*n'Abend*" – the only German to which we were prepared to commit ourselves. We roused a good many dogs on barges and in cottages, which alarmed us horribly at first, but we soon learnt that no one took any notice of them. We made detours round all the locks, hamlets and other places where more than a few solitary natives were likely to be met.

At the first streak of dawn we began to look for cover and were lucky in finding, without much searching, a large Dutch barn, full of straw and with no habitation near it. We climbed to the top of the straw, dug down between it and the end of the roof, put on all our extra clothing, and made ourselves as comfortable as we could. We had lost our waterbottle (a rubber air-cushion, with a funnel as filler) while collecting water from a ditch during the night, so had to carry up the day's supply in tins. We did this, of course, in the early morning before digging ourselves in. It was rather cold, but we spent a quiet day without any interruptions. During the day we got rid of the last traces of Prussian glory from Harrison's coat.

We allowed ourselves two hot drinks during the day, one of oxo and one of "Bivouac" cocoa. The daily ration worked out at about eight ounces of chocolate, four small Plasmon biscuits and half a tin of potted meat each, and the two hot drinks. We had a lot of malted milk and beef tabloids which we sucked on the march. This unpleasant diet provided plenty of nourishment but precious little bulk, and we soon learnt the value of tight belts. We had reckoned on reaching the coast in fourteen nights but we did it in nine, so were able to increase our rations towards the end.

This first day was typical of the next nine. We always hid in barns, in spite of the rather greater risk of discovery, because we did not care to face the cold and damp of the woods with such a long walk before us. Only twice more were we lucky enough to find isolated barns; the other days we had to spend in villages, in barns which were close to their owners' homesteads and often communicated directly with the kitchen. The barns were mostly very big and contained large stacks of corn or straw. Dug well in to the top of a stack, at the end farthest from the ladder, we felt fairly safe, The farm people often came into the barns, and sometimes worked in them all day, but only once were we in real danger of discovery. This was when we were in a small barn and lying in hay instead of the more usual straw (it was much warmer) and a farm hand came up three times during the day to get food for the beasts. The first time we were not expecting him and he nearly walked right on to us, and came much too close with his pitchfork. After that we dug down about six feet into the hay, and he might have stood on us without spotting us.

Harrison used to sleep like a babe nearly all day and could hardly keep awake long enough to have his hot drinks. I felt the cold and could not sleep, except for the first hour after we got in, when I slept from sheer fatigue.

It began to snow a little on the sixth night of our walk and at the same time a very hard frost set in and held to the end of the trek. For the last day and night it snowed hard and continuously.

We generally marched from dusk, about 5.30 p.m., till the first signs of dawn at about 4.30 a.m. Sometimes our start was delayed by the farm people working later than usual and preventing our breaking out. One Sunday morning we stayed out until 5 a.m., thinking the natives would lie in bed a little longer than usual, but we were nearly caught out by the farmer, who came in just as we got to the top of our stack, and we had to lie doggo for an hour or more before he left us to dig in in peace.

We generally halted for an hour or an hour and a half, if we could find some sort of shelter, at about 11 p.m., but it was too cold for us to get much rest.

We drank, if possible, from ditches and ponds, but sometimes had to tackle a pump in the small hours of the morning. We were often chased away from one farm after another by barking dogs when in search of a good barn.

All the barns which we used had big double doors of thin match-boarding. To open them, I used to lie down on my back and pull one flap with my hands while I pushed the other with my feet. In this way I could bend the boards and make a gap through which Harrison could crawl; he then lit a candle, found the fastening bar and let me in.

During one lie-up Harrison crept down during the day, armed with a chocolate tin, to rob a cow which we thought we could hear moving about in a stall somewhere below us. He did a long and careful stalk, practically in darkness and found – a bull.

After the first night's march we went north-west, on a compass bearing across country, to hit off the Rostock road about thirty kilometres north of Burg. We had made up our minds not to pass through a single village until we had crossed the river Havel (about seventy kilometres north of Burg), and we made detours through the fields round every one. There was a village every three or four kilometres. There was, however, a light railway which circled round the outsides of the villages, and by following this we saved a good deal of time, though the going was far from good. We thought there might be some kind of organised look-out for us on the bridge at Havelberg, where our road crossed the river, so made for the bank some distance below the town in the hope of finding a boat. We found ourselves in a marsh cut up by innumerable channels, and, being unable to find any sort of boat, had to go back to the road. There was a strong light on the bridge, thrown from some kind of engine-house which stood at the far side of it, and we could see several people moving about. As we approached the road from the marsh we passed through some gardens in which was a large pile of faggots. We took some of the biggest of these on our heads and staggered wearily across the bridge, exchanging the usual greetings with one or two men of whom, on account of our loads, we could see nothing except the feet. We left the faggots in the first yard which we passed. Probably someone had to do time for stealing them.

The road was nearly straight most of the way and fairly easy to follow, the greatest difficulty being to hit off the right one when emerging from big villages and small towns. We never hesitated in towns, but always walked straight through and, if we came out on the wrong road, we never turned back but went across country until we struck the right one. This sometimes lost us an hour or more, since the country close to the towns was very much enclosed. In the open country the roads are always flanked on both sides by trees, and are therefore, easy to find even on a very dark night. We did not have to use the compass much – always a slow process at night – since, until the last three nights, the sky was fairly clear, and as long as we could see the pole-star ahead of us we knew that we could not be far out of the right direction.

We put into one sack everything which would not stow comfortably into our rucksacks and took it in turns to carry it for half-hour spells. We walked about four miles an hour.

Three nights from the finish I acquired a very warm blanket-lined coat, which was a great comfort. Its owner, who had made a nuisance of himself by working in our barn all day, was thoughtful enough to leave it there when he knocked off for the German equivalent of tea just when it was time for us to be moving. When we were brought back to Burg the Commandant seized on this coat as conclusive evidence that we had been helped to escape by a German. (In civil life he was a judge.)

On the last night I had just got to the ground (we were in a very large Dutch barn) and Harrison was half-way down a very ramshackle staging when I saw two figures approaching through the snow with a huge covering of some sort over their heads. I whispered to Harrison, who kept as still as possible half-way down the scaffolding. I then dropped on my stomach at the foot of the staging. The two figures came into the barn, threw off the covering and disclosed themselves as young women. At the same moment Harrison's staging began to rattle violently, and the women, evidently in mortal terror, ran together and hugged each other. However, the rattling ceased and they began to peer about the barn, coming quite close to me and apparently looking straight at me, but seeing nothing. Then they picked up their covering, which turned out to be a huge mattress, and began hastily to fill it with unthreshed wheat from the stacks. Evidently they were robbing the barn and were just as anxious as we were not to be discovered, but it was not until some time afterwards that we realised this; at the moment we only felt sure we were spotted. I had another nerve-racking half-minute before they left us. The German peasant is nothing if not natural, and one of our visitors, having occasion to withdraw a little from her companion, chose – fortunately without examining it too closely – the very patch of darkness which was hiding me.

They went back to the road by the line which we had intended to follow, so, supposing that some habitation lay that way, we made off in the opposite direction – a change of plan for which we paid very heavily – meaning to circle round and get back to the road about a mile farther on.

For this last march we had no map, but we knew there was a choice of two roads, one running north-east through a place called Lage and the other north-west through Schwaan. We found neither place, nor did we get back to the main road until we were within two or three miles of Rostock. Between 6 p.m. on 26th November and 1.30 a.m. on 27th we covered about twenty-three miles, all either across country or on the worst of country roads – under a foot of snow. The result was that we arrived in Rostock completely tired out – a great mistake. In our later attempts we always planned to have a very short march on the last night so as to arrive at or near the frontier fresh and fit for any unforseen emergency.

The going on those country lanes was very bad; they had been cut into deep ruts the mud of which was frozen as hard as stone and the snow was so deep that in the dark the surface appeared to be quite smooth. The consequence was that we trod on a ridge and twisted an ankle more or less at every step. It snowed hard almost the whole night and was so cold that we only tried once to rest, and gave it up after a few minutes. We found no water, every ditch, stream or pond being frozen hard (the thermometer marked $-20°$ centigrade, they told us afterwards in Rostock), and we were forced to quench our thirst by sucking handfuls of snow – anyone who has ever tried this will know that it causes the tongue to break into a mass of small blisters, a most painful condition.

We came into the outskirts of Rostock at about 1.30 a.m. and there made the acquaintance of a most amazingly stupid German sergeant-major.

We were following the main road towards the docks when he stepped out from the shadow of some trees and called on us to halt. We shuffled on a few paces, but he roared again, and, not having a run left in us, we could only adopt the tactics on which we had agreed for this sort of emergency and pretend to be slightly drunk. We halted and stood swaying slightly and looking stupidly at the German.

I think I have said that we spoke no German; to be more exact, I had a very thin smattering of the language, and Harrison had an even thinner one, but we could both understand the gist of anything likely to be said to us in such circumstances as these.

The German stood under a lamp and ordered one of us to advance. I staggered forward and he began to bellow at me: "Who are you?" "What are you?" "Where do you come from?" "Where are you going and why?" etc., etc. I looked drunkenly at him, but did not venture on an answer. He followed up with the inevitable: "What nationality are you, and have you got papers?" – his voice getting louder and louder as he began to revel in the certainty of having found something really easy to bully. I began, between hiccoughs, to deliver a sentence in a mixture of languages which was meant to explain that we were Danish sailors from a ship in the docks, that we did not speak German, that we had left our papers in the ship, that we had been drinking with friends at the canal docks (we had just passed them and heard sounds of carousal), that German beer was very good and we were only poor sailors, and he was a dear good kind Prussian officer of very high rank and it was very cold. Good-night!

He seemed to follow my meaning, for he kept repeating my words, with corrections, at the top of his voice.

He tore open my coat and examined my clothes, finally running his finger down the seam of my trousers to feel for a stripe – which was there! Then he pushed me back against a wall and called up Harrison, who, during this performance, had been giving a wonderfully realistic imitation of a drunken man being sick in the gutter. Harrison let him roar half a dozen times, each roar angrier than the last, then staggered towards him, and, when he was right up against him, let go, with appropriate music, a full mouthful of chewed snow and chocolate all over the hero's manly breast. He was wearing a brand-new great-coat of the expensive pale blue kind which German under-officers are allowed to have made at their own expense. He screamed with rage, and, hurling Harrison violently away from him, treated us for three minutes to the choicest flow of obscenities to which he could lay his tongue while he scraped his chest with a piece of stick.

Then, to our utter amazement, he said something about having thought at first that we were prisoners of war and we could (not very politely) get out of his sight for a couple of blank, blank foreigners.

From start to finish we neither of us thought for a moment that we had had the slightest chance of bluffing that Hun – or any other – and had always agreed that, once fairly suspected, our only hope lay in running. Had our friend thought of looking in our packs he could not have failed to realise what we were. We learnt later at the police station that he was on the look-out for a couple of Russian privates who had bolted from a working party at Stralsund, but he actually knew that two British officers were reported escaped and that the Magdeburg Command had offered two hundred marks for the recapture of either.

After this incident we continued to walk drunkenly whenever there was anyone in sight. We often found the drunken walk useful during later attempts.

We made straight for the docks, and soon found a road which ran their whole length and quite close to the water-side. We had originally intended to have only a preliminary look at the docks that night and, unless we hit on the ferry-steamer at once and it seemed fairly easy to board, to push right on to the open coast and try for something in the way of a small boat the next night. But our cross-country trek had taken so much out of us that we decided to try there and then to get on board some kind of neutral steamer. We walked the whole length of the docks, meeting only one policeman, who was not interested in us, and seeing a great many steamers, several of which appeared to be neutrals.

It was an ideal night for our purpose, snowing and freezing hard, with a biting wind, and we knew quite well that any watchmen who might be posted about the docks would be in their huts with the doors closed and braziers going full blast. We moved without a sound over the snow. The docks were fairly well lit.

Eventually we hit on a small steamer lying alongside the quay, with a little smoke coming from her funnel. She had the Danish flag painted on her side and an obviously Scandinavian name under her counter. We looked her over from end to end, saw that there was no sign of a watch on deck and were on the point of creeping up her gangway when a big German police-dog rushed up from behind and jumped around us, barking noisily.

The door of a shed opened and a policeman walked up to us holding a whistle to his mouth. We tried the drunkard business, but we were up against a man of very different type to our sergeant-major friend. We were on enclosed premises, and in any case we could not run, so that was the end of our first attempt.

We were taken to the police station, where we shared the remains of our condensed rations with the police, who, for a small consideration, agreed to forget all about them. Consequently, when we were searched at Burg nothing was found to show how we had lived, and the Germans flatly refused to believe that we had walked from Burg or fed from our pockets. Moreover no suspicion fell at that time on the concentrated foods which continued to arrive in every parcel from home.

The police treated us very civilly. We spent the rest of the night together in a rather lousy cell, and, after a hearty breakfast of mangold soup next morning, were ordered to prepare for the journey back to Burg. This instruction was given to us by a handcuffed prisoner, who was produced to act as interpreter. He told us incidentally that he was a Swedish sailor and that he had been condemned to death the day before on charges of espionage.

We were taken over at the police station by an escort consisting of two of the most ferocious-looking sergeants I ever set eyes on – enormous men with fat, pink necks, bulging pink eyes and ginger moustaches on the model of the All Highest. They came to our cell, after we had been told to dress for the journey, and peremptorily ordered us out of it. Then each produced a firearm – one a revolver, the other an automatic pistol – which they ostentiously loaded, cocked and waved in our faces with the customary blood-curdling threats.

I mention this not because it was unusual but because of what followed in the train.

By the time we reached the station we had them half tamed, and they allowed us to buy – for all four of us – the most substantial meal which the refreshment-room could produce. We had to finish it on the platform because the head waiter unfortunately discovered that we were English pig-dogs and not poor deserters and kicked us out of the room. He got no tip. When we were in the train, however, our escort received some whispered instructions from the local equivalent of a railway transport officer, which brought on a fresh spasm of ferocity, and the pistols were again produced and their moving parts exercised for our benefit.

The result was that the automatic jammed at half-cock, with a cartridge half in the chamber and the muzzle within six inches of my stomach; but when I put out my hand for it and suggested to its owner in pidgin-German that he had better let me have it since I understood its works and he did not, he handed it over like a lamb, and only breathed freely again when I had removed the magazine and extracted the jammed cartridge. I told him it was a very dangerous instrument, and he thankfully followed my advice to put it in one pocket and the cartridges in the other and keep them as far as possible apart until he had had some more lessons in their use. In the next three years I learnt that these were quite a common type of home-serving German, but at the time we were both a little surprised.

We arrived at Magdeburg at 10 p.m., and Hauptmann Chessmann, the Burg Commandant, was so overjoyed at the thought of seeing us again after mourning us as lost for ever (and probably having been severely "strafed") that he came in person to meet us and held a preliminary inquiry on the spot while we waited for our connection.

We were rather roughly handled by the guard which took us on from Magdeburg to Burg – probably they had had a pretty thin time in consequence of our escape.

I should mention here that, when we were preparing to quit the camp, we wanted to make the Germans think, if we succeeded in getting out, that we had gone by train to Holland so that the look-out in the other directions might be less strict. Harrison therefore wrote a note which he addressed to an English officer, Templer, who was doing time for some trivial offence in Burg prison. In the note (which he mentioned would be smuggled into prison by a corrupted German) he said: "If we are not with you by the day after tomorrow we shall be in Holland. The Germans do not know that Cartwright speaks German so will never dream that we are going by train." He left the note among his belongings, where it was found as soon as we were missed. The Commandant swallowed it whole. It was dramatically produced at the official inquiry to prove me a liar when I denied that I knew the language. When I left Germany the following entry still stood in my "conduct sheet": "Speaks German perfectly, but will not admit it." This has been brought up at every court martial or court of inquiry at which I have had the pleasure of assisting since that date.

At the inquiry after our recapture a pair of English gloves and a tin-opener were produced as evidence against us. They were supposed to support a trumped-up charge of burglary. The things had been found in the garden where we did our first quick change – which, by a curious coincidence, happened to be the Commandant's own garden – and a broken board in the fence was the basis of the burglary charge. Harrison said he wanted the post office parcels register produced as evidence for us. Asked by the Commandant what he meant, he replied: "To prove that enough prisoners' parcels have arrived at the post office, and have not been signed for by the addressees, to outfit the whole population of Burg with English goods." We heard no more of the burglary charge.

The glove question was the only one which we answered at all, so that, since the Germans had not the slightest idea how we really got out, the inquiry was not a success. In subsequent interrogations and inquiries of the same kind we have both always declined to answer a single question. This makes the German very angry, since, failing evidence, he always charges a prisoner on "his own confession" if he has opened his mouth at all. Even if he has not he gets no peace until he has signed a long statement in German, alleged to be a verbatim report of the inquiry. I always willingly signed these novels, writing over my signature: "I do not understand the above." This too seemed to make them angry.

CHAPTER ELEVEN

CARTWRIGHT AND Harrison were caught on their first escape attempt together, but for them, like so many other determined escapers, this was merely the first round in a fight that was to last throughout their captivity. They did succeed in the end, getting away separately, and their joint book telling of their four secret and hilarious journeys is an all-time classic of escape.

*   *   *   *   *

British prisoners of war in Europe were as a rule treated humanely. They were held by men of their own religious and moral code, and the individual bully among their guards was the exception rather than the rule.

In World War II the white man who found himself the captive of the Japanese was up against something that at first he did not understand. Japanese military discipline is harsher than that of European armies, N.C.O.s slapping the faces of their subordinates as a matter of course. The prisoner, according to Japanese code, was a man as good as dead and not entitled to any consideration whatever, and treatment of prisoners by this backward nation was both negligent and deliberately cruel. At the end of the Japanese War, I was a member of one of the recovery teams which were sent to the Far East; I do not want ever again to see men reduced to the condition of those who had been held by the Japanese.

There were enemies in World War I who were almost as inhuman in their treatment of prisoners. Sir Thomas White records in *Guests of the Unspeakable* that of the fourteen thousand odd British and Indian prisoners captured by the Turks, not more than three thousand survived their captivity. In *Prisoners of the Red Desert* Captain Gwatkin-Williams tells of the hardships suffered at the hands of their Turkish and Arab guards in Libya.

Gwatkin-Williams was in command of H.M.S. *Tara*, a converted railway steamer which was torpedoed and sunk by a German U-boat while patrolling off the coast of Libya in November 1915. Most of her crew were taken aboard the attacking submarine, which was commanded by the German ace, von Arnauld de la Perriere. The U-boat commander proposed to hand his captives over to the Turks, but as Gwatkin-Williams was the only regular Royal Naval officer in the *Tara's* crew the German offered to take him back to Austria. Although the Englishman did not appreciate it at the time this was an act of kindness on de la Perriere's part, as he knew the mettle of his Allies. Thinking that escape would be easier from the Turks than from the Germans however, Gwatkin-Williams insisted on staying with his men, and was duly landed at Bardia and handed over to the Turkish commander-in-chief.

Then followed weeks of wandering in the desert, half naked, starved and beaten by the Arabs whom the Turks employed as guards. One by one the prisoners died and were buried by their comrades. At last Captain Gwatkin-Williams could stand it no longer and decided to try to escape and reach Sollum, which he believed to be held by the British.

R. S. Gwatkin-Williams

ON FEBRUARY 14th, the sick had all taken a turn for the worse, due no doubt in great measure to the wave of pessimism which had now spread over the camp, and also to the still dwindling rice ration, which was of the same bad quality of dirty and broken grains. Our hunger was very much greater than ever before, and officers and men alike now ate enormous quantities of snails. After a day or two of great depression, we began to cheer up again, for it is one of those curious anomalies of human nature, that the more wretched and painful existence becomes, the more does one desire to prolong it. We reasoned, moreover, that our gaolers would surely not have taken the trouble to keep us alive for three months and more, merely to let us perish now. We even welcomed the pangs of starvation, for we felt convinced that the very shortage of food would, in the end, compel them to release us.

The possibility of one or more of our number escaping, was now a common topic of conversation in the officers' tent, and one or two had loosely expressed an intention of trying to do so; but the general opinion appeared to be that it was quite impossible.

Various schemes were discussed, and for a time we almost settled upon what appeared a very simple expedient.

We had often noticed the extreme dislike of the Arabs to approaching a dead body. Once one of our number was dead, or even known to be seriously ill, no Arab would go near the tent where he lay.

What could be easier than to report that one of our number was dying, and a day or two later give out his death? We had already had three funerals at Bir Hakkim, and the mournful hymn singing procession to the graveside was now familiar to all our guards. We would have a mock funeral, and bury *something*, or at least appear to do so. Then, as soon as it was dark, the alleged corpse could, with ordinary luck, make good his escape, without the least fear of being missed and pursued.

But there was one fly in the ointment. Should the runaway, as was more than probable, ever be recaptured and brought back, his escape would at once implicate the whole of the other prisoners, who were likely to have a very "slim" time as a result of their little deception. The deception itself, too, in the first instance, would mean that every sailor in the camp would have to be warned beforehand, a necessary preliminary which would not help the cause of secrecy, and, among so many, there might well be one traitor, one who, to save himself from after-punishment, and to curry favour, might divulge the matter to Selim.

If only one could get through and make our pitiable plight known to the British, we felt assured that something would then be done.

But how? For the time being there seemed no practicable way. I cautiously approached the one or two officers who had expressed an intention of escaping, but when I directly mooted the subject, I found that it was an intention only, and that for the present, at any rate, they had no clear determination to carry it out. Wherefore I held my peace, and for the time being confided in no one except Basil and Apcar, who were necessary for my purpose.

Basil I employed to teach me a few words of Arabic, sentences which I thought might be useful to me, and these I wrote down carefully and phonetically, with their English equivalents, in a spare page of my diary.

Apcar was invaluable to me, for, through him, I was able to interrogate the two Indian horse-keepers, our fellow-prisoners. These men, having come all the way from Sollum, could give me a very good idea of the country lying between us and that place, a route which they described as being dead flat all the way, and they also stated most emphatically that they had encountered not a single human being in the whole journey. They could also give me some idea of the appearance of Sollum from inland, from Bir Waer, the Senoussi Camp which overlooked the place. I wanted to be able to recognize the latter at a distance if possible, so that on sighting it I could hide, and then endeavour to make my way through the beleaguering Turkish lines after dark. But in all matters which we discussed through the Indians I had to use the greatest caution, in order that they themselves should get no inkling of what was toward.

For the past two or three weeks I had steadily been getting into training so far as possible. I was always out with the firewood and snail collecting parties, and every evening I walked for some hours barefoot on a sandy patch near the camp, Basil acting as trainer. My Swedish and Sandow exercises amazed the guards, who took my prostrations and kickings as some new form of religious mania, and were deeply impressed thereby; one youth especially had always had great hopes of converting us to Islam, and I fancy he thought he had now at long last succeeded!

For a week I saved daily a quarter of my rice ration of three-quarters of a pound, a real test of fortitude in a person with naturally so hearty an appetite as myself. None of my brother officers said anything about this at the time, but I fancy the more observant noted it and began to suspect my intention. By this means, and by eating my stale rice, I had at the end of the week two days' freshly boiled rice saved. The trouble with the rice is that, once boiled, it readily turns sour, and becomes fermented and poisonous, and will not keep eatable for more than a very few days. It was necessary for me to take my food with me already cooked, for besides the danger there would be in lighting a fire, there were also the two additional difficulties that I had nothing to cook rice in, and also that I should be able to obtain no water on the way, as every well was sure to be guarded by soldiers.

Apcar also helped me in another material way; he had been sick practically ever since he landed, and therefore was virtually the only one of us who had not worn out his boots. His Arab shoes were also still in good order, and, himself retaining his European boots, he turned these native shoes over to me. With my bone needle and some thread from an old sail, I was able to repair them sufficiently for a journey, and I had in addition the remnants of my own European shoes.

Ever since the day we had landed, I had kept a very careful, if brief, record of all events of importance which had happened to us. Among these, I had put down the number of hours we had been on the march each day our journey to Bir Hakkim, and the general direction we had taken, and I also knew approximately the number of miles per hour we had moved at. These I plotted out carefully on a piece of ruled foolscap which I possessed, and for a sailor accustomed to navigation, it was an easy matter to get a good general idea of the direction and distance we had come from Port Bardia, the place where we had landed.

The trouble was that it was *not* Port Bardia I wished to get to. It was, in fact, the place which I particularly wished to avoid. Sollum, which I believed (erroneously) to be once more in British hands, was my objective.

With the greatest care I checked all the information available, both that obtained by Basil from camel drivers, and that which the Indians could give me. But the latter had taken little or no note of the direction, and the former always went on a more or less circuitous route along the line of the wells, whereas the path by which I wished to go was the most direct route available. My trouble was that I had only a very rough general idea of the configuration of the coast, and that I had no notion how far Sollum was to the south of Port Bardia. I guessed the distance at forty miles, whereas in reality it was only fifteen miles as the crow flies.

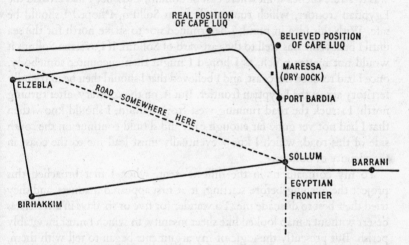

Another thing which also put my calculations somewhat awry, was the situation of Cape Lucq, the spot where we had spent the afternoon on November 18th, and whence we had obtained our last glimpse of the sea. I believed it to be the north-eastern point of Cyrenaica (the spot where in reality Ras el Mehl is situated), when, as a matter of fact, Cape Lucq is the northern point of that part of the coast and not the north-eastern, and is some twenty-four miles further to the west-north-west than I believed.

These two false premises biased my calculations as to the first part of our wanderings, and made Bir Hakkim appear closer to Sollum than in reality it was. Since those days, I have been able to check the real position of Bir Hakkim with some degree of accuracy, yet I find that my original calculations, based as they were on next to nothing, were surprisingly correct. The direction of Sollum east-north-east northerly was nearly right, and the distance which I estimated at eighty miles, though in reality it is a hundred and fifteen miles, was only ten miles wrong when taking the believed position of Cape Lucq as a departure point.

This old map with which I made my attempted escape is still in my possession; or rather, the greater part of it still is so.

My one great fear was that I should get into territory north and west of Sollum, which I suspected to be swarming with Senoussi; but in this matter I had one sheet anchor to help me in avoiding it. I *knew* that a road ran somewhere to the westward from Sollum, and that, if I struck this road, I should at once know that I was too far to the north, and should therefore keep a little further to the south on my easterly course. My main object was to strike the sea somewhere east of Sollum, and once I had crossed the Egyptian frontier, which runs south from Sollum, I hoped I should be safe. With this idea in mind, I determined not to strike north for the sea until I believed I was well to the eastward of Sollum. If I overran Sollum it would not matter much, as I hoped I might then encounter somebody, once I had reached the coast, and I believed that I should then be in friendly territory across the Egyptian frontier. But if, on the contrary, after turning north, I struck the road running west from Sollum, I should know then that I had not yet gone far enough east, and should continue on the south side of this road, which I knew eventually must lead me to the coast in the vicinity of Sollum.

To my companions in the officers' tent, when I first broached this project the evening before starting, it at first appeared madness, and they tried their best to dissuade me. To wander for five or six days in a waterless desert without a map looked like sheer insanity, in which I must inevitably perish. But presently the logic of my arguments began to tell with them, and they saw with my eyes, and began to hope, like myself, that such an escape really was feasible. What they doubted most was my own powers of endurance, but of these I never had the least qualms. Thanks to the best of mothers, and a life free from excess, I was, at the age of forty-one, in the prime of manhood. Bad and insufficient rice, with snails, may not appear to be an ideal diet to train on, and I certainly had not much reserve of energy; but it was probably much better for athletics than the life of the average town-dwelling European, with his tobacco, alcohol, vitiated atmosphere, late hours and fancy dishes. I was lean and muscular, accustomed to the climate, exposure and want, and above all, I was filled with hope and enthusiasm, that which no season ticket is a better passport for touring the surface of our globe. I had calculated the distance at eighty miles, or four days' march, averaging a minimum of twenty miles a day which I felt positive I could accomplish. And, supposing the distance were a hundred or even a hundred and twenty miles, I still felt confident that I could manage it. For I was now as inured to hardship as the Arabs themselves; I could go for a couple of days without water if necessary, and even without roots or snails as auxiliaries, I hoped I could endure four days without food. Latterly, we had discovered several edible roots, and they were of assistance in staving off the more acute pangs of hunger.

Matters then stood thus. I had saved two days' full rations of my own rice, and as Sunday, February 20th (the day on which I had determined to make my attempt), was the day on which rations were issued, I was able to draw an advance of two days more. I also spoke privately to Mr. Morris (the Chief Steward, who did the issuing), and obtained from him another ration from the general stock. The officers also gave me a ration, so that I had in all six days' rice rations. Unfortunately, when boiled, this was food of a terribly heavy nature to carry, for rice absorbs exactly twice its own weight of water, and the combined mass resulting weighed anything from twelve to fourteen pounds.

Two or three days anterior to the Sunday, I had it given out that I was seriously ill, knowing that those sick were occasionally allowed a little flour by way of medical comfort. The ruse was successful, and, by keeping out of sight, I obtained nearly a pound of barley-flour, which Basil quickly made into biscuits for me. My assumed sickness was also likely to keep any Arab from visiting our tent, and my absence would in all probability not be noticed for some days after I had left. "Holy Joe", the well-man, had also gone off on a journey for a few days, and, as he was by far the most observant of our gaolers, his absence gave a much greater freedom to my preparations, of which most of the officers, and none of the men, knew anything until the day itself.

Thus I had six or seven days' full food supply, including half a pound of cooked goat with which the officers' mess presented me, and also some fragments of biscuits, about a pound of dates, and a little sugar which Basil had somehow acquired in his visits as interpreter to the block-house. This food I did up into six portions in my spare pair of Arab cotton drawers, tying a string between each, and hung them over my shoulders, like two rows of sausages. Rice was in the two top cannon-balls, and the biscuit (which would keep) in the lower ones. I suppose this food weighed, with the dates and sugar, which I kept in a bag round my waist, some sixteen pounds. It was a very awkward kind of pack, but the best which, with the means at our disposal, we could contrive.

The other difficulty was water. I had to carry with me enough for six days. I have by me as I write the actual calculations which I made at that time, and I find I carried thirty-six of my little tomato-tins full with me. These tins run slightly under four tins to the pint, so I had something under nine pints, probably exactly a gallon. In the whole camp we could not find a single water-tight goat-skin bag. The new goat-skins, which had been prepared at Bir Hakkim, had, I fancy, been sent off for the use of the troops; at any rate, there were none to be seen anywhere. However, we selected the best small skin available, and into it I carefully measured my gallon of water which I proposed to carry on my back, Basil skilfully fitting loops to go over my shoulders, so that it was held something after the manner of a grip-sack. As the water skins were always wet on the outside, it was impossible to tell whether this skin was really leaking badly, as we did not finish fitting it until the last moment, it being always in use. But, in any case, it was the least porous skin available, and, as such, I had to use it and hope for the best.

I now had some sixteen pounds weight of food and ten pounds weight of water, and I carried in addition to these various odds and ends. An Arab horse-shoe for luck and also to use as a frying-pan for snails, my diary and pencil, a list of officers and men, half-a-dozen treasured matches and a stump of candle for night signalling, in case I should get in sight of friends near the sea, my pipe and tobacco pouch, in which latter I kept my bone needles and some thread, tomato-tin drinking cup, my spare worn-out pair of shoes, a few letters and the map I had prepared. I also carried Tarrick Bey's letter for use in case of re-capture, to prove that he had received my notice of withdrawal of parole, for I did not fancy being shot off-hand for such a disgraceful offence.

Altogether, I felt very well equipped for a ten days' journey if need be. I went through matters carefully with Apcar before leaving. He had the advantage of much clearer reasoning powers than most of the others, and never allowed his judgment to be warped by optimism; but even he had come so far round to my view, that he agreed the chances were at least even that I should not be at once shot, in the event of my falling into Senoussi hands. Of this latter contingency I had little fear, for the Indians had assured us that they had met no one on the whole journey; the real danger, it seemed to me, was death from thirst and exhaustion, had I miscalculated the distance and direction of Sollum.

The day before I left, Owen Roberts, one of the men, passed away from the accumulated effects of starvation, dysentery, and consumption, and we added a fourth cairn to the other three already there on the desolate wind-swept plain to the south of the camp. Poor fellow, his limbs were but pipe-stems when we buried him; there seemed not an ounce of flesh left on his body, in spite of the tenderest care from his companions. I had often been touched on visiting his tent to see how these starving men had set aside for him practically the whole of their combined day's meat ration.

The day before he died, we were given a small date ration, in addition to the bad rice. The sweetness of the dates, half caterpillar and dirt though they were, was a very great joy to us all, and the sick in particular were immensely benefited by them; but they came too late to help poor Roberts.

His death was the final link, if any further had been needed, to complete the chain of events that impelled me to act. If by any deed of mine I could hope to bring help, then I would endeavour to do it.

* * * * *

As before stated, Sunday, February 20th, was the day I had decided upon to make my bid for liberty. There were many reasons for going at that moment. I would not defer the matter longer, for I felt that my strength was diminishing every day; it was now or never, while the nights were long and the weather still remained cool. In the heat of summer, and with lengthening days, to have attempted it would have been sheer insanity, even if my strength held out until then. Hitherto I had been quite free from dysentery, but I could not be sure that this immunity would always continue, though I felt very fit.

Of my ability to keep in one direction in a straight line all the time I had no doubt. Every evening, when the stars were visible, we had spent hours in studying them, and I knew to a nicety at what points of the compass the principal constellations rose and set, and also the times at which they did so. It was obvious that I must travel by night, for the Bedouin of the desert had the keenest eyesight, and an ability for observation which puts to shame our telescopes and binoculars. To move in the daytime would be merely to invite capture; at night I should be more on an equality with my Senoussi neighbours. Let not the reader imagine, however, that the nights of the Red Desert in February are cloudless, scintillating with stars. The contrary is the case, and more often than not the stars are veiled by clouds. Having no compass, I had to depend on some other means than the stars for telling my direction. There was one other – the moon.

It was upon the moon only that I finally depended, and on Sunday, February 20th, 1916, the moon was at, or near her full. However cloudy it might be, unless it was very bad indeed, I might hope to catch glimpses of the moon shining through the clouds during the greater part of the night, and thus shape my course. Her light, in addition, would make the painful journey over that sea of stones somewhat easier, and it would not materially increase the danger of detection.

Everything seemed to be propitious for a journey. A number of our guards had left a week earlier and there now appeared to be very few but old men and boys left to look after us. We were rarely mustered, and an Arab's arithmetic is so weak, that if half a dozen of the men had been gone, they would probably have been unable to detect the fact. Of course, owing to my rank, I was a more conspicuous figure, and my absence would ordinarily soon have been noticed; but the pretence of my sickness would probably now defer this discovery for some days.

On that Sunday morning we were again encouraged to send letters by a mail ostensibly leaving for Sollum; for all we knew to the contrary none of our letters had ever reached England, and we had never had a reply to any of them; but I took this opportunity to send along my last will and testament before escaping. We were practically unguarded, the Arabs evidently regarding an escape as impossible; we had been marched to Bir Hakkim two hundred miles round three sides of a square, and trigonometry being to the Bedouin mind an unknown science, it never occurred to them that anyone would be able to find their way along the fourth side of the sqaure.

Having seen the caravan with our mails out of sight, and got Basil to report the exact direction it took, I spent the rest of this, my last day, in resting. Up till the last I was in doubt about one thing – should I steal the Commandant's horse? The old white horse which had come with us all the way was nearly always somewhere about – hobbled, poor beast – and eking out a precarious livelihood on shrubs. If I could catch him, he would undoubtedly give me a good lift on my way during the first night. But the danger was too great. We could not catch him until after dark, and even then there would be great risk of his hoof-beats being heard. Moreover, his track would be clearly visible, and, when I abandoned him at dawn, he would be a beacon to all the world to point out the way I had gone; a horse in the level desert is more visible than St. Paul's Cathedral! In the end, therefore, I decided to trust to my own legs, and hoped that even if I were pursued, they would think I had made for the Italian port of Tobruk, a place one-half the distance away that Sollum was, but one of whose location I had only the vaguest notion.

I was now very lean and sunburnt, with a brown and ragged beard. With my Arab clothes I could well hope to pass for an Arab myself, except on very close inspection. I would travel by night as far as possible, and if I found it necessary to travel by day, on sighting anyone, I would very slightly alter my direction to avoid the other. If, inspite of this, the stranger should close with me, I would pretend madness, religious devotion, or to be a dumb mendicant, whichever pose best seemed to suit my purpose at the time. By these means I hoped to avoid interrogation, and, if all failed, as a last resource, I should have resort to bribery. The Arabic sentences I had so carefully written down at Basil's dictation, explained that, though I had no money, I was specially under the protection of the Grand Senoussi and the Turkish General, and that, on my safe arrival at Sollum, my guide would be rewarded with a bag of gold.

I could think of no other contingency, and it was with a light heart that I stole out an hour after sundown on the Sunday evening, bearing with me the hopes and blessings of all such of my fellow-prisoners as were aware of my venture. I was much touched at the heartiness of the hand-grips as I left the officers' tent. Do not imagine we were all always friends, for we were constantly quarrelling; there was much jealousy, bickering and malice among us. But at that moment all our past feelings were wiped out, and I do not think they ever returned. All and every were with me at that moment, half regretting for their part that they were not accompanying me. Personally, I was very glad to be alone in the journey. A companion is a help, a moral support when one is cornered; but with two people there are always two opinions, and on such a matter of life and death I cared to defer to no one. With another with me we should have been like two greyhounds in leash, hindering, and not helping each other. When one was tired the other would wish to press on. When one wished to go straight the other would seek to turn aside. Besides the chances of two people being seen would be much greater than was the case with one, who could easily and quietly take cover.

Before going, I had arranged that, if I got safely through, I should get the ships at Sollum to turn their searchlights on to the clouds; we hoped that this would be visible, even at a distance of eighty miles. I had myself seen the glare of searchlights at sea, when more than two hundred miles distant from the port of Queenstown in Ireland.

Thus, with a stout staff in my hand, I stole out into the darkness. The camp fires were heaped high, the flames shot up, and the glare dazzled the sleepy and unsuspicious guard. In some twenty minutes I had lost sight of the last gleam from Bir Hakkim, as I rounded the slight rise to the east-north-east. The sentry had no ghost of a notion that I had gone, and I was stumbling cheerfully over the pitiless stones in the darkness.

All had indeed gone well.

*　　*　　*　　*　　*

My first feeling of exhilaration at so easily getting away undetected soon began to wear off, and it was not long before I became conscious of the ropes from my water-skin bag, which were cutting into my shoulders. I had padded myself against this contingency so far as possible, but even rags at Bir Hakkim were too scarce a commodity for me to have been able to borrow any from others, and my very leanness made the ropes bite into me all the harder. My back also was rapidly soaked through by the wet water-skin, and I greatly feared that my precious water-supply was leaking away, but of this I could not as yet be certain. However, the stones were so terrible in the dark that I soon forgot every other trouble and the pain of the ropes; all my energy and attention were required to prevent stumbling and falling.

Besides my Arab costume I wore also my naval uniform, not only for warmth, but also in anticipation that it might be of use to me as a protection if I were recaptured. At night I wore the dark uniform outside, but by day it was my white Arab shirt that I donned like a smock externally. They both were in the nature of protective colouring, smeared as they were by the soil of the desert. I had also, in addition, about ten feet in length of my fourteen-foot Arab burnous; four feet of it I had cut off, and left behind for lightness, at Bir Hakkim, before starting.

In less than an hour's time the sky began to lighten, and the full moon presently rising walking became very much better. I could avoid most of the stones, but the dim light was full of alarms. I am slightly deaf, and so had to trust more than ever to my eyesight, which, fortunately, is of the best; but at all times in the desert objects have a terrible monotony of appearance as well as of colour, and distances are always deceptive. At the unexpected appearance of any dark object I had to throw myself full length on the ground, and look at it against the sky-line, to observe whether it moved or not. After a time, feeling reassured, I would again rise and continue my march.

That such precautions were more than justified I soon had ample proof. It was about 4 a.m., and I suppose by that time the edge was getting worn off my vigilance. The moon was already low and behind me, so that I must have been sharply silhouetted against the western sky-line, whereas objects ahead of me were dim and misty-looking. Without the least warning I suddenly found I had tumbled right into a caravan of eighty of ninety camels, their ghostly shapes stealing silently down upon me both from ahead and on either side. It was too late then to avoid them, but I instantly did the next best thing, by throwing myself flat on my face, and drawing my sand-coloured burnous right over me. I suppose that by now my personal odour was similar to that of an Arab, for the animals went trailing solemnly by, without taking alarm or any notice of me. The camelman himself (I only saw one) followed chanting in high pitched nasal tones, and he passed within a few feet of me, but failed to observe me, although I was lying quite unconcealed in the open. Probably his thoughts were turned inwards, and were concerned mostly with his bad luck at being on night duty; if he saw me at all he probably thought I was some dead bush or sand heap; but, while he was passing, I was wondering all the time whether, if one of the camels trod on me, I should be able to avoid moving or crying out. It was all over in a quarter of an hour, and the last of the slow-moving grazing animals had gone past and faded once more into the silver grey of the sky-line; but by then the moon had become so totally obscured by clouds that I could no longer determine my direction, and had perforce to waste yet another hour until the sky had once more cleared.

I had taken rests of a few minutes at 9 p.m. and midnight, during which I had eaten a few dates, and licked the dripping hairs on the outside of my water-skin; but I think I was all the better for this extra compulsory wait of an hour, for it gave me time to survey damages. The shoes that Apcar had lent me proved to be a little too small, and I found when I took them off that, as I had for some time suspected, both my big toe nails had worked loose at the roots. To prevent them being turned right over backwards, I tied pieces of rag around both toe and nail; but this, though better than nothing, proved to be a very painful remedy, for the rag strips quickly cut into the flesh of my toe, so that both my feet were continually bleeding. I had, in addition, some pretty bad blisters on my heel, owing to not having worn foot-gear for nearly two months.

The rice also, which I had started out with, slung from my shoulders in front, I found hampered my movements a great deal, by banging to and fro against my body at every stride. I therefore, alternately carried it in my hand, or hung it from my staff over my shoulder; an irksome and awkward arrangement, but a very much better one than my original method. My shoulders also gradually became accustomed to the cutting ropes of the water-skin, which at first I had found so painful.

As I journeyed, I found that the country was by no means so flat as the Indians had represented it to be; but then, they had probably gone by a different route to myself. It was about 1 a.m., I think, that I passed over a low range of boulder-strewn hills, from whose summit I gazed down on to the wet, shimmering desert, which in the moonlight had the appearance of the sea. But I could find no pool of water in spite of the recent heavy rain, though there had obviously been puddles quite recently, and in places my feet sank deep into mud, leaving behind an unmistakable track, which caused me to take the precaution of keeping so far as possible, to harder, stonier ground.

But what amazed me and disquieted me most was the fact that there were numbers of other tracks, well-defined paths through the desert, which to judge by the fresh appearance of the camel droppings, had apparently quite recently been used; most of these tracks ran south-east and north-west diagonally across my own easterly course. The Indians had been most positive in their assertion that they had encountered no one on their way from Sollum; how then was I to account for this phenomenon, which seemed to betoken a much frequented neighbourhood?

Towards morning I began to feel very done with the heavy weight I was carrying, and the awful stones stubbing my mutilated toes; but the camel caravan incident helped to freshen me up considerably, and I managed to keep going at a steady pace.

At dawn I found myself in an absolutely flat and coverless plain, with nothing of any sort in sight, whereat I stumbled on yet another couple of miles, until I got to a place where there were shrubs some three or four feet high growing. There I set me down to make my calculations, and write up my log on the back of my map. I found I had done very well. It was as follows :—

Sun., 6.30 p.m. to Mon., 6.30 a.m.   = 12 hours.
Stopped to hide from caravan, 4 a.m. = 1 hour.
Stopped by clouds to rest   ..   .. = 1 hour.
Total, to 6.30 a.m., at 2½ miles per hr. = 10 hours = 25 miles.
Drank 4 tins of water; ate 1 day's rations

I spent all that day, Monday, hiding among the low shrubs; a very anxious day it was, and sleep a luxury quite out of the question, for, as soon as it was fully light, a number of large caravans passed quite close to me, with much noise and shouting of camelmen, and isolated groups of pedestrians often came within easy speaking distance; one group, a man on a horse and two women, I could easily have lobbed a biscuit on to, as they passed my frail cover. Luckily for me, they were busily engaged in heated argument, and therefore were not very observant, for the average Arab eyesight would certainly unerringly have detected me lying in hiding, the bush being too small to shut me out completely. I spent the whole day dodging round this bush, the largest of its kind, and dragging my water-skin and belongings after me, in my efforts to keep out of sight. By good fortune no two parties ever passed my bush from opposite sides at the same time, or I should inevitably have been seen by one or the other of them.

But my chief anxiety now was my water supply. There could no longer be any question that the skin was leaking terribly – there was no visible hole in it, it was simply a question of its age and general porosity; drip, drip, drip it went, and the precious fluid was lost in the sand. As I watched, I could see its bulk grow steadily less, already half of my whole stock appeared to have thus been lost. I put my mouth to it and kept licking the hairy outside, but this was really very little of an economy, for, what with loose hairs and congealed dust, I got more dirt than liquid into my mouth. Later on in the afternoon the stream of passers-by began to diminish, until at length there was no one in sight. All this time I had not dared to sleep, but nevertheless I felt much rested and refreshed; so an hour and a half before sunset, after a good look round, I got on the move again, wearing my Arab clothes over all. It was fortunate for me that I had done so, for I had gone but a short distance when, coming to the edge of an invisible shallow wadi or valley, I found myself unexpectedly in the immediate vicinity of eight Arab tents stretched in a row along its course, and about which there were several people moving. It was too late then to turn back, as they must already have observed me; I therefore had to trust to my disguise, and, by making a gradual detour, without going any closer to the tents, I gradually circled round them until I could once more proceed directly on my easterly course. Somebody at the tents actually waved to me, and shouted a something which I did not understand, probably a salutation. To him I replied by also waving and shouting in a similar manner; but it was with a very thankful heart that I at last lost sight of this camp astern of me. It must have been from thence that the caravans I had seen had taken their departure in the morning.

But where was the uninhabited country of which the Indians had spoken? This, which I was in, certainly could not have been it, and now I felt sure that they must have come by an entirely different route. But the solitude of the route was a matter of vital moment in all the calculations which I had made for a successful escape, and I already saw that my chances of getting through were greatly diminished.

There was rather a strong mirage before sunset on that afternoon, and I had several more scares before darkness finally set in, caused by my sighting some heaps of stones, the graves of long departed Bedouins, and a ruined building or two, which I took for another village. Distance in the desert where everything is much the same shape and the same khaki colour, is extremely difficult to judge, and consequently one is often unable even to guess the size of an object when first seen. A large saddle-shaped well-mound, an Arab tent, a humped camel, a grave cairn, a rock, a bush, a jerboa-mound, all look alike to the European eye. For a time, it is impossible to feel certain whether the object looked at is a well-mound forty feet high five miles off, a tent ten feet high one mile off, or a jerboa-mound showing just above a slight rise only a hundred yards distant; for there is nothing to compare them with, and they are identical in shape and colour, moreover, the mirage and the shimmer of the atmosphere cause the distant object often to show up more clearly and distinctly than the near-by one.

With nightfall, my troubles again began; fortunately the stones were not quite so bad as on the preceding night in the immediate vicinity of Bir Hakkim, and there were in addition more bushes, which generally indicate firm, level going; but, with my feet in the condition they were in, and nearly all my toe-nails now secured in place with rag and pieces of thread, any walking at all was an exquisite agony.

There were, however, many fires visible after dark, and the necessity for avoiding these helped to divert my thoughts from the mere physical pain; the sight of them was most disquieting, and I appeared to be in about as an uninhabited a neighbourhood as Hyde Park. Every now and then a dog barked at me, but fortunately Arabs are not, if they can help it, night walkers, and I encountered no one. I continued to tramp steadily along at about two and a half miles an hour until midnight, when I took a short rest.

From then on I continued with very short rests and occasional licks at my water-skin, at a gradually diminishing pace. There came a time when I could no longer lift my feet over the bushes and stones, my thighs got cramp from exhaustion and no longer responded to the impetus of my mind. I stumbled and fell ever now and then, and for a few seconds would be unable to rise. But I went on, somehow, until the first pink dawn showed in the eastern sky. It was the release I had been waiting for, and I literally fell in a heap into the nearest bush, unable further to move hand or foot.

Some beast of prey was coughing and snarling near at hand, love-making in the manner of the *felidæ*. I did not see him, for he was in a clump of bushes a hundred yards or so away; but I think he was a leopard by the volume and catlike quality of the sound. It may have been only some large wild cat, but Colonel Snow had told me that leopards occasionally, though rarely, visited the vicinity of Sollum. However that may be, I took no notice of the animal, nor he, for that matter, of me; we had both got better occupations. And presently, recovering somewhat I, ate some of the rice and wrote up my log. My entry is as follows :—

Started 4 p.m. and walked until 6 a.m., east by north, 2.3 miles per hour, with 2½ hours' rest. Drank 5 tins of water.

Total at sunrise on Tuesday. = 11½ hrs. at 2.3 m.p.h. = 26½ miles.

This appeared to be a good neighbourhood for hiding in, for it was uneven and covered with shrubs, some of the bushes being as much as five feet in height. Dragging myself to my feet, I hung my water-skin in the nearest bush, and put my drinking cup under it. The skin was now three-quarters empty, but not leaking quite so fast as before, and I hoped by this means to save some of the precious drops.

Then, in the dim twilight of the early dawn, I lay down once more, in the joyful consciousness that in two nights I had accomplished more than half my journey. I had come fifty-one and a half miles, at a conservative estimate, out of the calculated eighty miles. I at once fell into the dreamless sleep of utter exhaustion.

*   *   *   *   *

It must have been about an hour later that I awoke suddenly, conscious that something was happening; possibly it was a human voice that was borne to my ears. The sun was well up, and everything bathed in dazzling sunshine. Cautiously raising myself on my elbows, I gazed at my surroundings, the which the dim light of dawn had prevented my properly seeing before I went to sleep.

My heart gave a rebound and seemed to stand still. On every side of me were men and droves of camels moving in various directions; quite close at hand was a collection of twenty or more tents, with herds of sheep and goats, and I could see other similar groups in the distance. I was literally trapped, and had lain down almost in an Arab village; and, as I watched, I saw the children come out to play. Possibly I might even now elude the herdsmen, but sharp-sighted children, invading every quiet spot to play at hide-and-seek, I could hardly hope to escape.

But fortune had favoured me so much hitherto that I did not even then despair; lying as flat as possible on the ground, from behind my leafy screen I watched anxiously the course of events. I had not long to wait. A group of men with guns was passing by, when one of them suddenly stopped and looked intently in my direction; he then shouted to his companions and pointed towards where I was hiding. Feeling quite sure that he could not possibly see me, I looked anxiously round to discover a cause for this action on his part. I was soon enlightened, for there, plain for all the world to see, was my fatal water-skin hanging from the bush above my head and still drip–drip–dripping its precious drops away. I knew then, that I had thus unwittingly made a signal which would seal my own fate. It was only the dull stupor of utter exhaustion which could have made me do so foolish a thing, or have caused me to lie down so near a village; but now it was too late to remedy it.

The men – there were three of them – began to run in my direction. Covering myself all over with my burnous, I lay at full length, pretending to be asleep, having at the time some faint hope that they would hesitate to arouse an individual of whose identity they knew nothing, and who

appeared to be an Arab even as themselves. But an Arab has little sympathy
with anyone who is found asleep after daybreak. I felt sharp fingers clutch
into my shoulder and drag at me. I snorted and turned over again, as
though wishing to continue my sleep. It was useless, and I felt myself
dragged roughly to my feet.

I opened my eyes. At once there were loud ejaculations of astonishment;
for I have blue eyes, and blue eyes are not seen among the Arabs. On the
contrary, they are an object of derision and hatred, the sign of the accursed
foreigner!

The three men, as I now observed, were of the most villainous and cut-
throat type, quite the worst I had yet seen. Having got over their first
astonishment, and examined me and the water-skin, they started to shout
questions excitedly at me. As I was unable to understand them, they
shouted yet the louder, emphasizing the importance of an answer with
pokes of their rifle muzzles. As I was still unable to answer them, they then
settled the matter for themselves, by rapidly going over my person with
deft fingers to see if I had any belongings of value, and they were evidently
much astonished at the discovery of my tattered old naval uniform
under my outer Arab garments. I seized this opportunity to impress them
with my great personal importance, pointing out my tarnished gold lace
and the shreds of medal ribbon still remaining. I also got out my "book
of the words" and started to recite to them my prepared sentences of
Arabic, dwelling lingeringly upon my present poverty, but emphasizing
the immense quantity of gold which would accrue to the happy individual
who conducted me in safety to Sollum. But my captors were much too
excited to take heed at the time of what I was telling them, and I soon
found myself stripped stark naked, for the better examination of my
property; they then noticed that I was neither Mahomedan or Jew, and I
began to see my death warrant written in their avaricious eyes, as they
lovingly fingered their rifle triggers and looked meaningly at me.

It was at that moment that a diversion fortunately occurred. In so
populous a neighbourhood, such an incident as my capture could not go
unnoticed, and other groups were quickly making their way to the scene.
Before my first captors could proceed any further, some twenty or thirty
other Senoussi had come up, with the evident intention of participating in
the spoils. I and my belongings were pulled this way and that, and I was
seized by a new group who drove off my former owners, intimating to
me at the same time by a sign that the former would undoubtedly cut
my throat, a matter of which I had by then not the faintest doubt. But
my new captors were themselves little better; they also maltreated and
jeered at me, and the whole routine of apprizing and valuing my belong-

ings on their part, and of Arabic sentences and promises of future reward on mine, was gone through once more. For the moment I averted death; my Arabic speeches were gradually understood, and, perhaps, had some effect, and everything of mine which the natives touched, I roundly asserted was the special gift of the Grand Senoussi to me, or, failing him, of Nouri Bey. But I was by no means out of the wood yet. Hardly able to walk from exhaustion, but with a very sharp eye on my personal belongings, I was driven forward towards the tents, while every now and then, one of the Arabs in advance turned round and fired a shot at a few feet range in my direction. These shots were probably not intended really to hit me, but were meant to startle, and, if possible, to scare me; I fancy it was their idea of humour, a similar one to that used by the cow-punchers of the Wild West, when desirous of making a tenderfoot dance. If this were its purpose, it most signally failed, for by this time I was reckless with exhaustion, and openly jeered at this intimidating process. I felt, in fact, that it was time to assert myself and my importance once more. Among my most valued possessions there was a steel needle, a special gift from Selim to myself. One of the brigands, happening on this at the moment, at once annexed it. Instead of meekly submitting, as he evidently expected I should do, I at once seized him and shook him, and forced him to give it back. This done, I explained in pantomime to him that it was my own property. Having made him understand this, I then took the needle, and, with a great show of ceremony, solemnly presented it to him. So strange a thing is human nature that this cut-throat whom, only a moment before, was, I have no doubt, not only willing but eager to shed my blood, now felt a sense of shame. At first he would not even accept the gift; but, when I forced it on him, he reluctantly accepted it. It was a good move on my part; the rifle firing ceased, and my new friend, whom I took care to keep close at my side, kept me from a good bit of unpleasantness.

For the remainder of the morning I was dragged round and exhibited at the various tents, much as dancing bears used to be in England, and my uniform, and the tattoos with which my arms are covered were displayed with much pride. I smiled and endeavoured to ingratiate myself with the inhabitants, but my first smile was almost my undoing – for I have a gold tooth! The sight of so much wealth (for to these incredibly poor people, a gold tooth meant real riches) at once excited their cupidity, and they appear to consider that the removal of my head was the simplest method of obtaining the treasure. Seeing how the wind blew, I thereupon hastened to assure them that the object of their avarice was *not* gold, and I intimated that it was in reality brass or some such base metal; they believed me, for they could not credit that any human being would employ gold so extravagantly, but the display of my tooth was added to my other assets for "showing-off" purposes from that moment on.

It was now late afternoon, and I kept dropping from exhaustion and heat, when, approaching a new group of tents, there emerged from them two individuals arrayed in tattered khaki uniforms, who had evidently been aroused by the shouting from slumber. They were armed with somewhat ancient Martini carbines which they held in readiness, and at sight of which the Senoussi began to slink away. I soon tumbled to it that these were two Turkish soldiers billeted in the village. They themselves were evidently puzzled by my appearance, and at the facts which the Senoussi vociferously gabbled to them of my strange discovery. However, they at once annexed me as their own property, intimating to me by the usual gesture that my late companions intended to cut my throat. They then, like the others, proceeded to go once more dexterously over my person, with all the experience of old campaigners; but from this they soon desisted, realizing that what such pastmasters of the art of pilfering as the Senoussi had left untouched, was unlikely to have a value which amounted to anything.

My new Turkish friends then proceeded to interrogate me, an ordeal which, owing to mutual lack of knowledge of each other's language, consisted mainly of pantomime, I, however, worked off all my prepared Arabic sentences, to which they appeared to listen sympathetically. Perhaps, if Sollum had in reality been then in the possession of the British, as I believed, they might even, on the promise of unlimited gold, have taken me thither.

But, as it was, I got off very well in the end. The uncertainty as to my identity, and my own assurance in continually quoting the Grand Senoussi and Nouri Pasha as my friends and patrons, prevented anything of real value to me being taken. Even my diary was treated with the greatest respect and returned to me; for the Moslem mind appears to reverence written characters in any form, more especially when it cannot understand them.

In those days I had not witnessed that dramatic British work of art, "The Bing Boys"; if I had done so, I should certainly have recognized in my two Turkish captors beings eminently fitted to fill the title *rôle* of that play. They were both Cretans, I believe, one being called Ali Hassan, and the other Mahmoud. Of the two, Ali Hassan was short, thick-set, as broad as he was long, essentially vulgar, and of a dark and negroid type of countenance. The other, Mahmoud, was slim and good-looking, with regular features, of a more refined nature and able to read and write

Turkish with facility. Never did two men work better together, each supplying the qualities that the other lacked, their talents being complementary and not opposite. They played up to each other like the two comic villains of a pantomime, and they had become to each other so indispensable as to be inseparable. If it were a matter of robbery, intimidation or threat, then the bad old campaigner, Ali Hassan, with his bull neck, threatening brow, and ready rifle, was the chief actor; but when it was a question of gentle diplomacy, of trickery, or of sex dalliance, the "pretty boy", Mahmoud, became the central figure, and the burly Ali Hassan kept his ugly bulk out of sight. As I was destined to spend a whole week in the company of these two gentlemen, I had much opportunity for studying their merits. We three became very fast friends, and I was indeed sorry when we had to part. But I am anticipating.

My pantomime interrogation having finished, and my uniform ribbons, tattoos and belongings having been duly studied, Hassan looked at me and said the one word "Leglise". Having repeated it several times, I gathered that he meant that I was English, and to this statement I assented. They then both whistled loudly and flapped their arms after the manner of a bird in flight. There was no mistaking the pantomime this time; they were obviously gently suggesting that I was an escapee. To this I again gave my assent and mentioned the word Bir Hakkim, whereat Ali Hassan, with his forefinger drew down the lower eyelid of his right eye, exposing the red eyeball. This is the Eastern method of winking, or showing incredulity, and I responded by myself making a grimace. To my surprise, they both roared with laughter, and I was made to repeat the gesture, which was evidently new to them. Seeing their unfailing delight at its repetition, I then assumed several other facial expressions – hauteur, disdain, withering contempt, superciliousness, vanity, and the like. I was a made man! Never was "Charlie Chaplin" half so appreciated as I in that Bedouin camp of the Red Desert. My fame at once spread through the village, and I was once more taken from tent to tent, my uniform and tattoos now becoming only a side show; but as a facial contortionist, I at once rose to fame as the Star Turn of the Libyan Desert. No more did I squat humbly in the dust. I was given the seat of honour, and, having duly performed in turn to each delighted family gathering, I was liberally rewarded with handfuls of dates and bowls of milk. Even then, I could not help smiling to myself at the thought of how those grave and stately gentlemen who adorn the Admiralty at Whitehall, would regard this novel method of earning a living, especially by one in their employ, and who held, moreover, the exalted rank of Captain in His Majesty's Navy! But so it was, and I have many a time done far harder and less pleasant work for smaller reward. With all my other accomplishments, however, my gold tooth still continued to be an asset of value; thus are misfortunes often in themselves a benefit! Civilized dental treatment was in itself a marvel in that land of perfect teeth. I remember once, at Bir Hakkim, the amusement we prisoners all derived when Captain Tanner, sitting with some guards round the fire, allowed the upper plate of his false teeth to fall. The guards, seeing the teeth only and not the plate, suspended thus inexplicably without apparent support in the middle of his open mouth, at once fled in terror, as though the devil himself was after them.

That night I slept on the floor of a tent with my two Turkish guardians, each with a hand on my shoulder, his loaded Martini rifle sticking into my side, and a big camel rug over the three of us; for, with all their rough kindliness, they evidently still suspected me of an intention to escape. As though I had not already had enough exertion in the past forty-eight hours! As a matter of fact I was quite incapable of further movement, and could only feebly resent their notions of etiquette as to bed manners. My shoes I was compelled to take off, and my head-rag I was made to wear; against this dictum there was apparently no appeal, although my brow was burning and my feet were icy cold!

CHAPTER TWELVE

Aᴛᴇʀ Gᴡᴀᴛᴋɪɴ-Wɪʟʟɪᴀᴍs's recapture he accompanied the two Turks, a Bedouin and a camel-girl, on an apparently aimless journey across the desert, keeping themselves alive by stealing sheep which they roasted and consumed at one sitting. That the journey was not aimless became obvious when they arrived at a Turkish head-quarters encampment, and Gwatkin-Williams was handed over to Achmed Mansoor, his old commandant from Bir Hakkim. To the captive's surprise he was treated with civility when he had expected to be shot. (It was not until later that he heard of the Turkish defeat at Agadir, where the Commander-in-chief Jaffar Tacha had himself been taken prisoner. Here again the captor was restrained by the knowledge that his enemy held hostages; in fact, the power of Turkey in Libya was on the wane.) A few days later the new commandant of Bir Hakkim came to the head-quarters to report the escape of his senior prisoner, and was overjoyed to see him already recaptured.

Gwatkin-Williams was escorted back to the prison camp to find that not only were the prisoners starving but the guards as well. For some time they existed on snails, and herbs which they found growing in the desert. At last, when all the snails and herbs for miles around had been eaten, the prisoners revolted and told their guards that unless they were marched at once to some district where they could obtain food they would take matters into their own hands. This was the position when, on March 17th, 1916, the prisoners of the Red Desert were rescued by the Duke of Westminster and his armoured cars.

*   *   *   *   *

The prison camp of Yozgad in Turkey is well known to the reader of escape stories. It housed, among other well-known escapers, E. H. Jones[1] and H. G. Stoker[2]; and it was from this camp that a party of eight British officers set out on their four hundred and fifty miles march to freedom. The escape from the camp itself was not unduly difficult — the problem

[1] *The Road to En-Dor.*   [2] *Straws in the Wind.*

229

facing the escapers was how to cover those hundreds of miles which lay between Yozgad and "Rendezvous X" on the Mediterranean coast, where the leader of the party, a naval officer named A. A. Cochrane, had arranged with the War Office for a friendly boat to lie in wait. (A similar plan was also carried out by two German prisoners in England, who escaped from their camp, reached the rendezvous on the Welsh coast and flashed the signal light as arranged; but they could not be seen by the waiting U-boat because of an intervening rock, and they were recaptured.)

The journey of four hundred and fifty miles on foot across brigand-infested, difficult country, with little food and water, is an example of endurance and comradeship that is hard to beat. Cochrane and the seven others in the party – M. A. B. Johnston and K. D. Yearsley, who tell the story and are "Johnny" and "Looney" in the book; A. B. Haig, "Old Man"; R. A. P. Grant, "Grunt"; V. S. Clarke, "Nobby"; J. H. Harris, "Perce"; and F. R. Ellis – marched for twenty-three days and twenty-four nights before they reached the coast. The rendezvous time for the friendly ship was long since past, and the party planned to steal a boat and make their way to Cyprus. They found the coast patrolled by Turkish soldiers; and so, exhausted as they were, they made camp in a ravine which ran down to the sea, and settled down to recuperate and to await their chance to steal a boat. In a nearby deserted village they found a well, and in a barn about three hundred pounds of threshed but unmilled wheat. Luckily they also found an old coffee-grinder with which to mill the grain.

M. A. B. Johnston and K. D. Yearsley

FROM NOW onwards, for the rest of our stay on the coast, we settled down to a new kind of existence – in fact we may be said to have *existed*, and nothing more. Life became a dreary grind, both literally and metaphorically. For the next few days, at any rate, we thought of nothing else but how to prepare and eat as much food as we could. This was not greed: it was the only thing to do. None of us wanted to lie a day longer than absolutely necessary in that awful ravine, but we were at present simply too weak to help ourselves. To carry out a search for another boat was beyond the powers of any one.

Cochrane rigged up the coffee-grinder on the same afternoon as it had arrived – lashing the little brass cylinder to the branch of a tree at a convenient height for a man to turn the handle. A rusty saw, cutting like all Oriental saws on the pull-stroke, had been discovered in the village and brought down by the last party, and this proved useful now and on subsequent occasions.

Whilst one of the party worked at the mill, and another supervised the cooking of the next dixieful of porridge, the rest were busy picking over the grain in the hopes of removing at any rate some small proportion of the empty husks and the bits of earth with which it was mixed. Even so it was impossible to clean the dirt off the grains themselves.

Nothing, we thought, could be more wearisome than this never-ending task. Our misery was aggravated by the swarms of flies which incessantly harassed us as we worked. What right they had to be alive at all on such a deserted coast was never discovered. He whose turn it was to cook found in the smoke from the fire a temporary respite from their attentions; but they took care to make up for lost time afterwards. When the water was nearly boiled away, bits of porridge were wont to leap out of the pot and light on the cook's hands. The ensuing blister did not last long, for within twenty-four hours the flies had eaten it all away. We had no bandages left, and pieces of paper which we used to wet and stick on the blisters fell off as soon as they were dry. It was not many days before Old Man's and Johnny's hands became covered with septic sores. Unfortunately, too, most of us were out of 'baccy, as a means of keeping these pests away. Some took to smoking cigarettes made from the dried leaves which littered the stony bed of our unhappy home. Even the non-smoker of the party had to give way to the pernicious habit once, out of pure self-defence.

Nor at night was it easy to obtain peace. The flies had no sooner gone to their well-earned rest than the mosquitoes took up the call with their high-pitched trumpet notes. But of course it was not the noise which mattered, but their bites; and in the end most of us used to sleep with a handkerchief or piece of cloth over our faces, and a pair of socks over our hands.

Ravine life was most relaxing – partly owing to the stuffiness of the air in so deep and narrow a cleft, overgrown as it was with trees and scrub but perhaps still more to reaction, after more than three weeks of strenuous marching. So long as we had had the encouragement of being able to push on each day, and feel that we were getting nearer home, we had no time to think of bodily exhaustion: the excitement, mild though it was, kept us going. Now, unable to do anything towards making good our escape, it required a big effort to drag oneself to one's feet for the purpose of fetching a mugful of porridge. It required a still bigger one to go up in pairs to fetch water from the well, although it was essential for every one to do this at least once a day, merely to keep the pot a-boiling. This, too, was the only way of obtaining a deep drink; except for half a mug of tea made from several-times stewed leaves, all the water brought down to the *nullah* each day was utilized for cooking the wheat. Fortunately, to take us to the well there was the further inducement of a wash for both bodies and clothes. The latter by this time were in a very dirty and also wornout condition; but thanks doubtless to our having spent no appreciable time inside villages actually occupied by Turks, they were not verminous.

On account of the washing, visits to the well were apt at time to develop into lengthy affairs – anything up to five or six hours, which did not help towards getting through the daily tasks necessary to keep ourselves fed. Not only did this involve having reliefs at the mill for eight out of every twenty-four hours, but much work was necessary to keep up the supply of cleaned wheat to feed the machine. Necessity, however, is the mother of invention, and from the 5th September, acting on a suggestion made by Looney, we used to take the next day's wheat up to the well and wash it there in a couple of changes of water. There was a convenient stone trough on the spot. The chaff floated to the surface, while the earth whether in loose particles or clinging to the grains themselves, was dissolved. After washing, the wheat was spread out in the sun on squares of cloth brought down from the village, and when dry was fetched back to the ravine by the next water party.

Like most schemes, this one had its weak points. It was very extravagant in water, and in a few days our well began to show distinct signs of being drained to emptiness; in fact, only a puddle could have existed to begin with, though a larger one than that in the well near the tower.

The second disadvantage was that the grain, while left out to dry, might be discovered and give away our presence; but, in any case, one pair or another of the party was so often up at the well that the risk was not greatly increased; besides, there was not much to induce a Turk from the camp below to visit the ruins.

In the end we were seen, the first occasion being on the 6th September. That evening, Cochrane, Old Man, and Looney were up at the well, when an old fellow with a dyed beard – a Turk, as far as they could say – suddenly appeared, and eyed their water-bottles very thirstily. He accepted with readiness the drink they offered to him, but appeared to be nothing of a conversationalist. He was indeed almost suspiciously indifferent who the three might be. There was a mystery about that man which we never entirely solved. From then onwards. almost to the end of our stay on the coast, not a day passed without his seeing one or other of the party. To explain *our* presence at the well, the water-parties pretended they were

German observation posts sent up to watch the sea, over which, as a matter of fact, one could obtain a very fine view from that place. We usually carried up the field-glasses to have a look round, and these perhaps helped out our story. To live up further to our Hun disguise, we once told the man that really the place was *yessāk*. This is the Turkish equivalent to *verboten*, and, to judge from our experiences in the camps, is about as frequently used.

On another occasion it was sunset when some of us saw him. After his usual drink he washed his hands and face and said his prayers Mohammedan-wise. After his prayers he said he had seen two boats go past coming from the east and disappearing to the west. Little remarks like this made us think at one time that he might possibly be a British agent, landed to get information, or possibly for the express purpose of helping escaped officers like ourselves: for there had been plenty of time for the news of our escape from Yozgad to reach the Intelligence Department in Cyprus.

One day Grunt and Nobby deliberately went up to try to get into conversation with the mysterious individual. In the end they came to the conclusion that he must be some kind of outlaw. He told them that a friend and he had come from a place far inland to sell something or other to a coastal village, and he himself was now awaiting the other's return. They were going to take back with them a load of carobs, of which he already had been making collections under various trees. The beans seemed to be his only food, and he was obviously half-starving. This, combined with the fact that he relied on us to draw up water for him when there must be good water near the Turkish tents below, showed that he was in hiding for some cause or other. This was as well for us, as, if he had thought at all, he could not for a moment have been deceived by our story. Even if we were on watch, we should hardly trouble to bring up not only our own, but a lot of other men's water-bottles to fill with muddy water at a disused well. Whatever the explanation, the great thing was that he did not interfere with us. Two evenings before our final departure from the ravine, he told us that his donkeys would be coming back next morning, and that was the last time that he was seen.

A few extracts from diaries may serve to convey some idea of our feelings during these earlier days in the ravine:—

"*2nd Sept.* – Struggled up to well at 8 a.m. Had wash in mugful of water: temporarily refreshing, but exhausted for rest of day, and feeling weaker than ever before in spite of five brews of boulgar" (each brew was at this time about the half of a pint mug all round) "and one small chupattie each, made by Nobby. Flour for last made with much hard grinding after mill had been readjusted. Readjustment alone took two hours to do. . . . Flies awful all day. . . ."

"*3rd Sept.* – Locust beans quite good toasted over ashes, and make sweet syrup if first cut up and then boiled, but this entails a lot of work. Everyone cleaning and grinding wheat all day. As now set, grinder produces mixture of coarse flour and boulgar. Tried unsuccessfully to simmer this into a paste and then bake into thick chupatties." (All our efforts at this stage were directed towards producing something digestible with the minimum of work.) "Day passed very slowly, with occasional trips for water."

"*4th Sept.* – Most of us rather doubtful whether we shall be able to get back our strength on a boulgar diet, and flour takes more grinding than we have strength for at present – rather a vicious circle." Another diary for the same date says – "Feeling weaker now than I did when we first arrived; no energy for anything."

Next day the tide seems to have been on the turn.

"*5th Sept.* – Most of us slightly stronger, but held back by chronic lethargy. Continuous brewing all day. To save interruptions at the grinder we now feed in two parties of four, taking alternate brews: this means we get nearly a big mugful at a whack, at intervals of about three hours. . . . Most of us fill in gaps eating burnt beans. Charcoal said to be good for digestion! . . . One thing is, our feet are rested here, and blisters healed. We are also undoubtedly putting on flesh again, and if we can get rid of this hopeless slackness shall be all right. . . . Grunt, working from 1 p.m. onwards, made 1 large and 4 small chupatties each, so we are coming on." It was something to feel full again sometimes.

"*6th Sept.* – My energy as well as my strength returning a bit now. . . . Mill hard at it all day. . . . $4\frac{1}{2}$ mugfuls boulgar (1 pint each) and 6 chupatties ($4\frac{1}{2}$ inches diameter and fairly thick) the day's ration."

*   *   *   *   *

Our experiments at chupattie-making had led us in the end to grind the wheat in two stages – first into coarse meal, and then, with a finer setting of the mill, into flour. This meant less strain both for us and for the machine: upon the safety of the latter practically depended our survival, and frequent were the exhortations to the miller on duty not to be too violent with the wretched little handle. Standing there in the sun – for though there were trees in the ravine, they were not high enough to shelter a man standing up – one was greatly tempted to hurry through the task of twenty hoppers full of grain, and so risk breaking the grinder. A quotation which Looney had learnt from a book read at Yozgad proved very apposite on these occasions. It was from a label pasted on to a French toy, and ran as follows: *"Quoi qu'elle soit solidement montée, il ne faut pas brutaliser la machine!"*

When enough flour was ready, someone would knead it into a lump of dough, which would then be divided up by the cook and flattened into little discs. These were baked several at a time on the metal cover of our dixie. When enough chupatties were ready, the cook would pick them up one by one, while someone else, not in sight of them, called out the names of the party at random. This was to get over the difficulty caused by the chupatties not being all of quite the same size. Similarly, after each brew of porridge had been distributed into the mugs by spoonfuls, we determined who was to have the scrapings of the pot by the method of "fingers-out". It was necessary to scrape the dixie each time to prevent the muddy paste which stuck to the bottom becoming burnt during the next brew; and the way to get this done thoroughly was to let some one have it to eat.

On the 4th September, Nobby discovered a shorter way up to the well, by first going a little down instead of up the ravine we were in. From that date onwards, except for one night when it was necessary to be on the spot in case of eventualities, Looney and Perce, and on one occasion Johnny, went up at dusk to sleep near the well. Although the mosquitoes were almost as troublesome there, they found that the air was quite invigorating – a great contrast to that in the ravine, where no refreshing breeze ever found its way.

By this time hardly one of us had any foot-gear left worthy of the name, so we soaked an old *mashak* (skin water-bag) and a piece of raw hide, both of which had been brought down from the village on the second visit, with a view to using them for patch repairs. Both, however, proved too rotten to be of use, for they would not hold the stitches.

We had been a week in the ravine before any of us felt capable of farther exploration. To save time in getting to work again, on the last two evenings Cochrane and Nobby had had a little extra ration of porridge. Now at length, on the 6th September, they felt that it was within their powers to make another reconnaissance. Nothing more had been seen of the motorboat, but the bay in which had been its anchorage on our first night on the coast seemed to offer the best prospect of finding a boat of some sort. Accordingly at 5 p.m. the pair set off once again down the ravine, hoping to arrive near the end of it before dark. And so began another anxious time for all, as we wondered what the final night of our first month of freedom would bring forth. It had not been easy to keep a correct tally of the date during the march to the coast. More than once there had been no opportunity of writing a diary for three days at a time; whilst on the coast one day was so much like another that to lose count of a day would have been easy. One of us, however, had kept a complete diary, and so we knew that we had now been at large for a month.

To celebrate this we had decided, if all went well that night, to have something very good to eat on the morrow. Everyone voted for a plum-duff. Johnny had cooked a date-duff one evening during the siege of Kut, when his Indian *khansama* (cook) found the shell-fire too trying for his nerves. To Johnny then was given the post of *chef*. During the day each of the party did an extra fatigue on the coffee-grinder, with the result that by dusk we were able to set aside about two pounds of flour for the pudding. Its other ingredients were a couple of small handfuls of raisins and a pinch of salt. When Cochrane and Nobby departed operations commenced. The ingredients were mixed; the dough was kneaded on a flat rock and the resulting mass divided into two, for our little dixie was incapable of holding all at once. Each pudding was then rolled into a ball, tied up in a handkerchief, and boiled for two and a half hours. Thus it was close upon midnight before our dainties were ready for the morrow. The stillness of the nights in the ravine had often been broken by the melancholy chorus of a pack of jackals, usually far away but sometimes close at hand. We decided to take no risks of losing our duffs, and so slung them in the branches of a tree.

Meanwhile Cochrane and Nobby proceeded on their reconnaissance. We had made plans before they started in case of certain eventualities. One was that if the two were recaptured they should lead the Turks to the rest of the party; it was realised that otherwise they might be very hard put to it to prove that they were escaped prisoners of war and not spies. A more cheerful eventuality was the possibility that the motor-boat might have returned unobserved. In that case if a favourable opportunity of capturing it occurred, Cochrane and Nobby were to seize the vessel, make their way to Cyprus, and send back help for the rest four nights later. The rendezvous from which they would be fetched was to be on the headland opposite the little island on which stood the ruined castle. We eventually learnt that at the proposed rendezvous was stationed a battery of guns, so that it was well for us that this plan had never to be executed.

Our two scouts had many exciting moments in their reconnaissance that night. They went to within a few hundred yards of the mouth of the ravine and then, turning to the right, made their way up to higher ground by a side ravine. They climbed hurriedly, for the light was rapidly failing. From the top it was still impossible to overlook the bay which they wanted. They were moving along parallel to the sea when suddenly they heard voices. They could pick out four figures a little more than a hundred yards away, silhouetted against the sea on their left. These were Turks; they seemed to be looking out to sea, and after a minute or two squatted down on what appeared to be the flat roof of a house. At this juncture Cochrane swallowed a mosquito. Nobby says that to see him trying not to choke or cough would have been laughable at any less anxious time.

After this episode the two moved off with extra carefulness. It was now quite dark. They had not gone much farther when they again heard voices. This time the voices were quite close and coming towards them. Our pair took cover and waited: happily, at the last moment the owners of the voices turned off.

In view of the number of people who seemed to be about it was no good increasing the risk of detection by having two persons on the move; so, soon after, Cochrane left Nobby in a good place of concealment, and went on scouting around by himself.

Half an hour later he came back. He had been able to overlook the cove, and there were two boats there. It was too dark, however, to see of what sort they were, and as there was a shed with a sentry on duty close to the boats, the only thing to do was to wait for daylight. The two now slept and took watch in turn. At the first sign of dawn they moved down to a rock, commanding a good view of the creek. One of the boats appeared to be a ship's cutter, some twenty-eight feet long, the other perhaps twenty feet in length. Having seen all they could hope for, they lost no time in moving off, as it was now quite obvious that the house on which they had seen the four men on the previous evening was a look-out post; and it was now becoming dangerously light.

Instead of returning directly to the ravine, however, they made their way some distance down the coast to the S.W. They were able to see Selefké, and to recognise through the glasses a dhow in the river there, but it was some way inland. It was 11 a.m. before the reconnoitring party again reached the ravine. The news they brought gave us something definite to work for, and we decided that if we could finish our preparations in time we would make an attempt to seize one of the boats two nights later. That would be on the night of the 8th-9th September. But there was much to be done before then. Masts and spars, paddles and sails, and four days' supply of food for the sea journey had to be made ready. For the paddle heads Cochrane and Nobby had brought back some flat thin pieces of board which they had found near a broken-down hut; and also a bit of ancient baked pottery which would serve as a whetstone for our very blunt knives and the adze.

On the strength of the good news and to fortify ourselves for the work, we decided to wait no longer for our feast. The duffs were unslung from the tree, and each divided with as much accuracy as possible into eight pieces: in this way we should each have a slice from either pudding in case they varied in quantity or quality. Both were superb, and the finest duffs ever made. We commented on their amazing sweetness and excellent consistency. In reality a raisin was only to be found here and there, and the puddings were not cooked right through. When we had finished, Old Man asserted that he could then and there and with ease demolish six whole duffs by himself. This started an argument.

"What!" cried one; "eat forty-eight pieces like the two you have just had. Impossible!"

"Granted; twenty pieces would go down easily enough," said another, "and the next ten with a fair appetite. But after that it wouldn't be so easy. You might manage another ten, but the last eight would certainly defeat you."

Old Man, however, stuck to his assertion and refused to come down by so much as a single slice. As it was impossible without the duffs under discussion to prove him right or merely greedy, the subject was allowed to drop.

By this date Perce was the only one of the party who still had some tobacco, English 'baccy too, for he smoked very little. To celebrate the discovery of the boats, he now broke into his reserve. A single cigarette was rolled and handed round from one to another of us. It only needed a couple of inhaled puffs to make each of us feel as if we were going off under an anaesthetic. After the two of three puffs one thought it would be nice to sit down, and in a few seconds one felt it would be pleasanter still to lie down full length. That is what we did. The effect only lasted a minute or two, but it showed in what a weak condition we were.

On the evening trip to the nearer well it was found quite impossible to draw up any more water from it. It had been gradually drying up, and now the two on water fatigue could not scoop up even a spoonful of water when they let down a mug, so they had to go on to the well near the tower. This, too, was going dry, but still contained a little pool of very muddy water.

Shortly after four o'clock that afternoon Looney and Perce had started off on the third visit which was paid to the deserted village. They were armed with a long list of requisites: more cloth for sails; a big dixie for cooking large quantities of the reserve porridge at a time; some more grain; nails and any wood likely to be of use; cotton-wool for padding our feet when we went down to the shore; and many other things. They returned next morning at 9 a.m. with all the important articles, together with some hoop-iron and a few small poles. The latter were the very thing for the paddle-shafts. They also brought down some raw coffee-beans which they had found in a little leather bag; these we roasted and ground next day, and enjoyed the two finest drinks of coffee we remember having had in our lives.

Meanwhile we had started cooking our food for the sea voyage. It was to consist of small chupatties and porridge, but the latter would not be cooked until the latest possible date for fear of its going bad. Forty reserve chupatties had been set aside before we retired to rest on the night after the feast-day. From that day onwards till we left the ravine the coffee-grinder was worked unceasingly from 5 a.m. till 7 or 8 p.m. There was no question of a six hours' day for us; for while we ground flour and porridge for the reserve, we had still to provide our own meals for the day. We realised then, if never before, the truth of the saying, "In the sweat of thy face shalt thou eat bread."

Little of the 8th September had passed before we realised that it was hopeless to think of being ready by the following night. We therefore postponed the attempt, and settled down to our preparations in more deadly earnest. Cochrane decided on the size and shape of the sails, which were to be three in number. The rolls of cloth obtained from the village were about fourteen inches in width, and the biggest of the three sails was made with seven strips of the cloth. It was a good thing that we had still two big reels nearly untouched of the thread with which we had started from Yozgad.

When the strips had been sewn together, the edges of the sail were hemmed. Later, pieces of canvas from Ellis's pack, which was cut up for the purpose, were added at the corners for the sake of additional strength. No one had a moment to spare. Those who were not sail-making were doing something else, – either at the mill, at work on the paddles, cutting branches off trees for the spars, fetching water, or cooking.

September 9th was similarly spent, but again on this day it soon be-came obvious that we should not be ready by nightfall. By the time we retired to our sleeping-places, however, our preparations were well advanced. Two of the sails were finished, the spars were cut, some of the paddles were completed, and the larger part of the chupatties and porridge cooked. The porridge was put into one of our packs. It was not a very clean receptacle, but being fairly waterproof would, we hoped, helped to to keep the porridge moist; for our chief fear with regard to the coming sea voyage was shortage of water.

On the 10th we worked continuously from daylight till 3.30 p.m., by which time our preparations were complete. Before moving off we hid away all non-essentials, so as to reduce our loads. With the big cooking-pot half-full of water, and the spars, sails, and paddles, these were going to be both heavy and cumbersome. We also buried our fezes and the copies of the map, lest, if we were recaptured, they should encourage the Turks to think that we were spies. For the same reason, any allusions to what we had seen on the coast, and to our visits to the deserted village, were carefully erased from diaries. These precautions completed, we carried our unwieldy loads down the ravine to a point opposite the shorter path to the wells. Here we left our impedimenta, and taking only water-bottles, chargals, and the big cooking-pot, which had a cover and swing-handle, climbed up to the well near the tower and filled up. The water supply was almost exhausted, and it took an hour and a half to fill our receptacles and have a drink. It was impossible to practise the camel's plan, and drink more than we really needed at the time. It required a tremendous effort to force oneself to drink a mugful of these muddy dregs.

While the rest were filling the water-bottles, etc., Old Man and Nobby went off to a suitable point for a final look at part of our proposed route to the shore. Then all returned to the kits in the ravine. We had decided that we would move down to the beach in stockinged feet, so as to make as little noise as possible. For most of us this was not only a precaution, but a necessity, since our party of eight now only possessed three pairs of wearable boots between us. We accordingly padded our feet as best we could, and proceeded once more towards the sea.

The going was so difficult that we had several times to help one another over the enormous boulders which filled the bottom of the ravine, and down precipitous places where there had once been small waterfalls.

At 7 p.m. we were not far from the mouth of the ravine. Here, then, the party halted, while Nobby, who had been there on two previous occasions, scouted ahead. When he returned, reporting that all seemed to be clear, we crept on out of the ravine. It was now night. Walking very carefully, testing each footstep for fear of treading on a twig or loose stone and so making a noise, we came to a wall. This we crossed at a low place where it had been partially broken down, and a hundred yards beyond found ourselves approaching a line of telegraph poles and then the coast road. Up and down this we peered in the light of the young moon, and seeing no one went across. The ground here was level, but covered with big bushes and a few stunted firs, between which we made our way to the shore. It was grand to hear the lapping of the waves and smell the seaweed after nearly four years.

The creek, in which were the two rowing-boats, lay a mile to the west

of us. We had intended to strike the shore where we were, for by walking
to the creek along the edge of the sea the risk of stumbling against any
tents or huts in the dark would be reduced; but it took us longer to reach
our objective than we had expected. It was almost midnight when, a
quarter of a mile from the creek, and near a place where a boat could be
brought conveniently alongside, the party halted. Leaving the other here,
Cochrane and Johnny were to try to seize one of the two boats marked
down four nights previously, and Nobby was to accompany them in case
they needed help.

The shore line, which they now followed, rose rapidly to a steep cliff
forty feet or more above the level of the sea. When within a hundred
yards of the boat which they wanted, they found a way down to a narrow
ledge two feet above the water. The moon had long set, but they could
see the boat as a dark shadow against the water reflecting the starlight.
Here, then, Cochrane and Johnny proceeded to strip. They continued,
however, to wear a couple of pairs of socks in case the bottom should be
covered with sharp spikes, as has been the rocky edge of the shore for the
most part. They tied two pieces of thin rope round their waists with a
clasp-knife attached to each. Thus equipped, they let themselves down off
the ledge, and slipped quietly into the sea. Fortunately the water was warm;
but it was phosphorescent too, so they had to swim very slowly to avoid
making any unnecessary ripple.

As they neared the boat, which now loomed big above them, some
one in the shadow of the cliff a few yards away coughed. Next moment
they heard the butt of a rifle hitting a rock as the sentry (for such he must
have been) shifted his position. Hardly daring to breathe, they swam to
the side of the boat farther from him and held on to it. Here the water
was about six feet deep. After waiting a few minutes to let any suspicions
on the part of the sentry subside, they moved along to the bow of the
boat.

They had hoped to find it anchored by a rope, but to their great disappointment it was moored with a heavy iron chain. Speaking in very low
whispers, they decided that one should go under the water and lift the
anchor, while the other, with his piece of rope, tied one of the flukes to
a link high up in the chain. When the anchor was thus raised clear of the
bottom, they would swim quietly away, towing the boat. Accordingly,
Cochrane dived and lifted the anchor, while Johnny tied his rope round a
fluke and made it fast to a link as far up the chain as possible. They then
let go.

With what seemed to them a terrific noise, the chain rattled over the
gunwale till the anchor was once more on the bottom. Were they dis-

covered? Another cough! They did not dare to move. Could the splash of
the water lapping against the sides of the creek have muffled the sound of
the rattling chain? If only the chain had been fixed! But perhaps a short
length only had been loose.

Another attempt was made. This time it was Johnny who lifted the
anchor, while Cochrane tied his rope to it. Unfortunately he had the
rope still round his waist, and when the anchor dropped he was carried
down with it. How lucky that he had his clasp-knife! For though he was
free in a few seconds, he came to the surface spluttering out the water he
had swallowed. It was a near thing that he was not drowned. Where,
meantime, was the anchor? Little did they realise that it was lying
once more on the bottom and laughing at their efforts to carry off the
quarry that night.

Some point of the chain, of course, must be attached to the boat, but
it was risky to continue getting rid of the spare length by the present
method. Besides, there was no more rope with which to tie up the anchor
to the chain. As for getting into the boat and weighing anchor from there,
it would be sheer madness. The sentry would be certain to see them
naked and wet as they were.

By this time they were both shivering violently with cold, though, as
has been said, the water was quite warm. As a last attempt they tried to
take the boat out to the end of the chain by swimming away with it
farther from the sentry. Again the chain rattled over the gunwale, and
there was nothing for it but to admit defeat.

Slowly they swam back to the ledge where Nobby was awaiting them.
He said they had been away for an hour and twenty minutes, so it was
not surprising that they had felt cold. With numbed fingers they put on
their clothes and climbed gloomily up the cliff. By this time the walking
over sharp rocks had cut their socks and padding to pieces, so that they
were marching almost barefoot, a very painful operation.

On their rejoining the party, the sad tale of failure was told. As the
time was 3 a.m., the only thing to do was to get into the best cover we
could find near the coast and sleep till dawn. About a hundred yards inland we lay down in some small bushes beneath stunted pine-trees. There
we slept.

Our thirty-fifth morning found us in a state of great depression. There
seemed no chance left of getting out of the country. Lying in our hiding-
places we reviewed the situation in an almost apathetic mood.

We were on the eastern side of a W-shaped bay, a mile wide, and opening southwards. Its eastern arm was the creek, in which was the boat we
had failed to capture. There was a similar western arm, the two creeks

being separated by a narrow spit of land. From quite early in the morning motor-lorries could be seen and heard winding their way along the tortuous road. In several places this closely followed the coast line, and at one or two was carried on causeways across the sea itself. We lay on a headland on the seaward side of the Turkish encampment, and were overlooked by the look-out post on the cliff-side.

At noon a council of war was held. As we were lying dotted about some distance from one another, for the time being we all crept into an old shelter made of branches not many yards from us. There matters were discussed. Although several schemes were put forward, going back to the ravine in which we had spent so many wearisome days was not one of them. To return there would have made us into raving lunatics. The final decision was to make another attempt that night to seize the boat; this time there should be four of us in the water. If that failed, about the most attractive proposal was to go boldly on to the coast road and by bluff obtain a lift on a motor-lorry, demanding as Germans to be taken in a westerly direction to the nearest big town, Selefké: we might get a boat of some sort there. The chief lure of this scheme was that, should the lorry-driver believe our story, we should cover a few miles without walking on our flat feet. This was a fascinating thought indeed, for despite nearly a fortnight on the coast we had no wish to set out on the tramp again.

Two or three of us, however, thought we might sum up the energy to march eastwards along the road in the hope of finding a boat in the bay of Ayasch. But even if we did this there was still the difficulty about food and drink. Unless we replenished our supply we should have to undertake a sea voyage of at least a hundred miles with only two days' rations and perhaps a water-bottle full of water apiece. The consensus of opinion was thus come to that if we failed again that night we might as well give ourselves up the next day. We then went back into our old and safer hiding-places.

At about two o'clock in the afternoon we heard the sound of a far-off motor. This was no lorry. It came from a different direction. In a few seconds we were all listening intently.

"It's only another lorry after all!"

"No, it can't be. It's on the sea side of us!"

As the minutes passed, the noise became more and more distinct. Then our hearts leapt within us, as there came into the bay, towing a lighter and a dinghy, the motor-tug which we had last seen the day after we had reached the coast. Skirting the shore not three hundred yards from where we lay, the boats disappeared into the eastern creek.

Apathy and depression were gone in a second. Excitement and – this we like to remember – a deep sense of thankfulness for this answer to our prayers took their place.

The motor-boat was flying at her bows a Turkish and at her stern a German flag, but most of her crew of seven or eight looked to us like Greeks. In the lighter were over twenty Turks.

Another council of war took place, but of a very different type from the last. All were hopeful, and we made our plans in high spirits. Throughout our discussion, however, ran the assumption that some of the crew would be on board the motor-boat, and we should have to bribe them to take us across to Cyprus. It never entered our heads for a moment that any other scheme would be possible. In fact, when about an hour before sunset the dinghy with a few of the crew and some water-beakers on board was rowed across to a point opposite us on the western side of the bay (where there must have been a spring of fresh water), we determined to hail them on their return journey.

At one point they came within three hundred yards of us. In answer to our shouting and whistling, they stopped rowing and looked in our direction. They must have seen us, but they refused to take any further notice. Whom did they take us for? And why did they not report our presence when they went ashore? No one came to search for us; and as the mountain had not come to Mahomet, Mahomet would have to go to the mountain. Some one would have to swim out to the boat that night, and proffer bribes to the crew.

As the dusk of our thirty-sixth night fell, a ration of chupatties and a couple of handfuls of raisins were issued. A move was then made to the nearest point on the shore at which there was a suitable place for a boat to come alongside. There we waited till the moon set at about 8.30. In the meantime we drank what water remained in the big dixie. This left us with only our water-bottles full.

At this time our best Turkish scholar was feeling very sick. The last scrapings from the pack containing the porridge had fallen to him, and as all of it had turned sour during the previous night, Grunt's extra ration was proving a not unmixed blessing. This was a serious matter, as we relied on him to negotiate with the motor-boat's crew. However, at 9 p.m., he and Cochrane, the Old Man and Nobby, set forth on the last great venture. The others moved all the kit close down to the edge of the rock where a boat could come in.

An anxious wait ensued. The four had set out at 9 o'clock, but it was not till 11.30 that Looney, with his last reserve – half a biscuit – gone, saw a boat coming silently towards him. In a trice the other three were awakened. Was it friend or foe? She had four men on board: they were our four. The moment the boat touched at the rock the kit was thrown in. Cochrane had done magnificent work. He had swum round the creek, found out that there was no one in the motor-boat, cut away the dinghy belonging to the lighter, swum back with it, and fetched the other three.

Eight hopeful fugitives were soon gently paddling the dinghy towards the creek, keeping, so far as might be, in the shadow of the cliffs; for though the moon was down, the stars seemed to make the open bay unpleasantly light. As noiselessly as possible the dinghy came alongside the motor-boat and made fast. The creek here was about sixty yards wide. The tug, moored by a heavy chain and anchor, was in the middle of it. Some fifteen yards away was the lighter; on this were several men, one of whom was coughing the whole time we were "cutting out" the motor-boat. This took us a full hour.

On trying the weight of the chain and anchor, Cochrane decided to loose the motor-boat from her anchorage by dropping the chains overboard. He did not think it would be possible to weigh the anchor. Odd lengths of cord were collected and joined up in readiness for lowering the end of the chain silently when the time came. But success was not to be attained so easily. Boarding the motor-boat, Nobby and Perce had foot by foot, got rid of almost all the chain which lay in the bows, when another score of fathoms were discovered below deck. It would be quicker, after all, to weigh anchor, and by superhuman efforts this was at length achieved without attracting the attention of the enemy, our coats and shirts being used as padding over the gunwale.

As soon as the anchor was weighed, we connected the motor-boat with the dinghy by a tow-rope found on the former; all got back into the dinghy, and in this we paddled quietly away. With our home-made paddles and heavy tow we were unable to make much headway. With six paddles in the water, we could credit ourselves with a speed of not so much as a single knot.

Once clear of the bay, Cochrane again went aboard the motor-boat and this time had a look at the engine. We had remaining at this time about an inch of candle, but this served a very useful purpose. By its glimmer Cochrane was able to discover and light a hurricane-lamp. He told us the joyous news that there was a fair quantity of paraffin in the tank. Unfortunately no petrol was to be found, and it seemed unlikely that we should be able to start the engine from cold on paraffin alone. So weak indeed were we, that it was all we could do to turn over the engine at all. While frantic efforts were being made by Cochrane and Nobby to start her, those in the dinghy continued paddling. After three hours all were very tired of it, and very grateful for a slight off-shore breeze which gave us the chance of setting a sail. Cochrane rigged up our main-sail on the motor-boat; all then clambered aboard the latter.

Our speed was now quite good and many times that of our most furious paddling. Suddenly looking back, we saw the dinghy adrift and disappearing in the darkness behind us. Whoever had been holding the rope at the dinghy end had omitted to make fast on coming on board the motor-boat. The dinghy still contained all our kit; so to recover this, including as it did what food and water remained to us, Cochrane and Johnny jumped overboard and swam back to it. The sail on the motor-boat had been furled, and in a few minutes the dinghy was again in tow.

After this slight misadventure the engine-room was once more invaded, and Looney and Cochrane experimented with the magneto. There was a loose wire and vacant terminal which they were uncertain whether to connect or not, Eventually, with Nobby turning over the engine, a shock was obtained with the two disconnected. Two were now put on to the starting-handle. But the cramped space produced several bruised heads and nothing else as pair after pair struggled on.

At length at 4.30 a.m., little more than an hour before dawn, the engine started up with a roar, in went the clutch, and off went the motor-boat at a good seven knots. At the time when the engine began firing, Nobby, who was feeling very much the worse for his exertions in weighing anchor followed by his efforts to start the motor, was lying on deck in the stern. Startled by the sudden series of explosions, he thought for a moment that a machine-gun had opened fire at short range, till he discovered that he was lying on the exhaust-pipe, the end of which was led up on deck!

*   *   *   *   *

We reckoned that by this time we were some three miles from the creek, so we could hope that the roar of the engine would be inaudible to those on shore. On the other hand, sunrise on the 12th Spetember was a little before 6 a.m., so that dawn should have found us still within view from the land. A kindly mist, however, came down and hid us till we were well out to sea. As soon as it was light enough we tried to declutch in order to transfer our kit from the dinghy to the tug. But the clutch was in bad order and would not come out. The alternative was to haul up the dinghy level with the tug, with the motor still running, and then to transfer all our goods and chattels on to the deck. It was a difficult task, but it was done. We then turned the dinghy adrift. This meant the gain of an additional two knots.

It now seemed as if our troubles really were nearing their end. The engine was running splendidly, the main tank was full to the brim; there was enough and to spare of lubricating oil, and in a barrel lashed to the deck in the stern was found some more paraffin. A beaker contained sufficient water to give us each a mugful. It was brackish, but nectar compared to the well-water which we had been drinking for the last fortnight. We also allowed ourselves some chupatties and a handful of raisins.

Our principal fear now was of being chased by one of the seaplanes which we thought to be stationed at Mersina, not many miles away. We had seen one on two occasions during our stay in the ravine. Time went on, however, and nothing appeared. Instead of looking behind us for a seaplane we began to look ahead, hoping to come across one of our own patrol boats. It says much for the deserted condition of those waters that during our fortnight on the coast and our voyage of about 120 miles to Cyprus not a single boat was seen save for those five that we had seen in the creek.

Discussing the matter of the discovery of the loss of the motor-boat and the subsequent action of the crew, we came to the cheerful conclusion that probably the loss would not be divulged to the authorities for a considerable period. The rightful crew would know what to expect as a punishment for their carelessness, and would either perjure themselves by swearing that the boats had sunk at their moorings, or thinking discretion even better than perjury, disappear into the deserted hinterland through which we had marched. Should these two guesses be wrong, there was yet another course which we thought possible, though not so probable, for the crew to take. Thinking that the motor-boat and dinghy had drifted away, they would not mention their disappearance till a thorough search had been made of all bays and creeks within a few miles of the locality.

The cherry of this delightful cocktail of fancy was very palatable; whatever else happened, the occupants of the lighter, agitated to the extreme and dinghyless, would have to swim ashore, and this thought amused us greatly.[1]

Now for a few words about the motor-boat. She was named the *Hertha*, and boasted both a Turkish and a German flag. In addition to her name

[1]The following is an extract from a letter received from Lieut.-Colonel Keeling since we wrote the above: "At Adana I met the Turkish Miralai (Brigadier-General)—Beheddin Bey—who was in command on the coast. He was fully expecting the party (i.e., our party), and put all the blame on the men in the boat (i.e., the lighter) to which the motor-boat was tied. These men were all Turks, the Germans being on shore. The loss of the motor-boat was discovered before dawn, and at dawn a hydroplane was sent out to look for her; but she only spotted a small boat a few miles out, presumably the boat with which they had towed the motor-boat to a safe distance before starting the engine. Beheddin Bey drew me a plan showing exactly how everything had happened."

she had the Turkish symbol for "2" painted large on either side of her bows. Broad in the beam for her 38 feet of length, she was decked in, and down below harboured a 50-h.p. motor. In the bows of the engine-room we found a couple of Mauser rifles dated 1915, with a few rounds of small-arm ammunition; some of the latter had the nickel nose filed off to make them "mush-room" on impact. We also discovered a Very's pistol, with a box of cartridges; trays of spanners and spare parts for the motor, and two lifebelts taken from English ships whose names we have forgotten. On deck, immediately abaft the engine-room hatchway, was the steering-wheel, while farther astern was the barrel containing the extra paraffin, a can of lubricating oil, and various empty canisters.

Till noon the sea was sufficiently rough to be breaking continually over the bows, and three of the party were feeling the effect of the roll. To the rest, to be thus rocked in the cradle of the deep, borne ever nearer to freedom, was a sensation never to be forgotten. The motor was going splendidly, and we all took turns at the wheel, steering by the "sun-compass", and, with the exception of Cochrane, very badly.

By 1.30 p.m. we could recognise the dim outline of the high mountain-range of Cyprus: on the strength of this we each ate another two chupatties and a handful of raisins, finishing our meal with a quarter of a mugful of water.

But we were a trifle premature in our lavishness. Our troubles were not at an end, for half an hour later the engine began to fail, and, while Cochrane was below looking for the cause of the trouble, she petered out. The fault was subsequently traced to the over-heating of one of the main shaft bearings, the oil feed-pipe to which had been previously broken, and had vibrated from its place. Having satisfied himself that no serious damage was done, Cochrane decided to wait half an hour for the bearing to cool. During this time Old Man and Looney had a mid-sea bathe to re-fresh themselves, while Perce and Johnny tried to boil some water for tea. The fire was made on an iron sheet, on which some bights of chain were shaped into a cooking place for the big dixie. The roll of the boat, how-ever, though very much less than in the morning, proved too great to allow the dixie to remain steady on the chain, so the idea of tea had to be abandoned. We now had leisure to observe the sea, and we decided that its colour was the most wonderful we had ever seen – a clear purple-blue.

When the bearing had cooled, we tried to start the engine again. One pair followed another on the starting-handle, but all to no purpose. All four sparking-plugs were examined: the feed-pipe, separator, and carburetter were taken down. Except for a little water in the separator, all seemed correct. We refilled the tank with paraffin from the barrel on deck, but our renewed attempts still met with no success. Our efforts to turn the crank became more and more feeble, until, by 4.30 p.m., we lay down on deck utterly exhausted.

Just before sunset we decided we would make a final attempt to start up. Should that be unsuccessful, we would set the sails; but to our great relief she fired at the second attempt. Our joy was somewhat tempered by her refusing to run for more than a few minutes at a time. It was found that this was caused by the feed-pipe from the tank repeatedly choking, owing, no doubt, to grit in the oil obtained from the barrel, which, as we had noticed when pouring it in, was very dirty.

After dark, Cochrane did all the steering; while down in the engine-room were Looney as mechanic, and Old Man and Johnny as starters. Meantime, Perce sat on deck with his feet through the hatchway against the clutch-lever below him. By jamming this hard down, and tapping the clutch with a hammer, it was possible to persuade the cones to separate when required. For over four hours we spent our time starting and stopping. Our two best runs lasted for thirty and thirty-five minutes. Usually a run lasted for five or less. We took it in turns to tap the feed-pipe with a piece of wood, in the hope of keeping it from clogging; but it was of little use. Each time the engines stopped, Looney took down the separator and feed-pipe and blew through them, getting a mouthful of paraffin for his pains. When all was ready again, the two starters, though almost dead-beat, managed somehow to turn the crank.

By 10 p.m. we were becoming desperate. It was only Cochrane's cheering news that we were within two hours' run of the coast that kept the engine-room staff going. A run of five minutes meant a mile nearer home, so we carried on.

An hour later, Cochrane told us all to sit on the starboard side, for it was on this side that the feed-pipe left the tank. This was sheer genius on his part. From that very moment the wilful engine behaved herself, and ran obediently till we meant her to stop. As we neared the coast, at a distance, perhaps, of three miles from it, Nobby fired off a Very's light, in case there were any patrol boats in the neighbourhood; but no answering light appeared. Next day, in Cyprus, we asked the police if they had seen the light. They had not seen it, they said, but had heard it. This proves how wonderfully sound travels over water, for we would not for one second doubt a policeman's story. But, as is hardly necessary to point out, a Very's signal, like little children, should be seen and not heard.

Having had only our memories of the bearing and distance to Cyprus from Rendezvous X to guide us, we had worked out in the ravine that the bearing on which we had to steer would be S. 50° W. On sighting the island in the afternoon, we had found that this was too much to the west; so Cochrane had altered the course to make for the western end of the high range of mountains visible about due south of us. When about two miles from the shore we turned eastwards, and moved parallel to the coast, on the look-out for a good anchorage, if possible near a village. Finally, about a hundred yards from the shore, we dropped anchor in a wide bay.

On leaving Yozgad each of the party had possessed a watch, but by this time only two were in working order, and these were Old Man's and Johnny's. As the chain rattled over the side, the latter looked at the time, to find that the hand once more pointed to the witching hour of midnight. This timepiece served its purpose well, for it was not till an hour later, when it had ceased to be so essential, that it shared the fate of most of its comrades and was broken. It was interesting to find later, on comparing the Old Man's watch with Cyprus time, that there was only two minutes' difference between them. We had checked our time occasionally by noticing when one of the "pointers" of the Great Bear was vertically beneath the Pole Star; the solar time when this occurred on any night had been worked out before we left Yozgad. Fairly accurate time-keeping was of importance, for on this depended the successful use of both the "sun-compass" and the star-charts.

And so we had reached Cyprus, but we were all in too dazed a condition to realise for the moment what it meant; in fact, it took many days to do so. On arrival in the bay, Cochrane, with his keen sense of smell, had declared that there were cows not far off, and at about 3 o'clock we heard a cock crow. We said we would eat our hats, or words to that effect, if we did not have that bird for breakfast. There was not a single light on shore, and we had no idea whereabouts in Cyprus we had dropped anchor. As the stars disappeared in the coming light of dawn, we saw the coast more clearly. Then by degrees what we thought were ruins on the coast, rocks a couple of hundred yards east of us took form; later these proved to be the still occupied Greek monastery of Acropedi. Then a house or two near by stood distinct; then trees; and finally our eyes beheld not a mile away a large village, boasting churches, mosques, and fine buildings set in trees, and beyond a mountain-range rising sheer from the very houses.

With first light came a man to the beach opposite us. We shouted to him in English, French, and Turkish, but he appeared not to understand. Soon he was joined by two or three others. Then they started arriving in tens and twenties, men, women, and children. Mounted gendarmes galloped down. We shouted ourselves hoarse, but to no purpose. We tried several times to start up the motor, but we could not turn the handle.

Finally Cochrane jumped overboard in a shirt borrowed for the occasion, as it was longer and less torn than his own. He must have felt still rather undressed for the ordeal, as when he reached the water he shouted for his hat, which was thrown to him. Clothed thus he swam towards the shore. In two feet of water his courage gave way, and his modesty made him sit down. So situated he harangued the crowd.

Finally there appeared a gendarme who understood English. He said there was an English police officer in the village, which was named Lapethos; so borrowing a pencil and a piece of paper, Cochrane wrote a a note to the Englishman reporting our arrival. He explained to the gendarme that we wanted to bring the boat ashore, but that we could not start the engine. When this was understood several men at once stripped and swam out to the rest of us. Cochrane came back smoking a cigarette, which he passed round when he got on board. The Cypriotes too brought cigarettes perched behind their ear like a clerk's pencil, and these we smoked with great appreciation. The scheme was for us to weigh the anchor, give the men towing-ropes, and they would then pull the boat inshore. The men, though small, were well built. As they had started swimming almost before they could walk, it was no hardship for them to tow our heavy vessel. Laughing and shouting, they pulled us along until they thought a rest would be pleasant, then they came on board again. They shouted now and then in sheer lightness of heart; they were very cheery fellows. We were not towed straight inshore, but to a small natural jetty a hundred and fifty yards west of us along the beach.

Here we stepped on British soil, eight thin and weary ragamuffins. We know our hearts gave thanks to God, though our minds could not grasp that we were really free.

CHAPTER THIRTEEN

A PLEASANT epilogue to Johnston and Yearsley's story is provided by news item in *The Times* dated November 4th, 1919, reporting the finding of a Prize Court in London under the President of the Admiralty Division, who pronounced a decree condemning the Turkish tug and its cargo as prize. The President asked Commander Cochrane, "how it was that he had contrived to navigate her to Cyprus with the aid of officers of the army?"

*   *   *   *   *

The next story I have chosen is the third to come from a book written by two authors, but true to the escaper's tradition of originality no two of them take the same form. Harrison and Cartwright wrote alternate chapters of *Within Four Walls*, Johnston and Yearsley kept their individual authorship of *450 Miles to Freedom* anonymous, while Prittie and Edwards each wrote about half of *South to Freedom*. I am sorry I have not room for passages by Harrison and Edwards in this anthology, but I hope that the extracts by their co-authors will lead you to the books, and I know that you will not be disappointed.

Like Captain Haldane, Terence Prittie stresses the importance of taking the first opportunity to escape that offers itself. Captured near Calais in May 1940, he became one of the long line of weary prisoners marching slowly towards Germany.

T. C. F. Prittie

THE THIRD day's march brought us to Hesdin, a road and railway junction about half-way between Calais and Amiens.

On the whole, it was the worst day's march we had so far experienced. It began at four o'clock in the morning, lasted until five in the evening, and covered about twenty-five miles. The weather was hotter, the guards more hostile than usual. During the day I saw the first escape from our section of the column, Jack Poole, of the 60th, leaping over the low parapet of a bridge and disappearing from view below. Among others marching in my immediate neighbourhood, Alec Williams, of the 60th, and Tony Rolt, of the Rifle Brigade, were both obviously determined to go in the near future. Both did, indeed, leave the column on the following day. Tony was picked up within a few hours, and Alec got back to England after a month of adventure.

I had one unpleasant personal experience during the day. Getting tired of the terrible dragging pace at which we were marching, Tom Acton, Micky Smiley and others of us decided to march on quickly to the head of the column and then fall out in our own time and take a rest by the side of the road. There was no difficulty about this, as German sentries were perfectly satisfied as long as we kept moving on the middle of the road. We made our way through several hundred yards of column, and soon found ourselves well up in front, where there were few guards, and only French troops on the road. We were passing a gate into a field where some German vehicles were parked, when there was a sudden flurry and rush from behind the hedge, and half a dozen Germans in white canvas jackets – cook-house personnel, I imagine – dashed in among us with the idea of looting souvenirs. There were a number of sharp struggles, during which we lost a mackintosh and tin hat, and a couple of wrist-watches were smashed. In such circumstances a prisoner is in an impossible position and his struggles are inevitably weak and half-hearted. This incident was a further pointer towards the terms of honourable captivity!

We draggled into Hesdin in a very poor state at about half-past four in the afternoon. But outside the town itself, a signpost announced Boulogne 70, Abbeville 61 kilometres, and for the first time I was given a double check on my whereabouts from two towns whose positions I knew exactly. That evening we were able to buy rather more food than usual, while halted in the main street, and we slept for the first time on straw. Thus, although the start next morning was at 5.30, I felt, for once, something like fully rested, and set off far more alert and hopeful than at any period since capture.

Our road, leaving Hesdin, swung left-handed, going almost due east with Frèvent and Doullens signposted as the next towns of any importance. This change of direction was not unexpected, as we had heard that Allied troops were still along almost the whole length of the Somme. We were therefore moving parallel to the most obvious objective for anyone escaping, the line of the River Somme itself, and directly away from the next most probable avenue of escape, the English Channel. I had a strong feeling that this would be the vital day, if I was ever to achieve anything.

I had been marching with Charles Clay, of the Rifle Brigade, during the previous day, and he was perfectly prepared to make a break, although, like myself, he needed the first essential impetus to send him off. Charles was five or six years older than myself, a business man in ordinary life with a strong but very likeable personality. He had great hardihood of mind and was one of the very few on whom capture had, psychologically, little effect. On this fourth day we started off together. It was a particularly lovely morning, fresh and cool while the sun was still low in our faces. The first two miles ran through water-meadows along the valley of the Canche. While covering them I had a good look at the sentries, their spacing and general alertness. There seemed to be fewer of them than usual, roughly one to every twenty-five yards altogether, or one to every fifty yards on each side of the column.

Charles had kept his compass in spite of the preliminary search when captured. Otherwise, we had two small haversacks containing oddments of washing kit, two tins of meat and vegetables, some cheese and a dozen biscuits. I had about 400 francs left out of 800 which were not taken from me by the Germans at the outset, and a flask half-full of cheap French brandy. Between us we had a ground-sheet and gas-cape, and half a blanket. These were our total and inconsiderable assets.

About two miles out of Hesdin, the main road runs through the middle of a large wood with, I should think, a dozen acres of it on either side. Charles and I were still discussing possibilities when we came into sight of the trees over a slight rise. Half-facetiously, I remarked at that moment: "Look here, Charles, I've had enough of this performance. It's too damned undignified!" I think this wording of my thoughts finally settled our minds for us, as we looked round at the dirty, unshaven, unseeing faces round us, and the endless miles of stumbling figures that made up our column, stretching away into the distance.

Just short of the wood, I enlisted the help of Richard Wood, who entirely unknown to me and to the rest of us had kept going uncomplainingly with a bullet-hole through his shoulder. He agreed to move out on to the side of the road when I gave the signal, so that should a sentry notice any sort of movement out of the ranks and come up to investigate, he would find a man fallen out and tying up his bootlaces.

The front of the column was already far past the point where the road entered the wood. Gradually, we came up to the first trees, passed them and continued along in their shadow. Charles and I edged over to the right-hand side of the road, where there was a short, grassy downward slope, then a ditch with the first trees beyond, bounded by a wire fence. Suddenly, the grass verge disappeared, the ditch ran under the fence and the trees came right up to the road, within four feet of where we were walking.

Just ahead, I saw the first gap, a gate standing open and leading on to a narrow path which disappeared into the wood.

I gave the signal to Richard, looked round to place the sentries' heads, and slowed down as we came level with the gap.

The rest of the operation went through with absurd ease. Charles and I jumped straight through the gate, went like hell for forty yards down the path, then turned off to the right. We plunged into very thick cover, where we hurled ourselves to the ground, and lay absolutely motionless, hardly daring to breathe.

Out on the road there was no sign of excitement or interest. So many prisoners walked with their eyes turned hoplessly to the ground that I should not think that more than half a dozen people even saw us go. The column continued to shamble by in its thousands, and the cries and exhortations of the guards came to us clearly as we lay trembling, like a couple of mesmerised rabbits.

Within two minutes there was a beat of running feet on the path and a khaki-clad figure, bent nearly double and running with great determination, shot by us. I remember shouting: "Get off the path, for Christ's sake!" I had a confused idea that the sentries could see down the path itself, and might come along to investigate, and find us instead!

Nothing, however, happened, and we watched the rest of the column pass by, the rear brought up by a dozen Germans, who were harrying the inveterate stragglers, mainly elderly French officers with far more kit than they could conveniently hump along.

When they had all passed and the shouts of the guards were echoing away into the distance, we picked up ourselves and our belongings, and headed off into the depths of the wood. There, about three hundred yards farther in from the road, we found an ideal lying-up place, a little dell completely surrounded by a belt of fir-trees among the oaks and beeches of the main forest.

Here we washed, shaved, and took stock of our worldly possessions. Charles and I had between us about as much idea of what we really needed for escaping as a couple of the most junior boy scouts. As we had been very tired indeed for several days, we had an exaggerated impression of the desirability of travelling light. We therefore decided to scrap tin hats and gaiters, both of them articles which would show up in the bright moonlight of the fine summer nights. More important, we threw away not only our gas masks, but also my small haversack belonging to someone called 'Phillips', which I had picked up on the Calais sands after my capture. All these things we buried with minute and over-scrupulous care.

Apart from the clothes we were wearing, this left us with one haversack filled with washing things, food, and oddments of string and cloth, Charles' half blanket and ground sheet, and my gas-cape. Our food, we reckoned, would last us a couple of days, and we hoped, in the meantime, to get fresh supplies from French peasants. By throwing away a haversack we deprived ourselves of a much-needed article of equipment, as from then on our pockets were always crammed with food.

We slept about two hours in the dell, and woke up feeling much rested and keen to learn a bit more about our surroundings. We set out, therefore, to explore the wood, marching gaily and with a complete lack of caution down several paths which took us up the hill and farther away from the road. There were wheel-marks on the paths, of carts and probably of heavier vehicles too. There was indeed every reason to suppose that the wood had been, or even was still being used as a harbouring area, and after a time we left the paths and kept to the undergrowth.

Several times there were sounds of movement away to our left, and later we were to hear that a number of people escaped off the column into this particular wood. At any rate, we all gave each other many moments of abject fright during which we crouched low, listening with bated breath and then moving off very quietly once more.

After half an hour of this wavering and intermittent progress we reached the top or southern edge of the wood. From here a gentle grass slope stretched up another three hundred yards, cutting off any further view of the surrounding country. We reconnoitred up and down the edges of the wood, and then chose a second lying-up place about forty yards in from its upper side. This we camouflaged even further by planting fir branches and twigs, finally settling down to a long and much-needed sleep for the rest of the day.

We woke up about six o'clock, and after a really sound five-hour sleep. We had decided to put off any discussion of plans until we were properly rested and with a bit of food inside us. We were munching a biscuit when footsteps came very tentatively through the trees, paused, then came on again.

I never realised what sheer terror was until this moment. We had both jumped at once to the conclusion that this must be a German looking for us, and we lay quite motionless, with our mouths half-full of biscuit. My mind was cast back to the days when my nurse used to threaten me, a small and exceedingly trying child, "We'll get the Germans to come for you, if you don't do as you're told!" I cowered as the steps wavered, quested for a moment and then came straight and unerringly for our hiding-place. The next thing that either of us knew was the welcome sound of an English voice saying, "I'm awfully sorry to disturb you, but I happened to spot you an hour ago and I thought I'd come along to have a chat."

This was Dick Page, tall and hatchet-faced and a gunner 'regular' officer. He, it turned out, had left the column a minute or two after us, and it was at him that I shouted as he ran down the same path that we had taken.

He sat down, accepted a biscuit, and proceeded to tell us his story. Attached to G.H.Q. at Hazebrouck, he had been sent to Calais, alone on a motor-bike, on 25th May to find out what the situation was. He had driven straight into the middle of a German division astride the Calais-St. Omer road, and had been taken prisoner. Later in the day, however, he slipped away and got into Calais, only to fall again into German hands twenty-four hours later, when the siege came to an end.

Dick was a most reassuring type of person to meet at this stage. He was calm, matter-of-fact, entirely confident. So far there had been a complete unreality about our escape. Dick brought things into their true perspective. He was unworried and supremely English. I thought him very serious at first. But it only took a day or two to realise that behind his impersonal charm of manner was a very real naïve sense of humour. Meeting him was one of the happiest chances of my life. Since that day I have seen much of him, and learnt to appreciate his immense unsophisticated zest for life, and his spontaneous pleasure in the simple things that most of us take too much for granted.

Dick had shown far greater initiative than Charles and myself during the day, and had made a thorough reconnaissance of the top end of the wood. He had spotted two German anti-aircraft detachments, one of which was to pick up Tony Rolt and Charlie Forester during the night. He had made no definite plan, but we all three agreed that our first task was to get as far away as possible from the Étaples – Hesdin – Doullens lateral line of communications. As the map shows, we would therefore have to go due south, and reckoning to cover eight to ten miles during the short four and a half-hour night, we could defer until the next day a final decision as to our destination.

The remaining hours before dark we spent pleasantly enough chatting about home. Dick and I discovered that we had once played cricket against each other in Ireland, and for a time we managed successfully to forget the war and everything about it. Our spirits rose under the stimulus of Dick's infectious enthusiasm. His is the sort of mentality that rather

9

enjoys obstacles. He was quite convinced that we were going to get through, and hungry as we were, we soon reverted to the age-old formula of just what we should eat for our celebration dinner at the'Lion d'Or' in Rouen!

At about 10.15 it was pretty dark, and I went forward from the wood on the line that Dick had already chosen, straight between the German posts, with each of them about five hundred yards away. Eighty yards out from the trees I was completely invisible, Dick whistled me to stop, and the others, vague, shadowy figures in the gloaming, came out to join me. Dick took the lead, with myself as compass man twenty yards behind and Charles keeping a rough computation of the distance we did on each new bearing. We were all intensely excited now, fully alert and mentally quite restored to normal. The adventure had begun.

Walking by night under these circumstances is an exhilarating experience – at any rate up to one or two o'clock in the morning. Just as motor-car engines run more smoothly after dark, so one's legs and whole body seem to respond better to the strain of long hours of continuous walking. One's brain is more active, yet working with a calmer rhythm. The absence of light and of distracting noises seems to bring clearer thinking and a quicker nervous reaction to what is going on around. As one knows from experience, the ticking of a clock at night is a far more incisive, penetrating sound than the cheering of a crowd of fifty thousand at Twickenham or Highbury.

Since childhood Dick, Charles and I had all been out in the country at night, and this first march held for us nothing essentially novel in itself. But we were all keyed up to the importance of the occasion, to the knowledge that one mistake, one moment's indecision might end our chances of success for good and all. For myself, I can say that I walked at first in a state of continuous excitement tinged with fear, eyeing every bush and post with intense enquiry, and expecting an ambushing German to catapult himself out of every copse and hedgerow. Dick was a magnificient leader, quick of eye, sure of foot and setting and maintaining the steady two and a half-mile an hour pace which he no doubt, like myself, had first learnt on the Irish snipe-bogs.

For this night march we had arrived at certain preliminary rules. We would keep off all roads, save tracks which could not be used by anything faster than a farm cart. We would skirt any village on our route, and avoid walking through woods. Both these decisions were dictated by the liability of German troops to use houses and trees for billeting of troops or harbouring of vehicles. We had heard, too, that there was a 9 p.m. curfew imposed in all areas of France occupied by the enemy, and that this was being strictly observed. For obvious reasons we avoided all marshes and low-lying ground where there was a great probability of finding gardens, orchards and barbed-wire fences.

Everything went smoothly. It was a very fine, starlit night as still and clear as any I have ever known, with no whisper of wind or cloud in the sky. The going underfoot was excellent. This part of France is one of the richest agricultural areas in Europe, and rolling grasslands alternated with tremendous expanses of grain, already two feet high and planted in thirty to fifty acre hedgeless fields. We made a point of following along the edges of these, taking at first an exaggerated though commendable care not to trample through crops and leave a track which might be spotted from nearby roads or from the air.

During this first night we saw few woods and seldom had to change direction. We kept steadily on a due southerly compass bearing. Occasionally, far to the east, we heard the hum of a vehicle passing down the Hesdin-Frèvent road, and saw the faint reflection of its shaded lights. Charles and I talked a little, but most of the time we walked in silence, checking and re-checking compass bearings until the hourly halt came round and we could sit and rest.

About two in the morning the strain began to tell for the first time. With physical fatigue came a certain carelessness in picking our way. Several times we waded waist-deep through fields of clover and other crops that were already drenched with dew. We began to use by-roads for the first time and our careful reconnaissance-patrol formation gradually disappeared.

I think this is the invariable experience of those who make long night marches. The first feeling of excitement soon wears off and steadily changes after three or four hours to the beginnings of exhaustion.

I found myself growing strangely light-headed, unable to concentrate my thoughts or focus my attention on objects around me. Although I was still aware of the smallest sounds and movements I was not greatly interested. My only idea was to get on.

And slowly but surely my desire for sleep grew. For the first time I understood the efficacy of that American third-degree process employed against unconfessing criminals – that of keeping them "on the move". After a time its very lack will make sleep an obsession. Animal-need will always reassert itself. The dream that haunted me at three in the morning was not the British lines behind the Somme, the decks of the homebound Channel steamer or the groaning sideboard of my London club. Through the vague swelling lines of meadow and moor, and the black shadows of woods and hedgerows, I saw only one picture – that of a warm, cosy bed with clean white sheets. Charles and I took turns with the compass, and whoever was not using it gradually relapsed into a state of daze, trailing along at the back. What first seems a dramatic and romantic adventure becomes mere commonplace routine. Naturally, there is little incident when one's first object is to avoid incident of any kind, and ensure the safest and dullest type of progress.

At about three o'clock we came down a steep hill into the outskirts of a village. We worked our way round its eastern side until we reached its southern edge, but this operation took some time. It was now nearly half-past three and beginning to get light, and we decided to look round for a reasonable lying-up place.

On this side of the village, about a hundred yards from the nearest house and fifty yards off a country road, a few haystacks stood in the hollow of a field. Judged by later experience this was not a good place for our purposes. There was no cover, no means of moving at all in daylight, without being seen, and no water near. We were, however, all dead-tired by this time, drenched to the waist, shivering with cold and in no state to work out an alternative. We dug ourselves well into the side of a haystack, and arranged our triple "bed", as well as possible. Dick provided an overcoat and a small blanket. The overcoat served as a joint pillow, the ground sheet and gas-cape went beneath us and the two blankets on top, with a quantity of hay above that. On the whole, we might well have been more uncomfortable, and we had no great difficulty in getting to sleep.

At about 6 a.m. we were all woken up by the droning of an aeroplane which was passing and repassing very low overhead. As we heard later, this was a German "Fieseler-Storch" reconnaissance plane, and its job was to look for just such people as ourselves. The possibility of this dawned on us at once. When on the run there is an ever-present feeling that every man's hand is against you. We were fairly well camouflaged under the hay, but as soon as the aeroplane disappeared, Dick, with his usual gumption, hopped up and set off to take a look at the outskirts of the village with the object of finding a place where we could spend the day.

In twenty minutes he was back full of good news. He had spotted an old man pottering in a garden about a hundred yards off and had asked him for help and advice. Dick's French was very nearly the most atrocious I have ever heard, being largely limited to "*M'sieu, ou sont les Allemagnes? Sont-ils dans le jardin, ou non?*" He had no supplementary Latin gestures. But in some amazing way he always made himself understood, even when putting over some quite complicated demand. On this occasion he had scored a complete success. The old man told him first that there were no Germans in the garden, or in the village at all, which was called Vaulx and was ten miles from Hesdin. One German came in twice a day on a motor-bicycle to collect food. He never stayed more than half an hour. The village consisted of about a hundred cottages, with three or four hundred inhabitants, and the old man owned a barn only a couple of hundred yards away which he placed at our disposal. He was certain that we would be quite safe there.

Accordingly, we collected our belongings and moved off to the barn. Six o'clock is the really black hour of the day for the escaper on foot. At 4 a.m. physical exhaustion makes sleep possible in spite of cold and wet and an empty stomach. But by six further sleep in the open is out of the question and the hardness and dampness of the ground first make themselves properly felt. You will be cold, especially in the hands and feet, stiff in every limb and joint, and utterly miserable. The odds are you will have violent cramp, and it is quite certain you will wish you had never been born.

Under such circumstances the barn was better than any palace. Inside there were several partitions and the innermost section was quite dry and full of straw. We prepared an extra safety-device, piling straw up so that if anyone looked like coming into the barn we could cover ourselves in a few seconds. We could, too, peer out through several cracks in the walls, which gave us views of the main road and the path leading from it up to the barn.

In due course Dick and our old friend turned up. He was a short thick-set man of about fifty-five, quiet and rather shy, and utterly unlike the stage representation of the average Frenchman. After a few sentences I discovered that he was, in fact, a townsman and a refugee from Roubaix, which he had left on his own initiative in the first days following the German 'blitz' break-through from Sedan to the Rheims-Rethel bulge. I think he was Flemish, for he spoke a very terse, guttural type of French. He was, at all events, eminently helpful, and went off promising to bring back what food he could find, and a basin and bucket of hot water.

Dick and I began sorting out washing kit, and Dick, like a master-conjuror, produced of all things Charles' own haversack, which the latter had left lying in a house in Calais! By an extraordinary coincidence, Dick was captured in this very house and picked up the nearest haversack he could see. We now had a fine collection of razor-blades, sponges, soap and towels, amounting to real luxury.

The Frenchman came back a few minutes later with the hot water and a wonderful assortment of food, including ten eggs, bread, three-quarters of a pound of cheese, and half a pound of chocolate. In addition, he brought three bottles of *vin ordinaire*, one of milk, a half-bottle of brandy, and finally, a map! This latter was the best he could find, a small departmental map, sixteen kilometres to the inch and printed on the back of a railway and omnibus time-table. It showed only main roads and railways, had no contours, did not mark woods or hills at all, and rivers only very hazily. But for all that, it was a wonderful addition to our scanty geographical knowledge, and made a coherent plan for the first time really feasible.

After a marvellous all-over wash in hot water – our first for a couple of weeks – and an even more wonderful breakfast of new bread, eggs and cheese, washed down with red wine, we settled down to the serious discussion of a plan, There seemed at this stage to be three main possibilities.

The first was to turn east, and then north in the direction of Arras and Douai, which, according to our latest information (then several days out of date), were still held by the B.E.F. The consideration of this route brought home to us, with an ugly jolt, the fact that the British and Belgian armies must now be completely cut off from the main French forces. Had we but known of the overwhelming German superiority in tanks and aircraft we would have ruled this northern route out at once. Arras was forty miles north-east, and there was no indication that it was still in our hands. We imagined, however, that the B.E.F. and Belgians would fight hard to hold on to the ports of Dunkirk and Ostende, and Dick, from his experience on G.H.Q., had picked up a good working knowledge of the country from Arras north to the sea.

The main difficulty here seemed to be the fact that we would have to cross all German lines of communication, several bridges which would certainly be guarded, and finally a battle-area where troops might be closely concentrated and an actual battle was sure to be in progress. Allowing for divergencies, we would have to walk at least fifty miles. In the event of a British retreat, this distance might well easily be doubled.

As the map shows, the Somme at Abbeville and the sea at Quend Plage were almost equidistant, and their respective claims were also about equal. We suffered, of course, like everybody else, from last-war ideas of static warfare. Dick knew a certain amount about the possible tactics of the French defence. The lines of the Somme and Aisne together formed the last large natural obstacle north of the Seine. We could not envisage a retreat that would leave Paris, le Havre and Dieppe in enemy hands, and we felt therefore that a stand would be made along the Somme and the Chemin des Dames. As a complete German victory was utterly beyond our powers of imagination, we expected the Western front to be stabilised on these lines.

The need for quick action on our part was thus unduly emphasised. The Germans had in this area at the moment little more than fighting troops and advance supply services. But every day, we argued, would bring more Germans in. Police and Gestapo would inevitably follow, and the bridges, villages and roads would be brought under strict control. Every day made things more dangerous for us and reduced the possibilities of obtaining help from the French.

Such was our process of reasoning which, but for the complete breakdown of France, would probably have been correct.

The Somme, we thought, if held as a military line, would be, in theory at least, impassable. The use of bridges would be out of the question and boats must be reckoned to be unobtainable. Swimming or wading on a clear moonlit night did not seem a very good chance, especially if one had first to find a way through the German front lines and past their systematic patrols and listening posts.

Again, the whole area immediately to the north of the Somme would inevitably be swarming with tanks, motor transport and troops; and this applied especially to the Forest of Crécy, covering a large area of the north to Abbeville. There was a strong case, put forward by Charles, in favour of making for the Upper Somme, at Peronne, which should be narrower, shallower and possibly have French troops on both banks. This alternative, which in the long run would have given us by far our best chance of escape, was ruled out by reason of extra distance and entire absence of information.

There remained the sea. Between the mouths of the Authie and the Somme our map showed a number of towns and villages, at any of which there would be chances of finding a boat. With the help of our compass we could take a bearing on any point on the English coast. The wind was mainly in the south-west, and with oars and a makeshift sail we reckoned on doing fifteen to twenty miles in the night, and far more if we could find a Frenchman to navigate us. We could, too, row or sail south-west past the mouth of the Somme and so reach the Allied lines beyond. And there was always the additional chance that if we went out some distance to sea, we might be picked up by a British man-of-war.

Altogether the English Channel had most possibilities to offer, and its nearest point to us, at Quend Plage, was less than sixty kilometres away, which at fourteen to fifteen kilometres in the night was a matter of only four nights' march. This was our eventual choice of a plan, which was dependent, too, on crossing the River Authie at Le Ponchel, only a few miles away, and then turning due west for home.

The day passed quietly and pleasantly, with plenty of sleep in warm, soft hay beneath the sunlight that filtered through two large skylights. We ate two good meals, talked about home and everything under the sun, and dozed peacefully away to the sound of flies buzzing in the rafters. Once or twice we heard a motor-cycle hum past on its way into the village and out again, and occasionally farm-carts creaked down the roads, with French peasants wandering along beside them, talking and laughing, and apparently forgetful or utterly unconscious of the war. Our host from Roubaix came in several times, finally wishing us good-bye and good luck, and flatly refusing to accept any payment for his hospitality. The kindness of such people as this has remained a happy memory during the years that followed.

Once more, at about 10.30, we took the road, intent first on crossing the Authie at Le Ponchel.

According to our informant there was no regular guard on the bridge there, but a German cyclist went from Le Ponchel to another bridge farther down-stream several times during the night, and there was believed to be a section posted at the latter place. Once across the river we intended turning almost due west and making a bee-line for Quend Plage, fifty kilometres away. The bridge itself was our first serious problem.

As far as Le Ponchel we followed the road, keeping to the far side of the grass verge and ditch that bounded it. Again the night was beautifully clear and we made fair time, seeing no sign of life on the road until we reached the outskirts of the village. Le Ponchel was a larger place than Vaulx, and it contained a great number of narrow, winding streets, where we must have spent a quarter of an hour tiptoeing up and down before locating the bridge.

Here there was a serious hitch. The German section truck, reported to be at the downstream crossing, was drawn up on the right-hand side of the road and a few yards short of the Le Ponchel bridge.

Charles and I were both wearing heavy service boots, so Dick stalked the truck in his light shoes, came half-way back, and motioned us to come over quietly. As we went by there were heavy snores from inside the truck, and the wind created by the sleepers' breathing actually bellied the canvas tarpaulin of the vehicle to and fro. We crept by as quickly as we dared.

On the far side of the bridge the road forked, but the right-hand branch which we followed very soon bent back to the river, suggesting that this was the route followed by the German bicyclist on his nightly patrol. We therefore took a W.S.W. bearing from our compass, left the road and soon found ourselves in very difficult country, marshy and covered with a network of barbed-wire fences. Progress was slow, with Dick in front getting very wet. An additional source of worry was the fact that the main Hesdin-Amiens road was still nine to ten kilometres away running north and south straight across our line of march. As we had taken an hour and a quarter to get past Le Ponchel, we had less than three hours left to take us over this main road. As can be seen from the map, this road was bound to be an important German supply route for the Somme area, where a new battle was developing. There would be vehicles harbouring in the woods to either side, and anti-aircraft and observation-posts on high points. This main artery and the Montreuil – Abbeville road were, indeed, the two chief obstacles remaining between us and the coast, and it was highly desirable that we should give the widest possible berth to both of them during the daytime.

Naturally enough, we were all three convinced we could get across the road by three o'clock, and so have three-quarters of an hour left to find a lying-up place at least a mile beyond. As in a game of golf, there are few of us capable of deliberately playing short when there is a sporting chance of carrying the objective in one.

At first things went well enough. We were very soon out of the marsh, but woods held us up more than we noticed, and then at about two o'clock we came into a vast tract of heath, covered with a network of tracks, all winding crazily to and fro, often enough petering out in patches of watery bog. There were no houses, trees or landmarks of any kind. Charles and I, more particularly myself, were badly flustered with our compass work. A path leading due west would bend gradually to the north, veer west again, and then turn north or even north-east before coming to a dead end. Twice we took to the heath, but each time got bogged within a few minutes and were forced to return to the path that we had just left. At one period, under my guidance, we found that our general direction was actually south-east !

Dick, who had taken several heavy falls, was very tired, and Charles twice saved the situation, plumping strongly for his choice of roads at two "junctions-complex". At about 3.30 we came down a steep hill into a narrow lane that ran between hedges and grass fields, with the first trees we had seen in nearly four miles. The lane wound on into a valley, and following it down we passed through the fringe of a hamlet to within twenty yards of the main Hesdin-Amiens road, down which a German motorised column was moving at that very moment! Such was our state of exhaustion that we very nearly blundered into the middle of it!

All our worst fears were realised! We struggled back four hundred yards up the hill to where a row of deserted cottages stood back from the lane. One of the back doors was open and we made our way into an empty room, bare of all furniture and exceedingly damp and draughty. We covered the one window with sacking, jammed the door and lay down in a huddle on the cement floor, too tired to think of doing anything more.

Three hours later we woke up stiff and cold and very conscious of the dangers of the position that we had chosen. In the half-light of early morning the back room of the cottage had given an illusion of conceal-ment. By seven o'clock the sun was already up, and we now found that our window, from which the sacking had already fallen down, was in plain view of the road lower down, and that we could actually be seen moving about in the room. From the main road down in the valley came the con-tinuous buzz of traffic and occasional shouts of Germans loading up vehicles or backing them into temporary parking-places.

After two or three minutes' observation, Dick picked out the forms of several German soldiers silhouetted against the sky on the slope of the hill on the other side of the lane. They were less than a hundred yards away, and we decided from their movements that they were part of an anti-aircraft or observation-post just beyond our range of vision. If this were so, reliefs or parties bringing up food and water from the village below would use the lane, passing only a few yards from our front door. It would only be a matter of time before we were spotted.

Behind the cottages and away from the lane and its unconsidered sources of danger, the hill sloped sharply up, covered with scrub and small clumps of trees. Very carefully we made our way up its side, and there about two hundred yards away from the cottages, we found an ideal lying-up place. Here there was an impenetrable gorse and bramble brake, with a narrow path leading to a little clearing in its middle, and a number of trees around providing sufficient cover for us to stand up without any danger of being seen. We settled in at once. It was real "blitz weather", warm with a cloudless sky, but there was still dew on the ground and for the first hour or two we were very cold.

There was, of course, no question of moving out in search of food or water. The absence of the latter was the more serious disadvantage. On out first night's march we had drunk from any available spring or stream on our route, and from Vaulx we had kept one wine bottle and made a point of refilling in order always to have two or three pints in reserve. Latterly, in the wild heath country, we had found no drinkable water, and had drawn on this reserve. Now we were reduced to half a bottle between us and any washing or shaving became, of course, impossible.

We had plenty of food for the day, a couple of eggs, four or five biscuits, a piece of bread, and about an ounce of cheese each. For the next day we kept only half a dozen biscuits in all, a small piece of bread, and a few lumps of sugar. These latter we had been eating soaked in brandy at our hourly halts during the night, a valuable stimulant after one o'clock in the morning.

As far as we could make out from the inadequate map, we had not finally lost direction, but had covered less than eight miles. It was vitally necessary that we should not again be caught at such a disadvantage, and have to lie up beyond range of help, without possibility of movement. This day, indeed, provided an unforgettable lesson for the night marcher. Whatever the varying length of hours of darkness, a marginal period should always be set aside, to allow for half an hour's search for proper cover. That should be the first objective, and the six o'clock morning reconnaissance should provide for the finding of water and a better hiding-place for the day. The temptation to push on when it is already growing light is always very great. In Germany itself it was even more liable to lead to fatal results, and perhaps one walker in three was caught because he failed to observe this elementary rule.

The day passed uneventfully. Out plans for the night's march were necessarily vague. In the first place we could not tell to within a couple of miles where we actually were, and in the second place we had now crossed from the department of the Pas-de-Calais to that of the Somme. Our map took in the Somme department from Crécy, to south, as far as the mouth of the Somme to the west, but marked in practically no details. We would be more than ever dependent on correct compass work.

The presence of the German post on the adjacent hillside made a late start necessary, and we set off across country in preference to going down to the road-junction directly below us. There was still plenty of movement in the hamlet, and cars with dimmed headlights hummed through every now and then. We kept the houses on our left-hand side.

The first incident of the march was the sudden disappearance of Dick down a twenty-foot bank with a barbed wire fence at the bottom. This was the first of several such obstacles which we met during the next few nights. In the dark it was not possible to make out what they were, but they might well have been parts of old earthworks, as they were obviously artificial and of regular construction.

The first hour we kept north of west, with the main road on our left, and about midnight we crossed the road after a careful stalk up to it. Half an hour later we reached a large village which we took to be Vron – a place which was strongly occupied by German troops according to our information. We therefore changed our line of march to south-west in order to leave the village on our right.

The country now flattened out. There were no villages, hardly a house, simply unending fenceless fields of crops – wheat, barley and lucerne. By 2.30 we were becoming anxious. However careful your manipulation of the compass, this sort of situation always brings doubt and hesitation. I began to check the compass every fifty yards and even so to wonder whether we were not going in a circle after all. The absence of landmarks was very trying, for even a single tree can provide a guide for quarter or half a mile. Here there was nothing. Like men in the desert, we began to see mirages, not of silver towers, green palms and cool lake-water, but of a low, black fringe of trees on the skyline. One look up at the stars and the illusion vanished or turned into a two-foot hedge of gorse only thirty yards away.

At three o'clock we sighted woods at last. We were using a narrow by-road at the time, heavily rutted and potholed, and Charles, at the back, bending down to look at these tracks, discovered the unmistakable marks of tanks, which must have used this road during the last few hours. Shortly afterwards we came to a fork, where German traffic signs had been put up, and the tank tracks divided and multiplied themselves. Along the right-hand road was a small village nestling among orchards and almost in the shadow of the forest beyond. Outflanking clumps and thin plantations of trees came right up to the left-hand side of the road, giving plenty of covered approaches into the main woods. On the right or northern side of the village, the ground sloped gently up to a small, sixty-foot high mound.

Some strange dementia seized us at this moment for, instead of taking the quickest way into the forest, we decided to reconnoitre the village first. Certainly, we were bound to look for help to renew our supplies during the day, but this was hardly sufficient excuse for wasting time at such a juncture. We turned right, off the road, climbed the knoll (an ideal place for a German observation post, incidentally!) and peered vaguely into the grey shadows of the village in the hope of seeing some signs of life and movement.

Needless to say, we saw and heard nothing but only wasted a further precious quarter of an hour of our time. Returning from the knoll, where there was very little cover, we skirted the eastern side of the village, back to the same place from which we had started off on this meaningless little excursion.

Fifty yards nearer the village there was a low gate into an orchard, with trees immediately beyond. Being possibly the most tired and impatient of the party at this stage, I was in front when we reached the gate, which had high hedgerows on either side. I gave a push, it swung easily open, and I stepped through to let the others in.

At that moment I looked round and found, to my horror, that we were in the middle of a German tank park. There were twenty to thirty tanks round the edges of the orchard, all heavily camouflaged with branches. A sentry was, at that moment, walking quietly away from us down one of the hedges! We moved backwards out of that orchard rather like figures in a Mickey Mouse cartoon, with a first moment of sheer paralysis, then a violent dash with feet hardly touching the ground!

We literally ran down the road the way we had come with myself well out in front. Coming to the fork, we shot off to the right, down what appeared to be an avenue running to the gates of a private demesne. It was uncomfortably light now, and we did not pause for any considerations, but went straight through the gate and some distance on, turning off the avenue only when we saw the façade of a large country mansion in front of us.

After such a narrow escape we were not going to make any further mistakes, and, where laurels and rhododendrons of all colours grew thickly among young firs and larch trees, we chose a piece of cover so thick that even a rabbit would have had a job getting through it. Fir branches grew so low that we had to crawl on hands and knees, even so scraping our hands and faces painfully. We settled down to sleep in impenetrable gloom, with the rank smell of laurels in our nostrils, and in our ears the sound of water dripping somewhere nearby.

Charles was up in the morning before either Dick or I were properly awake, although from somewhere deep in our dreams we had heard once or twice the sound of a motor vehicle buzzing past. Leaving his jacket behind, Charles wandered off wearing khaki trousers and a dark blue pullover. Dark of hair and complexion and now unshaven and deeply sunburnt, he must have looked like any French peasant, a fortunate similarity, for no sooner was he properly in the open than a German motor-cyclist swept past on his way up the drive to the house!

The man, however, paid no attention to Charles, for, like any despatch-rider, he was travelling fifteen miles an hour faster than warranted, road-hogging along with his head bent between the handle-bars and deriving an obvious satisfaction from driving his bike into the ground.

Charles came back unperturbed but not altogether satisfied. He had seen enough to know that our present position, though safe enough from the point of view of keeping ourselves hidden, was not a suitable base from which to set out and find supplies. Evidently the country house was a

German H.Q. of some kind, for soon motor-cycles were going up and down the drive every few minutes, and a staff car once made its appearance, closely packed with square heads nodding and jolting on their way to the village.

Charles, however, had seen a French peasant in an adjoining field farther away from the drive. He now set off to contact him and was back again in a few minutes. The peasant had told him that there were two farms a quarter of a mile away across the fields, and had pointed out some of their outbuildings through the trees. He was going across to the smaller one himself, whose owner, a personal friend, he would warn of our impending arrival. He also gave Charles exact directions for getting there, through a belt of trees, down the side of a field of turnips and into an adjoining orchard.

Accordingly we waited for the motor-bike to make one of its periodic trips, and within ten minutes it shot by, scorching along with all the verve and noisiness of a Parisian taxi. We crept out of shelter, round the side of a high stone wall into a straggling fir plantation, through this again, over the field of roots to a lane that led into the orchard.

Here Dick went ahead to contact the owner. The farmer himself was out but his wife was very ready to help us, although during the last day or two there had been Germans in and out of all the farms, collecting eggs and potatoes. For these they paid in worthless paper money in order to preserve at least an appearance of rectitude!

Dick was shown a small hay-loft where we could take shelter, on the understanding that we pulled up the ladder behind us, and, if discovered, knew nothing about the farmer and his wife. This was achieved without trouble. The loft was about twelve feet square, and six feet high in the middle, with a roof sloping down to within two feet of the floor on either side. It was warm and cosy, with plenty of soft, delicious-smelling hay. There was a trap-door in the floor, and in due course the farmer's wife appeared below with a basketful of food, including white bread, a dozen eggs, half a pound of butter and bottles of milk and red wine. The highlight of the collection was, however, a large pork *paté*, rich-smelling and highly seasoned with garlic and onions. Unprepossessing in looks and smell, it was the sort of thing that one would have regarded with suspicion and insular contempt in the fat days of peace-time. For all that, it was one of the best things I have ever eaten in my life.

Pleasant surprises did not cease at this. The farmer himself turned up half an hour later, an ugly, cheerful and quite charming little man, who appeared delighted to see us. He brought a large pail of hot water, towels, a map of the Somme department and a lot of information.

Apparently we were between the villages of Ligescourt, Vironchaux and Wadicourt. We had covered twelve or fourteen kilometres during the night and had kept direction well. We were, too, I learnt later, within a few hundred yards of the battlefield of Crécy, but the farmer's memory did not travel far back enough into the past to remember England's one-time Continental ambitions, and he was one of the firmest supporters of the *Entente* that I have ever met. He was, too, among the small minority of Frenchmen who did not think the war was yet lost.

He was full of advice. He was convinced that we would find a boat on the coast and suggested Quend Plage as the most likely place. Berck Plage would have been even better, but to reach it we would have to re-cross the Authie, and there were rumours that the Germans at Berck had begun collecting all boats and putting them under guard. He knew none of the fishermen personally, for he and his family had come only a few months before from Marquise, in the Pas-de-Calais, but he was sure that we would find help.

After a quarter of an hour's talk, during which he looked several times at his watch, he suddenly slipped away, brought up a small son of about seven whom he left to entertain us, and then departed again. In a few minutes he was back, bearing a huge dish of roast duck, potatoes and vegetables *en casserole*, a wonderful and quite unexpected surprise.

During the day he and his wife each looked in once or twice, but most of the afternoon Germans were in the farm, requisitioning food, apparently with great politeness, and we had to lie very low indeed. In the evening a look-out was kept so that we could stroll about the farmyard talking to the family and feeling more like ordinary human beings than at any time since capture. The setting was no doubt an everyday one, the family gathered round us chatting, a farm labourer seated on the gate with a pipe in his mouth, chickens and geese straggling about our feet, and the farm buildings warm and mellow in the evening sunlight that streamed through the trees of the orchard. But it is one that stands out in memory, sandwiched as it is among the excitements and hardships of our escape. For this hour at least we could forget all our plans and troubles.

The evening brought a final surprise, a second basket of food, bread, butter, eggs, cheese and brandy. Altogether, it had been a grand day, with plenty to eat, time for sleeping, and the comfortable presence of friendly people about us. We were all very sorry to say good-bye to that family, who with typical generosity, refused to accept any sort of payment and only took a present of chocolate for the child under graceful protest.

As the first stage of our route lay through woods which were part of the northern fringe of the Forest of Crécy, we were able to make an earlier start at about ten o'clock. We expected a difficult march, as a number of villages lay directly on our way, and deviations were, in fact, wide and frequent. The country was very much more enclosed, with barbed-wire fences and thick, impenetrable hedgerows, and there were a number of high grass banks down which we all took heavy falls. There was little incident and progress was slow. Twice we saw German trucks parked in the fields, and gave them a wide berth. At about two o'clock we were once more in an endless stretch of bare moorland, entirely lacking in houses, trees or signposts, and after an unpleasant and tiring hour of compass work, we reached the edge of a very large village, which we took to be Quend, three miles short of Quend Plage.

On all the roads outside the village there were a large number of wheel-marks and very reluctantly we turned back to a thick clump of trees half a mile short of the place.

There are always compensations, and this time we found that the clump provided excellent cover and contained a quantity of dry bracken which gave us the most comfortable bed that we had yet found in the open. We slept soundly from four to seven.

Charles and I got up together in the morning, for Dick, who had done nearly all the leading and brain-work so far, was very tired. I reconnoitred the south edge of the wood, which afforded me a wide view of bare, deserted heathland with a few cultivated fields running down towards the village. At the other end of the wood Charles found a road, and met an old lady bicycling down it. She told him the name of the village, Villers-sur-l'Authie. We had trended steadily north during our march and were two or three miles off our intended line, besides being four miles short of Quend. We could not have covered more than eight miles during the night. The old lady said she would come back in the afternoon, bringing food and fresh water.

During the day we slept and ate plentifully, having more than enough food left over from what had been given us on the previous evening. We explored the woods thoroughly and found the remains of a number of Dutch newspapers. Later we heard how a body of Dutch troops had taken refuge there a few days previously, and how the Germans beat out the woods for them and caught the lot.

I met the old lady at the appointed rendezvous at about three in the afternoon. She was a stout, matronly type bursting with confident tales of the coming French counter-attack on the Somme, and full of abuse of the Germans who were occupying Villers. Requisitioning was being carried out on a large scale and food-rationing was threatened. She brought us two tins of sardines, a loaf of bread and a bottle of water, and she took our brandy bottle home, refilled it and returned it later in the evening.

Generally, it was notable how much more fighting spirit these French-women had than their menfolk. The average Frenchman seemed to take the German occupation philosophically – perhaps too philosophically – but the women were invariably full of tales of counter-offensives that would sweep "these ruffians" out of France. The hint of food-rationing alone was sufficient to flog up attempts at horror-stories, and threats of violent reprisals when the French armies invaded Germany!

There seemed no reason to change our plans in any way. Quend Plage was still our objective, and our slight deviation to the north placed us about ten miles due east of it. There were, however, a number of danger-points on our route. First came the Étaples-Montreuil-Abbeville road, which was the main German communication line between Calais and the Somme; then the Calais-Abbeville main railway line; and lastly the Abbeville-Fort Mahon Plage-le Touquet coastal road. There was also a steam-tramway in the Monchaux area, and information suggested there were more Germans along the coast than anywhere inland behind the battle-front.

Beginning our night march, we reached the far side of Villers by a détour round the northern side, but there we met with our first reverse, finding a broad highway running north-west, presumably to Montreuil, and unmarked on our maps. On one side was a high stone wall, on the other marshy ground, and we were obliged to follow along the side of the road for an awkward quarter of an hour. Had a German patrol come along, our only shelter would have been a shallow and quite inadequate ditch.

The wall, however, came in due course to an end and we turned directly west and cross-country again. The Montreuil-Abbeville road provided no difficulties. At midnight there was plenty of traffic on it, mainly travelling south to the Battle of the Somme. Interference from the air must have been slight at this time, for many of the vehicles had headlights full on; there was no German standing up or on the running-board to act as observer, and soldiers inside were singing cheerfully and tunefully.

Beyond the road we found ourselves in flatter country where heath alternated with cultivated fields, and there was a certain amount of water about in this area. Numerous irrigation drains intersected one another, and low grass-covered causeways ran between them, often coming to a dead-end and making counter-marches necessary. After a short time, we were driven on to the by-roads again, which, fortunately, were quite free of traffic.

On the outskirts of Quend we reached and crossed the railway line, leaving the town on our left and to the south of us. Quend was the largest place that we had met so far, and a considerable détour was necessary, which must have taken us a mile and a half off our line. Rather unwisely, we tried to correct this by taking a new compass bearing due south-west. One tends to forget how much ground is lost by two acute bearings, taken to correct one another.

Our course brought us into Monchaux, and anxious as we were to make up time we decided to walk straight through the village. This was an unhappy decision. At the very first house a dog started barking, and his hysterical warning was taken up by every dog in the village. The chorus gradually swelled as we arrived at the end of the long, narrow main street, and continued to echo through the night long after we reached the open country at the other side of the place. Beyond Monchaux the road turned north for Fort Mahon, and we left it to continue west, looking for the steam-tramway, which should, according to the map, have run straight across our front.

The steam-tramway, however, resolutely refused to turn up, and we began bearing south of west again to correct a purely imaginary error. Only the next day were we to learn that the steam-tramway did, in fact, no longer exist.

At three o'clock we took a lane which led us to an ideal camping place, pine-woods with plenty of cover, and a small group of cottages nearby placed handily for the morning. Somewhere in front we could, at last, hear the far-off murmur of the sea. The breeze, blowing in our faces, brought a tang of salt and a sweet freshness from the English Channel. We slept there, with the distant music in our ears, telling us of the rolling sand-dunes ahead, the grey welter of the waves beyond and, farther again, home and journey's end.

*   *   *   *   *

This time Charles and I made the morning reconnaissance, knocking smartly on the door of the nearest cottage and stepping inside. We found a very frowsy little couple in residence, an old peasant and his wife, who were sitting over their breakfast. They were horrified to see us, chattering wildly in an unintelligible patois, and upsetting quite a lot of their breakfast in their excitement.

It appeared that the Germans had sent three truck loads of soldiers out to these cottages only the day before. They had asked for details of escaped prisoners in the immediate neighbourhood, and receiving no satisfactory answer, off-loaded several machine-guns and blazed off whole magazines of ammunition into the woods. A number of Allied soldiers had then come in from the undergrowth with their hands up and, said the peasant, *"Il y en a des cadavres là-bas, beaucoup, beaucoup, beaucoup!"* pointing at the same time to the place where we had been peacefully sleeping for the last three hours!

The little man gave us some coffee which, even to us, tasted pretty foul, and offered to share his bowl of porridge. He was quite friendly but obviously scared out of his wits, and he had only two ideas in his head, the first being that we should leave at the earliest possible moment! He seemed to know nothing about the war, and barely understood which side the English were fighting on. His general mentality seemed to be that of a peasant of the French Revolution days!

His wife, a small, shrivelled and gibbering counterpart, was equally ignorant, even dirtier and little better than a cretin. They were both convinced that our only policy was to search out a man called Réné, gamekeeper to the local *Seigneur* who owned these woods, and preserved their shooting. Réné apparently had all the answers, could deal with the Germans and, if necessary, ship us off to our own country, wherever that was. He, and not the *Seigneur*, was evidently their local deity.

We were hustled out of the tumbledown cottage, and Réné's house was pointed out – a lodge standing at the gates of an avenue, which led presumably to the *Seigneur's* country house. We saw the last of the two little old people as they stood watching us off the place, occasionally scuttering up and down, looking round corners, presumably for Germans, and assuming hunched hunted attitudes.

At the lodge gates there were a number of Belgian refugees, encamped round two farm-carts. They gave us some coffee, while one of them fetched Réné, who was evidently regarded by them, too, as a considerable personage. Réné duly made his appearance, a swarthy, bearded man of middle age, looking very much as I have always imagined Richard Coeur de Lion to have been, with a bit of Douglas Fairbanks, senior, thrown in. I expect, by the time I write this, that Réné will have long since ceased to be, and some member of the *Maquis* will have found him a suitable target for shooting practice. For Réné was pro-German to the core, an out-and-out *collaborateur* even at this early stage of the war.

He began by telling us that there was no object in trying to escape. *"Les Allemands,"* he said, *"sont des gens tout-à-fait aimables."* We had far better give ourselves up. He added, "I was a prisoner in the Great War, and I ought to know that I was decently treated." This part of his discourse ended with the inevitable reminder, *"La guerre, c'est finie."* He had no doubt that we British, too, would soon make peace.

He went on to say that it was out of the question for us to remain on his master's land, as that might implicate him in the event of our being caught there. He made no offer at all in the way of giving or selling us food, and he made us very conscious of the fact that he was doing us a big favour by talking to us at all.

A certain amount, however, transpired during this conversation. As an inducement towards giving ourselves up, he stressed the fact that all boats from Fort Mahon Plage, Berck Plage and Quend Plage had been gathered in by the Germans and put under strong guard. He did not know anything about St. Quentin-en-Tourment, three miles south down the coast, but he suggested that if we must go anywhere, this was probably the best place. He was also ready to show us the quickest way off his master's land.

After a short talk, we decided to take immediate advantage of this offer, gathered up our belongings, and followed him for several hundred yards through the pinewoods. There he left us, after giving further directions. He was almost friendly when we crossed the boundary of his master's demesne, and waved us an insultingly cheerful good-bye. We continued through the trees and over undulating sandhills, which were coloured deep red in the early morning sunlight. Twice we caught glimpses of the sea during a very pleasant twenty minutes walk, which brought us to a large farm-house, standing just clear of the woods.

The daughter of the house, a dark-eyed girl of thirteen or fourteen, was standing out on the road, and at my request went in and fetched her father, an extremely pleasant, upstanding ex-soldier of about forty. He immediately confirmed the news about boats. The Germans had constructed a large road in the sand-dunes, running the whole way from Berck Plage to Le Crotoy at the mouth of the Somme. They had put the whole coast-line under military control, allowing no fishermen out, kept all French-men off the sea-shore, and gathered all boats into the port of Le Crotoy. He believed that north of the Authie they had done the same thing, using Le Touquet and Étaples as their depots.

St. Quentin was useless. As far as he knew, there were no boats hidden that we could use. Those at Le Crotoy were under guard, but just how efficient that guard was he could not say. He thought that there were too few German soldiers there to do the job thoroughly, and that these could be avoided or even bribed.

He brought us some food at once, eight eggs, bread, milk, cheese and paté, and refused payment. As an afterthought, he led us off five or six hundred yards through the woods to a little hut, which he said was quite safe, as the Germans had just searched the area thoroughly and would not return again.

There he left us, promising to come back at 9-30 that evening and put us on our way to Le Crotoy.

We decided to camp a hundred yards away from the hut, in which he had told us there were some Belgians living. After half an hour I paid them a visit. Much to my surprise, they turned out to be in uniform, being Red Cross medical personnel. They were as fantastic a trio as I have ever seen, all with ten days' growth of beard, dilapidated, dirty and smelling horribly. They all stood up and greeted me with immense formality, introducing themselves in order of size, one being a six-footer with red hair and whiskers, and another little more than five feet high, with a vast black spade-beard. The third was a fat, lugubrious looking individual with a marked resemblance to that member of the "Three Stooges" comedy team – who is always being knocked about by his companions. He had the same high, thin voice, pendulous cheeks and pale, plaintive eyes.

They had plenty of information, some of it useful. About boats they knew nothing. They simply had seen none and did not know where to look for them. It was possible, however, to get across the Somme estuary, five kilometres wide, by foot, improbable as this may sound. Apparently at low tide the whole estuary is wadable, with the exception of the Abbeville-St. Valéry canal, which is cut only a hundred yards from the southern bank of the river. Three days previously the trio had themselves started wading in company with several hundred refugees and a number of soldiers. They set off at three in the morning, and at five were two-thirds of the way across, when they found themselves under German artillery and machine-gun fire.

This fire came from the German bridgehead opposite Noailles and south of the river and forced them to turn back, after several people had been wounded and others drowned. This was the first we had heard of German troops on the south bank of the Somme, but the Belgians had no doubts on the matter and added that there was a larger German bridgehead south of Abbeville. Le Hourdel, directly opposite Le Crotoy, was believed to be still in British hands.

After this reverse the three Belgians gave themselves up, but the Germans, with insufficient men to spare for the guarding of non-combatants, set them loose again. They then collected as much food as they could find, ate it, and gave themselves up again, receiving this time a sharper rebuff. They had twice since repeated this performance and were now reduced to a two-pound slab of bacon, which they reckoned would last them two days longer. Personally, I thought this an over-estimate of at least thirty-six hours, for while I was there those who were not talking to me kept getting up, cutting a generous slice of bacon, swallowing it and lying down again.

They had just heard of King Leopold's capitulation, and this piece of news had determined them to give themselves up once more and ask the Germans to send them back to Belgium!

Our story intrigued them immensely, and two of them asked to be allowed to come with us and have another try at getting away in earnest. This request we were obliged to side-track, in spite of the fact that they had already begun making overtures of friendship by cutting us slices of bacon from the fast diminishing flitch. Jerome K. Jerome might have got plenty of copy out of them, but for our purposes a more useless and improvident collection of people would have been hard to find.

The rest of the day we spent sleeping on a beautifully warm sand-bed under the sun, with occasional visits to the hut for conversation, and to a nearby spring for water.

At 9.30 the farmer arrived at the rendezvous on the fringe of the wood. He took us along for half a mile, and then gave us our itinerary to Le Crotoy, his directions being slightly complicated by the alternations of "à droit" and "tout droit" (straight on).

Charles, however, managed to memorise it all, and everything went according to plan. We crossed one main road, found the bridge over the Tourment stream, which we knew to be unguarded, and at a road junction, with a calvary, turned right-handed and south-west for the sea.

Here we were using a small by-road which ran along a narrow causeway between wide stretches of watery marsh. Although our thoughts were concentrated mainly on the route and the danger of meeting someone, I shall never forget the beauty of that marsh. Far away to the right we could hear the booming of the sea out beyond the sand-dunes, and the waters and weeds of the marsh shone silvery pale under the moonlight. They were alive with bullfrogs that kept up an incessant chorus, harsh and guttural close at hand, but from a distance as light and musical as the chirping of crickets. The skies were cloudless and the moon very bright – too bright indeed from our point of view. At first there were occasional dark clumps of trees dotting the bog, but these grew ever rarer, until the only landmarks left were the poplars and willows along the banks of the causeway.

For over an hour we walked along through the marshes, almost dropping off to sleep on our feet. Three miles from Le Crotoy we came to the little village of La Bassée, a line of fishermen's cottages on the left, with the marsh and sea-flats still on the right-hand side of the road. Here and there, glistening lanes of clear water stretched down to the sea, pitch black at their edges, and silver shot with palest gold in the middle, where slanting rays of moonlight struck down. Outside La Bassée culti-vated ground reappeared on the left, with not a sign of cover. As the brightness of the night was being slowly reinforced by the first pale greyness of dawn, we twice made sorties to look for a camping-place. Once we nearly decided to use a thick, bushy hedgerow, as we were determined not to be caught by daylight in the open. Wisely, as it turned out, we pushed on this time, and Dick, from his six feet three inches, was first to see a dark clump of trees up the gentle slope of the hill to the left.

In ten minutes we reached the place and found it to be a square ten-acre wood very similar to the one which we had used outside Villers. With plenty of time before daybreak, we made a thorough reconnaissance, and found a large farm on the south side. Returning to the thickest cover, which we had chosen for a lying-up place, we nearly blundered into a truck backed among the trees and from which a loud snoring proceeded. There was no sign of sentries, and we came to the correct conclusion that it contained refugees. At three o'clock we settled down to our earliest, warmest and best morning sleep so far.

In the morning, Dick found out that we had landed up at an ideal kicking-off point for the final dash. We were just over a mile from Le Crotoy, and from the hill on which the farm stood could get a fair view of the lie of the land running down to the Somme estuary and of the sea beyond. Unwittingly, too, we had chosen as our headquarters the largest dairy farm in the neighbourhood. Rationing had already been introduced here by the Germans but so far only in a mild and unsystematic form. We could have all the milk we wanted, and were given literally gallons. For once, after much argument, we were allowed to pay – a happy arrangement in this case, as we had no scruples about asking for more!

There were a large number of people about, an employ of twenty farm labourers, several French families in the house, and twenty to thirty Belgian refugees camping in trucks and barns. The farmer gave us as much bread and butter and as many eggs as we wanted, and we were able to set aside as much as four days' rations for a boat journey, which we felt would be enough to keep us until picked up out at sea.

During the day a number of people from the farm came to visit us. There were two Belgian sisters from Charleroi, the husband of the elder, who was a French electrician, this man's married sister and her two small children. The farmer's son also looked in twice to see if we had everything we wanted, bringing an Abbé with him the second time. All had infor-mation of some kind and were immensely interested, the younger Belgian girl making us her particular charge and bringing us small snacks of bacon and porridge during the day, and tea and coffee in the evening.

The Abbé, a very charming and amusing man, had a tolerably clear idea of what was going on in the world outside. He gave us the latest news available. The battle of the Somme was now, apparently, under way, as we ourselves could hear from the continuous rumbling of the guns beyond Abbeville. Up till the previous day, the English had held Le Hourdel, directly opposite Le Crotoy, and on the southern shore of the Somme, but the Germans had enlarged their bridgehead beyond Noailles to include St. Valéry-sur-Somme, now in flames following very heavy fighting and bombardment from the air.

In Le Crotoy itself was a small German detachment of fifty men, but they had instituted rigid control of the port, where all boats from the neighbourhood were concentrated and packed into as small a space as possible. No one could approach to within fifty or sixty yards of the boats, as there were several sentries in the adjoining square, the Place Jeanne d'Arc. The Abbé thought it might be possible to procure a boatman and said he would consult a friend that evening. He felt, personally, that there was a better chance of wading the estuary. Two days before, a couple of British officers and a sergeant had turned up and made the attempt. The sergeant was caught and paraded through the streets of Le Crotoy. Nothing was known of the fate of the two officers.

Late in the afternoon the younger Belgian girl went down to the town and bought us sardines, chocolate, paté and biscuits, and collected more chocolate from among the Belgian refugees. This latter gift we tried to refuse, as it was Belgian Côte d'Or chocolate which they had saved up, but they were determined that we should have it. Sad to relate, I have lost the address and may never be able to repay her kindness.

British aircraft were active over the estuary, and bombs were actually dropped on Le Crotoy itself, aimed at but just missing the German radio-station and hitting several of our precious boats in the harbour! Away to the east, heavy gunfire was intensified during the day, and by evening was almost continuous. The Abbé, on his return, could give us little fresh news. His friend in the town could not get a boatman for us, or a guide to take us across the mouth of the Somme by foot. He had, however, procured maps and tide-charts, from which there was much to be learnt.

To set off by boat, we had to leave at or after midnight, when there would be sufficient water in the ordinarily very shallow harbour. A four kilometre row would take us to Le Hourdel, and the same distance would clear the point beyond Le Hourdel and bring us into the open sea. If we waded, we could not leave until shortly before low tide, at three o'clock, and with luck might reach the canal along the southern shore in an hour and a half. There were several bridges marked across the canal and it would probably take us another half-hour to find one of these. The whole undertaking was far from easy, as there were patches of quicksand and deep pools, but we were far more worried by the consideration that we would reach the opposite shore in broad daylight.

As to whether British or Germans were now in occupation of that shore, the Abbé could give us no definite answer. He felt that it was most probably in German hands, as there had been no firing there since the previous afternoon, while a battle continued to rage south and south-west of St. Valéry.

There was a wireless in the farm, and Winston Churchill's speech had just come over, praising the defence of Calais. But Hitler had also made a speech, announcing the beginning of a great new German offensive, between Amiens and the sea. The Abbé had no pretensions to being a strategist, but he thought the Somme battle might prove the decisive point of the whole campaign. The vital question was whether the French had gained time to re-form their lines, following the German breakthrough to the Channel ports. If they had, a French counter-attack would develop. But if not, the battle would degenerate into a running fight through the whole length of France.

Late in the evening, several flights of Wellingtons came sweeping down the line of the Somme, a grand sight as they flew wing to wing in perfect formation. Almost opposite Le Crotoy, Messerschmitts appeared, cutting down behind them, turning, climbing and diving again. We heard once more that awe-inspiring noise of machine-guns in the skies, small, controlled bursts of thunder suggestive of the voice of God in one of William Blake's visions. By St. Valéry, anti-aircraft batteries opened up, and thick little puffs of smoke began to burst in the sky, apparently directly below the German fighters. The Abbé thought that this meant that St. Valéry was once more in Allied hands. In point of fact, the batteries were firing too low, and the smoke-puffs were seconds late to our eyes. Subsequently we learnt that they must have been firing at the British planes, which disappeared in the direction of Abbeville.

The Abbé was, at any rate, certain of one thing: that we should stay the night and await further developments. If Allied forces counterattacked and succeeded in crossing the Somme we were clearly best off sitting where we were. If the Germans drove south, we could not land at Le Hourdel, and lost, in this way, one of our two chief gambits. There might still be a chance of getting a boatman or, at least, more detailed information about the port. We were tired and had not had a proper

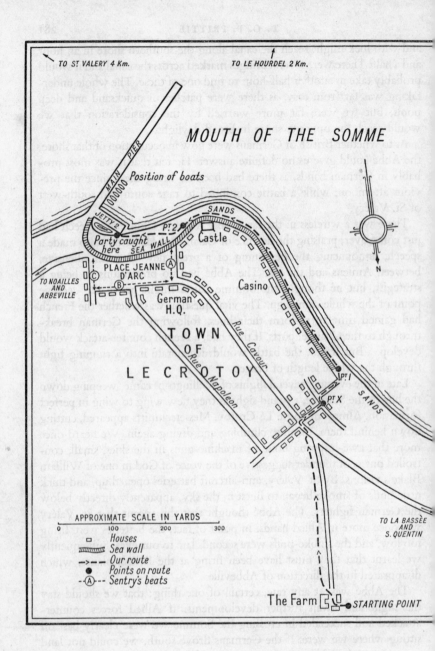

MOUTH OF THE SOMME

TO ST VALERY 4 Km.

TO LE HOURDEL 2 Km.

MAIN PIER

Position of boats

SANDS

JETTY 2

PT. 2

Castle

Party caught
here

SEA WALL

PLACE JEANNE
D'ARC

TO NOAILLES
AND
ABBEVILLE

German
H.Q.

Casino

TOWN
OF
LE CROTOY

Rue Cavour

Rue Napoleon

PT 1

PT X

SANDS

N

TO LA BASSÈE
AND
S. QUENTIN

APPROXIMATE SCALE IN YARDS

0   100   200   300

☐ Houses
Sea wall
-->--- Our route
● Points on route
-Ⓐ-- Sentry's beats

The Farm

STARTING POINT

night's rest for nearly three weeks. One always imagines that seven or eight hours' sleep during the day should be a simple thing to achieve. In fact, one does not at once become acclimatised to the exchange of day for night, and sleep in the open on a bright day is neither sound nor satisfactory.

All these arguments pointed towards doing as the Abbé suggested, and finally this was what we decided to do. In the light of later knowledge, it was probably the correct course, and we would have benefited most fully had we then settled down quietly until the whole battle shifted farther to the south. Many escaped prisoners in France were eventually to get home by following the simple advice of the Chinese philosopher Lin Yutang, to "take it easy".

At the time, however, it was difficult to take the long view, obsessed as we were with the Boy Scout mentality of getting on with the job.

From one aspect, at any rate, we did not regret taking the Abbé's advice. The farmer gave us quantities of straw and hay to put in a very high, half shut-in farm cart, and we enjoyed a wonderfully peaceful night, sleeping nine solid hours in the greatest warmth and comfort.

The next day we spent in making and developing our plans. One big change was apparent from the moment we woke up. The noise of battle was very much farther off, away to the south. The faint, intermittent rumbling seemed to come mostly from south of Abbeville, and at lunch-time German wireless stations announced the immediate success of the new offensive between Amiens and the sea, which had resulted in advances varying between twenty and thirty kilometres the whole way along the line.

This news ruled out any idea of wading the Somme estuary. It had, moreover, the effect of forcing us to make an immediate attempt, as the line was now twenty kilometres back from Le Hourdel. This withdrawal necessitated a sea-trip of at least thirty-five kilometres if we were to sail round to the coast-line of France, south of the Allied front line. This still remained the most likely chance. Heading straight out to sea offered the possibility of meeting a British naval vessel, but there was every chance of German reconnaissance planes spotting us before we were half-way across. We had seen no British fighter aircraft since our arrival in France, and the tremendous local German superiority in the air was self-evident.

Obviously, we could not afford to wait another night, when the Allied line might retire another twenty kilometres, and so be completely out of reach. Zero hour, we decided, would have to be during the course of the coming night.

The younger Belgian girl now made a great effort to help us. She walked down to the Place Jeanne d'Arc just outside the port, and when the sentries tried to turn her back, continued diagonally across the square, pretending not to understand and shouting back a jumble of nonsense at them. Finally a sentry chased her and turned her away, but she had by that time seen enough to give us some valuable details off the map.

There were three sentries on the square, in the positions marked a, b and c on the accompanying sketch; (A) had a shelter thirty yards in from the seawall, and his beat ran along the western side of the Place Jeanne d'Arc; (B) took the northern and (C) the eastern sides of the square. Inside the port, and running at right angles from the main pier, was a subsidiary wooden jetty marked Z. In the outer angle formed by the two piers, and so beyond jetty Z, were the first of the boats. The nearest two boats had no oars, the third was dilapidated, but the fourth had oars and a rudimentary mast.

The route we chose is marked on the map by a line of dots. From point (1) onwards we would be in the shelter of the sea-wall, in places only three feet high, but rising to ten or twelve feet beyond the Casino and always affording sufficient cover for an emergency. At point (2) we would have a long halt, locate the sentries, particularly (A) just above us, and choose our moment to slip under jetty Z.

Here a second halt would be necessary, when we would have to watch the main pier and the boats for any sign of danger, before making our final move to point (3) where lay the boat recommended to us.

We could row on the ebbing tide, setting our course by compass for the entrance to the deep-water channel ahead. There we would, if possible, hoist sail, turning W.S.W. to keep parallel to the coast. Taking correct bearings should present no difficulty, for all the previous night St. Valéry had been a lake of fire, and thick smoke continued to rise throughout the day.

Food supplies were bulky, as we were taking more than enough for four days, together with four large bottles of water, and our haversacks and pockets were crammed full. Bottles had to be packed singly, owing to the obvious danger of two or more of them knocking together.

At eight o'clock we were told that there was no sign of Germans in the neighbourhood, and we paid a visit to the farm-yard, partly to stretch our legs, but primarily to thank those who had helped us, particularly the two Belgian girls. Everyone wished us luck, there were quite tearful good-byes, and after giving back our surplus food we returned to the bushes for a short doze.

At 10.15 it was dark enough to start. There were a few clouds in the sky, making it the darkest night for over a week, a happy augury. From the farm we followed the by-road down to the La Bassée-Le Crotoy main road, keeping fifty yards out in the fields. Reaching the main road, we turned left, then right-handed towards the sea and arrived at point X, where there was a temporary check, Dick having a strong bias to a by-road, which led, I think, back towards La Bassée. After a time, we continued on to point (1).

Here we took off our boots and tied them tightly round our chests, so that they should not swing about. Dick now took over complete control, going into the lead with Charles and myself about eight yards behind. We arranged – an elementary enough rule – to keep our eyes on him, stop when he stopped, listen while we were stationary and only move up to him then if we had something of interest to report. The sea-wall was, in most places, over five feet high, and we could walk slightly stooped forward, bending double and sometimes crawling at the really low places, and pausing short of the occasional flight of steps that ran up from the beach to the level of the streets above.

The moon was beginning to peep out from behind the clouds, looking lovely enough above the smooth, shimmering sea, but showing up our silhouettes uncomfortably clearly. To neutralise this we kept as close in to the wall as possible, but sometimes large boulders or heaps of shingle drove us down to the water's edge, nowhere more than twenty yards out from our line of march. Progress was slow but sure along the mile stretch to the castle on the point, but just before arriving opposite this we were surprised to see a blind lifted three times quickly from the window of a long, low building which we took, from our map, to be the Casino.

Each time a light flashed out, and then far out to sea an answering light winked back. During this performance, quite unintelligible to us, we remained flat on the ground, waiting several minutes afterwards before going on again.

Opposite the castle we were forced almost into the shallow water by a high ridge of shingle deposited by the sea against the point. Progress became very slow as we approached the Place Jeanne d'Arc. Dick stopped frequently, all of us listening with bated breath and trembling with excitement. Once I heard one of the sentries call something up above, but he was some way off, and there was absolutely no sight or sound of sentry (A). The moon was very bright at this moment, and all the clouds had swept away to the east.

Now we were past sentry (A), and now only twenty yards from the jetty, where pale water glimmered under the black wooden groins. We crossed a dangerously bare stretch of sand. Nearer and nearer we crept, and Dick was under the jetty. Charles and I were almost in its shadow. I could see the boats through the wooden struts of the jetty, one, two, three stretching away down the side of the main pier, with the nearest a bare forty feet away.

Suddenly lights flashed from the sea-wall to our left, and a guttural voice shouted, "*Da! da! es gibt was darunter!*" (There! There! there's something down there!)

Another voice, slow and sleepy, replied to the effect that it was only shadows flickering on the water. There was a bit of an argument, while we waited absolutely still, crouched deep in the shadows of the jetty.

There was no possibility of making a dash for it. On the one side was the sea, in which, laden as we were, we could have made no sort of progress. Behind lay the brilliantly moonlit strip of sand which we had just crossed, and now actually nearer to the Germans than to ourselves.

For a moment I thought they would go away, but a second later heavy boots grated on the shingle and two Germans came straight for our hiding-place flashing torches to either side, stepping right up to us, and then turning their torches full on our faces. One was a young lieutenant, the other a sergeant. The latter it was who had discovered us.

The lieutenant spoke to me in broken French, "*Qui est-vous? O'est défendu d'être sur le plage! Qu'est ce que vous faites ici?*"

I answered at once, gesticulating and jabbering as fast as my French would allow, saying that we had lost our way, and had then thought we could stroll down the beach to the Place Jeanne d'Arc.

Neither seemed to recognise the fact that we were all in uniform, and for a few seconds it looked as if they would be satisfied with my extremely improbable explanation. But the sergeant, at that moment, saw that Dick was holding something behind his back. He made a grab and pulled away Dick's tin-hat, which had played a useful part in our journey so far, serving on occasion as a cup during the night marches.

The hat was waved in front of the lieutenant; they both recognised it for what it was, and like all Germans began screaming with excitement.

Out came two revolvers. "*Herr Gott, soldaten! Hände hoch! hoch! höher, oder ich schiesse! Höher, höher, Sakrament nochmal!*" (My God, soldiers! Hands up! Up! Higher, or I'll shoot! Higher, higher!)

The next few minutes were distinctly unpleasant. We were marched up against the sea-wall, and while the lieutenant went through our pockets, the sergeant kept us covered, with frequent shouts to lift our hands higher.

Out came all our stuff in a heap, and the lieutenant then asked us what we were doing on the beach and why we had been flashing signals out to sea. I answered in German that we had no means of flashing signals, that we had been surprised by them ourselves and had taken cover at the time. This explanation, surprisingly enough, he accepted and they marched us up into the Place Jeanne d'Arc.

Here the sentries were panicking badly, shouting back and forth at one another, and holding their rifles at the ready with fingers twitching on the trigger, ready to blow us or their own officers at any moment to kingdom come. I have a distinct memory of one of them (A, I think) taking a rush at us as we reached the square and being curtly ordered back by the sergeant.

We were marched across the square to the German headquarters, a large private house in the north-west corner.

There we were taken in and sat down in a comfortable drawing-room, where our interrogation began. This could hardly have been a success from the German point of view. Both the lieutenant and his sergeant had been drinking freely and were now at the merry stage. They were also far more interested in telling us about themselves than in asking us questions.

A few details as to our rank and appearance were taken down and then a babel of general conversation broke out.

After a time we had positively to lift our voices to make ourselves heard!

Apparently we had avoided sentry A successfully; just how, the lieutenant could not make out, but he was not vastly concerned about it. He and the sergeant belonged to an anti-aircraft detachment of the German Air Force. They had done the rounds of the guard at 11.30 and decided to stay on for a smoke and a stroll along the pier, an unfortunate decision for us! The sergeant spotted us quite accidentally (he said, of course, that they would have caught us, anyway!) and the lieutenant admitted that he had been certain at first that we were either shadows or rats! Personally, with drink inside me, I always tend to see things much larger than life.

They were both very friendly and charming people with whom to pass an evening. Within a few minutes, plates heaped with sausages and bread were set before us, and a large box of chocolates put within everyone's reach on the middle of the table. Bottles of red wine were cracked in quick succession, with apologies for the fact that it was only cheap local wine. Conversation was animated. The detachment cook was sent for and produced a newly-baked cake, from which five thick slices were cut, and we were asked gravely how it tasted. The cook refused to agree that it was first-class and persisted in saying that he had not put in enough sugar.

Twice R.A.F. bombers came over, and three or four small bombs landed several hundred yards away, hardly a pleasant experience for us!

After being caught at midnight, we did not finally turn in for the night until three in the morning, tired and terribly disappointed, but pleasantly full of good, warming food and wine. Long after lights out the corporal continued to talk from another corner of the room. He had been a member of the "Condor Legion" in Spain, and had an inexhaustible fund of reminiscences. I drifted comfortably off to sleep to the sound of his voice, droning on incoherently about the bombing of Barcelona ... Madrid ... women of Catalonia are ... and war is a pity ... Madrid ... (shut up, Gustav!) ... I always liked the English ... Madrid ...

So ended my first attempt at escape.

CHAPTER FOURTEEN

TERENCE PRITTIE failed in his first break for freedom but it was only bad luck that stopped him, as it stopped so many others, from making his escape complete.

Roy Farran is another escaper who did not waste much time before he made his first, and successful, attempt. Eighteen years of age at the outbreak of war, he crammed more adventure into the following eight years than most men; and his book *Winged Dagger* is so packed with danger and excitement that the escape he describes here forms but a brief part of it.

Wounded in both legs and an arm in 1941 during the fighting on Crete, he was taken prisoner and sent to Greece in a German ambulance plane for an urgent operation on one of his legs, which was becoming gangrenous.

Roy Farran

THE PRISONER-OF-WAR hospital, a large white building on the outskirts of Athens, had been a girls' school before the war. It was a modern structure built in the shape of a Cross of Lorraine in a wide open space near Kokinia, the Covent Garden of Greece. About half a mile away, amidst the houses of the suburbs, sick prisoners were confined in some old Greek barracks.

The hospital was run largely by captured British doctors under German supervision and the treatment was generally good in spite of the shortage of anaesthetics. The wards were crammed full with British wounded from Greece and Crete, but as they became fit enough to be convalescent they were evacuated to the prison camp.

The hospital and the camp were both under the command of the same German officer – a humourless Sudeten Czech – who insisted upon iron discipline. At first our relations were good, but after the first escape he began to reduce our privileges with a clumsy and tactless hand.

The food in the hospital was bad, but we could not blame the Germans for not having made more adequate arrangement to deal with such an unexpected number of prisoners. Our breakfast consisted of mint tea, our lunch of a slice of bread and a piece of goats' cheese, and our dinner of a cup of soup with a piece of bread. It was enough to keep alive prisoners who were lying in bed all day, but it was not sufficient for those who were able to walk about.

The New Zealanders had a number of band instruments and organised many concerts in the wards. At first the Greek Red Cross was allowed to visit us with presents, but later the Germans stopped them when they suspected that it was a means of our contacting friendly organisations outside. We were allowed to write a short letter home every ten days and after the first six weeks we began to receive replies.

On the whole the morale in the hospital was not good. Many of the occupants were bitter about the misdirection of the war, which had led them into Greece and Crete; many were glad to be safe from the Stukas and the air raids to return to their loved ones at the end of hostilities; and many were just completely demoralised by our crushing defeat. Generally speaking, the senior officers were the worst, and I think it is true to say that one is inclined to risk less as one grows older, although it is difficult to notice this tendency in the normal run of the army machine. For instance a plan was hatched for a mass break-out from the prison camp. A thousand prisoners were guarded by four sentries, and the total guard only amounted to thirty. All the Greeks round about were friendly and with the arms of the guard we might have been able to seize a destroyer in the harbour. All the naval experts were there to sail it back to Egypt and there were airmen who were prepared to have a go at the aerodrome at Tatoi. It was admittedly a desperate plan, but with New Zealand and Australian executives, it stood a fair chance of success. It was abandoned because the senior officers were afraid of reprisals and the consequent loss of life. They could not be made to realise that as prisoners we were of no further use to the war effort anyway.

We passed our days in recounting the disasters of the battle and in looking forward to the next meal. We were paid a small sum in marks each month which could be spent at a canteen run by a Greek contractor. Later, the marks were exchanged for special talismans when it was realised that we had managed to change them into the local currency.

As we became more fit, we began to discuss the chances of escape. Many talked about it, but few were prepared to put a plan into execution. In our corner of the ward a Commando officer formed an "escape group," consisting of one other Commando, myself and a New Zealander. His name was Robin Savage, a regular soldier of the Queens, and the others were Ken Maxwell, Sinclair the New Zealander and myself. Savage and Maxwell were only suffering from superficial wounds caused by the truck, in which they had been captured, overturning. Sinclair had been shot through the face and found it difficult to eat. I was the worst with the gaping wound in my thigh, although I was improving rapidly since a German doctor had cut out the gangrene.

Our plans were very imaginative and largely impracticable. We discussed the possibility of stealing a seaplane from the harbour at Phaleron, but I am glad that we were never stupid enough to try it. In the main, our meetings concentrated on the pooling of information about the state of the sentries round the hospital and the chances of escaping from the prison camp. We generally agreed that we were in no condition for a march overland to Turkey and that our only chances of getting away from Greece were by sea. There were rumours of a friendly organisation in Athens, which was prepared to help escaped prisoners, but at that time we were by no means certain of the attitude of the population as a whole. Robin Savage agreed to try to get information up to me from the prison camp (to which he would no doubt soon be transferred) through the medium of the working party which came up every day to clean the floors in the hospital.

The first definite information we received of the friendly attitude of the Greek population was when a concert party was allowed to come up from the prison camp to amuse the patients in the hospital. Pipe-Major Roy of the Black Watch played his pipes on the way up, to the delight of the Greeks in the streets, and the Germans were only able to avoid a riot by a firm show of strength.

Then began a series of escapes, which brought down reprisals on the heads of the prisoners in the hospital and camp alike. The first was a brave attempt by two New Zealanders to escape in the dirty laundry from the hospital. They wrapped themselves up, each in a bundle of sheets, and were carried down to the steps of the hospital by German soldiers, who strangely did not seem to remark upon the weight. They told us later, that they lay on the steps in the hot sun for some two hours, until they were near the point of suffocation. When at last the laundry van arrived they were thrown into the back. It was an unfortunate end to a gallant attempt that they should choose to abandon the van at the moment it was passing the gate of the Italian barracks. They were badly beaten up and returned to the hospital.

The next attempt was more successful. Jim Creagh, a New Zealander, and two others effected an escape from the prison camp by crawling between the sentries on the wire.

A few days later, towards the end of July, two Australians escaped from the hospital by an elaborate plan. The walking patients were allowed in the compound between the hospital and the wire for half an hour at four o'clock every evening. The Australians usually passed the time playing a game of chance on the toss of two pennies called "two-up." One British soldier, who had lost both legs, was an artist of considerable talent and he had curried favour with the guards by painting their portraits. On the night of the escape he occupied the attention of the sentry at the back of the hospital by drawing his caricature. Under the cover of the "two-up" game these two Australians wriggled through the wire to conceal themselves until dark in two holes we had noticed from the roof. Although they could not be seen from ground level, it was quite easy to see them from the top floor and we had to exercise great restraint not to peep through the windows to see how they were getting on.

This successful escape was the cause of considerable reprisals to the remaining prisoners, who responded with a long period of obstinate ill-discipline.

Until then the Germans had only attempted to wheedle us into making gramophone records which could be broadcast to our people at home. Many seriously wounded prisoners, whose resistance had been weakened by pain, forgot themselves enough to agree to send a short message. I am ashamed to say that I was one of them, having succumbed to the honeyed words of a German who said that he had been educated at a Quaker school near Birmingham. Fortunately, we were all warned of the true purpose of the offer by the healthier prisoners, and I think everybody withdrew their agreement before the records were made.

Now the Czech Commandant turned on every device known to prison commanders. Two spies were introduced to the hospital in the guise of R.A.M.C. orderlies, but their excuse of speaking English with an accent because they had lived a long time abroad was easily seen through. One night four Australians beat up one of these informers and locked him in the cells. The wire was strengthened and there were frequent searches. The Commandant pulled off all our bandages in his rage, seemingly convinced that some of us were not wounded at all. This was the last straw as far as we were concerned, and we resolved upon a programme of passive disobedience.

The walking wounded in the hospital and the fit prisoners in the prison camp had always made roll-call difficult by moving from one rank to the other, or answering somebody else's name. Now they refused to fall in until they were prodded by bayonets.

Rotten tomatoes and bits of paving stone were dropped from the roofs on to the heads of sentries, who countered by firing at any one they could see from the ground. The tyres of the bicycles belonging to the guard were constantly being deflated and rude slogans were chalked on the walls. We were once treated to the spectacle of the Czech Commandant opening the silver paper on every one of a box of chocolates, convinced that we were in contact with the outside through the medium of the supplies which came into the hospital canteen.

We were ordered to salute the Czech Commandant on sight and any infringement was punished by three days in the cells. At the beginning of August I was just able to walk with the aid of a pair of crutches. I failed to salute the Commandant in the corridor one morning and he ordered the sergeant of the guard to give me a kick in the pants, which sent me sprawling in the corridor. I was so angry that I resolved to do something which would really pay him back. I had noticed some packing cases full of straw in one of the courtyards and that evening I put a match to them. It was, perhaps, a stupid trick, for it served no useful purpose except to exasperate the Commandant further.

As a punishment he forbade smoking in the wards and threatened to give any offender three days' solitary confinement on bread and water. Great notices signed on behalf of the Supreme Command of the Reich were posted on the walls, but they only had the effect of further reducing our small reserve of cigarettes. Everybody smoked. The cells were soon full to capacity and the Czech Commandant gave up the unequal struggle.

Our concerts were stopped when "Run, Adolf, run," and "Hang out the Washing on the Siegfried Line" were included in the programme.

An Australian and a New Zealander pulled off one of the most spectacular escapes of the war, when they pole-vaulted the wire in the prison camp. Although many bullets were fired at them they got clean away. Robin Savage came to visit me with the working party the same day. He was very excited, telling me that he had been able to make contact with certain Greeks outside. He would not tell me any of the details at that moment, but promised that he would get a message to me the day before he escaped. At the time he was contemplating a break from the working party half way between the prison camp and the hospital.

During the night there was a fierce storm in which the wind blew so that you could barely hear yourself speak and the rain came down in torrents. Thirteen officers and thirteen men escaped through the wire from the prison camp. A spectator told us later that they were passing through two separate holes like a long line of rabbits. A German sentry shone a torch on one officer as he was half-way under the wire, but failed to see him. Included in the escapees were all my friends—Savage, Maxwell and Sinclair—and Pipe-Major Roy, who left with his pipes in full marching order.

I did not know whether to be furious or happy when I heard the news the next morning. I felt deserted in a way, for they had promised to give me some information before they left, and now I was all alone in the hospital.

The Czech Commandant was furious. He told us all that he would lose his job if there were any more escapes, and that he was going to make it his business to see that there were not. He placed eight machine-guns round the prison camp, strengthened the wire and doubled the guard. The wire at the hospital was also strengthened. Greek boys had been in the habit of swooping up to the wire on bicycles and throwing packets of cigarettes across, but this was now stopped by deliberate rifle-fire. Ten Greeks were shot within sight of the prison camp—as an example— when a sentry reported that someone had fired a rifle bullet at him.

After a fortnight I felt that I could walk well enough to begin to take active steps towards my escape.

*   *   *   *   *

On the face of it, it appeared that the hospital was more difficult to escape from than the prison camp. It was in an open space of ground, about a thousand yards square, and the wire consisted of a normal fence, eight feet high with close vertical and horizontal strands, connected to a roll of concertina wire by a diagonal sheeting. One sentry stood on each corner of the wire, and after dark a patrol walked round the outside. At the camp, from which there had been many more escapes, the Greek houses were only separated from the wire by the width of the road. The perimeter was longer and the ground inside the wire was quite broken.

I resolved to make my first reconnaissance in the prison camp. The large wound in my thigh was still far from healed, but I persuaded one of the English doctors to pass me as fit for the camp. The rumours of an impending move to Germany or Italy lent additional urgency to my plans. The march down was most fatiguing and I found my leg so stiff that it was difficult to walk for two days.

I was disappointed by the outlook in my new abode. The Germans had tightened up their security measures considerably since the big break, and I could see no obvious way of escaping. A lovely Greek girl with a beautiful voice used to sing "South of the Border, Down Mexico Way," from the roof of a house opposite at the same time every evening, and once we glimpsed the red hair of one of the New Zealand escapees through the window. Unless it was a Gestapo trap, this house was certainly friendly.

I had been in the camp for two days when a Scots doctor whispered that he would like to see me outside the hut during the evening exercise period. When I met him, after a cautious look round about, he said that he had a message from Maxwell. I was to get in touch with a certain New Zealand corporal in the cookhouse.

I found this friend the next morning, but he stoutly denied that he knew anything about Maxwell or anybody else. After I had argued with him for some minutes, he took me aside and whispered, "If you really want to escape, I can get a message to some people outside. You see, I go in with the ration truck every day. When the German gets out to open the gate of the dump, I can pass messages into the crowd. Are you fair dinkum on the level? O.K.! Leave it to me. Come and see me on Tuesday."

I met him again on the Tuesday and he said that if I escaped certain friends would be waiting in a ruined house five hundred yards from the wire on Thursday night. He told me to confirm that I was going on the Thursday morning.

It was a tall order since I had no idea how to elude the sentries, and my leg was not really in any condition for acrobatics. To escape is difficult enough, but to have to get away by a certain time is too much for even the most expert of escapers. On Thursday morning I reluctantly told him that I was unable to make it.

The defences at the camp were so strong that I now resolved to try my luck with the hospital, where the sentries were not quite so alert. A bout of sand-fly fever helped me to convince the German doctor that the wound in my leg was deteriorating. He was so taken in by my groans of pain every time he touched the wound, that he railed against the doctors who had been stupid enough to discharge me. I was carried back to the hospital on a stretcher by four Germans, although I would have been quite capable of walking.

When I had got back to my old bed in the ward, I began a week of intensive organisation. I had already converted my store of marks into three thousand drachmæ at the Greek canteen. I also saved up odd scraps of food which I scrounged from the kitchen. A wounded padre had an ordnance map of Greece of which we all took a tracing on lavatory paper.

The main problem apart from the actual escape was how to acquire civilian clothes. I dyed a suit of pyjamas dark blue with the gentian violet ointment used for sprained ankles. Somebody sold me a white shirt and I obtained a pair of Australian brown boots in exchange for my overcoat (or rather the overcoat which Jim Crewdson had put over me when I was first wounded in Crete). The boots were too obviously new, so I cut them about with an old razor blade. A Greek plumber was repairing a pipe in

the hospital and I tried to persuade him to give me his panama hat. He
was terrified, saying that the Germans would shoot him, but later in the
day, when he took it off for a moment, I stole it.

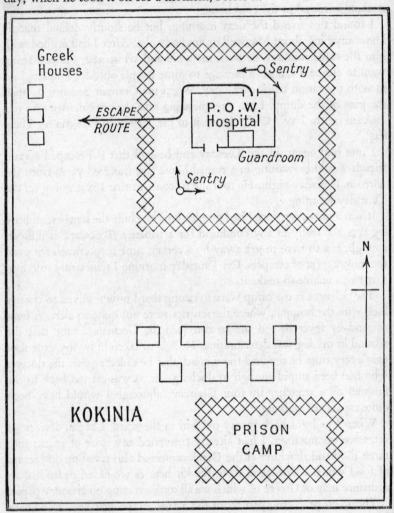

All these items of escape kit I concealed in a pillowslip under my bed.
My first idea was to hop into the ration truck which came in every day
through the main gate. Although we were not allowed to sit on the front
steps, I used regularly to sit there on my pillowslip, half-reading a book
and half-contemplating the chances of getting into the truck. The sentries
would move me away at first, but I always came back, and I think the

blank look on my face eventually convinced them that I was a harmless lunatic. If I could get into the driving seat and start the truck, there was little doubt that I would be able to steer it through the gate. But I could never face the possibility of the engine not starting with the first press of the button.

I was taking a course of sunbathing on the roof in the afternoon to try to cover myself with enough tan to pass as a Greek. One afternoon in the middle of August I suddenly noticed that the sentry on the gate (who was also responsible for the west side of the wire) was gazing at some Greek women digging for food in a rubbish heap. He seemed half-asleep and I knew him of old as a rather stupid man with one eye. This was an opportunity which I could never forgive myself if I missed. I ran down to the ward, grabbed my pillowslip, scurried down the stairs and out through the back door. I was still clad only in a pair of shorts and I think the sentry on the back must have thought me a member of the fatigue party about to put some rubbish in the dustbin, although we were not allowed into the compound until four o'clock.

I walked out of his sight round the corner of the building. The sentry on the gate was still looking in the opposite direction. I walked straight up to the wire and crawled through it. Something had snapped in my brain and I cannot remember actually wriggling through the tangle, although I think that I did not touch it once with my body. The dressing had come off my leg and I limped slowly across the open space, keeping one eye on the sentry. Just as he turned, I threw myself into a convenient rivulet, but by then I was five hundred yards from the wire.

I lay there panting, overjoyed with the astonishing ease of my escape. After a few moments the sentry turned to gaze at the Greek women once more. I stood up and ran, half-limping, towards the nearest Greek cottages. I glanced back once to the hospital and saw somebody wave a handkerchief from the roof. I waved back.

I was too far away to be recognised now, so that I began to walk. I came into a narrow unpaved street behind the cottages, where some women were bargaining around a fruit barrow. At any other time I would have been embarrassed, but now I was too excited to care. I began to change into my civilian clothes in the middle of the street. The women stopped their chattering and stared at me, transfixed. An old peasant came up to me and beckoned for me to follow her. I walked behind her into a cottage, holding up my trousers with one hand, and finished my changing under cover. In sign language she asked if the Germans had seen me escape. I shook my head. A little girl with trachoma in one eye took me by the hand and led me out into the street.

I walked with her, preceded now by a boy, to another little two-roomed cottage in the centre of the village. A rather attractive peasant woman, whose name I gathered to be Maria, was painting the ceiling from the top of a pair of step-ladders. She evinced no surprise at the news and led me into the front room, where she left me alone with about eleven babies.

Most of the room was occupied by a brass-knobbed double bed, which was crawling with babies of all ages. There seemed to be children everywhere. A mantelpiece was decorated with empty shellcases and I noticed that one of the babies was playing with an anti-gas eyeshield of English manufacture. I sat there on the chair, waiting and still panting with the excitement of my escape.

She had pulled the curtains and locked the door, but I was suspicious and started up at every sound. Once I heard a truck outside, and thought that they had sold me to the Germans, but it turned out to be only the sewage truck from the camp.

After about an hour visitors began to pour in with presents. The first was Maria's husband, who was an orange-seller and could say "oranges very good one bob" in English, which was not much of a help. I explained by means of a diagram on the back of a cigarette box how I had escaped. Others came in and kissed me on both cheeks, hugging me with joy. They pushed an enormous plate of macaroni before me and filled my pockets with packets of Woodbines. Some sang a national song and danced a sort of jig around me. Then they brought in another pretty girl, who unfortunately only had one eye, and pointed out the most attractive parts of her body. She rubbed both fingers together and pointed to the bed. It seemed that she had lost her husband in Albania and wanted me to till the garden. Maria noticed that I was looking embarrassed (for, after all, it was a bit fast) and told her husband to wait until later. They seemed very pleased when I said that a blonde baby was "an *inglesi*."

I felt that I was too close to the prison camp to be safe, and, in any case, I was in no mood for settling down to married life, so I decided to pay a visit after dark to the friendly house near the prison camp. The orange-seller was broken-hearted and Maria wept, but I was quite adamant about wanting to find my friends.

In the evening I walked with the orange-seller past cafés full of carousing Germans to a street near the prison camp. I made one navigational error in the dark and nearly ran into one of the sentries on the wire. At last I climbed over a stone wall at the back of the house. A man in a white cloth cap was pruning a tree in the garden and he dropped his shears in amazement when I crept up and whispered "English" into his ear. He signalled to me to beware of the large house next door, which apparently contained *fascisti*, and pushed me into a small gardener's cottage. The most beautiful girl I have ever seen came into the room. She was dressed in a neat, white summer frock and was barefooted. I suspected that she was the girl who used to sing "South of the Border, Down Mexico Way," to the prisoners. At first they were suspicious, but when I asked them if they had seen my friend Maxwell, they went into peals of laughter.

The girl caught me by the shoulders, and, pulling me towards her, kissed me full on the lips. I blushed scarlet like a self-conscious schoolboy. She whipped my panama hat off my head and gave me a new cloth cap. Then she explained to the chagrined little orange-seller that I must go to join my friends. I was sorry to leave him, for he was the first of many kind helpers. I think it is true to say that we would have received the same help at nine Greek houses out of ten in Athens at that time. It is, without doubt, the kindest and most hospitable race in the world. If I could do anything to save them from the agonies they are undergoing at this moment, I would gladly give my life to do so.

They went into a huddle in the corner and whispered plans in Greek, with shrugs of their shoulders and waves of their hands. After a few moments I found myself in the street with the girl and her mother. Her brother went on ahead.

We walked a long way down lighted streets and past the Italian barracks, where a soldier was playing upon a trumpet at the gate. One Italian soldier cast a keen look at us and I began to fear that he had seen through my disguise, when I suddenly realised with relief that he was more interested in the girl than in me. We came to a shopping centre, where the streets were full of people and the windows were brightly lit. The brother came back with another Greek, who told me that his name was Sortires, and who put some very shrewd questions to me. He asked me where I lived in England and I said Birmingham, which was untrue, but sounded more convincing than any other town he was likely to have known. He asked me where I had been captured and the name of my unit. At last he seemed convinced that I was not a Gestapo spy and told me to follow him. I had walked several paces before I remembered that I had not said good-bye to my new-found friends, but when I turned round they had gone.

Sortires led me up a flight of stairs, opened the door and pushed me into a room. I was still blinking my eyes to accustom them to the light when somebody shouted my name. All I could see was a polished table around which sat three Greeks, none of whom I could recognise. And then one of them was slapping me on the back. It was Maxwell, who had dyed his hair black and had grown black sideboards and a thin moustache. It was a perfect disguise, and I was staggered by his transformation.

I was overjoyed at my astounding luck in meeting up with my old friend once more. It was nearly a month since the others had escaped and Maxwell was full of their experiences. We exchanged reminiscences far into the night, while the Greeks fussed around us. It was explained that the fat man was a dentist called Tino, who owned the house, and that Sortires was a coster, who had organised his friends into a gang to aid escaped British prisoners. I learned later that his patrons were one Valisaki, a captain in the Greek Navy, and Papastratis, the famous cigarette manufacturer. Tino's wife was a good-looking blonde, who seemed to me to be making a dead-set at Maxwell, which could not have been good for the success of our schemes. She had a bonny child, which Maxwell made a great fuss about, teaching it to say "Kakomania" or "Bad Germans" in Greek baby talk.

Robin Savage was in a jeweller's house in Piraeus and Sinclair was hiding in a house by the harbour. It seemed that they had great hopes of obtaining a caique to take us to Turkey or Egypt, but the plans fell through before I had been there a day. Altogether, during my month in hiding in Greece we had fifteen different false alarms for escape by caique or submarine. Our disappointments became so regular that we began to suspect that the Greeks were not interested in our escaping to Egypt, but rather they wanted us to stay to be of use in a rebellion. I now think that these suspicions were unjustified, but when one is in hiding for long periods at a time one's ideas are liable to get out of proper perspective.

After I had had an enormous meal, my hair was dyed black by the dentist's wife with some sort of quick-taking dye which oxidised into a metallic black as soon as it had been applied. The colour lasted for the whole of my sojourn in Greece and caused me great embarrassment when it began to grow out in Egypt two months later. I can still remember the shocked whispers of Gezira lovelies, who thought that this "frightful subaltern" had dyed his hair. The piebald colour did not altogether disappear for another six months.

Ken Maxwell and I talked long into the night, but at last we went to bed. We were aroused at an early hour the next morning by Tino, who said that German soldiers were searching Kokinia. He did not seem in the least bit alarmed and told us that we could watch them from two deckchairs on the balcony if we wished.

I was quite apprehensive, since it was quite obvious that this search was consequent to my escape, but Maxwell stilled my fears. Italian soldiers in tin hats were patrolling the streets in fours, while Germans were debussing from trucks to search the houses at the end of the street. We saw them turn out all the idlers from the coffee houses and arrest those who had not got identity cards. When the searchers reached the next house but one, Tino told us to come inside. He showed us a drain-pipe through an open bedroom window and then hid us under some floorboards in the room. But there was no need to worry. Tino told such convincing lies to the German officer at the door that he did not bother to search the house.

Sortires arrived later in the morning in a very agitated state. He said that a German officer had called at his brother's house at four o'clock in the morning while Sortires was away from home. Elias, his brother, had been arrested, while his wife, who was seven months gone with child, had had a miscarriage from the shock. Sortires was now on the run and he said that it was important that we should move to another house in Athens without delay. These two brothers were good brave boys, but they liked to endanger our position by bragging of their achievements in the cafés. Elias endured unspeakable tortures at the hands of the Gestapo, but refused to talk, so convincing them that they finally released him. There were many cases of Greeks withstanding torture rather than disclose what they knew of the whereabouts of British prisoners. One woman had matches thrust up her finger-nails, and was later released. She came to see us in Athens and we were horrified by the sight of what the Gestapo had done to her. I have never quite understood why the risks Greeks underwent for British soldiers were not more publicised in the newspapers at home.

In the evening a girl called Dolly arrived to guide us to our new home. She was an ugly girl, but the stories of her bravery were legend. She was said to spend her spare time in manufacturing coloured paper "V's", which she put on the seats of German staff cars. Maxwell went with another man and I followed with Dolly out into the street. We walked down to the bus-stop in the market-place past hundreds of soldiers taking the air. I at first shrank away from the Italians, but Dolly led me right up to them until our shoulders brushed. We got into the bus and she bought our tickets. I noticed a man in a white gabardine coat who was staring at me with blue, penetrating eyes, so that I began to fear that he might be a Gestapo agent. Dolly dug me in the ribs and told me to "look out", whereupon I became very agitated until I realised that she meant me to look out of the window. I am afraid I am very stupid.

When we left the bus at Piraeus, I noticed that the man in the white coat was following. We took a turning to the left and he turned as well, keeping about fifty yards behind. I told Dolly and she bade me to keep on walking, while she dodged into a shop window. A few moments later she caught up with me, saying that it was all right. I did not dare to ask her what she had done, for she was quite capable of sticking a knife in his ribs.

We arrived at the house of Mr. Kazarsis, the jeweller, where Robin Savage and I met again for the first time in a month. He apologised for having left so suddenly without warning and lauded Kazarsis to the skies. He was an old man of about sixty, with grey hair and a faultless appearance. His shoes were so brightly polished that you could see your face in them. He prided himself on being more English than the English, and his conversation was like a quaint old Victorian book. He had served as an interpreter with our armies at Salonika in the Great War, a record of which he was very proud. Savage agreed that Kokinia was getting too hot to be safe and suggested that we spend the night with Robin Sinclair, before moving on to Athens the next day. He himself would stay in Piraeus to maintain contact with our friends.

It was explained that a rival society in Athens had been agitating to replace Sortires and Co. as our protectors. We did not understand why they should be so anxious to have us (not realising at the time that they were part of the same organisation), and when the leader, a Madame Kareeyani, sent her ravishing blonde daughter Electra down to talk us into moving, Savage's suspicions were aroused. I cannot quite remember the details of the intrigue, but it was something to do with a Greek Air Force officer called Angelo, a shining light in the rival society, who had been arrested by the Gestapo. However, it was agreed that beggars cannot be choosers and that it would be better under the circumstances to accompany Dolly to Athens.

It was a long walk to the house in which Robin Sinclair was staying and by the time we had reached it the wound in my leg was bleeding profusely. We rang the bell at the heavy iron gates of a large house overlooking the harbour. It was opened by a funny old man in Asiatic clothes, who proved to be Mr. Constantinedes, an Albanian charcoal merchant and our new protector. Inside we met Robin Sinclair, who had dyed his hair red and was wearing a blue shirt with white flannels like a Hollywood film star. It was plain to see that he was having an awkward time with Aliki, the patron's daughter, who obviously adored him. She was the rather spoilt daughter of a rich man, but was quite attractive in a way in spite of her large tummy. I felt very weak – too weak in fact to eat the splendid meal they had prepared for us in the palatial dining-room. Mr. Constantinedes retired upstairs to leave us to the tender mercies of Aliki. We had long resolved to avoid amorous entanglements, appreciating the risk of betrayal by a jealous suitor, but it was not always easy. Ken Maxwell and I were quite relieved to reach the seclusion of our bedroom.

The next day was spent in frivolous games with Aliki and her girl friends, amongst whom was a beautiful brunette called Felicity. Only by dint of the greatest tact did we avoid complications, which might have wrecked all our plans. It was easy to understand the setting for an ideal romance – young British officers being sheltered by brave, beautiful women. It was indeed fortunate that the pain from my wound prevented me from responding too much to their overtures. We played a game called "the bottle," which consisted of the girls spinning a bottle on the table and kissing the man to which it pointed when it came to rest. Sortires arrived in the afternoon and it was obvious that he intensely resented Aliki's attentions to Sinclair. Here were the first smoulderings of a fire and only our move to Athens saved us from a large conflagration.

When evening came, Dolly arrived with two other boys to take us to our new home. I was to play the urchin with one of the boys, which suited me well. We set off walking in three pairs, the boy and I leading by some fifty yards. Contact was maintained by whistling "Koreetho Mussolini," a patriotic song to the tune of "The Woodpecker Song." Dolly was a great expert, because she had a broken tooth in front.

We passed many sailors on the water-front, two of whom stopped us to ask the time. The boy was quick to answer. I made a careful note of the number of destroyers in the harbour in case it might be useful. At the underground railway station the boy bought our tickets and gave me a Greek newspaper. We swaggered about with our hands in our pockets on the platform, occasionally spitting nonchalantly on to the track. We took pains not to recognise each other when we got on the train, although all the pairs were in the same coach. I unfolded my newspaper and sat in a corner, but I was completely nonplussed when a Greek tapped me on the knee to ask a question. Again the boy quickly intervened to answer.

At the terminus we passed many German soldiers before we walked across Ammonia Square to the tram-stop. We kept on the outside of the tram where the lights were dim, but, even so, I felt that the Greek opposite me was staring rather hard. I began to calculate my chances if I jumped off while the tram was on the move. Still the Greek stared, until my face went scarlet and it seemed that his eyes were boring through to my back collar stud. Suddenly he dismounted at a stop (in point of fact the one before ours), and as he swung off the tram, he winked one eye and put up his thumb. So much for my disguise!

We walked down the streets to the bungalow in which we were to spend the next ten days. It was already occupied by five other escaped prisoners – the renowned Pipe-Major Roy, two Australians, a Polish Jew called George Filar and another Palestinian called Christo. All these escapees were being looked after by Dolly and her mother under the supervision of Madame Kareeyani. They had various incredible stories of escape to tell. George Filar had been a sergeant in a Palestinian Pioneer Company and had led a party of Jews to escape down a sewer from Corinth Prison Camp. He had also demonstrated his bravery by aiding the escape of four New Zealanders from our own camp in Kokinia. He was to prove a trusty and reliable member of our party, especially since he had learned to speak Greek so rapidly. I little thought at the time that I was to fall out so much with the Jews six years later. The two Australians had swum ashore off a prison ship bound for Salonika. They had been forced to kill a German with an iron bar to effect their escape from the docks at Piraeus.

So many friends came in with presents of clothing and food that we began to fear that our new home was less secure than the last. Madame Kareeyani was a splendid woman with enormous breasts, who could not do enough for us. She was executed by the Gestapo on the day that the Allied parachutists landed on Megara airfield. Since her death there has been great controversy as to whether she really was a brave woman, but all I can say is that I vouch for the fact that she took great risks on our behalf.

I was much amused by the pains Pipe-Major Roy took to preserve his other-rank status. He frowned on attempts at familiarity, obviously believing that it was bad for discipline. The Greeks loved him.

We had a lot of trouble with Christo, who would insist upon going abroad at night, although all the others had agreed not to take un-necessary risks. Even worse, we could not cure him of expectorating out of the window.

After about ten days, a Cypriot stranger arrived with news of a sub-marine and promised to take us to the rendezvous in a taxi the next night. We could not wholly trust him, although he was probably quite genuine. During the day a Greek Intelligence Officer called "Jackson" arrived with certain information which he asked us to memorise in case we should get away. When the appointed time drew near, our nerves were so frayed that we were all ready to bolt out of the back door at the slightest sus-picious sound. As it happened, a perfectly innocent motor car did pre-cipitate two of us into the back garden. The taxi did not turn up, thus leaving us all in a state of agitation. Robin Savage had concocted a plan for stealing an E-boat from the harbour, which I considered to be not worth the risk. He planned to row out to the torpedo-net in a dinghy and there to pull the plug out of the boat. He calculated that this would call down a patrol boat, which he intended to capture with grenades and pistols (all of which were available). Consequent upon this small disagreement and the failure of the submarine venture, we decided to split forces. Four was too large a party in any case. I asked Madame Kareeyani to find a new billet for Sinclair and myself, while Savage and Maxwell moved off to new friends. We still maintained contact through the medium of George, the Polish Jew.

Robin Sinclair and I were lodged in a new home owned by one Aristedes. His two half-sisters, Elpice and Kathia, and his mother were living in the same house. Elias, his brother, was a merchant captain whose ship had been sunk and who occasionally called in to see us. It was a pleasant home and we were very happy. Every morning the old mother would wake us up with two figs and a glass of milk. "*Kalli mera*," she would say, "how are you?" By then we had obtained bogus Greek identity cards and each morning Elpice would put us through a catechism of questions. I was Costas Nicholaides, a bank clerk from Samos.

"What is the name of your father?"

"My father's name is Giorgio."

"What is the name of your mother?"

"My mother's name is Maria."

"Where do you live?"

"I live at Number Six, Stadium Street."

"No, Costas, you say it like this . . ." and she would mouth a difficult Greek word.

We were becoming quite proficient in the language and could already carry on a simple conversation. We played cards all day, becoming great experts at a version of "Piquette." In the evenings we sometimes went out for exercise. Once we went to the cinema and I sat next to a German officer. They were ridiculous films – a newsreel about Russians being mown down in thousands, and a stupid melodrama in which a flower-girl sang a song called "Bloomen." We had great fun throwing cigarettes in the air on the way back, when they told us that it was bad luck not to stamp them out. They were laughing, happy days. Elpice conceived a great attachment for me, which was difficult to resist. I can remember now how we sat on the roof in the moonlight, looking at the stars behind the Parthenon, while she stroked my hair and softly crooned a Greek love song.

One night there was a big R.A.F. raid on Tatoi airfield, which received heavy damage from bombs bursting in the hangars. We watched it all from the roof and were overjoyed at the fires which were started, although our friends' faces fell a little the next day when they learned that many Greek civilians had been killed. Even so, they tended to exaggerate the

German losses. The extraordinary thing was their never-failing conviction that the English would soon return.

It was about the middle of September when Elias, the merchant sailor, first spoke to us of the chances of an escape. He said that several Greeks desired to get to Egypt, but had not enough money to hire a boat. They would be prepared to take us if we could raise some cash. George, the Polish Jew, who could speak Greek so well by now that he was able to walk about in daylight, was our only contact with the outside world. I instructed him to contact all the heads of the organisation to see if he could raise money on the strength of promissory notes signed by me on behalf of the British Government. Our chief benefactor was a polished gentle-man called Averoff, once an officer in the Greek Navy, and he was good enough to give us something in the neighbourhood of a hundred and forty pounds in drachmae. The President of the Anglo-Hellenic League, an old Etonian called Palis, also visited us with offers of help. I paid a visit by day, wearing dark sun-glasses, to Robin Savage, who was living in great luxury in a flat in the centre of the town. His female ward also gave us a large sum. Savage and Maxwell did not wish to accompany us for some obscure reason (I think because they had little faith that the caique would ever materialise), and we said good-bye to each other. Robin con-tinued to take an interest in our venture up to the moment we embarked and even sent down Mr. Kazarsis to make certain that we were not being sold a pig in a poke.

When all the plans were ready, we moved down to a fisherman's cottage in Piraeus. There we met Lefteris, the engineer who was to coax the engine across the Mediterranean. He was a handsome, hefty Greek with a captivating smile and quite an air of solidity about him. We drank coffee in his house for some hours, discussing the details of the voyage. Our old friend Elias was to accompany us as the captain. We moved to the house of one Pantorelli, who was another friend of Lefteris. He was living in a house in great poverty with his aged mother and a young brother, who was christened "Spike" by virtue of his close-cropped hair. I have omitted to say that during these preceding two days we had picked up two other British passengers for the boat – an Australian sergeant and a staff-sergeant in the Service Corps called Charles Wright. The Australian was a tough egg who had run a dance-band in Sydney in civilian life. They had both walked across the mountains from Corinth and Wright had contracted some terrible sores from bad water. Spike became very attached to the Australian, who used to sing to him in a rich bass voice.

Then began the usual mist of politics and intrigue which surrounds all Greek schemes. Yani, the owner of the caique, said that he would not part with the boat unless we gave him another hundred pounds. He came to see me in the house and I pleaded with him to see reason, but he was quite adamant. I offered a promissory note but he insisted upon cash. He was a horrible-looking rogue and he stank of fish and wine. I feared that he not only wanted to bleed us dry, but also intended to collect the reward for our capture from the Gestapo.

Averoff came to the rescue again with a promise that the money would be paid in cash in Athens the moment he received a code message on the Cairo radio to say that we had safely arrived in Egypt. After a petulant show of ill grace, Yani agreed, fearing to incite the wrath of a powerful man like Averoff.

In the evening Pantorelli arrived in a great state of excitement to say that Lefteris and another Greek had been arrested by the police. We gathered at first that it was because they had been loading black market diesel oil on to the boat, but I believe from what I have heard since that it was for drunkenness. It seemed that all was lost.

The next day Lefteris arrived with a Greek policeman, grinning all over his face. As soon as Lefteris had told them that he was aiding some British officers to escape, he was released. All they wanted to know was why he had not told them in the first place. The policeman brought us some loaves of bread, and, with tears running down his face, gave me his pistol. He also promised to picket the docks while we stowed away on board the boat. I was very pleased at the turn events had taken, for it meant that there would be no further monkey business from Yani.

We sneaked down to the quay in ones and twos at about eleven o'clock, long after curfew. It was important that we should make no noise, since German sentries were sleeping on an army caique two boat-lengths away. The ten Greek passengers had got there before us and were crouched together in the tiny hold. They whispered that they were having some trouble with the boy, Spike, who had stowed away during daylight. I tried to persuade him to land, but he told me through his tears that he was only a burden on his mother, that he was only another mouth to feed and he wanted to be a soldier. I tried pulling him out by the legs, but he threatened to awake all Athens with his screams. Pantorelli pleaded with him from the shore, but he clung tightly to the front stanchion without saying a word. Another attempt to drag him out met with the same result. In desperation, I assured his brother that I would take care of him like a son when we got to Egypt.

"But you do not understand, he is very sick."

"I will pay for all the doctors in the world."

"Yes, but he must have injections every week. He has syphilis."

"Whatever he has got, I will see that he is cared for."

Pantorelli turned abruptly on his heel and stalked up the hill.

Just before dawn we cast off and allowed the tide to take us out into the middle of the harbour. When we were well clear of the shore, Lefteris started up the engine with the aid of a blow-lamp.

It was only a small vessel – perhaps thirty feet in length – and the fourteen people were crammed tight in the hold, their mouths amongst the cockroaches. There was a gaping hole where the mast should have been, so that we were relying entirely on our diesel motors. We calculated that we should have just enough fuel to reach Alexandria in four days if all went well. For navigation, we had an old school atlas which showed the shapes of the islands we were to follow as far as Crete. From there it would be plain sailing due south. There was only a sack of crusts and a few onions on board, for the famine was already tightening its grip on Athens. We christened the ship *Elpice*, which not only reminded us of our benefactress in Greece, but also represented the spirit of the voyage.

Most of us writhed in the agonies of sea-sickness in the first two hours, but we soon became accustomed to the roll of our tiny craft.

Off the first island, we sighted a patrol boat, which sent us all scrambling into the hold. Elias cast the nets overboard and we safely passed the danger point without incident. On the second day a German aircraft dived down to look at us, but it must have been satisfied because it resumed its course.

We glided happily through the calm sea between the islands, lying on the deck and trailing our hands in the water. Everything was going well until the second night, when Giorgio, another Greek, had taken the tiller from Elias. He mistook the shape of an island and took us far out of our course. I suddenly noticed that the islands were not corresponding to the shape of those in the atlas and woke up Elias. We held to the same bearing for some time, until at last he agreed. We decided to anchor in the lee of a rock until daylight. Just as we were chugging into the shadows, somebody noticed a dark shape which looked like another boat. Lefteris switched off the engine and we sat there for a long time, holding our breaths, but the shadow did not move. Daylight revealed it to be another rock.

It was a serious business this loss of course, since our fuel supply left no margin of safety. Anxiously we counted up the cans. To our horror, we discovered that someone – presumably Pantorelli – had stolen three tins. There was no turning back now and all we could do was to pray that we might meet up with a British ship on the other side of Crete. For the next two days we made good headway through the beautiful calm seas of the Aegean. There is no place in the world which quite reaches the beauty of the Greek islands in the spring and the autumn. We lay back on the deck, basking in the sunshine and thinking how infinitely better this was than our clandestine life in the suburbs of Athens. As a novice to the sea, I was quite astonished to find how long it took to reach an island which looked comparatively close. The sunsets were breath-taking in their loveliness. As the shadows lengthened, the rocky islands took on a purple tint and our tiny craft became a speck of gold on a shining lake. I thought of Flecker and expected the caique to burst into a rose at any moment. The most moving thing was the all-pervading silence, only broken by the "phut phut" of our motor.

In the planning stage, we had always reckoned that the danger point would be the straits between the east end of Crete and the Rhodes Islands. We knew it to be patrolled by E-boats and had therefore decided to pass through during the hours of darkness. The mistake in our course had taken us a full day off our bearing, so that we were already completely out of schedule. I was beginning to regret that I had voted against sailing for Turkey on the grounds that it was highly probable that she would soon be invaded by Germany. Now there was nothing for it but to soft pedal so that we would pass through the straits on the fourth night out from Piraeus. We badly needed more water and food and I therefore agreed with Elias that the best course was to sail for Santorini, a large island commanding the entrance to the straits.

We reached what we thought to be the island early on the morning of the fourth day. There was no sign of any movement on the side from which we approached, so we took the caique right up into the calm sea between the rocks at the base of the cliff. There was no question of going round to the port which the atlas showed to be on the east side, since it was extremely likely that there was a German garrison on the island. Christos, a young Greek sailor, dived over the side with a knife in his mouth, bent on climbing the cliff to kill a sheep. He looked like an ancient pirate as his naked body swarmed monkey fashion up the rocky cliffs. He was gone some time and when at last he reappeared, the news he hailed down to the boat was most disappointing. The island was not Santorini, but was an uninhabited islet four miles to the south. There was a better anchorage on the east side.

Elias guided the boat round to the other side of the island and we all waded ashore to see what we could find. It was plain that the place had been inhabited at some time, perhaps only seasonally during the harvest, because a large part of its surface was covered with recent wheat stubble. By now we were very hungry, so that we were pleased to collect odd ears of corn we found on the ground. Over on the south side, I found definite signs of habitation. Rude square dwellings had been carved out of the rocks and were fitted with wooden doors. There was even a tiny chapel on the hill with all its equipage in a fine state of preservation. I genuflected and said a short prayer before the altar, putting my remaining drachmae in the offertory box before I left.

A delighted shout from Christos heralded the discovery of a cistern full of sweet fresh water. We filled up our olive oil barrel and the stone chatty we had brought from Piraeus. We all drank long draughts, throwing the cool water all over our bodies, until our bellies were distended with the pressure. Looking out over the sea towards Crete, we could see two tiny fishing boats tossing on the waves. The Australian sergeant found two baskets full of fruit hidden in the rocks by the shore, which obviously belonged to the fishermen. All my prayers had been answered. I was for taking both baskets, but Elias insisted upon our only taking one, firm in the conviction that we would be violating some unwritten law of the sea. We left all our remaining Greek money in the other basket as some compensation for what we had stolen.

We resumed our voyage and during the fourth night we began to pass through the straits. A lighthouse could be plainly seen on the eastern tip of Crete and we could also see aircraft landing on the Heraklion airfield. When we were half-way through the dangerous stretch, a thick fog came down. At first we blessed it, but when it developed into one of those sudden storms characteristic of the Mediterranean at this time of the year, we began to fear for the safety of the boat. The sea grew from a slight choppiness to a boiling cauldron in under an hour. Elias grimly held the tiller so that our bows struck the enormous waves as our tiny craft was driven before the wind. We were carried at will by the storm for a day and a half, riding the forty-foot waves like a celluloid ball in a shooting gallery. If any of those waves had hit us broadside, we would have certainly capsized. Elias held on to the tiller for forty-eight hours without rest. Only an expert sailor could have brought us through to survival in such a sea. He would give the tiller a flick on the tops of the waves to take full advantage of the movement of those great walls of water. As it was, many waves crashed over the side to fill the hold with water. While we held the sides with one hand, we tried to bail it out with jam tins with the other. At times it was all we could do to remain in the boat. She would be carried along on the white foam at the top of a great mass of water, her propeller threshing madly in the air, and then we would crash forty feet below into the slough in the writhing sea between two towering white-flecked cliffs. It was plain from the sun that we were being carried too much to the south-west towards Benghazi, in spite of Elias's efforts to bring her round on the tops of the waves. What was even more serious, our diesel oil was being rapidly consumed with the rough usage the propeller was receiving. We could not turn off the motor because it was only our small amount of headway which enabled us to run with the waves.

After a day and a half of pure misery, the storm abated as quickly as it had risen. We found ourselves once more in a calm sea, but with the difference that now we were drifting powerless with the current. Our last stocks of diesel oil had gone. I was completely dismayed to find that almost all our water and every scrap of food had also disappeared. I cursed myself for my carelessness in not rationing it more strictly. We were all in the depths of despondency and lay half-conscious in the sun, overcome by our exertions in the storm. I ordered strict rationing of the water to one-third of a jam tin per man per day and set myself down with a drawn pistol by the barrel. It was cold in the night and we fought for a corner of one of the two blankets.

Our lethargy degenerated into argument on the morning of the sixth day. George, the Polish Jew, was disappointing for the first time since I had met him. He hurled recriminations at Elias for not having checked the oil before our departure, and even accused Lefteris of having had a hand in stealing it. When the time came for the water ration, I quarrelled with the Australian, who swore that he had not had his share although I knew full well that he had. He struck me on the chin and the Greeks threatened to throw him overboard. Most of the Greeks seemed to collapse in resignation to their fate, but Lefteris just sat in the stern staring moodily out to sea. He roused himself sufficiently to help me make two square sails out of blankets at about midday, constructing a mast from boards torn from the bottom of the boat.

In the afternoon we divided ourselves into two parties and tried to paddle with boards and planks, but we soon collapsed exhausted into the bottom of the boat. We tried again in the evening, but we were too weak to make it effective.

We were all very weak by the seventh day, when the time came round for the last water ration. I was quite touched by Spike's trying to refuse his, saying that he had no right to it since he had embarked without permission from Piraeus. It was a brave gesture, especially since he was the most sickly member of the crew. Of course we made him drink it, even giving him more than his ration. I hope he is happy now. When I last heard of him he was an apprentice in the Greek Air Force.

The most active member of the crew, in spite of his sores, was Staff-Sergeant Charles Wright. He timed how long it took for a cigarette packet to pass from the bows to the stern and thus calculated that we were making about one and a half knots with the current. He also made a rough estimate of our position with the aid of an angle made of two sticks. According to the shadows, he judged us to be about a hundred miles north of the African coast.

Those who bothered to move spent most of the day keeping themselves cool by dousing themselves under a bucket of sea water. We also tied soaked shirts round our heads. Some of the Greeks gave in to the temptation to drink sea water, but I think they regretted it. One at least developed some form of madness and sat on the side rolling his eyes at the sea.

By the eighth day we were all far gone with thirst and exhaustion. Our lips were cracked, our tongues were swelling and we could only crawl about on our hands and knees. I have always heard that when one is expecting imminent death, one dreams of the loved ones at home, or of heaven and the happy days of one's youth. I did not. All I could think of was a glass of cool Pilsener beer with a plate of steak, fried tomatoes and chips in a little café in Alexandria. So much for romance.

As the sun was going down on the eighth day, we suddenly heard the sound of aircraft engines. We waved white towels and handkerchiefs over the side, and I scrawled "no water" with dirty oil on our white blanket sail. We had already decided to signal to any craft we heard at night, German or British, aeroplane or ship, since it was now not only a question of escaping from prison, but was more a matter of saving our lives. We had tied oily rags round pieces of wood as torches for the purpose. A seaplane came over and we laughed to see the circles on its wings. It saw us and began to circle round. It dived twice over the caique and the pilots waved. We waved back, stuck up our thumbs, shook each other by the hand and grinned helplessly at each other in our joy. It looked as though it was going to land, but I think the sea was a little too choppy. Instead it waggled its wings and flew off into the sun.

We were all confident that in an hour or two destroyers would appear on the horizon. When night fell and there was no sign of rescue, our spirits fell a little, but we all felt sure that daylight would bring help. As the ninth day dragged on with no sign of the destroyers, we sank from the heights of joy to the depths of despair. We were all so weak now that we could only move with the greatest effort. Our mouths were so deformed that we could only croak and even that was sheer agony.

I had suggested the possibility of making a distiller earlier in the voyage, but the others had poo-poohed the idea with a mass of figures to prove the great quantity of heat energy required. I mentioned it again – not so much as a suggestion, but more as a faint hope of something which could never be. Staff-Sergeant Charles Wright pulled himself along on his elbows without saying a word, until he was alongside the engine hatch. I noticed that he was trying to unscrew a copper pipe from the engine and, hopefully, I moved along to help him. We hacked a petrol tin in half and punctured it with holes to make a stove. Another closed tin was half-filled with sea water to make the boiler. We led the copper pipe from the boiler into a stone chatty, sealing the junctions with pieces of rag. Then, around the outside of the pipe, Wright made a cooling jacket with a piece off the bilge pump. The chatty was cooled by wrapping a wet shirt round it. We stuffed pieces of wood and oily rag into the brazier and set a match to it. After a few minutes steam began to escape from the junctions, but some must have been going through the pipe. Frantically we poured cool sea water into the water jacket and held the pipe tight into its socket to get the maximum amount of steam. We could hardly believe it when drops of water began to trickle into the earthenware chatty. When the others saw it, they all roused themselves to help by gathering fuel. For an hour's work we made enough to give us each about three mouthfuls of water. We were saved. There was no doubt about it, we were saved. We felt that we could go for weeks without food now that we had water and sooner or later we must strike land.

Three nights before, we had heard German aircraft flying over to bomb the canal and we resolved to signal if we heard them again during the night. We divided ourselves into watches and all the flares were made ready. At about one o'clock in the morning I was shaken by one of the Greeks, who said that he had heard the throb of engines. I listened and thought that I too could hear aircraft in the distance. We lit the first flare, waving it backwards and forwards.

After a few minutes, when the engines were growing louder, our hearts nearly stopped to see two long black shapes coming towards us out of the darkness. They were ships. We shouted as loudly as our swollen tongues would admit. We lit two more flares and waved them back and forth over the stern of the caique. The long ghostly shapes, which were now quite plainly men o' war, glided slowly by, keeping to their course. They seemed to ignore our signals completely. We screamed and wept to see them pay so little heed to us and then at last the rear destroyer of the three turned back towards us. It came close enough to hail.

"Ahoy there! Who are you?"

"British prisoners of war escaped from Greece."

There was a pause for a few moments as the searchlight was swung on to us.

"How many of you are there?"

"Four British, a Pole and ten Greeks. Who are you?"

"The *Jackal*. Stand by, we are coming aboard."

The destroyer came close alongside and bluejackets came aboard to carry us up the gangway. Lefteris elected to stay on the caique, which was brought into Alexandria under naval supervision. We were surprised to learn that we were only forty miles north of the port. I had ten rashers of bacon and eight eggs for my breakfast the next morning.

CHAPTER FIFTEEN

URING WORLD WAR I escaping from Germany had become a science, and by the end of that relatively restricted mêlée over thirty British prisoners had slipped out of their carefully guarded camps and had either crossed the border into neutral Holland, Switzerland or Denmark, or taken a boat to Sweden. A few had made their way back through the lines of battle into Allied territory.

The choice of route for the escaper in World War II was rather more limited. There was, for instance, only the Swiss land frontier for him to cross. Unless he was held in Italy, from the evacuation of Dunkirk until the Second Front in 1944 there were no lines of battle through which to make his way. The police forces and quasi-military organizations of Nazi Germany had gained valuable experience in rounding up foreign workers and fugitive Jews.

In World War I the escaper could be helped enormously in his task by the efforts of friends both at home and in nearby neutral countries, but in the recent War the prisoners lived in a state of absolute communism. No one had more in the way of material possessions than his neighbour. Private food parcels for individuals were not allowed, and in most camps pay was pooled and used by the British camp authority for the benefit of the community. The state of communism, as is usual, depended on machine-guns and barbed wire to define its boundaries.

Escape from this featureless communism of the modern prison camp became rather more than an individual effort, and although the methods used were often similar to those of World War I the escape from an established camp was now organized as a military operation. It was still up to the aspirant escaper to discover a weakness in the enemy defences, but having done so he was bound to take his idea to the Escape Committee who, if it approved, did everything in its power to support the originator of the scheme. Once outside the camp, the escaper's success still depended entirely on his own efforts and individual luck.

*   *   *   *   *

The tunnel through which Robert Kee escaped from *Oflag XXIB* in Poland had its entrance in the side of a trench in one of the latrines. I myself was privileged to play a very minor role in this tunnel, acting as a stooge and keeping watch while the spoil was hauled in large jam tins to the surface. From stooge I graduated to become a "disperser of excavated earth." Apart from the actual escapers, a great number of prisoners were helping in the scheme. The tunnel was a very fine one and remained undiscovered, I think, by virtue of its mephitic starting-place.

Although to the escapers went the excitement of the journey beyond the wire, those who remained in the camp enjoyed the triumph of the morning roll-call when fifty-two men were found to be missing. The inevitable reprisals followed, but they were well worth while; and as the days passed and it became more and more likely that some at least of the escapers had got away the whole camp felt that the victory was theirs to share.

In the following extract from *A Crowd is not Company* Robert Kee tells what happened to him and his companion on their journey.

Robert Kee

ONE INCIDENT stands out like an oasis in this desert, fresh and clear and, by contrast with the surrounding time, magic and unnatural.

Lying on my stomach in the dark tunnel, smelling the earth and keeping touch with the heels of the man in front, I still could not believe that I was going to escape.

It was nearly four months before that we had begun this underground life, wriggling down through a lavatory seat and a hole cut in the brick foundations to hollow out a chamber and start a tunnel. Late autumn, midwinter, and now premature spring – in all weathers we had made the furtive journey to the large lavatory block and crawled in through the hole, or received the cans of earth for dispersal, pouring it down through the seats and ramming it into the filth with long poles, or stood about in the gloom, watching for the inside patrols and conversing with those prisoners who came and sat long on legitimate business. The routine had become part of us, and though we often hated it and grudged the time, we felt affectionate and possessive about it. There was something stimulating about the hours spent digging at the tiny face, tugging on the rope for the earth to be dragged away and receiving the faint answering tug from the other end, or squeezing backwards cursing to join the rope where it had snapped under the strain. When we came up to the familiar tea and the squalor and the faces it was as if we had spent the afternoon in another planet.

And very slowly, almost unnoticed, something had grown out of it all. The rope on the trolley became longer and the pull became harder. Soon it was necessary to station someone half-way down the tunnel to help the man pulling from the chamber, then two men at intervals. Unintentional deviations in the level became noticeable: the lamp carried by the workers at the face was no longer in sight from the chamber. People began to measure the amount of tunnel already dug, and as the weeks went by the imperceptible progress of each day consolidated in astonishing "footage": thirty feet, fifty feet, seventy feet. People began to measure it the other way round: the amount of footage still to be dug. But it seemed impossible that it would ever lead to an escape. No one really thought about that very much; it was all just a daily routine to be worked through. And then a mathematician went down with a set-square and a lead weight tied to a piece of string and found that the tunnel was fifteen feet deeper than it was meant to be. Nobody believe him so he did it all over again and got the same result. So the tunnel started to go upwards, while people stuck probing sticks up through the roof for safety. And one day one of these sticks came up above the ground and it was exactly where the mathematician had calculated it would be, many feet outside the wire.

And so on, until one night I found myself listening in the darkness to my heart beating against the packed earth of the floor, clutching an attaché case filled with escape food and fingering a pocketful of false papers, but still not really believing that I should escape. The inside patrols would discover the trap. There would be a snap roll-call in the blocks. Somehow, I was sure, the alarm would be given before anyone had got away and we should all be hauled ignominiously out again. Or if that didn't happen someone would be seen scuttling across the open field to the cover of the wood before my turn came to emerge. There would be a shot, a thumping of heavy boots down the path over our heads and then, provided that the guards did not start more shooting, fourteen days solitary in the "cooler".

Sammy and I had drawn places No. 16 and 17. We were lucky in so far as there were thirty-five people after us, but as we were both certain that something would go wrong before our turn came, wherever we were, it made little difference to us whether we were Nos. 16 and 17 or 51 and 52.

The first two needed complete darkness to dig the final break-through. There was half an hour of light left. Even when they had started digging it might take them another half hour if their calculations of the amount still to be dug were wrong.

Sammy, lying behind me, pulled at my ankle.

"I wish they'd hurry up," he said, "this is bad for my claustrophobia."

Occasionally messages were passed down the tunnel from the chamber to the head or vice versa. As we were lying about half-way down it and it was necessary to speak in whispers we knew that the messages we received bore little relation to what had originally been said or to what would arrive at the other end. But we passed them on.

The man in front of me, whose name was Warburton, turned his head as much as it is possible to turn a head without moving one's shoulders and hissed:

"The Emperor says, there's simply got to be more air."

I passed it on to Sammy, who said:

"I don't know who the Emperor is, but I couldn't agree with him more."

I heard him amend it into:

"People are fainting; there's got to be more air."

Certainly the air was bad. There were about thirty people lying in a hundred and fifty feet of tunnel, and another twenty waiting in the chamber. Somewhere in the chamber there was a man working himself into a state of exhaustion on an air pump made out of a kit-bag, but in the middle of the tunnel it was difficult to believe in him while, at the head, people were obviously convinced that they were being suffocated.

"Are you passing these messages on?" hissed Warburton furiously; "more air for Christ's sake."

Once there was the dreaded sound of boots running overhead. My heart beat so loudly that I couldn't tell which was boots and which was heart. Sammy took my ankle.

"We've had it," he said.

But ten minutes passed and nothing happened. Then Warburton said:

"It must have been the patrolling goon trying to keep warm. You don't need to pass that on, by the way."

For a long time we lay there in silence. I hardly thought at all about the weight of fifteen feet of earth above us or the impossibility of going backwards or forwards if the tunnel collapsed. There had been moments of suppressed terror when we first started the work, but the cumulative effect of nothing going wrong day after day for four months was to build confidence. Now I thought as little about the possibility of the tunnel collapsing as I used to think about the possibility of the wings falling off an aeroplane when flying. I lay there wondering whether there wasn't perhaps a chance that we might get away after all.

Sammy passed up another message:

" 'How much longer before they break?', and there's to be less smoking. The latter probably a free translation of talking."

I changed it to "talking" and passed it on.

About ten minutes later the answer came back.

"It's in the chamber."

"What is?" I asked

"I don't know," said Warburton peevishly. "I'm just passing it on."

"Yes, but what are you passing on?"

"How the hell should I know? It's the answer to the last message, I suppose."

"But the last message asked when they were going to break."

"Oh, shut up."

Five minutes later the proper answer came. It was a draught of cold night air.

"Thank God for that," said Sammy.

Very slowly we began to crawl forward.

It was not a continuous progress but a series of rare tiny jerks. Sometimes we remained stationary for five minutes at a time and often I decided that at last something had gone wrong. But always we moved on again, and each time we moved on the possibility of escape became more real and exciting.

A message came down from the head of the tunnel:

"Seven men out."

Sammy said: "Good God, only seven! This seems to have been going on all night."

I was sweating. My elbows, sore from weeks of work in the tunnel, were becoming more and more painful. I badly wanted to stretch my neck.

After a long time I noticed that we were jerking uphill. That meant that we were on the last stretch. I told Sammy.

"Quiet, for Christ's sake," said Warburton, much louder than I had spoken, "I can see the sky."

It seemed to me that it was getting very much more difficult to move. There was no longer room for my attaché case by my side and I had to wait until there was sufficient space between me and Warburton before I could push it ahead. The walls of the tunnel were becoming narrower and narrower. My shoulders were pressing hard against them on each side and every time I moved my back brushed the ceiling, bringing down a fine shower of earth.

Now I understood the reason for the long pauses in our progress. The earth which had been dug away to break the tunnel had not been sufficiently dispersed in the excitement of success and as a result the tunnel, like a bottle of hock lying on its side, grew elegantly narrower towards the exit. Each man had to stop and fight his way out. I could hear Warburton panting and wrestling with the walls and realized that it would be my turn next. Occasionally he kicked earth into my face as he fought for the pressure to be free. I lay wondering if I could maintain the tension inside me long enough to get myself out. Every second it was necessary to screw it a little tighter and success now seemed to depend solely on time. If I did not get out before the tension snapped I should never get out at all. At this rate I gave myself about ten minutes.

It was some time since Warburton had kicked earth into my face. I looked ahead to see if he was through. There was only blackness. I thought he must have got stuck in the exit. Then I looked up and saw, light by contrast with the inside of the tunnel, the blue of the night sky. I had expected the exit to be as gently sloped as the whole of the last ascent. I now saw that it went vertically upwards into the night. Warburton had probably left some minutes ago. Guiltily, I heaved myself up.

To my surprise I got my head and shoulders out quite easily. There was a strong wind blowing and the night was overcast. The mathematician and the two who had broken the tunnel had worked accurately. I was looking out of a ditch that ran close to a potato-clamp. It was perfect cover. I was about thirty yards outside the wire.

I saw the patrolling sentry coming down the wire towards me. He stood out clearly in the light of the arc lamps and I thought I must stand out just as clearly to him. But he passed by the place where he could have seen a head and shoulders planted in the stubble and, humming and stamping his feet, ambled down to the other end of the wire. This was my chance.

I tried to pull my arms through and found that I was stuck.

For a long time, I knelt there, pinioned by the noose of earth. Then I succeeded in getting down and starting again. This time I put my arms through first but stuck at the waist. I was wearing a thick cut-down R.A.F. greatcoat and the pockets were stuffed with food. Anyway I had forgotten my attaché case so I went down again. I pushed the attaché case through first, then my arms, and again stuck at the waist. I could hear the sentry coming back up the wire. I struggled wildly, thrashing with my feet in the earth below me. I wondered what Sammy was thinking. The sentry was only about twenty yards away down the wire and coming up it fast. He would be bound to see me this time if he looked my way because so much of my body was above the ground. I made a final effort. I thought that I should break in the sides and spoil the chances of the people coming after me. I got through just before the sentry came level with me. I lay flat on my stomach in the ditch and waited for the shot.

The sentry ambled by, whistling this time, to the other end of his beat. I had about a minute's worth of tension left inside me.

I scrambled along the ditch on my hands and knees to the end of the potato-clamp. There was some open ground to be covered before reaching another ditch and another potato-clamp. I turned to look at the camp. From this distance I could see both ends of the stretch of wire under which the tunnel had passed. In the tall towers at each end the sentries occasionally switched on their searchlights, passed them slowly up and down the wire, swept them, like someone sweeping crumbs off a table, across the camp itself and then switched them out again. They never seemed to think of turning them on to the field outside the wire.

There was no sign of the patrolling sentry so I crawled out of the ditch and across the open stubble to the next clamp. We had been told to crawl with our stomachs flat to the ground for safety, but I wanted to get to the next ditch as soon as possible. As a sop to my conscience I went on two legs and one hand (the other carrying the attaché case) with my bottom high in the air. Just inside the next ditch someone lay on his stomach panting with exhaustion. It was Warburton. I crawled over him, hurried to the end of the ditch and again looked back. This time the camp had shrunk considerably. It seemed to hang in the darkness on the chain of lights which shone at regular intervals all round it. I crawled out of the ditch, under a flimsy wire fence and into the next field. There was still about two hundred yards to go to the wood, but the field sloped downwards about a quarter of the way across and once in the dip there was no danger of being seen from the camp. I moved forward as quickly as possible, this time not even bothering to touch the ground with one hand but running with my knees bent and my body crouched forward. I was suddenly aware of several other figures running across the field in similar positions. We went over the rise into the dip like soldiers of the '14-'18 war going over the top.

Inside the dip I threw myself down and rested. In the open space that still separated me from the wood I could see other dark smudges against the light earth of the field. We lay there for a while panting, like fish that had jumped out of a net on to the deck of a fishing boat.

I had arranged to meet Sammy on the edge of the wood. It was typical of our lack of belief in such a meeting that we had arranged nothing more definite. When I got there the wood was alive with English voices.

"Hist – Percy?"

"No."

"Hist – George?"

"Hisst!"

"Hist!"

"That you, Taft?"

322   THE ESCAPERS

"No."

"Hist!"

"Percy! Percy!"

I was leaning against a tree and thinking that I should never find Sammy when he came straight up to me out of the field.

"Wait till I get my breath back," he said and collapsed beside me.

I looked at the square chain of lights and relaxed. It was safe to relax now. This was the beginning of something else.

"How did you get on?" Sammy asked.

"I wouldn't have believed that the same five minutes could be both so bloody and so wonderful."

Sammy had less breath.

"I got stuck," he said.

I realized how small the opening must have been for he was a little man and very agile.

A figure tip-toed past a few feet away from us.

"Percy! Percy!" it whispered and disappeared into the trees.

"Let's go," I said to Sammy.

"When I've got my breath back."

"The sooner we put some distance between us and the camp the better."

"I quite agree, but I can't do that without any breath, can I?"

I realized the strain that was going to be placed on our partnership. Our fate and actions were now linked together as closely as those of Siamese twins and every decision contained a potential quarrel.

"All right," I said.

I pulled off the old black-dyed pyjamas I had worn over my clothes to keep them clean in the tunnel, and threw them away into the wood. Then I pulled out the cap which a man who normally spent his time reading Lucretius had made for me out of a German blanket, and tidied myself up.

"How do I look?"

"O.K. Let's go."

Sammy pulled out a naval officer's cap with the badges removed. I could only see his outline against the cloudy sky, but I knew what he looked like from the dress rehearsal we had carried out the day before. In daylight he intended to wear a pair of dark glasses because his face had been burnt when he was shot down and he was afraid that this would attract attention. He was better dressed than I was. His threadbare naval uniform with civilian buttons, the green half-length overcoat which he had bought from the Pole who drove the sewage cart, and his cap, were at least consistent and plausible. He did not look well-dressed but he did look like the sort of person you would expect to meet in trains and railway stations and take no notice of. He was described in his false identity card as a "machinist" and he had something of the seedy confident look of people who spend much time with oil-cans and machines. His dark glasses even gave a hint of his having once had some quite advanced specialist knowledge and for a time we considered describing him as an "engineer". But my own appearance would have been inconsistent with anything so ambitious.

"I'm afraid it'll have to be machinist after all," he said resentfully when he first saw me in my clothes.

He seemed to take it as quite a blow to his pride. Certainly I did not look convincing. In addition to my blanket cap and my cut-down R.A.F. greatcoat, I wore a pair of naval trousers, a tie which I had often worn as an undergraduate and which had somehow not been confiscated from one of my clothing parcels, and a dyed R.A.F. airman's tunic which we hoped I should never have to reveal because it was so obvious that I had altered the cut. Altogether I had a mad artificial appearance. I looked like some-one who had dressed up.

But it was my boots that worried me most of all.

"Be sure to see that your boots are all right," Sammy had said to me about a week before.

I had been in a hurry to book my place in the library for the morning and, looking down at the boots I was wearing, had decided that they would do.

"Yes, of course," I had said crossly.

And then, on the afternoon of the break, my toe had appeared through the top of the leather. For half an hour I had scurried round the blocks trying to borrow another pair. Eventually I found a pair which fitted me and which the owner was prepared to lend.

"The only snag," he said, "is that I stuck the sole of the right boot on with glue and I shouldn't like to guarantee it."

"That'll be all right," I said confidently.

But what if it wasn't? Could anything be more bogus or more para-lysing than a boot without a sole?

I tried to forget about it.

As we set off I said to Sammy:

"You know, I think we look quite good really."

"Yes," he said, "in the dark."

* * * * *

Sammy had a luminous compass and we started to walk north-east in the direction of the Bromberg railway. It had looked quite simple on the map: some open country first, then up a secondary road until it turned in the wrong direction, more open country, across a main road and then the railway line. The field we started to walk across was very muddy and we moved slowly. It was necessary to skirt the camp, and the boundary lights were visible all the time a quarter of a mile away. There was something nightmarish about our heavy mud-clogged steps and the continual presence of the camp from which we were trying to escape. After we had crossed the field we came to a sort of heath. Sometimes the grass was long, sometimes short, sometimes there was gorse and sometimes there were little winding paths which led nowhere. All the time the boundary lights pricked out the shape of the camp just over our right shoulders.

"The balloon doesn't seem to have gone up yet," said Sammy.

"I'll feel happier when we can't see the camp any more."

"I think we'd better walk separate – one about fifteen yards ahead of the other, so that if we run into someone one of us will have a chance of getting away. I'll go first."

"All right," I said, "but don't go too far or I won't be able to see you."

It was very dark and the wind made the night darker. Neither of us had yet fully understood the fact that we were free and we expected to be caught at any moment. The darkness seemed to be full of clever Germans with excellent night vision who knew all about us and were biding their time. The ambitious plans that we had made for our journey now seemed more hopelessly unreal than ever. ". . . make our way to Bromberg before it gets light . . . catch the early morning train to Berlin. . . ." And here we were after half an hour, still floundering about in the darkness scarcely out of reach of the searchlights.

Sammy stopped. I wondered if there was something wrong and stopped too. After about half a minute he came cautiously back towards me.

"Is that you?" he said.

"Yes."

"What are you doing?"

"I stopped because you stopped."

"Well, for Christ's sake – I stopped because I wanted you to catch up with me."

"How was I to know that? I thought that something had gone wrong."

"Well anyway," he said, looking at his compass, "what I wanted to say was that we've got to keep further over to the right."

"But that's the direction of the camp."

"I don't care. That's where we've got to go. If we don't hit that railway line we'll get hopelessly stuck – wandering about like this until morning. Once we get to the railway line we don't need to worry about direction any more. We just walk straight up it to Bromberg."

"All right."

He set off in front again, leaving the path. The camp lights grew larger. I could even pick out the silhouette of one of the guard towers.

We had found another path and had been walking along it without difficulty for about ten minutes when I heard a noise. I saw Sammy stop and crawl quickly away into the long grass. I did the same and listened for the sound of footsteps. My heart beat loudly and irregularly so that I was afraid the sound might give me away. But no one came. Very carefully I crawled forward to find Sammy. I almost crawled on top of him before I saw him.

"Didn't you hear someone?" he whispered.

"Yes."

"Sh."

We listened together.

"There doesn't seem to be anyone there now."

"Perhaps they're waiting for us to show ourselves."

"We'll have to go on. We've wasted nearly an hour already."

"All right."

This time I went ahead. The compass was reassuring in the darkness like a pilot's instruments in bumpy cloud. I noticed with surprise that the camp was now behind us although at no time did we seem to have passed it. Once, when we went down into a hollow it disappeared from sight altogether. But it was there again the next moment, though the lights were smaller. They looked almost small enough for the wind to blow them away altogether. I stopped and waited for Sammy.

"Anything wrong?" he asked.

"No. We should be getting to the road soon which will be a relief."

"Good. Look out where you're going though. I seem to remember from the map that there's some marshy ground close to the road."

"What about having something to eat?" I said.

"Already?"

I was troubled by a secret fear that we should be caught before we had had time to eat any of our specially prepared escaping food. If we were caught after eating, at least we should feel that we had got something out of the escape. Otherwise the thought of all our confiscated uneaten food would torment us for months when we were back in the camp.

"Just to keep our morale up?" I said. I could not help smiling.

Sammy smiled back.

"I think we might allow our morale a few raisins," he said, "but we ought to keep moving."

We munched raisins as we walked.

I was still leading when I saw the dusty white secondary road just ahead of us and a little to the left. I was so relieved that I left the path we were on and made straight for the road. There was a slight slope for a few yards. I ran down it. Falling suddenly, like a drunkard, I was up to my waist in thick muddy water. I trod furiously, splashed with my arms to save myself from overbalancing. I got out again on to the path. My boots and trousers were heavy with muddy slime. Sammy ran up.

"Oh Christ," he said, and stared at me appalled.

The water was soaking through to my skin and I felt the beginning of a clammy despair. The only consolation was that I had not lost my attaché case.

"We'll have to hope the mud dries before morning," said Sammy, "and we'll try to brush it off."

We both sat down while I emptied the water out of my boots. Then I took off my trousers and we wrung them out. After I had put them on again I dried my feet with a towel and put on a clean pair of socks out of my attaché case. The touch of the dry wool was comforting. I laced up my boots and felt better. I hoped that the dampness round my stomach and at the small of my back would go as I walked. The stimulus of recovery from mishap was flowing through me and although, logically speaking, we were now worse off than before, because the whole bluff of our appearance was prejudiced, I felt more confident than at any time since we had started. I picked up my attaché case and we followed the path on to the road.

"Good," said Sammy, "now up here for about a mile, then cross-country again for a bit, over the main road, and we should hit the railway."

I had gone a dozen yards when I heard a queer flapping noise as I walked. I looked down. The front part of the sole of my right boot had come unstuck with the water. I did not dare to tell Sammy.

We walked close to the side of the road so that we could leave it quickly if we heard someone coming. But the whiteness of the road made it easier than before to see that no one was coming and our progress was less neurotic. It was no longer possible to pick out the lights of the camp individually. There was just a big distant glow and this too was comforting. I even began to think that we might reach Bromberg, but the idea of buying tickets and catching trains still seemed ridiculous.

When we came to the bend in the road where we had to strike across country again, Sammy said:

"What about a rest and some food?"

We sat down on open ground a few yards away from the road and unpacked raisins and chocolate. The camp had become a faint white glare in the sky from somewhere just below the horizon. As we lay on the grass, eating unrestrainedly for the first time for years, watching the black clouds chase each other across the starlit sky and hearing nothing but the wind in the darkness, something began to thaw inside me. I was aware that I was free. No voices – arguing, shouting, whining, asking, telling. No cramped little room. No cramped little brain. No demands. No obligations. No covering up. Just myself and the sky and the dark empty countryside and the wind blowing over it to eternity.

After about half an hour Sammy said:

"I suppose we'd better get on."

"I suppose so."

We started walking again.

The glare from the camp disappeared altogether below the horizon.

The going was easier than I had expected. We found a path that ran beside some ploughed land and followed it until we came to a different type of country. There were fields with hedges, mostly pasture, and there were woods dotting the rising ground. It was like parts of England. For me our journey became like a dream. The dark fields and the blurred trees against the syline seemed to contain a great mystery. I felt that I could never be happier. I wanted to be allowed to wander through the night and this precious cold landscape for ever.

We walked down a sloping triangular meadow, enclosed on two sides by deep black woods. This place, I thought, is the heart of the earth.

I looked at my watch. It was half-past one.

"We'll have to hurry up if we're going to catch the eight o'clock from Bromberg," I said.

"My feet hurt," said Sammy, "I want a rest."

"Let's rest when we get to the railway line. We'll know how much time we've got to waste then."

"Oh, all right. But my poor dogs!"

We were walking together now. There did not seem much chance of meeting anyone in open country and we both felt more confident. I was almost dry and had even stopped worrying about the sole of my boot. I could not hear it flapping so often on the grass as on the road.

We discussed our plans.

"We've got to get to Bromberg before it's light. We mustn't be seen wandering about here in daylight."

"No, especially with you covered in mud."

"It depends on when the alarm is given. I suppose they might not discover the escape until morning appel. But even then it wouldn't be safe in

Bromberg after about ten. Anyway I think we would look suspicious wandering about like this whether the alarm was up or not."

"The next train after the eight o'clock is not until half-past one."

"We'll just have to make the eight o'clock then."

"What worries me is: how are we going to get through the cordon which they'll obviously throw round Bromberg as soon as the balloon goes up?"

"We'll have to hope it doesn't go up. Anyway, that's the point of walking up the railway line instead of the road."

We had talked about all these things a hundred times before, but it eased our minds to talk about them again now when the unknown was so soon to become known.

Once we stopped by a ditch full of water and Sammy bathed his feet. I was thirsty and had already drunk all the water from the little medicine bottle I had brought with me, so I drank from the ditch. It was stagnant but not unpleasant.

We went on again.

After a long time we walked over a rise and saw a light below us in the distance.

"What the hell's that?" said Sammy.

We sat down under a hedge and he struck a match and looked at the map.

"Christ, I suppose it's that railway crossing," he said, pointing at the crumpled piece of paper. The wind crackled the edges. "It's much further south than we ought to be. Almost due east of the camp. Still, it means that we're nearly at the railway line."

A few minutes later we found a path which led us to the main road we had expected. We stopped and listened before crossing it, and then ran over it quickly as if we were under fire. The light we had seen was brighter now and a dog was barking. We made a small arc to the north.

"I don't see any railway line," said Sammy.

"It must be here somewhere. The ground rises in a minute."

I stared at a single tree on the skyline just in front of us. Then I realized that it wasn't a tree but a railway signal. For some reason we had expected to find the railway line running flat across the countryside as it did on the map.

We ran up the embankment. It was high and very steep. Sammy stopped half-way up for a rest and I was glad to sit down at the top. We could still see the light, only fainter again, down the line to the south.

"We must have a look at the map," said Sammy. He took it out of his pocket and tried to strike a match.

I knocked it out of his hand.

"For God's sake be careful."

"What the hell are you panicking about?"

"I'm not panicking, but it's mad to strike a light up here."

"Well, we've got to see where we are, haven't we?"

"But there may be people about, especially close to that crossing."

"Oh, balls."

"Well, I'm not going to stay here while you do it."

I walked away up the line. After I had gone a hundred yards I looked back. There was no sign of Sammy or the match. I felt mean and a fool. I went back. Sammy was folding up the map.

"Sorry," I said, "where are we?"

"That's the level crossing all right." He pointed towards the light. "It means we've about eighteen kilometres to do up the railway. What's the time?"

"Just after three. That leaves us about four and a half hours. We should just do it."

"Oh Christ," he said, "my poor dogs!"

We set off. It was a single track and we again decided to take it in turns to walk ahead.

I soon discovered the disadvantage of walking along a railway line. The sleepers were too close together for it to be possible to walk a normal regular pace. The same thing applied to the spaces in between them, and it was impossible to put one foot on a space and another on a sleeper because the spaces were irregular in depth and always lower than the sleepers. I tried walking along the narrow path between the rail and the embankment but this was continually disappearing or leading off down the embankment. In the end I became resigned to a short mincing step over the sleepers. This was ridiculous and tiring.

I found Sammy sitting by the side of the line.

"God, this is hell isn't it?" he said.

"Hell."

"I'm just going to take off my boots for a minute."

"All right."

I looked at my watch.

"We might as well have a few raisins while we're about it," he said.

He knew how to win me over.

We stopped like this two or three times during the night. Once we even left the line altogether for twenty minutes and sat in a little copse eating biscuits and cheese. We knew it was unpractical but at the same time it seemed madness not to enjoy food and freedom while we had them.

"We don't want to let ourselves get run down," said Sammy.

Once we stopped to wash in a pond by the side of the line, and Sammy tried to brush the mud off my trousers and the bottom of my coat. My feet were sore too by that time and they felt better for being washed.

Once we passed through a deserted village station. The concrete platforms rose up to our shoulders on either side and there was a blurred building on one of them which presumably held the ticket office. It pleased me to think of the respectable citizens who would stand on these platforms next day, waiting for their train with tickets in their pockets and knowing nothing of the two figures that had passed through during the night.

We knew that about seven kilometres from Bromberg there was a bridge where the railway went over the canal. We expected it and dreaded it. It was generally supposed that all railway bridges in Germany were guarded. On the other hand people who had escaped often came back and talked of finding them unguarded. For weeks we had tried to find out about this bridge over the canal. We had gone to Vincent, the "Intelligence" man.

"I think you can assume it's guarded," he had said.

"Why assume it if it's not though?" said Sammy.

"Why not assume everything you can?"

"But we don't want to assume it," I said.

"Oh, I see. Well, in that case I'll try and find out for you."

"Don't strain yourself," said Sammy.

Then we had tried asking Jack Nopps' tame German.

"English or American?" I had said, offering him a cigarette.

"Thanks." He took a fistful of both.

"Supposing one ever succeeded in escaping from here, would it be safe to go over bridges – say, railway bridges – or would they be guarded?"

"Fatal. Guarded night and day," he said, putting the cigarettes away into an inner pocket and lighting the stubbed out end of an old cigar.

When I told Sammy he said that he too had asked him the same question.

"What did he say?"

"He said they weren't guarded."

"What did you give him?"

"Some chocolate."

"I gave him cigarettes."

"That brings us down to: 'Which does Jack Nopps' goon like best, cigarettes or chocolate?' "

Then, just before the tunnel was due to break, Vincent had come to see us.

"I've got some information for you two," he said. "About that bridge you asked me about – I've collected a good deal of evidence and it seems impossible to say categorically one thing or the other. On the other hand I should say there is a tendency for it to be guarded and should avoid it at all costs."

I could see that Sammy was going to say something rude.

"Thanks," I said, "thanks very much."

And now it was only a kilometre away. Sammy caught up with me.

"I wonder which way it's tending at the moment," he said. "We'd better go slow and approach it very carefully. If we see it's guarded, we'll have to leave the line and try and get across the canal some other way. We'll toss up to see who goes first. Whoever goes last can stay well behind. If he hears a fuss he can run off into the darkness."

He picked up a stone from between the sleepers and held out his hands.

"Left or right?"

"Left."

"Sorry."

He let the stone drop from his right hand.

"O.K.," I said, "keep well behind."

I set off.

I expected to come to the bridge so often in the next ten minutes that when it did loom out of the darkness ahead of me, like a prehistoric monster lumbering out of primeval slime, I was surprised to find it so close on top of me. I began to crawl along the side of the line towards it. I kept stopping to listen for the sound of a sentry but could hear nothing. The steel structure looked enormous from so close to the ground. When I was about ten yards away I saw the faint glitter of the water in the canal. Then I heard a solitary definite "plop". I stayed quite still on my hands and knees. A fish? Or a bored sentry throwing in a stone? I lay flat on my stomach and listened. There was no other sound. A minute passed and I was afraid that Sammy would be catching me up. Suddenly I could stand it no longer. If there was anyone there I should know in fifteen seconds. If there wasn't, there would be no harm done. I stood up quite noisily and walked quickly towards the bridge.

No one at this end. The girders rang with the sound of my boots. The sound echoed up from the water beneath. But that was all.

There was no one on the other side.

I ran back to tell Sammy. We crossed together.

"Good old bridge," said Sammy, slapping the ironwork affectionately as if it were a horse. "Of course you must give the man his due, he did only say it had a tendency that way."

When we got to the other side we sheltered in the dark hollow under the bridge. Sammy lit a cigarette. He brought out the map and read it by pulling hard on the cigarette and then putting the glowing end close to the paper.

"Well, there we are," he said, pointing to a place on the map where the caterpillar railway line crossed the worm canal.

It was comforting to know our position as definitely as that. It made me feel that in spite of confusion and Sammy's feet and my muddy trousers and flapping sole we had been competent.

It was a quarter past six. We had seven kilometres to go and about another hour of darkness.

"I don't think we're going to make it," said Sammy, stretching himself flat on the bank.

"We've bloody well got to."

"I don't think we will all the same."

"We'll have to walk the last bit in daylight if necessary."

"Risky," he said.

"Well, don't be so bloody objective about it. It's you it's going to be risky for as well as me."

"Oh, I know, I know."

"Well then do something about it."

"Oh, shut up."

Our voices rose and boomed fatuously under the bridge.

Sammy lit another cigarette.

We sat in silence until we both began to get cold.

"Come on," he said.

It was half-past six. We might just catch the train but we had no chance of getting to Bromberg in darkness. Sammy realized this too, but we said nothing as we walked on together.

Even so the dawn surprised us. Somehow I had expected to see it coming and to be able to put on a spurt to beat it. But before it was possible to say definitely that night was going it was suddenly not night at all but day. We walked on without speaking, Sammy a few yards ahead. I could see him clearly now. His small hunched figure with its little legs prancing nimbly over the sleepers had a queer mad quality. He looked like an Edward Lear illustration to a Limerick. He turned round and looked at me.

"Oh, my God," he said, stopping and doubling up with laughter. "Oh, my God! I wish you could see yourself."

"What's the matter?"

"You look absolutely mad. And bogus as hell."

He went on chuckling to himself under his dark glasses for some minutes.

All this time it was getting lighter. We knew that we looked suspicious, especially walking down a railway line, but we were both too tired to bother much and just walked on. Sandy pinewoods stretched away on either side of the line. They had the dirty worn-out look of parts of Surrey.

"These woods are on the map. They're about two and a half kilometres from the town."

We were walking on carelessly so that we forgot all about the line crossing the main road until we were there. The shock woke us up.

"What the hell are we going to do?" said Sammy. "We can't go on like this, we look too awful."

"I think we'd better hide up in the woods for a bit and get ourselves tidy. We'll have to give up the eight o'clock to Berlin. Perhaps there'll be a local one going in the right direction later in the morning. We can get some sleep that way."

"It'll be risky in these woods. They don't look very thick."

"The whole thing's pretty risky by now. Anyway we haven't done badly to get this far."

Sammy thought for a moment.

"Let's go up the railway line rather than along the road anyway," he said.

"All right."

As we crossed over the road we saw a man coming down it towards us. Neither of us looked at him. We walked on and across the line. The road ran away from the line at a slight angle and after a minute I could see the man staring after us. He obviously thought it odd that we should choose the railway line in preference to the road. When we were enclosed by trees again, Sammy said:

"I can't stand much more of that. Let's hide up."

We turned off into the wood. It was now quite light though the sun was not yet up. There were bushes in parts of the wood, also patches where small trees grew close together. Even so it looked much thicker from a standing position than when we were actually lying down in it. The woods were covered with intersecting paths as if people walked there often.

"It doesn't matter," said Sammy lying down under a bramble bush, "we haven't done badly to get this far".

I lay down too. I couldn't remember whether it was he or I who had said that before. I was very tired. I expected to be woken up by a policeman or a forester. But I didn't care. I went to sleep.

*   *   *   *   *

The first thing I noticed when I woke up was the green purplish colour of Sammy's burnt face in the early morning light. A minute later long dancing fingernails of sunshine probed into the wood from the horizon. It was very cold.

Sammy moved a long curling bramble away from his eyes.

"What's the time?" he asked.

"A quarter past eight."

He let the bramble fall again.

I went to look for some water. We seemed to be in the thickest part of the wood and there was no sound of anyone else. I found a stream and came back to tell Sammy and to fetch my washing things.

After we had washed and cleaned our teeth, and eaten great quantities of bread and butter and corned beef, we felt better. Sammy brushed my trousers again.

"Is it coming off?" I asked.

"I don't think so, but it's going in which has much the same effect. It doesn't look too bad."

We allowed ourselves some chocolate and sat down and talked about what we were going to do next. We both felt a pleasant recklessness about the future. Our original plan had collapsed and theoretically we were now due to be caught. But we had not been caught yet and every additional minute was a triumph in itself.

We decided that the woods would be one of the first places to be searched when the escape was discovered and that we ought to leave as soon as possible. We agreed to try and bluff our way into Bromberg by walking openly down the main road.

"Somehow I don't think they'll expect to find escaped prisoners walking down a main road in daylight."

"We'll try and look like two ordinary chaps going to work."

"When we get to the station we can find out the time of the first train going west, and then hide in the lavatory until it goes."

Such a plan would have sounded hopeless and lunatic the day before. Now we both accepted it as reasonable and set off with confidence.

We had to cross the railway line to get to the main road and as we came out into the clearing a little train rattled up towards Bromberg. We stopped to let it pass, trying to look as if we always came out of a wood at that time of the morning. One man in a corner seat looked at us and then turned away, taking us for granted. This increased our confidence and we walked happily over the line to the main road.

We had gone about a hundred yards when Sammy noticed the flapping noise.

"What the hell's that noise?" he asked.

"I think it's the sole of my boot. It's come unstuck."

"Oh, my God!" he giggled. "Oh, my God!"

It did not seem to matter at all now. It was just one more contribution to the illogicality of our still being free.

It was pleasant to walk along a flat road after the railway line. We passed through a small village. A woman was hanging up some washing. A boy was sitting on a doorstep. A man, dressed rather like Sammy, was bending over a car in a garage. The sun shone. The air was clear. There was a quiet background of country sounds.

"Remember the name of that village," said Sammy after we had passed through. "We can say we've come from there if anyone asks us."

A horse and cart was coming down the road towards us. We mumbled incoherently at each other to give the impression of conversation. As it passed the man who was driving said: "*Morgen.*"

"*Morgen,*" shouted Sammy heartily. This frightened me because his accent was arrogantly English. But the man on the cart didn't look back.

"For God's sake, don't do that again," I said.

"Sorry, I really meant it in a way."

The cart had had a little notice printed on the side: "Heinz Renner, Friedrichstrasse, Bromberg."

"We'll say we're going to work for Heinz Renner," I said.

The pine woods came down to the road on each side. Soon we would be seeing the outskirts of Bromberg.

"The aerodrome's somewhere near here," said Sammy, "if there's a barrier across the road anywhere it'll probably be here."

I again became conscious of the flapping sole of my boot.

A short burst of tommy-gun fire ripped the quiet of the woods and Sammy jumped high into the air. There were shouts in the wood and I could see grey Luftwaffe figures in steel helmets running through the trees. There were more shots.

"Keep on walking," said Sammy under his breath, "but I think we've had it."

I was far too frightened to do anything but walk.

An N.C.O. with a tommy-gun ran out of the wood on to the road about twenty yards ahead of us. His face was red and sweating and his helmet had slipped on to the back of his head. He ran up the road towards us. Other soldiers ran after him. There were more shots in the wood.

"Jesus Christ," said Sammy, "I don't like this. Quick, look as if we're having a conversation."

I opened my mouth but could make no sound at all.

The N.C.O. and the soldiers ran straight past us into the wood. There were more shots and a whistle blew. Then there were no more shots. There was no more shouting. Bored and panting, the soldiers fell in by the side of the road. A few hundred yards lower down we passed the aero-drome.

My heart was beating so heavily that I thought I should have to sit down.

I don't know which was the greater shock: the first sound of the shots or the final realization that it was all only part of a military exercise and had absolutely nothing to do with us at all.

We walked down the hill into Bromberg.

I felt so confident that I stopped a Pole and asked him the way to the station.

"First on the left over the bridge. Second on the right."

"Thanks very much."

"*Bitte schön.*"

"Too easy," said Sammy.

We arrived as the station clock struck a quarter to ten.

*   *   *   *   *

The more people we saw the more confident we became, for no one paid any attention to us. There was a large bustling crowd in the hall of the station and we wandered through it trying to find out the times of the trains going towards Berlin. Our chief difficulty was communication between ourselves. I was described on my identity card as a French worker and Sammy on his as an Italian, these being the languages each of us knew best. Sammy's Italian was excellent, but I knew none at all. Sammy's French was elementary and mine was very little better. At first we tried talking together in a heavy schoolboy French, but we misunderstood each other so often that we were reduced to mumbling in English. This must have given us a furtive appearance as we had to withdraw from the crowds to discuss what we read on the notice-boards.

Finally we decided to catch a local train to Schneidemühl, about fifty kilometres away to the west. It was due to leave at twelve o'clock.

I had left Sammy and was moving across to the booking office when a little man in S.S. uniform came up to me.

He rattled a money-box.

"*Eine kleine Spende.*" The Party made regular collections for winter relief.

I had no coins. The money which we had got in the camp was all in notes. I stuffed a one mark note into the little slot. The man looked surprised. I stuffed in another. He looked more surprised still.

"*Danke schön, danke schön.*"

I shuffled quickly away.

I was nervous buying the tickets and gave a whole five mark note too much. But the man, his eyes glazed with the bored superiority of the petty official, merely thought that I was stupid and slapped the note back to me.

When I told Sammy about the man with the money-box he giggled.

"Of course he was surprised. An interpreter in the camp once told me that no goon ever gives more than ten pfennigs."

We went up to the barrier.

"Your train doesn't go for another two hours," said the ticket inspector.

"We'll wait."

He punched the tickets and we passed through.

There was a long concrete subway underneath the station and steps led up from it at intervals to the separate platforms: one, three and five down one side; two, four and six down the other. We followed the sign for the lavatory.

A man was adjusting his bow tie in front of a mirror. This made it impossible for us to talk to each other. We took off our coats and washed. We took towels from our attaché cases (furtively, to avoid disclosing unnatural quantities of chocolate) and dried our hands and faces. The man was still there fiddling with the ends of his tie. I noticed that Sammy had "Gift of the British Red Cross" stamped across his braces, and I put on my own coat quickly, hoping that he would do the same. But he was being purposely slow and played maddeningly with the taps.

Then the man at the mirror undid his bow tie altogether, pulled it off his neck and stuffed it away into his pocket. He pulled an ordinary tie out of another pocket, tied it quickly, turned down his collar and left.

We began to whisper.

"For God's sake put on your coat."

"Quick, get in there."

"We mustn't talk unless we're certain no one's about."

"All right, but get in."

"And we'll stay until the train goes."

"O.K."

When I went to the door of the first cubicle and saw the little semi-circular "*Besetzt*" on the outside it was as if someone had dropped a stone into the bottom of my stomach. A man must have been sitting inside listening to us. A feeble hope made me push the door and it swung open with a creak: the lock was broken; there was no one there. I hurried to the other doors. "*Frei.*" "*Frei.*" "*Frei.*" Sammy and I locked ourselves in next to each other.

Soon I saw a piece of paper being pushed under the partition between us. "If you've anything to say, write it down."

A few minutes later a large biscuit followed with some cheese and a note on the top: "For the morale."

I tore off a sheet of lavatory paper, wrote "Thanks" on it and pushed it under the partition. Then I ate the biscuit and stared at the pornographic drawings on the wall.

Tiredness emphasized the strangeness of our position. A phrase which my grandmother always used when discussing the unorthodoxy of other people's behaviour went echoing through my head: "Where will it all end, my dear? Where will it all end?"

I began to be frightened in a new way, in a way that was no longer either amusing or exciting as well. Perhaps it was because we were now quite trapped if anything should go wrong, or merely because I was tired, but I now began to understand the full strength of our enemy. It was no longer just a matter of a few guards to be outwitted. A whole society was against us and for practical purposes that meant all society, the whole world.

The main door into the lavatory opened. There was the clatter of a pail and the slobbering of some sort of rubber mop on the floor. The station char was on her rounds. In a few minutes I heard her in the next cubicle to mine, slamming up the seat and pulling the plug. The dirty water from her mop edged its way under the partition into my cubicle. She tried my door. I rustled the lavatory paper. She tried Sammy's door. He was more realistic. She moved away, singing to herself and slobbering around with the mop somewhere else in the room. Then she came back and rattled our doors impatiently. I realized that if she was determined to come in we should have to leave, but I could think of nothing to do but wait to see what she would do. I could hear her waiting and breathing on the other side of the door. She waited for about two minutes and then kicked the door and shouted in a German which I did not understand. I pulled the plug and left with a show of dignity.

She was fat and short and her thick black hair was done up in a bun at the back of her head. She muttered at me as I passed. I heard Sammy pull his plug and went outside to wait for him in the subway. The same S.S. man as before came up to me.

"*Eine kleine Spende.*"

I gave him some of the change I had got with the tickets.

Sammy came out and we went towards our platform. I slammed my feet as we walked so that the echoes rang in the hollow place. Somehow it released some of the tiredness in my head.

I bought a newspaper and we went and sat in the waiting-room. It was almost empty. There were two or three genuine foreign workers, whose dishevelled appearance gave me confidence. There was a tired-looking young mother, a pale father and a screaming baby. A middle-aged woman in black was pushing plates along a marble-topped counter and flicking crumbs off it with a duster.

"We'll be able to have soup later," said Sammy.

With the exception of fish it was the only unrationed food in Germany. We sat down at a table which had fresh coffee stains on it.

"I'm going to sleep," said Sammy, "I think it's safer."

I began to read the German High Command's communiqué in the newspaper.

"Between Tripoli and Mareth our rearguards . . ."

Tripoli. Somewhere between Tripoli and Mareth the world changed. Somewhere in that desert there was a point beyond which it was no longer necessary to disguise personality, hide in lavatories, fear everyone who passed. Tripoli didn't seem to have anything to do with this stuffy Polish railway station. The two worlds existed but there was no link between them. We were sitting on the Polish railway station and our world was one of humiliation and deceit.

Tiredness was like a bog into which I was sinking. The use of my muscles was becoming difficult. It was a great effort to put down the newspaper, to shift my bottom and to move my head. I saw the dark green glasses on Sammy's false-looking nose and the pale father slapping the baby and the mother watching in despair. Then I was sucked into the sour sticky blackness of the bog.

*   *   *   *   *

Though I was awake for most of the next two days I never completely shook off sleep. The few short intervals of sleep which I did get, such as this one of an hour with my head slumped over my arm on the coffee-stained table of a station waiting-room, were never sufficient to absorb more than a small quantity of tiredness. Tiredness grew continually. Each sleep made me feel better than before I went into it, but always worse than after the previous sleep. For two days my limbs grew heavier and heavier. Material things became more and more remote as if held at a longer and longer arm's length. My mind had to work harder and harder for less and less result. I walked and thought in a cocoon of frustrated sleep, and people and incidents often took on the fantasy of a morning dream.

The waiting-room was suddenly full. There were people sitting on their luggage in the spaces between the tables and chairs. A big woman with a rucksack was looking down at me as if she expected me to offer her my seat. There was a waiting-room hum, occasionally broken by the yell of a child or someone trying to order coffee from a hot waiter.

Sammy leant across the table. His eyes flickered furtively under the green lenses.

"*Une demi-heure encore*," he said slowly. "Too much of a crowd for soup, I think," he added.

It seemed the next minute that he leant across again and muttered: "Ten minutes to go."

Just after that we began to step over people and luggage on our way to the front door. The big woman sat down on my chair.

On the platform were two British soldiers in clean battle-dress, side hats and well polished boots. They were walking up and down in step, like officers waiting for a parade to begin. Their escort must have been close by but I could not see him. I wanted to talk to them, to say: "Pst – you think I'm a German civilian, but I'm really an R.A.F. officer," but somehow they looked forbidding in their correctness as we slunk past, content to be despised by them too.

At the other end of the platform, standing discreetly at the back of the crowd in a check cap and a smart blue mackintosh, was Willy Myers.

It was such a surprise to see him that at first it did not seem a surprise at all. Then I looked quickly, guiltily away. I knew Sammy had seen him too because he said "Good God!" quite loudly beside me. I allowed myself another look at Willy. He gave me the sort of smile one gives people one meets every day but wants to keep at a distance. Sammy and I turned towards the line and waited for our train.

"It's Willy Myers, did you see?"

"Er-*oui, je l'ai vu*."

I think the dark glasses must have made it easier for Sammy to keep control of himself.

An official wearing a blue peaked cap came up to us.

"Where are you going to?"

"We're going to Schneidemühl. We're . . ." I reached into my pocket for our papers.

"That's right," said the official, "this is your train coming in now."

We pushed our way into a third-class carriage through elbowing widows and old men with baskets.

It was a long carriage without compartments and the brawl for seats continued inside. We sat down together among four soldiers. I wondered if Willy Myers had got a seat. The soldiers were combining their contempt for civilians with the joy of going on leave by talking very loudly and bouncing about on their seats as if there was no one in the carriage. Occasionally the eyes of one of them would stray to see what sort of impression he was making.

The train started.

The jolting of the carriage and the hardness of the wooden seat worked into my disjointed dozing. I thought that I ought to keep awake and was continually forcing my head up and my eyes open. Every time I awoke the world seemed freshly raw. I was hot and sticky under my thick coat. The stuffiness of the carriage had a foreign smell. All round me German voices talking of market and rationing and bombing reminded me that I had no place among these people. One of the soldiers started to whistle an old dance tune called "Goody-goody." Sammy had taken his cap off. A woman was eating some bread and a pink juicy sausage.

We stopped at a station. Nakel. I remembered staring at the name on the local map.

I started thinking about the tunnel and our journey of the night before. I wanted to digest the experience. But it changed into a game I was playing at school. Someone was "He" and we all had to go and hide. I went down into the fives courts, through the swimming bath, past the rifle range and out on to the main road. Where was I going? I wanted to stop. I was afraid.

We were at another station.

No one seemed to get out, but a lot more people got in. A soldier took out a mouth organ and began to play "*Lilli Marlene.*" Several women held string bags full of vegetables. The train started again.

To market, to market to buy a fat pig, to market, to market jiggedy jig. My own *Lilli Marlene*. There was a shout down the compartment behind me. I was wide awake.

People were fumbling in their pockets. I knew I looked calm but I tried to feel it too. After all, our papers were perfectly forged and Sammy swore that they were copies of an original.

It was only the ticket inspector. He clipped our tickets and passed on. Sammy never even woke up.

The next time I woke up I realized at once that I had been asleep for a long time. The carriage was almost empty. It was as if most of the people had been made to vanish by the wave of some magic wand. Even the soldiers had quietened down. I was refreshed. I looked at my watch and saw that we were almost due at Schneidemühl.

This, I thought, is quite an achievement. We are more than fifty miles from the camp.

Sammy was sitting upright, looking pleased with himself too.

On the platform we met Willy Myers again almost at once. He was greatly agitated because although he had bought himself a second-class ticket he had got into a third-class carriage by mistake. This had offended the ticket inspector who had insisted that he moved. When he had moved into a second-class carriage he had found himself sitting within a few feet of one of the camp interpreters going on leave.

"Phew," he said, "it was a nasty couple of hours."

"It serves you right for travelling second-class," said Sammy.

Walking slowly with Willy towards the station time-table Sammy and I discussed our plans. Our long-term plans had always been extremely hazy, mainly because we had not believed that we should ever be in a position to use them. Sammy had talked mysteriously about some contact he knew of on the Belgian frontier. "We'll make our way by train to Aachen," he had said, authoritatively one evening in the camp, "and then go on to this address I know." And he had gone off to play roulette until bedtime. (He won £500 that night, but the money was just about as unreal as the train to Aachen. You could not buy food or clothes or books with the £500 and you did not need a train when the furthest you could go in any direction was two hundred yards.) A day before the tunnel broke he had sewn a map of the Belgian frontier into the lining of his coat, but after that we were too busy with immediate practical problems to think anything more about it.

Now magically we were on a railway station fifty miles away from the camp. Though the Belgian frontier was not yet by any means real it was clear that reality was changing and that we should have to adapt our ideas to meet it.

"If there's a train going to Berlin to-night," said Sammy, "we'll go through with the old plan. We could always spend the night in the waiting-room of a big station without being noticed. If there's not, we'll think again."

We nosed round one of the time-table boards.

There were no more trains to Berlin that day.

There was a train to Stettin with a change at Küstrin, in three hours time. Sammy and I withdrew to discuss it.

"Why not?"

"O.K."

"We'll try and get a boat. At least we'll have made a shot at it that way."

"O.K."

Willy Myers had disappeared. We looked for him for a few minutes and then decided to spend part of our three hours wait in walking round the town. We gave up our tickets and went out of the station. Half-way up the hill we saw Willy.

We caught him up. He seemed rather annoyed to see us.

"Couldn't you wait for us?" asked Sammy.

"You looked so bloody furtive whispering together. Besides," he pointed at my trousers, "look at that mud. Socially, it's not giving me a chance."

He stalked on offended. For a moment it was difficult not to believe in this prim bourgeois Dane (he had been the only one out of fifty to pose as a Dane) in his neat clothes and well-polished shoes.

"What are your plans?" I asked.

I thought it was up to me to make amends in some way. He was flattered.

"Well, as a matter of fact," he said, "I haven't told anyone in the camp my plans, but I don't mind telling you two now, in the circumstances."

We had passed over the railway bridge and were walking down a row of seedy but pretentious villas.

"I know a German family somewhere up on the coast north of here. I shall go and see them and get them to give me a rowing-boat to go to Denmark in. Once in Denmark, of course, I'm all right. I've got plenty of connections there."

"Where does this family live?" asked Sammy.

"Well as a matter of fact I don't exactly know the name of the village. You see I never actually stayed with them. I was staying with a family somewhere inland and we just went up to this other family once for the day."

"Oh," said Sammy.

We walked down another row of villas. We told him our plan. Although to me it seemed no more impractical than his own, he was sceptical. He made the most of our having completely changed our plan en route.

"I've had this plan of mine worked out for nearly six months," he said.

We walked about for an hour and then came back to the railway bridge.

"The dogs are getting tired again," said Sammy. "Let's go into the station and sit down."

"There's another two hours to wait."

"We can have some soup or something."

"Oh, all right."

"I think I'd better get out of town and find somewhere in the woods to sleep," said Willy.

"So long, then. All the best."

"Good-bye," said Willy, raising his cap politely. "Good luck."

Sammy and I went back into the station.

CHAPTER SIXTEEN

R OBERT KEE and his companion were finally caught by the Gestapo, but they were not ill-treated and they were returned to *Oflag XXIB* ten days later. One by one all the British escapers were brought in except Lieutenant-Commander Buckley. We were told by the Germans that he had been "found drowned" on the Baltic coast. His death remains a mystery to this day.

It is to Robert Kee's bad luck that we owe his second book *The Impossible Shore*, in which he gives a most moving account of the liberation of his prison camp by the Russians. He, I think, more than any other writer, has caught in these two books the wry humour and desperate frustration that make up the strange half-life of the prisoner of war.

*   *   *   *   *

Escape from P.O.W. camps in all civilized countries is regarded by both military captor and his captive as a legitimate sport. Provision has been made for it in the Geneva Convention, and were it not for the escaper's opportunities to collect surplus food, civilian clothes and other equipment many of the stories in this book could never have been written.

Spencer Chapman, in his escape from the Japanese, had no such opportunities, nor could he expect his treatment on recapture to be softened by any rules of war. He was aware, however, how difficult escape would be once he reached a permanent prison camp, and he was resolved to make his break at the earliest opportunity. In a recent letter he tells me, "Having read most escape stories, when the time came for me to put my theories into practice, the interesting thing was that I had absolute confidence in my ability to escape; the only problem was to choose the auspicious moment."

Spencer Chapman is typical of the British civilian turned soldier who made such efficient guerilla fighters during the recent War. Posted to Singapore in 1941 as an instructor in the school of guerilla fighting, he stayed behind after the Japanese occupation and fought for three and a half years behind the enemy lines. Knowing at first nothing of the country nor its people, Colonel Chapman, often sick with blackwater fever, malaria, pneumonia and tic-typhus, harried the Japanese with home-made bombs and booby-traps, trained Chinese Communist guerillas and did much to raise the morale of the inhabitants and restore their faith in the British.

In 1944, while trying to make contact with Pat Noone, another Englishman who had been working with the guerillas, Spencer Chapman and Lim, a member of his band, arrived at what they thought was a Chinese guerilla headquarters. But it turned out to be the hiding-place of Chinese bandits, who stole their revolvers and ammunition, and kept them prisoner. Spencer Chapman sent Lim, who was less closely guarded, back to headquarters with a message while he himself remained behind to recover the revolvers. Before he could do this he heard from a friendly Chinese vegetable-grower that one of the bandits, Rat-face, intended to sell him to the Japanese; and he decided to escape.

F. Spencer Chapman

IT WAS now May 10, my fourteenth day in the camp and my thirty-sixth birthday. It seemed an auspicious day to escape. A month's rest and adequate, if simple, food had made me extremely fit, and I thought I could get home in a week even without any help from the Sakai. That evening I surreptitiously packed up all my gear in my big rucksack. Though it was not their turn, Rat-face and the stooge were on duty. Something had made them suspicious. The guards would drink coffee until far into the night. Then they would take it in turn to keep awake, but usually morning found them both sprawling fast asleep across the table.

In those days we always carried with us an "L-tablet" – L for lethal, in case we should be captured by the Japs and have to face torture. I had long since lost my tablet, but Davis and Broome had given me some morphia pills which could be used for the same purpose. I had no intention of killing my sentries. I just wanted to make quite sure they would sleep soundly. Unfortunately I had no idea how much to use. My lethal dose consisted of eight tablets. I decided to give them four each. That evening I joined them at coffee, and having previously crushed up the little white tablets, it was quite easy to slip them into their mugs before they stirred the sugar. I waited till they had drai e d their mugs and then, feeling singularly elated, I left them and clime d the ladder to my loft. They talked noisily for some time. Quite suddenly, there was silence. Whether they ever woke up or not I do not know – or care.

To make doubly sure, I had already rembuved part of the *atap* wall in one corner of the hut so that I could slip straigoht out into the night without walking past the sentries. Shortly before midnight I tiptoed down the ladder from the loft, pushed my bulky pack through this gap and crawled out after it. It was a pale starlit night with a clear white moon riding high above the silver tree-tops. There was a low pall of ground-mist over the river. Never have I been so conscious of the brilliance of tropical moonlight, made more intense by contrast with the inky shadows of the jungle. As I picked my way between the dewy sweet-potato plants, I felt like an aircraft illuminated by the beams of innumerable searchlights. When I reached the jungle I took out my torch, which was fitted with a green filter. It gave enough light for me to follow the track and place my bare feet carefully, for I dare not wear shoes lest I should be tracked.

I had some difficulty crossing the Korbu river, as it had been raining and the water was waist deep and very swift. Without the steadying weight of my pack I should probably have been swept away. As it was, I had to inch my way across, leaning into the strong current for balance. I had no difficulty in retracing the track past the old headman's house and up-river whence we had come. Here, padding along the footpath in absolute silence, I almost walked into a herd of pig which crashed away in the jungle with loud sharp barks, sending my heart into my mouth. I then had to recross the Korbu and follow the slippery rock slabs on the further bank. Having crossed the tributary Larek, I climbed the hill by a slippery path which was hollowed out and deeply pitted with footmarks of elephant. A thin soaking rain was now falling steadily, and the steep clay path was very difficult to climb with my bare feet. I had always imagined that leeches slept at night, but I was wrong and got so badly bitten that I was afraid that if it stopped raining I should be tracked by the trail of blood.

Above Bras' house I had to leave the track I knew, and it took me some time to find the pre-war elephant track up the hill to Larek mine. At last I came out on to the old mining-ground. This was most remarkable country. The various branches of the Larek river flowed out of a wide basin surrounded by a circle of high mountains. Although this valley was in the very heart of the jungle and had not been visited by anyone except the Sakai for several years, it showed everywhere signs of man's hand, especially in the bed of the river, which in many places the miners had tried to control with neat containing walls of stone or wooden breakwaters, now derelict. For a long distance on either side of the river, the jungle had been cleared many years ago and there were large areas of open level sand and bare red laterite hillocks, where bracken, ferns, and magenta and white ground orchids flourished. In some places Straits rhododendron and other flowering shrubs had taken root in the light red sand, and these were clustered with the grey nests of the tree-ants. Everywhere were pig and *rusa* tracks, some of them quite fresh. I felt like an explorer suddenly discovering the remains of a former civilization.

All at once I heard a dog bark and realized there were Sakai about. I tried to find them, but they were not used to the presence of other human beings in this remote place and fled, probably thinking the hated Japs were after them. This was very disappointing, as a Sakai could so easily have led me back on to my old trail and in any case they are always good company. I wasted most of the afternoon tracking Sakai, but though I once thought I could smell a trace of smoke, I could not find their houses or camp-fires. That night I slept in an old Sakai lean-to hut in the middle of a mile-wide stretch of bare sand where there was less danger of surprise than in the closed jungle.

Next day I cooked my breakfast of rice and curried prawns long before dawn and was away as soon as it was light enough to travel – about half-past five o'clock. I followed the Larek river until it divided, and then took the right-hand branch, because there was at first a faint trail beside it. Here the river had been painstakingly built up with stones to ensure a good flow of water for the tin mine, and higher up there were several conduits bringing in additional water from side streams. Soon the gradient steepened, as is usual when approaching a watershed, and the vegetation became increasingly thick and thorny.

When I at last reached the summit of the ridge I suffered a bitter disappointment. Although the map showed that the boundary of a Forest Reserve ran along the watershed, there was no vestige of a path. Instead, the going was of the most impenetrable kind. I had either to worm along the ground, parting the grass and mosses and crawling beneath the vegetation like a wild boar – sometimes, indeed, actually following their tunnels – or clamber along the top of it like a monkey without touching the ground at all.

For some hours I fought my way along this ridge, making pitifully little headway with my bulky pack. Ahead I could see the high peak of Chon-dong (4,803 feet) still separating me from the Korbu-Gajah watershed, where I had hoped to pick up my outward track. So killing was the going that I thought it would take me at least another day and a half of heart-breaking toil to reach it. I therefore decided to go down the other side of the watershed into the Ulu Chemor, where the map showed evidence of plenty of Sakai settlements, to find a guide to take me over to the valley of the Kinta river and back to the country I knew.

At midday I stopped on the Larek-Chemor watershed and ate the cold remains of the rice and curried prawns that I had saved from breakfast.

The descent to Ulu Chemor was as difficult as jungle going can possibly be without being actually impassable. A few saplings had been neatly sliced off by *parangs*, just where the isolated runnels of water joined to form the first rill of the Sungei Chemor, so I imagined that it was a regular Sakai highway. Thus I was misled into following the stream downhill, instead of doing what experience had taught me, namely to forsake the stream for at least the first thousand feet of its mad tumble to the plains, and to follow down the crest of the spur between two watercourses.

As the volume of water increased, so did the angle of descent. At first it was easier to follow the granite bed of the stream, lowering myself from rock to rock, and sometimes relying on the roots or branches of trees, than to traverse the steep muddy banks above. But soon a roar that I had hoped was the wind in the tree-tops turned out to be a series of waterfalls, and here, wherever I tried to climb out on to the bank, I was always forced sooner or later back into the spray-filled gorge of the river. Once I half fell, half lowered myself down the almost vertical gully of a side stream only to find myself cut off by a wall of steep rock and roaring water. Fortunately I had wound a length of rattan round my waist for just such a contingency, and was able to climb back up the side stream and pull my rucksack after me. I then determined to have no more of the watercourse and climbed laboriously uphill for half an hour until I came out on to a steep *atap*-covered ridge. As I had hoped, there was a Sakai track running up and down the ridge. Footmarks led upward, and I followed them for an hour until the path finished at an empty hut where somebody had recently cut some pineapples, and where a black cat was still in possession.

I had now been travelling for ten hours and was extremely tired. As I had had to discard my rubber shoes so as not to slip while clambering down the stream, my feet as well as my shins were cut and bruised, and the weight of my rucksack had rubbed a great deal of skin off my shoulders and waist. After a good rest I followed the track downward for a long time until it returned to the Chemor river. Here to my horror it crossed over and went straight up a steep ridge on the further bank. Luckily the Sungei Chemor had now lost much of its former impetuosity and it was possible to wade down it.

It had started to rain, and the evening was closing in. My back and shoulders were so sore that each step was most painful. I was very tired indeed. However, it seemed easier, if not wiser, to go on in the probability of reaching the warmth and hospitality of a Sakai house than to stay in the rain, build myself a shelter of banana leaves, light a fire, and cook my solitary meal. I cursed myself for not having left well alone and stayed at the empty Sakai hut on the ridge.

Suddenly I saw the track of a heeled boot in the sand beside the river. My first thought was that it was a Jap, but I knew I was many miles from the outside and I was certain Japs would not come so far into the jungle except perhaps to attack the guerillas. Though I knew there was a camp at Chemor, I thought it was many miles from here and I had not heard that they had had any trouble with the Japs. I came to the conclusion that either a Sakai had got hold of a pair of boots left behind by British soldiers, or that a patrol of Chinese guerillas, wearing boots taken from the Japs, had passed this way. I decided I must not camp and light a fire until I had solved this mystery.

Very soon afterwards, at about 5.30 p.m., I came round a corner of the river and saw two Sakai, bathing naked in the water. This was luck indeed. I approached very cautiously, keeping well in to the bank, as Sakai are very timid and I was afraid they would run away if I gave them half a chance. When I was about twenty yards away, I stepped out from the bank and said quietly in Malay, "Don't be afraid. Don't be afraid. I'm not a Jap: I'm an Englishman and I want you to help me." At the sound of my voice the Sakai stood still. I saw somebody move on the further bank. He was wearing a high-crowned jockey cap with a yellow star on the front – a Jap cap. He looked like a Chinese, and my first thought was that I had stumbled into a guerilla camp – they often wear captured Jap hats and use Sakai guides.

Suddenly the truth dawned on me, and I began to edge towards the bank. The man I had seen – a Jap sentry – started jumping from foot to foot, shouting at the top of his voice and waving the muzzle of a tommy-gun at me. When I continued to move towards the bank, he raised the gun to his shoulder and shouted, "Hands up! Hands up!" I obeyed. What else could I do? I had no weapons. I was completely exhausted after twelve hours' hard going. With my rucksack I could not have run a yard, and I should have been shot if I had tried to slip it off and dive into the jungle – anyway I was surrounded by now by a crowd of gesticulating Japs and bearded Indians. All at once I started to laugh, because, in all our plays in the camps, the Jap comes on to the stage grimacing, waving his arms, and shouting, "*Killy-kollack; killy-kollack!*" And here were Japs, dozens of them, all grimacing, waving their arms, and shouting, "*Killy-kollack; killy-kollack!*"

The Japs closed around me and jostled me up the river bank into their camp. Several prodded me with rifles and tommy-guns, and one, braver than the others, rushed out of his tent and hit me over the head with his rifle. Fortunately the stock snapped with a loud crack and the butt broke off, so the blow did not hurt at all, though I fell to the ground as a precaution. I struggled to get up again, but finding it impossible with my rucksack still on, I started to slip the straps off my shoulders. At this the Japs thought I was fumbling for a weapon or preparing to escape and several of them threw themselves on to my feet and held my wrists to the ground. In doing this, one of my captors discovered my wrist watch and was just about to take it off when an officer came up and, parting the crowd, started to question me excitedly in English: Who was I? Where had I come from? Was I alone? Where was my gun? Where was I going to? Meanwhile others were patting my pockets in search of weapons and starting to undo my rucksack, and another effort was made to remove my wrist watch. Seeing this, the officer pushed the man back and, waving the crowd aside, took me over to his tent.

I estimated that there were about a hundred Japs and two hundred Sikhs and Punjabis in this party, though I had no opportunity of making an exact count. About fifty Japs, including the officers and N.C.O.'s, slept under a single long lean-to of canvas, while the other Japs and all the Indians had similar shelters, though made of leaves. In front of each tent a large fire was burning, and they had just finished their evening meal. The Indians stood around in attitudes of sullen hostility, almost indifference. The Japs seemed to ignore them, as if they were mere coolies.

The officer in charge, after assuring himself that I was alone and un-armed, put a guard over my rucksack and started to question me. He was young, clean-shaven, pleasant-looking, and very polite. He spoke fairly good English. His first words were, "You are English gentleman: you must not speak lie." That was all very well, but I had rather a lot to explain away and I asked for a drink of water to make time.

I did some quick thinking. I had two empty holsters but no weapons of any sort. I had maps of the whole area marked: Reprinted in India, 1942 – therefore obviously smuggled in somehow since the occupation – and, idiot that I was, with my route marked in pencil. I had a letter, from Davis, dated April 12, 1944, introducing me to Noone, and my Singapore identity card as "Major Chapman" with a photograph which was an obvious likeness. I also had a very detailed diary of events since leaving our camp at Pa Kasut's. Most of it consisted of pages and pages of ethnological details of the Sakai, bird and hunting notes, and tirades against the bandits. Fortunately all security details were written in Eskimo, and any place names were in a code of my own which worked on the association of ideas – my associations – and therefore virtually uncrackable. But the Sakai names were written in clear. Though I had no desire to protect the bandits, I would have risked my life to protect the Sakai who had helped us. Clearly I must get rid of this diary.

I had finished three cups of water and my captor and a Malay-speaking
N.C.O. interpreter were getting impatient. They were filling in time by
going through the contents of my rucksack.[1] The food – alas! for my
precious curry powder and fresh chillies – was given to the Indians. The
diary was examined and put back together with the maps, and the identity
card carefully scrutinized. Now, for the first time, the officer seemed to
realize I was a soldier and examined my "uniform." I was wearing an old
pair of *kampong*-made sheet-rubber shoes, and khaki trousers and shirt.
On the shoulder-flaps of the latter were leather crowns which I had cut
out myself and sewn on. As soon as the officer read that I was a major and
recognized my crowns, he jumped to his feet and saluted – surely the
height of Japanese politeness!

I started speaking in Malay, thinking that if I lied myself into too much
of a muddle I could always blame my lack of command of the language.
I got on very well with the N.C.O., and he paid me the compliment of
saying that, as I spoke such good Malay, he imagined I must have lived in
the country many years – anybody who knows just how good my Malay
was in those days will realize what a very polite people the Japanese are!
However, just as we were really beginning to get on well, the officer, who
knew no Malay, insisted on carrying on the interrogation in English.

I told him a long story. I *had* lived with the Chinese guerillas in Pahang
some years before, but they were Communists and were even more of a
danger to the British than the Japanese. I had quarrelled with them and had
had to run away from their camp with a man called Davis – an officer
who had been cut off and left behind by our retreating forces. Davis and I

---

[1]Here is an exact list of what was in my frame rucksack.

Ground-sheet.	Waterproof bag for clothes.
Blanket sewn into a bag.	Guerilla cap (less red star and peak).
Pair of khaki drill trousers.	2 khaki shirts.
Pair of cotton pants, 2 vests.	Sarong.
Gym. shoes (worn out).	Small bottle gun oil.
.38 holster and belt.	.45 holster and belt.
5 sheets of inch-to-the-mile Ordnance Survey.	4 sheets of $\frac{1}{2}$- or $\frac{1}{4}$-inch maps.
Composite maps, drawn by myself, showing route.	Letter from Davis to Noone.
Diary and pencils.	Malay vocabulary (my own).

Copies of *Adrift in the Pacific* and *Weavers of Webs* (I had collected these at Jalong and was
   taking them back for the others to read).
$250 in notes.

Bamboo-root pipe and cut tobacco.	1-lb. roll of dried tobacco leaves.
Valet razor with strop and blades. Soap. Tooth-brush. Small towel.	
Cooking-pot and lid.	Mug, spoon, pocket knife.

Clinical thermometer, 2 first field-dressings, 3 tins of quinine (surplus for Noone). Some
   suphathiazole tablets and acriflavine solution made up in a gun-oil bottle.
Salt, pepper, dried prawns, a few salt fish, curry powder, fresh chilies, onions, garlic, ginger.
8 lbs. rice in raffia bag.
Collection of seeds of wild flowers and some pressed plants (intended for Kew Herbarium).
3 boxes matches and scraps of rubber for lighting fires.
I also carried a *parang* in wooden sheath on a rattan belt.

had gone to live with the Sakai near Bidor, but we had quarrelled and, as Davis knew Noone, he had given me a letter of introduction to him and I had set off to Grik to look for him. At Jalong the Sakai had told me that Noone was not in north Perak so I had turned back. At Larek I had met some Chinese robbers and they had taken my weapons, then let me go. I was now trying to find my way back to Davis, though I was afraid he had probably gone back to Pahang.

The officer listened very carefully to me. He made a few notes, looked some facts up in a file, and conferred at length with another officer. Then he started firing questions:

"Do you know Mr. Robinson?"

"Yes, but he has died of fever."

"That is so. And Mr. Quayle, why has he left that camp and gone away?"

"I do not know. I have heard of him and want to meet him. He has probably quarrelled with the Communists."

"Where is Mr. Noone?"

"I do not know. Do you?" (No answer.)

"Do you know of a party of Englishmen living near the Cameron Highlands?"

"No. I have heard of them and have been looking for them, but I hear they have all gone over into Pahang."

"Who told you?"

"Oh, some Chinese."

"But I thought you said you had parted company with the Chinese?"

"Yes, but these were the Chinese robbers at Larek."

"Do you know an Englishman called Colonel Chapman, who is leader of all the Communists?"

This was indeed a two-edged compliment! When I went into the jungle I was a major, but the Corps Commander had said that in order to have more prestige with the Chinese guerillas, I should have the honorary (unpaid) rank of Lieutenant-Colonel. I had, when dealing with the guerilla leaders, called myself Colonel Chapman until I joined Davis and discovered I was still only a major. I knew that in 1942 the Japs had put a price on my head – though, I thought then, and still think, an inordinately small one! Apparently he had not connected my name with that on my identity card. But he had it in front of him and was bound to find out sooner or later.

"Yes. He is my elder brother. Have you any news of him? I heard he had been killed in an ambush in Pahang."

And so it went on. I explained that I was sick of living with Sakai and eating rats and tapioca, and how I hoped they would let me come down to Ipoh with them where I could see some pretty girls again and drink Japanese beer. And how nice it was to be among civilized people once more. I hated the Communist guerillas. After all, they had turned me out of their camp and insulted me, and I would give my hosts any information they liked on the following day, but now I was terribly tired. All I wanted was a good meal and a night's rest. When we got to Ipoh, I would tell them anything they wanted to know. This all went down very well, but they were still rather worried about my family relationships and were busy scrutinizing my identity card and comparing the photograph with the original.

I had discovered that we were going down to Ipoh on the following day, and after some thought decided I would escape that night rather than try to slip away *en route*. This would mean that I should get only one meal and a short night's rest, but 2 a.m. is the best time to escape unless one has a very long way to go before dawn. Oddly enough, I never had any doubt whatsoever that I should be able to escape. It was just a matter of choosing the most auspicious moment. Consequently I had no sense of fear, only a feeling of excitement that a new adventure had fallen so fortuitously in my path, and extreme annoyance with myself for being such an idiot as to walk right into a Jap camp. On the other hand – how was I to have known it was a Jap camp? They had had no sentries out, and it was unprecedented for the Japs to be camping away into the jungle like this, at least two days' journey from the nearest road. My extreme and utter weariness must explain both my carelessness and my subsequent light-headed fearlessness.

The officer, while questioning me about the Larek "robbers," had produced his own map and on this was a pencilled, arrowed route – I was not the only fool that marked my maps – running from Chemor over the Chemor-Larek watershed a few miles south of where I had crossed it, and down the elephant track to Jalong, and another arrowed route ran in from Sungei Siput to converge on Jalong. Now I understood the aeroplanes that had circled so assiduously over Jalong. Probably the usual exaggerated rumours had got out that there were "hundreds of Englishmen" in Jalong, and the Japs were taking action. I assumed that a small party would escort me to Ipoh while the rest carried on with their original plan.

I knew that I could travel twice as fast as the Japs in the jungle, especially as I should have to leave my rucksack behind, and I planned to double back along my tracks to Jalong and warn the Sakai of the impending attack. I should be able to make it in a single day. The bandits could look after themselves. It was the Sakai I was worrying about.

The first thing to do was to get hold of my diary, which was reposing in the bottom of my rucksack, and to put on the strongest clothes I had for the morrow's journey. I knew I should not be able to wear my rubber shoes because the Malay-speaking Jap had shown great interest in them, asking where I had got them from and how much they had cost. They had rubber bars on the sole and made a very conspicuous pattern. I should have to go barefooted. They had no objection to my having a bath, though six armed guards stood round me while I waded naked into the stream and poured the ice-cold water over me. I noticed that my shoulders and hips were bruised and bleeding from the rucksack, and my legs were scarred with scratches and leech-bites. After the bath I put on clean under-clothes, my stoutest shirt with long sleeves, and a pair of khaki drill trousers. Then I sat in the officer's tent by the fire and was given as much rice – lovely white rice from Siam – and salt fish as I could eat. My host apologized for the lack of variety and for the absence of whisky, but said he would make up for that when we got down to the plains.

I then asked if I could get my pipe out of my rucksack and was allowed to fumble inside it while several guards watched me closely. Fortunately the top of a rucksack is narrow, so although they were observing me care-fully, I was able to find the small soft-backed notebook in which I kept my diary in tiny writing, to roll it up, and put it inside a handkerchief. I then produced the handkerchief, wiped my nose with it to show what it was for, and asked if I could put it in my pocket. This was allowed. The other two things I needed for my journey were my compass and medical set – especially quinine to ward off my fortnightly attacks of malaria, and suphathiazole powder to treat the scratches and leech-bites on my legs and prevent them developing into ulcers. The map I could do without, as I had memorized the lie of the hills and watercourses. Unfortunately I could not palm the compass and medical set, so took them over and showed them to my host and asked if I could take some quinine. This was a tactical error, as he got very excited, thinking, I presume, that I wanted to poison my-self, and he put the medical set and compass in his own pocket. He was very interested in the latter, apparently not having seen a prismatic oil compass before – he himself wore an ordinary dry compass strapped to his wrist.

It only remained to burn the diary which I had extracted from the hand-kerchief and rolled tightly up. In order to get a little shadow from the brilliant light of the bamboo fire, I asked if I could hang up my blanket to dry. Then, having found my old bamboo-root pipe – which was not difficult as I had hidden it under the ground-sheet – I filled it and went to the fire to light it. I carefully chose a fair-sized bamboo brand, then, standing in the shadow of my blanket, lit the pipe and at the same time pushed the rolled-up diary inside the hollow stem of the bamboo. Having lit my pipe, I threw the brand back into the fire, where it was soon consumed.

I made one more effort to regain my compass by asking the Jap if I could show him how well its luminous patches showed at night. This delighted him, but he was careful to put it back in his pocket. I then spent a pleasant half-hour smoking my pipe and looking through Japanese illustrated periodicals – full of pictures of the stupid British. By way of conversation I asked him if he knew the whereabouts of two Japanese I had known at Cambridge: Prince Hashisuka the ornithologist, and Kagami the skier. Though he seemed flattered by the nice things I said – quite sincerely – about his countrymen, he could give me no news of them.

Once he asked me what future I imagined there was in staying with the Sakai in the jungle, as the British had already lost the war. I replied, without thinking, that I was waiting for the British to return to Malaya, when I would come out of the jungle and join them. At this he gave a scornful snort, and thought the story so good that he passed it on to the others, who shouted with laughter.

At about ten o'clock we turned in for the night. I was very relieved to see that my host showed no inclination to do anything so unmannerly as to tie my hands. We wished each other a very cordial good-night and soon there was no sound but the cracking of the fire and the heavy regular breathing of my bedfellows.

*   *   *   *   *

Although my hosts did not attempt to tie me up, they took no other chances. There were three sentries who seemed to be particularly interested in my welfare. An N.C.O. carried a pistol – I saw him take it out of its holster, cock it, and push it into the belt of his raincoat. A sentry with fixed bayonet strolled up and down beyond the fire in front of the tent. Another with a tommy-gun hovered on the edge of the firelight and seemed to be watching the jungle as if they expected my friends might attempt a rescue. Alas! how little fear there was of that!

The N.C.O. stood on the far side of the fire and seemed to be in charge of all the guard, as other sentries appeared from beyond the range of our fire, took orders, and disappeared again. All were practically, if not smartly, dressed in leather – usually nailed – boots, puttees cross-gartered with their tapes, loose-fitting breeches, shirt and tunic, high cloth caps of varied design, and a useful-looking belted raincoat with a hood that pulled up over the cap.

My tent-fellows slept in all their clothes, including boots, and were thus able to dispense with blankets. I lay between my English-speaking friend and another officer in the centre of the tent and therefore directly in front of the fire, which was only a few yards from my feet. It was quite light enough to read, and the encircling jungle night looked inky black by contrast, though I knew there would soon be a moon. My neighbours seemed to fall asleep instantly, but were restless and noisy sleepers. We were so crowded that one or the other often rolled against me or put a knee affectionately over mine and I had to push them back, observing with satisfaction that no amount of manhandling seemed to disturb them – though my guard showed signs of disapproval.

In the days when I was a fieldcraft instructor I had read every book on escaping and used to lecture on the subject. But none of the methods I had advocated seemed to be of much practical use now. My first plan was to pull up the canvas at the back of the tent and to slip out that way. But it had been tightly pegged down and my bedfellows were too close to allow me to work at it. My next plan – the obvious one – was to go to the edge of the jungle to relieve nature and then to make a dash for it. I rehearsed this, but the N.C.O. on guard called up two sentries with fixed bayonets, and they stood so embarrassingly near me that nature refused to function and my guards were obviously suspicious.

My next idea – one of desperation – was to set the officer's clothing alight and then to slip away in the ensuing hubbub. I was allowed to smoke my pipe and managed to put some bamboo embers among my neighbours' spare clothes, but there was insufficient draught and nothing came of it. After this I went to sleep, thinking that after all I would have to escape on the way down to Ipoh.

At about one o'clock I woke up. The N.C.O. on duty had been changed and the new one did not seem so vigilant. I watched him closely, and while pretending restlessly to stretch my arms, I was able little by little to ease up the canvas behind my head. Before I could continue operations I had to do something about the fire which, in the chill early morning, had been made larger and more brilliant than ever. I now had an inspiration which traded most ungenerously, on the natural good manners of my hosts. After a few preliminary hiccoughs, I got up, retching horribly, and pretended to be violently sick. I had saved up spittle for some time and the results, especially the noise, were most realistic. The N.C.O. was quite sympathetic and I explained that the heat of the fire was so great that I was unable to sleep and was indeed – as he had seen – very ill. He immediately called up the sentries and together they damped down the fire and raked it further from the tent.

From there the firelight still shone on to my blanket sleeping-bag, but

I was able to put on my rubber shoes (which I should have to wear until daylight) and then to collect some of the miscellaneous gear belonging to my bedfellows – a haversack, a tin hat, some spare boots, and a dispatch case (which, unfortunately, I could not open and which was too heavy to take away), and pushed them down into my sleeping-bag, tastefully arranging the boots to resemble my own feet thrust into the corners of the bag. Meanwhile, with legs doubled up, and watching the guard through half-closed eyes, I worked myself further and further back into the angle of the tent. A Japanese rifle caused much discomfort to my backbone. I thought how careless it was of them to have left it there, and wished I could have taken it with me, but it would have been too much of an encumbrance.

I waited till one sentry was out of sight, the other at the far end of his beat, and the N.C.O. not actually looking at me. Then, in one movement I thrust myself violently through the opening at the bottom of the canvas. I heard a "ping", as a peg gave or a rope broke, and a sudden guttural gasp from the N.C.O. – and I was out in the jungle.

I crashed through a bamboo thicket, raced in brilliant moonlight along the trunk and branches of a huge fallen tree – a balancing feat I could never have accomplished in cold blood – dived through some undergrowth, then half fell into the river. I slithered down between the rocks for a short distance, then stopped to listen. There was not a sound, not a sound of any sort: no shooting into the jungle, no voices, not even the snapping of a twig. I could only imagine that my captors were listening too, and I slid a long way further down the stream – once going right up to my armpits in a deep pool. It was then that I discovered that my watch was missing – a disaster for my subsequent navigation: the leather strap must have caught on something in my dash for freedom.

I was now below the camp. My plan was to make a fairly wide detour, to strike the river above the camp, and then to follow it up until dawn, by which time I hoped to get on to the Sakai path I had found the day before and to follow it over the watershed to Larek.

I clambered out of the stream and felt my way up through the steep undergrowth on the far side, for only an occasional gleam of moonlight filtered through to the floor of the jungle. When I was some distance above the noise of the river, I paused to listen. There was still no sound of pursuit. After half an hour I struck a good track and came out into a moonlit clearing where stood, among the tall wet grass, a long-deserted Sakai house built some eight feet above the ground. The thatched roof gleamed in the brilliant moonlight, accentuated by the deep shadows beneath the eaves and under the house. It was so still that even the huge black and white banana leaves stood motionless and there was a sweet fragrance of some forgotten flower growing in the clearing. I could see the moon now and the constellation of Aquila with its bright star Altair, so could get my bearings accurately, as I still had a fair idea of the time and knew from experience in what quarter of the sky Aquila would lie at that hour of the night.

I decided to follow up the stream, keeping well up on its right bank, and was delighted to find a Sakai path starting off in the right direction. However, it soon ended in two very small graves with little *atap* roofs over them and I had to take to the thick jungle with the stars lost to sight and only an occasional glimpse of the moon to check direction. At last I came upon a wide but overgrown path along an *atap* ridge, but as I kept on losing it in the darkness, I lay down to await the dawn, for travel, even if it is not exactly in the right direction, is ten times as fast along a path as in the thick jungle.

As soon as it was light enough I took off my shoes and followed the track eastward. After an hour's excellent going, I came to a track heading steeply downhill to the south. Perhaps this would join the one I had discovered yesterday and I ventured a long way down it, but dared not follow it as far as the river because I was still too near the Jap camp and I was certain that at earliest dawn they would send patrols up and down the Sungei Chemor. I therefore returned to the ridge track and followed it in a north-easterly direction until it fell steeply for a thousand feet and I came to a large river. To my horror this river, instead of flowing from left to right, was flowing in the other direction! There was a fine cave here beside the river with many signs that it had been used by Sakai. I spent some time drawing a map in the dust and ashes, trying to work out where I had gone wrong.

I retraced my steps up the long steep hill and followed a path eastward down to another rather smaller river, but still the water was flowing in the wrong direction, and realizing that I had now left it too late to follow the Sungei Chemor with impunity, even if I were to find it, I determined to follow this river up to its source and then to cross the Chemor-Larek divide further north.

Dusk found me on top of the watershed. It would be very cold up there at night, especially as my clothes were soaked through with sweat, so I retraced my steps to a sheltered dell I had noticed, to bivouac for the night. Since I had no knife, I could not make much of a shelter but managed to hack off some wild banana leaves with a stone, and putting some below me and others above, I was soon asleep, and though it rained hard in the night I was no wetter than when I had turned in.

As soon as it was light I went up to the top of the ridge and started to run down the other side, hoping soon to see the great scar of the Larek mine or perhaps the high cone of Gunong Korbu. The jungle was very thick here and, though I was going steeply downhill, the tree-tops obscured what lay below. It was not until I found a clearing where several trees had fallen that I had any view and then, to my consternation, instead of Larek and the inner jungle, I saw the west-coast plains and the Malacca Straits beyond. I could have wept with disappointment. Once again I sat down and tried to work out where I was and how I had got there.[1] The problem was completely inexplicable and I knew that the only certain solution was to retrace my footprints over the watershed, then follow the river back to the neighbourhood of the Jap camp, there to work out my plans afresh – possibly to slip southward on the edge of the jungle.

This plan entailed grave risk, but I felt certain that the Japs, having given up their search for me in the vicinity of the camp, would follow their original plan and go over to Larek, cutting a wide track which I might later be able to utilize. Though I was not yet beginning to lose strength, I did not expect to be able to travel at this rate with only water as a diet for much more than a week, and once really lost one can wander indefinitely in the great jungle, each day becoming more exhausted and correspondingly less vigilant. The Sakai all seemed to have fled, and there was little hope of finding them, so I spent the rest of the day in vain search for a path crossing the watershed and returned that night to my shelter of banana leaves.

Next day, with some difficulty, I retraced my steps to the cave beside the river and prepared to sleep in it. But I found that the Japs had already visited it in their search for me. It was covered with boot-marks and littered with paper. As they probably knew I had been there, although I was going barefooted at that time, I did not dare to sleep in the cave, though it was raining again, and made myself another shelter of banana leaves. Nearby I found some plants of tapioca, and though there were no roots on them I ate the leaves. I had often eaten them cooked and imagined they were edible raw. But I was mistaken, as I had terrible pains in the night, accompanied by a morbid thirst.

By the middle of the next day, May 16, I had made my way back to the deserted Sakai house a quarter of a mile above the Jap camp and was

[1]Careful examination of the map later gave me the solution: I had kept too far to the left (my invariable habit in fog or jungle) and descended to a northern tributary of the Chemor—hence my bewilderment at the reversal of the current. I had followed this stream due north to cross the watershed where it runs east and west and to descend a tributary of the Sungei Kuang in a north-*westerly* direction—hence the view of the plains (actually near Jalong and Sungei Siput).

sheltering inside during a torrential downpour. Judging by the litter, the Japs had been here too since my last visit, but there was no sound or sign of smoke from their old camp in the valley below. As I was still feeling very ill as a result of eating the tapioca leaves, I found a hiding-place beneath the derelict sleeping-bench and was soon asleep.

After some time, I was woken up by voices underneath the house and looking through the cracks in the floor I saw some Japs and Sikhs – I could not count how many. This must have been a patrol which had stayed behind to look for me. Possibly they had seen my naked footmarks underneath the hut, though the rain would have obliterated them outside, for two of the Sikhs climbed laboriously up, with loud-voiced encouragement from the others, and entered the house. But the floor was so rotten that they satisfied themselves with a perfunctory glance round. After sheltering for some time and talking loudly, they at last set off in the direction of the plains. Judging by the size of their packs, they were going for good.

An hour later, just as evening closed in, three naked Sakai came running along the track which passed beneath the house. I dared not call to them, and in any case they would have fled; but the mere fact that there were still Sakai around gave me fresh hope. I tried to track them, but it was too dark, and by next morning, after I had passed a very comfortable night in the hut, the rain had obliterated all but the heel-marks of the Japs' boots.

Next morning was the fifth day since I had escaped from the Japs. Since then I had eaten only a few rattan berries and the tapioca leaves which had made me so ill, but I was drinking enormous quantities of water. Unless I was going to leave my bones in the jungle – with or without the help of a Japanese bullet – I had to do some serious thinking, and it was symptomatic of my physical state that I was very reluctant to do this, being much more inclined to rush on, anywhere, instead of pausing to work out a coherent plan. Surprisingly enough I was not at all exhausted, but I felt curiously light-headed – as if the top of my skull were a foot higher than normal. On three of the four days since my escape I had travelled furiously, with hardly any rest, from dawn till dusk – more than twelve hours – but in spite of always going to bed soaking wet, I had slept right through each night and oddly enough was really enjoying myself. I had no doubt whatsoever that I could carry on for many days yet, even without food. I knew enough about the Japs – their paper-chase trail and enormous heel-marks, their loud voices and their bad eyesight, and, if it should go as far as that, their bad marksmanship – to feel quite confident that I could get the better of them. I was certain that the main body of the Japanese had gone over the watershed to Larek and Jalong. Though I was still anxious to warn my Sakai friends, I knew I should catch up the Japs or run into their rear-guard if I went that way just yet.

When day dawned, I heard a cock crowing far below on the other side of the ridge from the Jap camp by the Sungei Chemor. I was pretty certain that it was a jungle-fowl, and that indicated the presence of an old clearing, and as Sakai are in the habit of visiting their old houses and gardens, I hoped a track would lead me to the present settlement. As soon as I left the track I was involved in a series of extremely steep rocky gullies, choked with thorns and rotten vegetation. After an hour of very precarious scrambling and the usual drill of lowering myself down on a rattan line, I came to a wide path pock-marked with heel-prints and littered with cigarette wrappers and empty food-bags. This was clearly the path that the main Jap patrol had followed on their way to the camp where I had been their ungrateful guest.

This wide path soon brought me to a very large Sakai village with six or seven beautifully built houses capable of holding about a hundred and fifty people. Goats and fowls walked about in the sunshine. There were clumps of pineapples and banana trees hung with bunches of fruit, and on the opposite side of the valley were several clearings carpeted with the soft even green of tapioca bushes. Looking down the wide Chemor valley, I could see the blue foothills of the plains framed between its variegated jungle-covered sides.

The village was of course deserted and the presence of the very dead bodies of a young girl and an old woman showed that the Japs had come this way. I was certain that as their goats and fowls were still here, the Sakai would return, so I lay up in the jungle edge to watch, being rather disturbed by the noise of a Jap plane which spent the whole morning circling low over this part of the jungle, perhaps – I flattered myself – searching for me. Sure enough, I soon saw two tousle-headed dark faces peeping out of the jungle on the other side of the clearing and I went across to talk to them. The Sakai were very friendly but literally shaking with terror. They told me that some days before, the Japs had suddenly appeared and attempted to surround the houses. The Sakai had started to flee into the jungle, but the Japs opened fire, and as well as the dead I had seen, many were wounded.

They gave me some ripe bananas and a *parang*, but they could not spare me a flint and steel. I tried repeatedly to persuade them to take me over the watershed to the Kinta valley, but this they absolutely refused to do, saying that they must try to collect their womenfolk, who were scattered all over the jungle, and that there were still parties of Japs and Indians about. I tried to follow the route they described and spent several hours following up a tributary of the Sungei Chemor, but night found me high up in a trackless area of waterfalls, steep rocky outcrops, thorn-scrub, and a tangle of heart-breaking undergrowth. Fortunately I now had a *parang* and was able to make a comfortable shelter of *atap* in which to spend the night. Next morning, May 18, I again tried to get over the watershed into the Kinta valley, but though I fought my way to the summit ridge, there was no sign of a track. Since the descent seemed even steeper and the vegetation more thick and thorny, I retraced my steps to the Sakai village.

As soon as I got near, I could hear that something unusual was going on. Peeping through the edge of the clearing, I saw several Sikhs running about trying to round up the remaining goats. Apparently the Japs had established a regular patrol between Chemor and the camp from which I had escaped, and probably over the top to Larek and Jalong also. If this was so, not only was it unhealthy for me to stay in this area, but I could expect no help from these Sakai.

When I had been trying to follow the Sakai's directions over to the Kinta, I had noticed a wide path leaving the left bank of the stream and going uphill to the south-west. I now followed this over a high ridge and down to another stream, where the track disappeared. Sakai tracks have a way of following streams, where the going is often easiest, but if one is unaccompanied by a Sakai it is very difficult to find where the track leaves the stream and takes to the hills again. So it was on this day. Presently I picked up an overgrown track, and soon came to a steep valley where the jungle was being cleared. Soon the track was wide enough for a car, though grass-grown, and I turned aside to walk in a rubber estate, which gave more possibility of a safe retreat. Presently I found myself overlooking the head of a motor road, where were several large vegetable gardens with Chinese women hoeing, wearing black blouses and trousers and huge conical huts. I saw one larger house, apart from the rest, and creeping round through a forest of tapioca bushes I went in at the open doorway.

Here I found six Chinese men, who seemed delighted though somewhat astonished to see me. After a bath in the stream (while one of them kept watch on the road) and a large meal of rice cooked with sweet potato, a stalky green vegetable and dried fish, one of them gave me a small home-made pipe and we settled down to talk. It appeared that I had come out near Kinding Tea Estate, about three miles above Tanjong Rambutan. The men said they could put me in touch with the guerillas, but in the present disturbed state of things it might take a week or more. They told me it was quite impossible for me to stay there and took me back to a tiny hut on the very edge of the jungle. There were half a dozen other fugitives in this small house, underfed and dressed in rags, several of them in a high fever from malaria.

I gathered from them, and from stories I subsequently heard, that at this time the Japanese had just started a drive against the *kampong* Chinese on the jungle edge the whole way from Grik to Kuala Kubu – about 150 miles. This was probably the most savage of any of their organized massacres. Each morning two or three two-engined planes would circle low round and round the area between the main road and the edge of the jungle. At the same time a cordon of trucks full of Indians and Malays would be placed every fifty yards along a section of road to shoot anybody attempting to break out. The cordon would close in. Young able-bodied men were taken away and seen no more – probably they were ordered to go and fight elsewhere for the Japs or to work in the labour camps, and murdered if they refused. Girls, even children of twelve or thirteen years, were often raped at once or taken away to fill the military brothels. An enormous number of Chinese were tommy-gunned or bayoneted. Others were driven into the *atap* houses and burned alive. Everything in the houses that was of any possible value was taken away – every cent of money, watches, trinkets, clothes, cooking utensils, even the vegetables from the gardens.

Next morning, May 19, I watched these Jap planes circling round and round so low that I could see the pilot's helmeted face looking down, and I wondered how they could manoeuvre their large two-engined machines so low among the steep valleys and wooded foothills. I even went out to the edge of the rubber and, though I could not get a view over the *kampongs*, I could easily hear the noise of firing and the heart-rending screams of the victims. While I was there several half-demented fugitives came running up the lane into the jungle.

At midday one of the six men at the tapioca *kongsi*-house came up and told me that a thousand Sikh police had been posted along the jungle edge to intercept and kill anybody who tried to escape that way, and that though they wanted to help me, it was impossible just then and I must go back into the jungle. Of course I did not believe this story, but I determined to go right back past the Sakai village and the Japanese camp to Larek, and to strike my old trail somewhere at the head of the Korbu valley. True, it was a very long way round and straight into a dangerous area, but I felt certain the Japs would by now have cut a trail which I could use, and I hoped that as it was a week since my escape they would have given up the search.

The same afternoon, May 19, I left this stormy refuge. They could give me only a few pounds of rice, half a cigarette tin of salt, a handful of ground-nuts, an old sack to use as a blanket, and eight home-made matches. At the same time the dozen or so Chinese fugitives who were there, believing the ridiculous scare about the thousand Sikhs, set off, carrying their miserable possessions, to return to the hell that was still going on in their *kampongs*. I wondered which of us was being the more stupid.

I retraced my steps to the Sungei Chemor, and made one more effort to force the track over the watershed to the Kinta valley. But I failed again, so I spent the night in a small Sakai shelter I found beside the Chemor river. I suffered a bitter disappointment here, as the home-made matches that the Chinese had given me would not light. After wasting four of them I decided to keep the other four and dry them out in the sun before trying them. I ate my ground-nuts together with a pocketful of sweet-potato leaves which I had picked in the Chinese garden.

Early next morning I visited the Jap camp to look for my wrist watch and pipe – without success – and followed an excellent track which the Japs had cut over the top, about a mile north of my route to Larek. In the middle of the sandy wastes, where I had camped on my way over from Jalong, I counted the cold ashes of fourteen large fires, but the Japs had built no sort of shelter. There had been no sunshine by which to dry my remaining four matches. Indeed, it had rained solidly all day, and though I managed to make one splutter by the old trick of first rubbing it up and down the short hair of the nape of my neck, I was unable to make it burn.

Next day, May 21, I followed the wide Japanese track past another of their camps, as usual littered with paper, and right down to the Sungei Korbu where they had turned downstream towards Jalong. I went upstream and at last came to a Sakai hut right up in the hills on the right bank of the Korbu river. I walked into this house before the occupants had time to flee, and found there several of the headmen I had stayed with five weeks before. Instead of giving me the usual cordial "*Tabe tuan*" (Greetings, sir), they bowed to the ground and gave me the formal "*Selamat datang*" (Peace attend your coming). At first I could not account for this change in their attitude, but it gradually appeared that my bandit friends, after my escape, had told the credulous Sakai that I was a Jap agent. They naturally thought that it was I who had brought all these disasters to their peaceful valley. But I was soon able to make matters clear and to hear their story.

It appeared that a few days previously the Japs had suddenly appeared in the jungle – the Sakai had no idea whence they had come. They had captured several Sakai alive, shot others, burned down the houses, and either removed or destroyed the huge stores of rice which had been collected for the bandits. Bras, the young and intelligent headman, had disappeared: perhaps he had been killed. The Sakai were very disgusted with the Chinese, who had fled at the first sign of danger and not stayed to protect their jungle allies. All the Sakai were in a bad state of nerves, and for my own safety as much as theirs, wanted me to go to a still higher and more remote hideout for the night. But I was very reluctant to do this, as I was very tired and my feet had been rather badly cut about after travelling so far barefooted without having had time to harden them properly beforehand, and usually at such speed that I could not pause to avoid rough and thorny places. In any case, there was little possibility of the Japs coming up as far as here.

I was given as many plates of delicious dry fragrant Sakai rice as I could eat, together with a huge bowl of pumpkin cooked with salt, pepper, curry, chillies, and shoots of wild ginger – certainly the best dish of pumpkin I have ever tasted. We smoked until dark, and I was just beginning to think I had never enjoyed food so much or eaten such a quantity in a few hours, when I saw that my hosts were about to kill no less than six old roosters. They were afraid that their crowing would betray the presence of the house to the Japs. Among us we finished off all six fowls, though they were terribly tough, and enormous quantities of rice.

The next morning, May 22, I set off early with a guide. Before I went I managed to persuade the Sakai to give me a flint and steel and some tinder. We reached the house which Lim and I had called the *jagong* (maize) house, because it stood in a clearing planted with this grain. Here my guide failed me – the only time a Sakai let me down. After waiting some time for him to return I realized that he had abandoned me. The next morning I set off on my own to find the elusive watershed, but after twelve hours of exhausting travel through the worst sort of jungle, I found that I had moved in a large circle, finishing up within a few hundred yards of my starting-point. Next day I had no better luck, and in addition felt the first warnings of a bout of malaria. I realized that I had to find my way back to the *jagong* house and lie up there. Soon, as the fever got hold of me, my strength ebbed, and for the last part of the journey I had to crawl on my hands and knees, eventually arriving long after dark.

I reached the *jagong* house on the night of May 25 and was very ill there with malaria for more than a fortnight. I was able to keep account of time by cutting a notch each day on the pole beside my bed and, though I had the usual alternations of uncontrollable shivering and high fever with a racing pulse, I was never, as far as I know, actually delirious. My chief trouble, other than the fever, was twenty or thirty running ulcers on my feet and legs and one over my hip-bone, which resulted from many deep cuts and leech-bites. Since I knew I should be completely immobilized till these were better, I forced myself to bathe them four times a day with a solution of boiling water and the last few grains of my salt. I would then cover them with maize leaves to keep out the dirt.

The Sakai did not discover my presence for the first few days, but subsequently they used to visit me from time to time at odd hours of the night, usually to split and dry bamboo torches for fishing. They were far too frightened to come so far down into the valley during the hours of daylight, as they were still dominated by terror of the Japanese, who, they said, had made their headquarters at Kampong Jalong and were gradually working up the Korbu valley searching for guerillas and Sakai and burning down any houses they found.

I had been very uneasy on this score myself, and had taken elaborate precautions. My bed was on the floor in the far corner of the hut. I had made a small doorway in the *atap* wall so that I could slip through and crawl down the trunk of a felled tree which was there and into the edge of the jungle. I had also made a screen of maize stalks so that the tree-trunk would be invisible to anybody approaching the house along the main track. There was a small dun-coloured terrier bitch which seemed to belong to the house, though like most Sakai dogs it completely ignored my presence and refused to make friends. But the owner told me it hated Japs and would bark as soon as they came near.

On June 2, the dog started growling, and going to the door of the house, I could hear voices and the chop-chop of *parangs* coming from down the track. As no one but a Jap would want to make the perfectly adequate path wider, I smothered my fire with a pile of ashes I had kept for the purpose and slipped out through my getaway into the jungle. Peeping through the leaves, I saw two Japs and about a dozen Sikhs enter the hut. The small dog barked furiously and one of the Japs had two shots at it, but missed. The party spent some time inside the house, then set it alight and left it. Fortunately it had been raining all night, and the *atap*, being soaked, was reluctant to burn; I was able to beat it out with a stick, so that the only damage was a large gap in one wall.

On June 8 my fever reached its climax, and for some reason I was quite certain I was going to die. It was an unpleasant sensation to lie there alone in the depths of the jungle, convinced that I had only a few hours to live. My chief feeling was one of annoyance and frustration that the great efforts I had made since escaping from the bandits had been entirely wasted and that no one would even know how hard I had tried.

Next day I woke up long after sunrise. I found that the fever had completely left me and I was ravenously hungry. Though I was still very weak,

I could now walk across the house without holding on to the roof-beams. My ulcerated legs had practically healed during my enforced lying up, and I felt I might be able to set off after a day's rest. I went out into the clearing, collected some maize, scraped the grain off the cobs with a rattan-thorn grater, as I had seen the Sakai do, and roasted it inside a bamboo. The result was delicious, and I ate till my stomach was distended.

That evening one of the older Sakai came in to cook some tapioca, and after considerable argument I persuaded him to take me up-river to the house at Kuala Termin. He warned me that this house had been burned down by the Japs, but I could not believe they had penetrated so far into the jungle; in any case I hoped he might be able to contact the Sakai there and persuade them to take me over the watershed to the Kinta valley.

On June 11 - exactly a calendar month since I had escaped from the bandits - we set off. I should really have rested for a few more days, but I felt so much better that I was impatient to be off. I went terribly slowly, especially uphill, but rallied when the old man said it was no good going on and we should return. Towards evening we reached the clearing near the Kuala Termin house, but instead of crossing the Korbu by the "Himalayan" bridge, we struck straight uphill, following a typical *atap* ridge. This was too much for me, and I lay down and slept while my guide went in search of Sakai. Just as it got dark he returned with two men whom I remembered, and between them they pulled me up the hill with a rattan line. I could still walk along the level, but uphill my leg-muscles simply refused to work. After climbing for at least a thousand feet we reached a small empty but newly built *atap* hut, hidden away off the ridge in the middle of a thicket. The Sakai, apparently, had fled still further into the hills.

While I was examining the house and the food that they had left for me, the three men disappeared. I never saw them again, though I waited till well after daylight on the following morning. It poured with rain all night and I felt rather miserable, as I was not at all certain that I could find the bridge across the river, much less the house at Kuala Termin, which would set me off on the right track. And even if I found the track it was one of those that meandered up a succession of small streams and would be very hard to follow.

I therefore set off with some foreboding. I was surprised to find how well my legs went after a long sleep, and I could even keep a good pace uphill. I found the house without difficulty. It *had* been burned right to the ground, but I satisfied myself from the lack of litter and the absence of boot-marks and fresh cutting along the tracks that no Jap had ever been near here and that the fire must have been entirely fortuitous. The Sakai are very careless with their fires, and it was pure chance that the conflagration had coincided with the Jap drive against Kampong Jalong further down the valley.

I chewed sugar-cane in the clearing near the house until my gums were sore and then set off to retrace the way by which Lim and I had arrived two months before. Luckily a Sakai had gone the same way earlier in the morning (though the two men from here had assured me that none of them knew this route) and I was able to follow his naked footmarks and to cast back when I lost them. Evening found me near the house which commanded such a magnificent view over Tanjong Rambutan, and I hoped that I should be able to find the pig paling which ran along the ridge and that this would lead me to the house. However, I was unlucky here. As it grew dark I lost my Sakai's footmarks, could find neither fence nor house, and had to sleep out in the jungle.

The following day, June 13, I ate some sugar-cane that I had brought with me and spent another hour or two searching for the house. As I could not find it, I determined to drop downhill to the Sungei Gajah, follow it down to where it joined the Seno-oi river, then follow up the latter until I reached the huge house where Lim and I had had trouble with the oratorical Sakai. I found the Gajah without difficulty. It ran at the bottom of a valley whose steep sides were scarred with old clearings that came right down to the bank. The river was very swift and deep and in some places flowed through gorges, and I had to find my way overland. Once I was swept away by the current and was carried down some distance and badly bruised before I could regain the bank.

I joined the Seno-oi about midday and tried to follow it up, but the volume of water was enormous and I could find no sign of a track on either side. I therefore returned to the main river, feeling that I had done all I possibly could to find the Sakai, and with a clear conscience started to look forward to the good food, security, and companionship of a Chinese *kongsi*-house. I had been following down the joint streams for some time when the character of the river changed. The rapids ceased and I was now able to let myself be carried down at the edge of the current, occasionally checking my speed by clinging hold of boulders. This was a somewhat precarious but extremely rapid method of descent.

When I pulled myself ashore once to rest, I saw some fresh footprints in the sand. A large party of Sakai had been there only a short time before. I determined not to lose these tracks and followed the sandy marks where the little men had jumped from boulder to boulder and again when they took to the shore. In the late afternoon I came upon them and approached cautiously so as not to give them a chance to run away. When I spoke to them I recognized some of the men from the large house up the Sungei

Seno-oi, and on inquiry discovered that it was now deserted, though the Japs had not been near it. They resolutely refused to let me go back with them to their new house in the hills, but said that if I followed down the river I should soon come to a Chinese *kongsi*-house at the head of a pipe-line. I was still trying to persuade one of them to show me the way when I realized they were already disappearing into the jungle, and soon I was alone again, with two small cooked fish and some tapioca that they had left for me.

After eating this I continued to follow the river down. There was, as the Sakai had said, a good track. At first, to avoid another rapid, it led parallel to the river in and out of side valleys and round rocky spurs. Then it crossed the river, led through a large and very pleasant bamboo grove, across a swamp, over several deserted clearings, and at last to a couple of timber-built Chinese houses at the head of a bicycle track and pipe-line.

In this house were five Chinese. They promised to put me in touch with the guerillas, but as Malays in the employ of the Japs were liable to visit the house at any hour of the morning, they refused to let me sleep there. After giving me some food they took me to an overgrown clearing half a mile down-river, where there was a hideout which had been built for two Chinese fugitives. It was raining heavily, and although they lent me a four-foot-wide conical umbrella-hat, I was soaked to the skin by the time we reached the refuge, and during the night I had a relapse of malaria. I stayed in this hut for three days and was very glad of the rest and security, for I was so weak that if I got up too suddenly I had a complete blackout and fell down again, and only came to from the pain of hitting the ground. Each evening the Chinese would bring me a meal of rice and sweet potatoes with fresh fish, sweet-potato leaves, and other vegetables, and I used to keep enough to eat in the morning, though at this time my appetite was poor and I could not sleep well as I was suffering from violent toothache. There was a hot spring near the hut, just the right temperature for a bath, and this was a great luxury as well as being very good for my cuts and bruises.

On the third night in this refuge, being unable to sleep, I was sitting on a log outside listening to the hunting cry of a tiger, when my attention became fixed on what I thought was a singularly bright and constant fire-fly. Suddenly I realized it was a light which was gradually approaching. In case it was an enemy, though this was unlikely in the middle of the night, I hid in the jungle, but soon recognized the voice of the leader of the pipe-line Chinese and came out to meet him.

With him were another oldish man and a young and very charming Chinese who was introduced to me as Ah Sang. I was in touch with the guerillas once again.

CHAPTER SEVENTEEN

I DO NOT KNOW if the six British Generals who escaped from Campo 12 in Italy in the spring of 1943 had read the story of the Confederate Generals' escape in the American Civil War – the inspiration for which came direct from the escapes of Jean Valjean in Victor Hugo's *Les Misérables*.

General John Hunt Morgan, the leader of the American escape, was a mere thirty-eight years of age – a chicken compared with the British officers who were mostly in their fifties. He was captured on the 26th July 1863 by General Shackelford of the Federal Army and imprisoned with the rest of his officers in a civilian gaol in Columbus. The officers were confined at night in the small cells designed for convicts, but during the day were allowed to leave their cells and walk about in the wide corridor. Captain Hines, one of General Morgan's staff, suspecting the presence of an airduct beneath the floor of his cell, dug a hole beneath his bed and found himself in a long narrow passage which ran under the floor below the entire row of cells and terminated in an iron grille. A team of officers at once began tunnelling their way from this airduct, through the foundations of the building, towards the prison yard. To do this they had to cut through two foundation walls five and six feet thick. Since they must emerge from their tunnel under cover of darkness, after they had all been locked in their cells for the night, it was necessary to make an entrance from the airduct into each cell. This was done by breaking through from the passage under the floor until only a thin crust of cement was left. While the digging team worked in the tunnel, General Morgan's brother made a rope from mattress covers and a grappling-hook from an iron poker.

The prison yard towards which they were tunnelling was surrounded by a high wall, and the escapers were unable to see what lay outside. They therefore began a heated discussion among themselves on feats of physical strength, and a Captain Taylor boasted that he could climb a ladder hand over hand without using his legs. The warder who was drawn into the discussion doubted this, and he was invited to produce a ladder, which he did. The ladder was placed in a strategic position, and Captain Taylor performed his feat. He was able to see over the wall, and reported the lie of the land to his fellow-escapers.

On the night of 27th November 1863, a night of heavy cloud, Captain Hines broke through the thin skin of cement into each cell and the escapers assembled in the airduct, crawled up the tunnel and emerged into the prison yard. With the aid of the home-made rope and grappling-iron they scaled the wall and were free.

* * * * *

The following account of the escape of the British Generals in Italy is taken from the late Brigadier Hargest's *Farewell Campo* 12. The escape has also been described from different angles in Lieutenant-General Sir Adrian Carton de Wiart's *Happy Odyssey*, Lieutenant-General Sir Philip Neame's *Playing With Strife* and John Leeming's *Always To-morrow*.

There is something rather splendid for me in the thought of these high-ranking officers dyeing and sewing civilian clothes, hoarding their chocolate ration, digging for hours in a damp tunnel and finally crawling out through it and away from the castle in which they had been held prisoner.

Brigadier Hargest told the story of his imprisonment with simplicity and at times great beauty. It is the story of a brave and kindly man.

James Hargest

AUGUST CAME and went without any progress. The fruit season was in full flush and would soon be over, while on all sides we saw the potato crops being lifted. Soon the autumn would come, and falling leaves would strip the woods of the cover essential to us if we were to walk two hundred and fifty miles to the frontier. We became a little desperate.

So far the Italians' whole attention had been directed against an attempt over the walls, and the new precautions had effectually ruined our prospects in that direction. It became a question of a tunnel or nothing. It was de Wiart who proposed the new scheme. One day he said to me: "There only remains the chapel. Can't we find a way into it from the men's dining-room?"

I went straight down and made a reconnaissance, with no results; but we determined to pursue the matter further by doing an exhaustive examination. The chapel formed the outside of the castle at the north-west corner and was directly under the high square tower. Its one door faced on to the courtyard, but had been bricked up, and even a scratch on the surface would have been detected by the Italians who passed close by it many times a day. The fourth side was against our dining-room and separated from it by a small landing and the lift well, the lift being used only for the carriage of food from the kitchen below. During the exploratory examination Neame discovered that by lowering the lift and using it as a platform we might be able to pierce the wall into the chapel on our own floor. After that we could make up our minds on the best means of going on. The advantages of this idea were patent immediately. The lift well was dark and might easily conceal a man in the event of a surprise visit, and in any case, we would be on the ground floor and a hasty retreat could be made either down to the kitchen or through our living rooms to the main stairway to our rooms. Hope rose strongly within us at once and almost without discussion we were agreed to give it a try.

Once we had decided on the general method we rapidly organized our forces and got down to work. Of course we had to feel our way as, although we had a fair knowledge of the general habits of our custodians, we had not so strictly observed them in regard to their early morning movements, their reactions to strange noises, etc. We set out on a close study of all these details and every day or two met to discuss our plans as they developed. We placed Boyd in charge of the operations and agreed on working from two-fifteen till four-fifteen p.m., the time when a number of us were out walking and there was a good deal of movement around the place. People playing games or chopping wood or merely walking were always good cover for noise. It was decided to work in pairs: Boyd and Miles, Combe and Todhunter, Stirling and I.

We started in on breaking through the wall behind the lift into the chapel. The tools we had were few and primitive, the principal one a large kitchen knife I had found with a broken handle. Boyd put a good wooden handle on it and it lasted right through the seven months of heavy work. We also had the cut iron bars I have already mentioned. They were about five-eighths of an inch in diameter and sharpened at one end by Sergeant Baxter, who used the kitchen range as a furnace. Ranfurly made a small shovel from a piece of sheet iron and placed a handle on it and we had a sharp-pointed ice trowel which was next to the knife in order of usefulness. At the beginning we used ordinary garden buckets for carrying away the spoil, but as we approached the outer wall we made canvas ones to reduce the noise.

We stood on the lift and started on the first wall, chipping and cutting the plaster and then scraping out the mortar from between the stones. It was slow work, and the noise seemed to be terrific in the confined space. Every movement of one's arms or body shook the lift, which boomed like a great drum. The first day's progress was not substantial; neither was it discouraging, and we were learning the technique of cutting through solid walls with the tools at hand. On the third day we had progressed about two foot six inches, and before it ended we could see light through a crack between the stones. On the fourth session we were through. We put the slimmest man in and his report was encouraging. The chapel was quite sizable and had a good deal of room for spoil. The windows were so high above the floors that no one could see in from the outside. No charge of desecration could be brought against us for the chapel and porch were full of stored stuff – pictures, furniture and, not least, a case of champagne and a bottle of whisky. It says a little for our singleness of purpose that in the six months that followed we used the champagne case as a seat for the man not actually working on the face and we left it intact, also the whisky. If we were caught, we were not going to run the risk of prison for petty theft.

There were a few days' hold-up after this. The plaster dropping on to the motor had made the lift defective, and we daily expected an electrician in to repair it, not without some anxiety. I had one of my fairly frequent bouts of hip trouble at this time and was laid up; but Miles and Stirling worked at the hole and enlarged it sufficiently to let in the biggest man. The dimensions had to allow for Boyd's shoulders and my hips.

The next step was to camouflage the hole and make it as nearly as possible invisible. Here Boyd's skill as a joiner came in. I cut into the plaster with a knife, deep enough to take the three-ply false panel forty-five centimetres square which he made. Once it was fitted he and Ranfurly made a contraption consisting of a hollow tube of wood large enough to allow a bottle to run up and down inside. The bottle was filled with water to give it weight, and then attached to the panel by a cord. When the panel was fitted the weight of the bottle held it tightly in place hard against the counter sinking in the plaster. To open the door one had merely to pull the panel out and lower it down the lift well out of the way, while to replace it one raised it and fitted it in – the bottle did the rest.

This done, Ranfurly, our painter, washed the face of the whole wall, including the panel, with plaster wash until it was uniform in colour. From time to time he had to go over it; but it was highly satisfactory. A still further precaution against detection was carried out by Sergeant Bayne, our electrician. He "fixed" the lift so that it could only be lowered by pressing the button at the bottom, working on the presumption that only a very extraordinary Italian would lower the lift from this point and mount the spiral staircase to see if there was anything amiss at the top. His judgment was right – no one ever did go up to see. As a still further precaution the light at the top of the lift was put out of order so that in case an Italian did look in when the lift was down, he would be gazing into a very badly lighted lift well.

All this was wisely done before the actual work began on the major undertaking. We all inspected it in turn, and Neame as an engineer was called in to give expert advice. The chapel was about twenty feet square with an altar and a very high ceiling. Between it and the sealed-up door into the courtyard was a small porch about seven feet square, and lower by three steps than the chapel itself. It was very dark, having only a small grated window beside the doorway, too high for people outside to see through. We were able to open it while working but closed it at all other times. To ensure obscurity we pasted brown paper on the inside.

We decided to sink a shaft through the porch floor alongside the outer wall, next the driveway, the dimensions to be a metre square by ten feet deep, unless the foundations of the wall went further down, in which case it would be necessary to go deeper. From the bottom we would drive a gallery at right angles to the wall straight under the driveway and the outer wall, that is, the battlement. We estimated that this gallery would need to be thirty-two feet in length to the near end of the wall, and we proposed to incline it on a grade of one in eight, so that at the far end it would be fourteen feet below the level of the driveway, low enough, we hoped, to take us below the bottom of the outside walls. In all this preliminary work we leaned heavily on Neame, who, though he had no data to work on (he could not dare even measure the distance from wall to wall for fear of detection by the two sentries on the walk above), made an almost perfect job of the layout.

On September 18th we began work on the shaft. The honour of taking up the first tile in the floor fell to Combe and me. While we worked, Todhunter and Stirling toiled noiselessly in the chapel, stacking the furniture high around the walls and fitting lengths of coconut matting found there around the edges of the cleared space so that the earth would not spoil the pictures.

John and I made an early discovery – that the Italian workman who laid that floor knew his job. It was the tightest fitting tiling I have ever seen, and although we cut through the cement packing it was hours before we could make any impression. Even when we had made a hole for the point of our levers it took all our strength to crack off little chips. In the meantime the watchers on the floor above were panic-stricken by the booming noise and sent down word that we were rocking the tower, so we had to ease off a little. When knock-off time came we had moved only a couple of tiles; but at least it was a start.

After that we had some days off owing to a scare which caused us to expect a sudden search; but nothing happened. We filled up this period by a careful planning of the task of watching. For the first days we had placed a man in the dining-room to watch the two gateways and another in Rudolph Vaughan's bedroom on the first floor to watch the sentries. Now de Wiart took over the command of the watchers, and decided that the best vantage points were Vaughan's bedroom window for the gateways, and his bathroom window for the sentries. To enable the watchers to see without being seen the wooden slatted shutters in the bedrooms were closed and the watcher was able to look down on an angle at the gateways. It worked perfectly.

To maintain contact between the upper floor and the workers he placed a man in the dining-room to receive messages and pass them on. This worked for a start, but it was found that the strain of watching for two hours on end was too much; so three men were sent up, one at each of the windows, and one resting. Every twenty minutes the man resting relieved the watcher at the window, who went to the bathroom, and the man there came into the bedroom to rest and act as messenger to the man in the dining-room. We had two workers and four watchers all through the months we were engaged. Another great improvement was effected in inter-communication. Sergeant Bayne connected the electric bell in Vaughan's room and the bell in the bathroom with a buzzer in the chapel porch. Odd lengths of lead salvaged on our explorations permitted of this. The buzzer was placed near the working face within easy hearing distance, and some signals were decided upon. One buzz meant "stop temporarily," two buzzes "carry on again," three "alarm – come to surface and prepare to evacuate," four "really serious, be prepared for anything."

The dearth of candles in the castle provided no difficulty once we found a lighting point in the chapel. Sergeant Bayne gave us electric light at the surface, and as the work progressed a lead was taken forward permitting us to work in an excellent light provided gratis by the Italian Government.

Another improvement was made in the method of entry into the porch. A wide plank was placed across the lift well into the hole in order to obviate the rumble. To enter, someone had to put this in place, so that the workers could lie flat on it and propel themselves along into the porch. Out of consideration for our tummies, which ran the risk of collecting a splinter in the forward dive, Boyd planed the plank, and six months of sliding along it made it as smooth as glass. We became expert at going in and out, and a horizontal dive from the lift side into the porch became part of the daily routine. It was essential to stop at the right moment, as otherwise there was a risk of going straight down the shaft to the peril of one's neck.

Stirling and I gave an unwitting demonstration of a rapid exit when we were about six feet down the shaft. De Wiart, as officer in charge of watchers, was not satisfied that we workers acted on the signals with sufficient speed, so he decided on a test with a stop-watch. Without warning he called out: "Someone is coming – come out quickly." Stirling was at the top and, closing the porch window, shot out and disappeared through the dining-room. I climbed the six-foot side, put out the light, shot through the hole, pushed the board back, started the lift on its upward journey and closed the door in preparation for headlong flight to my room when Carton said: "Not bad – forty-five seconds."

At about the end of September O'Connor came back and took over the command of "operations" so far as the actual work went. Teams were organized to remain on a permanent basis. He and Combe made one, Boyd and Miles another, Stirling and I a third. We decided to work two shifts daily if possible – one from seven till nine-thirty a.m. and the other from two-fifteen to four-thirty p.m. As we had made fairly severe calls on men as watchers – men who could not benefit from our success – we insisted that the morning watch would be taken by those of the six escapers who were not working. It meant that of those six, five were working or watching and one was resting. Because of his inability to work due to injuries from the last war, de Wiart insisted on watching both morning and afternoon during the whole period. He is one of the coolest men I have ever met; yet in the six months that followed there were times when even his nerves were frayed by the incessant strain.

We all took the job very seriously – there was never any suggestion of hesitancy on the part of anyone; on the contrary, if there was a shift lost from any cause the party who were due to work felt themselves aggrieved. I don't believe any party of would-be escapers ever worked harder or more consistently than ours, and this included all those grand fellows who helped for the sake of helping with no hope of participating in the final break-out.

*   *   *   *   *

After we had cleared away the floor tiling we came on rubble, which was easy to move; but once through this we struck hard grey rock and heavy clay intermixed, packed tight under the huge weight of the castle. It tested our bodies and our tools; but we grew accustomed to working in the confined space of a square metre and our technique improved. The square edges of the shaft had to be cut with the long knife, but in the centre we used the ice-trowel and sometimes the sharpened bars. The last-named, however, being blunt produced the effect of knocking which the watchers could hear from above, and we resorted to their use only when absolutely necessary.

At six feet we came on a domed rock that spread itself all over the floor and seemed impossible to move. We christened it the Dome of St. Paul. Eventually we passed down one side and undermined it so that it was possible to work levers round. Then we found that what appeared to be a solid block of hard stone was really a cone of granite with rotten rock encrusted round it, and by stripping it we reduced it to a manageable weight. We passed two ropes round it and four men hauled it to the surface.

As the shaft went down so our heap of spoil rose. We knew that we would have difficulties in disposing of it all, and from the beginning we stacked it carefully. First we made a stone wall round the shaft to keep back the soil, leaving a working platform clear. A very heavy statue of the Virgin Mary served as a guard on one side. We removed it from its base which we placed alongside and used as a kind of bollard. Until we were the full ten feet down we did not use a ladder, but pulled ourselves up by a rope passed round the bollard, with toeholds in the sides of the shaft. We had a thin rope looped at one end for raising the buckets, which were then carried off and dumped behind the stone curbing.

As the spoil heap rose we extended it into the chapel and built it up until at the end it was easily ten feet high and pressed down hard. We aimed at being down to the ten feet level by October 31st, but reached it some days earlier, thanks to occasional bits of soft going and our increased skill. It was a good, workmanlike job. Then we turned outwards and began our tunnel at right angles to the wall. We had long since passed the seat of the foundations, which surprised us by their shallowness, for we had expected that the huge tower of stone might easily have foundations many feet deep, whereas they only went down a short way, due I suppose to the natural solid rock formation of the hill. The dimensions of the drive were set at four feet by two, but as we advanced we found we could work in much less space and reduced the height to three foot four. This gave us headroom, but at the far end restricted the flow of air and made working very hot. At the beginning we had beautiful going of clay, with a solid strata of rock just above making a perfect roof that required no timbering; but as we went down in our incline of one in eight we struck two bands of solid rock each over a foot in thickness. These had to be moved.

Progress was very slow and laborious, and sometimes it seemed impossible to get on. The rock appeared to be quite solid and beyond the scope of our tools to deal with; but we learned much as we went. Caused either by the castle's great weight, or by an earthquake, the rock was always found to be fragmented if we persevered long enough. First a thin line would appear on the surface of the stone, indicating the place to work on. Much scratching with the knife would outline a crack that could be developed. Alternately scraping and clearing away the debris and cutting into the very tight clay above and below permitted the placing of a lever under the point of the stone; then, by dint of much worrying, the stone would loosen and perhaps fall out. Most of the rocks were triangular, nearly always with the point facing the workers, making the freeing process more difficult still. Sometimes the outgoing relief would pour water over a rock in the hope that it might disclose a crack not otherwise discernible; but the advantage was offset by the resultant mud which stuck to one's clothes and boots, and would have made detection easy in the event of a sudden appearance before an Italian, so we dropped the practice.

In the chapel we found a five-ton lifting jack which we sometimes used to put pressure under a stubborn rock; but that meant digging a hole in the floor to get the necessary length, and was rarely worth while. Our difficulties were principally caused by the lack of space in which to work levers, and the need for quiet. Each group of watchers was sure that the others were noisy and endangered the scheme. We found from practice that the sound of voices or the dropping of a bucket did not carry; but a heavy blow with the trowel or an iron bar reverberated all round the walls and up to the tower. When we came near the battlements where the sentries were overhead we used only the knife.

Our pace was slow. Some weeks we made only a very few inches; in some we made as much as three feet. Every Sunday Neame went down and measured the dimensions and the incline, making any recommendations he believed necessary. He devised an excellent inclinometer by getting Boyd to make a V-shaped apparatus, which he put into the bank horizontally. The top of the V was dead level, while the lower arm was shaped at an angle of one in eight. On this were nailed two pieces of cane which when at rest were swung into the V, but when needed could be opened out and used as sights. Someone held a marked stick upright at the working face and by sighting along it Neame could check the rate of incline to an inch. It worked so successfully that when we had reached the wall our incline was exact – we had gone down four feet.

By Christmas Day, after four months' work, we had travelled nearly twenty feet, and to reward the helpers among the officers and men we opened the workings for inspection in pairs. They were all suitably staggered at the scale of the undertaking. Most of them had thought we were a few elderly gentlemen full of enthusiasm but rather harmless as miners; but after this inspection they realized we were in earnest. The size of the rocks we had brought up impressed them. Our work achieved a new status.

The art of watching was perfected, and we brought everything down to a sort of drill. In the morning one of the servants – generally Collins – did a quick survey of the whole castle to see that there were no Italians about. This could not be done by an officer, who might have found it difficult to explain his being up so early in the day. Collins would report to the chief watcher who then placed his sentries in the bathroom and bedroom respectively, while Collins went down to the dining-room to be ready to assist. Then the workers waiting in one of the bedrooms in their working clothes were summoned and, proceeding to the lift well, were allowed through and the panel replaced. Before they went down the shaft the signal buzzer was tested. After that they were free to work.

The watchers knew from practice what to expect and when. At half-past seven an N.C.O. came in by the small gate and put out the light above the cloister steps. Then he opened the door of the courtyard. This called for one buzz; three buzzes meant that he had entered the courtyard. At seven forty-five the new guard relieved the old in the yard beyond the white wall, and a close watch was kept to see that the officer of the day did not enter our yard. At nine o'clock a soldier brought the milk into the kitchen by the small gate. During the five minutes he was there the workers were on one buzz. On certain days the laundry came, and on Saturday mornings at eight-thirty the shopping sergeant brought in the weekly flowers for Stirling to put into vases for Sunday's service and for the tables. On Sunday morning the three or four Roman Catholics were taken to church at seven forty-five, and we arranged that they were always ready and standing near the main gate. So it went on. We knew the habits of nearly every one of the sentries and just what they would do. Some found a patch of sun to stand in; some came down to the end of their beats and talked to their comrades; some read their letters; some just dozed. The ones we disliked were those who stood right opposite the bathroom window without moving, compelling the miners below to reduce their work to pushing the knife in and cutting out small bits – a very slow job.

We had many alarms – in fact few shifts passed without one. On many days they were serious. The gate would suddenly be approached by a *carabiniere* escorting a workman bringing in his tools to start on some job. This would necessitate the workers staying below or seeking a chance to slip out unseen. Sometimes an officer would come into the castle unexpectedly and just hang about, to our acute discomfort; sometimes a *carabiniere* would turn up from nowhere and appear to direct his attention on the very spot he was most unwelcome. One thing always intrigued me – the fact that for several hours every day for over six months all of our gaolers in the castle precincts were under the closest observation without being aware of it. And yet they were highly nervous of us. Nearly every night there was a search in some part of the castle. The living-rooms, the kitchen, the bathrooms, all came in for frequent scrutiny. Sometimes we would see them in the garden late at night turning over the refuse or poking about among our growing plants; but we never left anything there to arouse suspicion. All our efforts were bent on lulling them into apathy.

With the New Year our plans began to take definite form and our preparations were pushed on. We hoped to complete the tunnel in mid-March and settled on March 20th as the earliest date we could leave. My hip was troubling me – tunnelling was not the best activity for it – and I applied to have it X-rayed and treated. I had to go down to a hospital in Florence for the X-ray and on each occasion I persuaded the driver to go by a slightly different route, enabling me to mark down road junctions and piazzas. From the top of the Quarries we could pick out these points, and we were eventually able to choose a first-class route from the castle to the railway station. I had massage in my room. It used to amuse me that the Italian masseur should work on me so painstakingly to fit me for my job in the tunnel. The cramped position in the heat, alternating with the chill of waiting at the shaft, was the real cause of my trouble.

In late January a dampness in the rock, which we knew must be the result of seepage from a water table, told us we were close to the outer wall. Timbering was necessary and Boyd and Miles set to work. While it was in progress Stirling and I used our shift to widen a short length as a by-pass for up and down traffic. There was a division of opinion over this and over a later by-pass; but on the last night they justified their construction. Sergeant Bayne, our electrician, carried the light along the wall beside us as required, and during the whole period not a bulb was broken.

We drove on until there could be no doubt that we were under the battlements; then we worked upwards by taking away the top and treading it underneath our feet. On the second day we found what we sought, the hard base of the wall – huge, square blocks of stone joined together by very hard concrete. They made an excellent roof, and we travelled along under it easily and safely for almost six feet, and beyond it for another two feet, when we were actually outside the limits of the battlements.

The next thing was to find just how far we were below the surface. We knew that we had fourteen feet of cover inside; but the ground fell away steeply and we had no means of being certain. It was imperative that we should drive upwards to within easy handling distance of the surface. Equally important was it that we did not approach it too rashly and risk a subsidence before we were ready to go out. While the other two shifts cleared up the tunnel and made another "sitting-out" place under the wall itself, Boyd and Miles, assisted by Ranfurly, made and put in place what proved to be a very satisfactory device. The excavation beyond the wall was two feet wide. In this they placed three pieces of sawn timber on either side of the new upward shaft, with a gap of about four inches between each, and pieces of timber above each one as a ceiling. As progress was made the ceiling pieces were removed one at a time, some soil gouged out and the piece replaced. By this means we always had a firm roof and there was no danger of subsidence. As the shaft was pushed upwards other pieces of sawn timber were fitted inside and as they took the strain of the roof they were screwed into the outer uprights without noise. So each day the shaft ascended, very gingerly, but safely and almost noiselessly.

The next problem was to find the exact distance necessary. Neame solved this by taking a hollow stair rod, sharpening one end and driving it ahead. To do this meant noise, and noise was dangerous under the sentries' very feet; so every three or four days a diversion was created in the drive-way or in the courtyard. Heavy timber-sawing, the men playing football in the confined area, much bumping of the wall against the battlements, were all part of the scheme. When the sentries were nicely placed the General would drive his stair rod upwards, until one day daylight appeared. On measurement it was disclosed that we had nineteen inches to go in the total upward shaft of seven feet. From then onwards the greatest care had to be taken; but at last Boyd reported that the surface was only five inches away – easy cutting distance when the moment came. A ladder was fixed in position to facilitate the climb, the roof was reinforced and packed tight against pressure from the top. All was ready.

At the end we had one scare. There was a torrential downpour of rain. A regular river flowed down the tunnel forming a lake. Two of us went down and made a sump to hold as much as possible, and to place timber so that the water ran rather than dropped. In a few days the shaft dried out again.

Final preparations were pushed on. Kits were overhauled and everything possible was placed in the chapel where it was reasonably dry and safe from search. We knew that discovery there meant discovery everywhere. Food necessities were computed and chocolate and compressed tablets were in demand. Miles and I suffered a severe loss at this time. With the exception of broken fragments we had never allowed ourselves the luxury of eating chocolate, but stored it away in our cache until we had accumulated ten pounds. We used tins, each holding several pounds, and sealed the lids with adhesive tape. One night I brought mine up and opened it, to find that the whole lot had become mildewed and quite uneatable. There was nothing for it but destruction and at once I began to

feed our stoves with it. In a few minutes the whole of the top flat reeked
with the stench of burning chocolate. I was fearful that one of the guards
would come in to investigate; but nothing happened and when Miles
came up to bed the smell was dying down. Fortunately at this time I
received several large tins of chocolate from my wife and was able
partially to replenish our stocks.

We settled our routes and as a corollary the rough date of departure.
De Wiart and O'Connor adhered to their plan of walking to the frontier,
while the remaining four of us decided to go from Florence by train to as
near the Swiss frontier as we could. We planned for speed. Apart from
anything else we did not want to take a large amount of food. The
walkers, on the other hand, had to take all the food they could carry.
Their proposed two hundred and fifty mile walk more or less fixed the
earliest date we could set off, for as they would have to live mainly out of
doors, sheltering by day and walking at night, it was desirable that we
should allow the spring to advance as far as possible to give them the advantage of the warmer weather. We decided that we would make March
20th zero day, and that we would leave on the first suitable night after
that. To us a suitable night meant a wet one, preferably a windy, wet one.
Heavy rain was essential to keep the sentries overhead in their boxes, and
wind would assist in deadening the noise. As we all had our own ideas on
suitability we agreed to hand the responsibility over to Neame, whose
decision would be final.

Each night now I packed and unpacked my kit – a cheap little Italian
suitcase Howes had given me; and almost every night I dressed in my
room. In the kit I placed only Italian articles – soap, towel, shaving gear,
scarf, spare underclothes and pyjamas. Food was to be restricted to two
eggs, bread and cheese, and some food tablets. In the pockets of my raincoat I carried chocolate and some milk tablets, both English. My aim was
to appear as a workman cleanly but carelessly dressed, going away to a
new job equipped for the journey by a faithful wife. Miles was to go as a
carpenter, Boyd as a workman and Combe as a commercial traveller. I
would wear my jacket and cap, a green shirt Ranfurly gave me, a cheap
tie Howes got from one of the boys, and heavy black boots, with my raincoat over my arm. I used to pay special attention to the set of collar and tie
and to maintaining a certain facial expression.

As we intended going out through the tunnel entrance in heavy rain,
we could expect copious mud and we all provided ourselves with over-
dress. I had an out-sized pair of pyjamas to pull over my clothes, including
the raincoat, and a large handkerchief to tie over my cap to keep it clean.
We had soft outer material to keep our boots clean and to reduce the

noise. Some sewed up large felt overshoes; I slipped two felt soles under my boots and held them in place by two pairs of huge socks which protected my trouser-legs as well. We each had sufficient money and a map, and most of us had compasses.

We also had our identity cards. Over these, G.-P., our official artist and map-maker, rose to superb heights from which the fact clearly emerged that if he had not chosen to be a respectable major-general he might have had a successful career as a forger. Sketching and painting being his hobbies he was allowed a fairly good assortment of brushes, fine pens, paper, inks and colours. After we had obtained possession of a real Italian identity card he did not seem to have much trouble in matching the paper and copying the crest, stamp-markings, printed lines, and the signature of the issuing official. He spent hours mixing inks to get exact shades, and improvising stamps. Somehow he managed to procure special glasses which made the fine work possible.

We thought photographs would stump him; not a bit of it. For his weekly gramophone recitals it was necessary to buy records, and by a queer chance he discovered that the artists' photographs in the catalogues were the exact size of, and printed on similar paper to, those on identity cards. He sent for further catalogues and set up a small committee to choose likenesses. The results could not have been better – all six of us seemed to have more or less of a counterpart in German or Italian opera. They found me a celebrated German tenor, and G.-P. gave him my moustache more painlessly than I cultivated his right-hand hair-parting.

I called myself Angelo Pasco, after my old friend the fish-merchant in my native town of Invercargill; there was no chance of my forgetting it, and it was easy to pronounce. I came from Bologna, and you could see that I was a bricklayer if you looked inside my case and saw trowel and plumbline lying on top.

To provide six identity cards was a long and arduous task. Before they were all ready even G.-P.'s happy disposition showed signs of strain; but they were six perfect replicas – it was impossible for the lay eye to tell the counterfeit from the original.

Miles had acquired a useful tool – a pair of pliers. One day he came to me with the news that a workman had left his pliers on the ground a little distance from his job. By that time we were no mean snappers-up of unconsidered trifles. Miles carelessly threw an old gardening sack over them and after the man departed we hurried them into hiding.

The next matter of importance, and it was very important, was the one-thirty a.m. check. Every night the officer on duty accompanied by a sergeant, came round our rooms and saw us all in bed, the servants as well.

We could not expect to leave before nine o'clock, which would only give us four and a half hours' start. On the other hand, if we could evade this check we would not be missed until eleven in the morning at the earliest. We decided to use dummies. As a preliminary, Neame protested against the practice of the inspecting officers of coming right into our rooms; he insisted on their staying in the doorway and using their torches from there. After weeks of squabbling we got them used to this. Then as spring approached we applied for protection against the mosquitoes, and nets were put up, great canopies completely covering each bed and reducing the rays of the torches to impotence.

Then we concentrated on our dummies. They were little masterpieces – all of them. Each had to be different and required different materials. Boyd was grey-haired, O'Connor and Combe fair, I dark and Miles and Carton bald. We persevered to such an extent that we produced tolerably good likenesses. I let my hair grow, and when Howes cut it we stuck it on a handkerchief saturated with glue, not overlooking my bare spot on top. We fixed the handkerchief over a stuffed balaclava and sewed on an ear and the job was complete. Sometimes when we made up the bed it was difficult to believe that I was not really in it. Each week we had a small exhibition of dummies in bed, everyone interested being invited to throw in suggestions.

The last piece of rock was removed early in March. We were ready. All that was necessary was the suitable night, and we settled down to a period of waiting.

*   *   *   *   *

On Sunday, March 28th, it rained hard. As the day advanced we made ready. There was, of course, a certain amount of tension, and when at church service we found that G.-P. had included the hymn "Through the night of doubt and sorrow onwards goes the pilgrim band," we were all a little moved. Right up till seven-thirty we thought there were great possibilities; but with night the rain eased and Neame cancelled preparations. Needless to say there were divergent opinions; but we had agreed to abide by his decision, and there was never any question of the wisdom of this.

Monday morning was fine; but as the day advanced clouds came over and by six o'clock it was raining hard, a silent rain, but very close to what we needed. I was on my bed resting about 7.30 p.m. when Neame looked in and said: "I think you had better dress, Jim; it looks as though to-night will be a good one."

At once we got to work and in a very few minutes I was ready. Ran-furly had reserved some sandwiches and hard-boiled eggs for each of us, and at the last I opened a bottle of rum which Stirling and I had kept for this occasion for over a year. I filled six two- or three-ounce medicine bottles, one for each man. There was also room for a small bottle of wine in my case.

Then came the hardest moment of the whole adventure: saying good-bye to Howes. For three years we had been together, in England and in the east. We had fought together; on all my leaves, however short, I had taken him. In the Greek and Cretan campaigns he had never left me for one moment, no matter how weary he was, and in our last fight he had shared my slit trench. He was a big, quiet young fellow who inspired confidence; in Vincigliata every officer and man liked and respected him. Of course he wanted to come with me; I would have given much to take him; but the risks were great and the chances of success so small that I did not feel I had a right to endanger him. So we said good-bye. War is hard in its good-byes.

Dinner was a quarter of an hour earlier that night and we sat down all together for the last time, some of the boys mounting guard to prevent surprise. While we were dining Neame and Ranfurly passed through the hole into the chapel, Neame to see that all was right in the tunnel, Ranfurly to pull down the timbering at the far end and cut away the remaining earth up to the surface. He took the long knife and made a perfect job.

We were all waiting rather tensely, trying to conceal it beneath the veneer of small talk, when the last alarm came through from Vaughan's room: "Officer coming." We six escapees took up our cases and fled upstairs through the living-rooms. It was only an N.C.O. making his round of the battlements. We trooped back to the dining-room. Things ran smoothly from then onwards. We said our good-byes lightheartedly and one by one filed into the lift-landing and slid for the last time through the panel into the chapel porch. I was fourth man and when I got in the first three had disappeared down the shaft. Ranfurly was sitting, naked except for a pair of shorts, at the head of the shaft, and when I went to shake hands he said: "For heaven's sake don't touch me, I'm just one greasy slimy mess from head to foot." Taking out those last five inches of mud had been a dirty business.

I found Neame sitting in the by-pass. He reported that all was well. He had a shaded light there, and I could see Boyd's legs disappearing up the ladder. Each of us had a special task once we appeared on the surface. John Combe went first carrying his suitcase, a stout rope and a blanket. The blanket he spread on the ground to act as a carpet to avoid obvious marks a sentry could see when daylight came. The rope was to be hitched round a post on the top of a stone wall just down the hillside from the

13

battlements. It was our last obstacle, five feet high on the uphill side and about ten feet on the downhill or road side. The rope was to steady us; we could hang on to it while descending. A huge iron gate about twelve feet high opened on to the road. As we had never seen it used in all the time we had been there we had no reason to hope that it might not be locked. Once over, John was to help Miles, who was then to be his assistant on the road. Miles, second man up, was to take a measured three-ply board reinforced for strengthening, to be used as a lid for the hole when the last man was out. Boyd was next and had just his kit. He was to get on to the road and act as scout while the rest came over.

I was number four and in addition to my suitcase had the hooked rope we always used for haulage and a sandbag full of pine needles and soil. I pushed the case up ahead of me, and dragged the sandbag up with my free hand – not easy in that confined space with mud oozing out from every side. When I emerged I had a shock. Instead of the darkness we had expected a couple of concealed lamps made it almost as light as day. Had an Italian been on that side he must have seen each of us as we came up. As it happened, the light certainly made our exit easy.

It was a tremendous experience. Not even the need for action could suppress the wave of exaltation that swept over me. Here was the successful achievement of a year of planning and seven months of toil. I remember thinking, with a new kind of awareness, that whatever the immediate future held, at this moment I was alive and free. I have never been able to recapture in retrospect the fullness of that moment.

I put down my case and sandbag and passed the rope back into the shaft, hook downwards. A tug, and I began hauling up. Carton's large pack appeared. I unhooked it and fished again, this time for O'Connor's pack. All this was according to plan and I had hauled in and was waiting for a head and shoulders to appear when a whisper came up: "The rope." A bit surprised, I tried again; up came two walking sticks – I hadn't heard about them. De Wiart came surprisingly easily. As he surfaced I placed his pack on the stump of his left arm and off he went. O'Connor, following, disappeared into the darkness. I threw the carpet back down the shaft and clamped the board over the hole. It fitted perfectly and stood my weight as I pressed it down. I emptied my bag of pine needles on it and smoothed the surface. I even found a few stones and some chickweed to give it a natural appearance. The last job was to level off any remaining footmarks. Then, taking up my case, rope and empty sack, I decamped. It was exactly half-past nine.

They were all waiting at the foot of the little wall. We had had unexpected good luck, as the door to the road was not locked, and we passed through. I gave my rope to Miles, who cached it along with the other one in a place already chosen, not too conspicuous, yet not too well hidden. When our flight was discovered we hoped that they would be found and give the impression that we had come over the top. We wanted to keep the secret of the tunnel as long as possible. Once through the door we found sufficient shadows to make the going safer. We began crossing the road. John, finding the door difficult to close, slammed it; the noise seemed to shatter our freedom.

We filed down through the wet woods in complete darkness, then across a fence into an olive grove. Thick brambles made the terraces difficult to negotiate; but we got down somehow without noise. Half-way down to the deep valley we were making for we stopped and hid our over-clothes and my sandbag in some bushes. Six hundred yards lower down a roadway ran at right angles to our path. Here we said good-bye to O'Connor and de Wiart, who were using this as a starting-point for their long walk. We shook hands, and the darkness swallowed them up.

The rain had stopped, and we had no trouble in seeing our way down-hill to a bridge above a mill, where we came on a tarred road. We threw our overshoes into the swollen stream. I felt terribly dirty, and seemed to be mud all over, so I soused my suitcase in the running water and cleaned off the worst of it. Then we set off on our six-mile tramp. The road offered no obstacles, we knew it so well from observation, and we tramped along it like a police squad in pairs, our heavy boots making a tremendous noise. It was the first time in many months we had walked on a road unaccompanied by a guard, although I don't think we gave much thought to that at the time.

Once we got on to the lower ground nearer the city we began to meet people carrying torches or on lighted bicycles. We were a little tense at first; but no one took any notice of us and we soon became accustomed to them. We were dressed in very heavy clothes because we felt certain that if we succeeded in reaching the mountains near the frontier we would find snow and might have to sleep out in it. In addition we wore our greatcoats and before long we felt the heat and perspired like oxen. For some reason Miles and Boyd, who were leading, cracked on a very fast pace that seemed unnecessary and even dangerous. I caught them up and suggested slowing down as we had three hours from the start in which to do six miles, and it would be preferable not to arrive too early and too hot. They were afraid that we might miss our route, and wanted some time in hand. As it was, we arrived at 11.35 p.m. After a little careful reconnaissance, we went boldly into the huge hall of the station.

The ticket gate was at the far end, guarded by *carabinieri* and railway officials. We did not stay together but moved about separately to get the lie of the land. I wanted to see whether I drew any special attention, so took up a position close to some soldiers in the middle of the great hall; but neither they nor anyone else looked at me or my dirty boots, so I gained fresh confidence and ceased to be afraid of being detected through my dress.

We drifted outside and met in the shadow, Boyd going off to buy three third-class return tickets to Milan. In a few moments he returned rather perturbed. In response to his request the ticket clerk had asked a question or told him something, and Boyd had fled. We thought it could be nothing more serious than instructions about changing at Bologna, so Miles went over and bought the tickets without further trouble. Combe who was better dressed travelled second-class and bought his own ticket. The waiting was trying. The relieve the monotony we walked about the streets in pairs, coming back at intervals to see if there was any alarm. At about twelve-thirty we sauntered through the gates. It was quite simple. Adopting the slowish gait of an elderly workman I walked up and, looking each official in the eye as I reached him, passed safely through.

Then began a long wait. The train did not come in until 1.45 a.m. It was to have left at 12.35 a.m. Contrary to report, Fascism could not even run the trains punctually for us. All that time we walked about the cold, wet platform, afraid to sit down in case we sat on something forbidden – there were no regular seats. When the train arrived it was crowded to the doors, and the chances of getting aboard seemed remote. The seething crowd on the platforms surged towards the doors in solid masses, preventing anyone from alighting. I saw a new technique in train-boarding. Men and women ranged themselves along the platform opposite the compartment windows; a man would heave his lady up until she got a hand-hold which enabled her to go through the window. Then she reached down and hauled in the baggage which the man held up to her, afterwards taking his arms and pulling him up and in. We were well separated by this time and I had no one to haul me in. I determined that if anyone was left behind it wasn't going to be me, and tucking my bag safely under my arm I charged in. I don't know how I managed it, but eventually I got one foot on the step and the crowd behind did the rest, depositing me well into the corridor with Boyd not far behind. All this was done to the accompaniment of shouts, curses, and fierce arguments, in none of which I took part; but I was on board. I did not ask for more.

The Italians are wonderful people. At one moment they can hurl piercing diatribes at each other; at the next they are smiling and all politeness. In five minutes they were laughing and teasing and making room for each other like happy children. My only discomfort was due to the fact that the man next to me, not six inches from my face, was the *carabiniere* in charge of the carriage. After a while he began to talk to me. I ignored him, but he spoke again. I bent over and said in a whisper such as I've often heard deaf people use: "I'm sorry, but I am very deaf." This was in Italian and probably very bad Italian, though I had practised hard; but it was effective and he left me alone.

The train was fast and we did the forty-five miles to Bologna in an hour, arriving at 3 a.m. The slow train to Milan was due to leave precisely at that time, but actually it was twenty minutes past five before we got away. Another weary wait on a cold platform without any seats. Our efforts to find a refreshment buffet were fruitless. Once when the others were seeking food and I was watching the luggage, a policeman came up and asked me if all the bags were mine. I said they were and he walked off. Several people asked me about platforms or trains, but my chief anxiety was the delay. It was growing lighter and our features would become easier to distinguish. We had hoped to be in Milan by six o'clock and at Como by eight; we seemed to be stuck here indefinitely.

When the train did come in the scrimmage was fiercer than at Florence. By this time I had learnt from experience and, putting my head down, drove in, using my elbows on all who came alongside. By this method I got on to the step and mounted to the top; but then disaster overtook me. Someone clutched at my poor little suitcase and tore it out of my hand, leaving me only the handle. I had to make a quick decision – to retrieve it or leave it. I decided on the former, and kicking my legs clear I dropped straight down on the crowd struggling to mount the high steps. The cursing reached a high standard; but I found my bag and butting ahead with it climbed up again. This time I was further along the corridor. I could see Miles's tall figure at the other end and Boyd about six feet behind me. We ignored each other.

I repaired the handle of my bag with a boot-lace, and standing with my back to the outside wall held it behind my neck so that it would not be trampled on. My legs straddled a pile of suitcases on the floor. As soon as we started a little elderly man nearby spoke to me and threatened to become chatty. I looked straight at him with what I thought was a little smile, but was probably more like a foolish grin to him, and said nothing. When he persisted I repeated my formula about being deaf.

He turned away to find another audience, whom he amused by making jokes at my expense, all of which, of course, I had to ignore. He was a mean little man and I would have loved to wring his neck. The train stopped at every station and the journey seemed endless. I had memorized all the larger stations so that in the event of a hasty detrainment I would know where we were in relation to other places and to the frontier. I ticked them off as we passed: Modena, Parma, Piacenza, Lodi – they came and went horribly slowly. From the beginning I had prayed that if we had to run for it we would at least be over the river Po; at last we crossed it. The heavy rain beat drearily across the Lombardy plain. Every stream was in spate, in every hollow lakes had formed; the Po itself was wide and muddy.

In the corridor there was an air of jollity and no one seemed to resent the overcrowding; on the contrary, they enjoyed it. Near the door was a ladies' toilet and as we progressed the women in the carriage kept coming down to it, squeezing past everyone with the greatest difficulty. One cheery old fellow installed himself as doorkeeper and as one woman came out he would call: "One more!" If a lady overstayed a period he thought reasonable he would knock on the door and urge her to hurry. Everyone enjoyed him. As each woman passed me at my corner I had to crouch to make room and this brought my weight down on the cases below me. After a while I saw my troublesome old man look down intently. He struck a match to see better and held it near my feet. I looked down and a dreadful sight met my gaze. My weight had split the two or three cheap cases from top to bottom and out of the cracks appeared ladies' lingerie, gloves, etc.; worst of all, there was a sickly red mess on the floor that was either red wine mixed with mud or strawberry jam – the match went out before I could decide. My position would have been bad if the old man or anyone nearby had been the owner and involved me in an argument of which the results could only have been disastrous. I prayed hard. The old man looked at me and winked. Obviously the bags weren't his. I determined to be well out of the carriage by the time the real owner could get to them.

At Lodi, the last stop before Milan, a nice-looking young woman and her husband got in – I don't quite know how they did it. Anyway, she was full of personality and in a very few moments she was the centre of much chattering. She seemed to be re-telling some joke the old man was making at the expense of Lodi, and tried to draw me into the talk. I smiled back weakly, and the old man came to my assistance:

"It's no use talking to him. He's deaf. Anyway, I think he's a German."

*   *   *   *   *

We reached Milan at 8.20 a.m., the exact time a train was scheduled to leave for Como. The remarkable thing was that it left punctually. By the time we had all met and got our bearings on that huge station several minutes had elapsed, so we had to form another plan, a very difficult thing to do when we dared not stand together for any length of time. We threw in suggestions as we passed and re-passed, and each of them seemed to be opposed to all the others.

I wanted to take a taxi as far along the Como road as we could, but that was rejected. Miles refused to believe the time-table which said that the next train ran at a little after mid-day, and went and bought four tickets for Como; but when we arrived at the ticket-gate we were told to come back at twelve o'clock, so we strode off and I chewed up my ticket as I went. I couldn't think of any other way to get rid of it. We took a stroll round a square and met for another discussion. John urged that we try the North Station, the terminus of a private line to Como situated some distance away. The majority agreed, and Boyd and Combe set off. We saw them run for a tram and, as far as we could see, they caught it. We never saw them again. We waited for a few minutes and boarded another tram from different ends. There was a little lady near me who appeared friendly so I asked her if she would tell me when to get off. She herself was going to the North Station; so I edged along and whispered to Miles to watch when she got off. I had always wanted to see Milan, especially the Scala Theatre and the Cathedral. That morning I saw them both; we passed by the Scala, and caught a view of the Cathedral as we crossed a piazza.

It was five minutes to ten when we arrived, and we saw that a train was scheduled to leave at ten-thirty for Como. No sign of the other two; we thought they might have bought their tickets already and gone through the gate. While Reg. bought ours I went into the buffet and ordered coffee and newspapers, securing a window table from which we would be able to see the platform and any sign of the others. Reg. was horrified when I opened my case and took out a sandwich for each of us; but I felt that it was safe to act naturally. It was ten o'clock, and this was the first time we had sat down since leaving the dinner-table at eight-thirty the night before. We were feeling the strain. Earlier, in the train, I had watched both Boyd and Miles wilt and go grey, and my hip was troubling me a good deal. Whilst at the main station Miles had said as he passed: "My God, im, you look terrible! Pull yourself together." When we met again I said: "The next time you pass a mirror have a good look at yourself." The ruth was that we were all feeling it.

A few minutes before ten-thirty we passed through the barrier and went on board the rickety little train of five or six partly-filled carriages, and punctually at the half-hour we left the station. There was still no sign of Boyd and Combe. We began to fear for their safety, but there was nothing we could do. We ran out of the city into very beautiful country with the sun shining brightly. I enjoyed that part of our journey, and the fact that we were sitting instead of standing added to my pleasure. We reached Como at five minutes to twelve, just about the time when we thought the hunt would be really up. I would not have been surprised if the station had bristled with police; but all was quiet and peaceful.

Reg. went down to the exit while I waited at the rear of the train, but as Boyd and Combe did not appear I went down and joined him, surrendering our tickets. All hope of meeting them now left us and we determined to do the best we could for ourselves. We walked straight down to the lakeside and along the waterfront to the left. Already it was hot and we felt the weight of our heavy clothes.

There were crowds of people about; but nobody took any notice of us and we soon became accustomed to passing soldiers and police without the least tremor. The road left the lakeside and passed through a residential area. Here a minor calamity befell me. The lace handle of my bag broke and the bag fell on the footpath. When I retrieved it a red gush of liquid poured out – my wine. I hastily opened the bag, heaved the broken bottle over somebody's fence, and went on again. We were to feel the loss later.

The road from Como to Chiasso, the frontier town about five miles further on, rises steadily for some kilometres, then goes steeply upward. Rich villas with lovely gardens stand on either side. On this hot day the road felt like an oven. Just as we left Como a party of police and soldiers met us in the narrowest part of the street, and passed on. Miles was keen on taking the road towards Chiasso, then leaving it as early as possible and going south up on to the San Fermo Pass in preference to going up the lakeside, and then striking due west as we had intended. I agreed; to the south the houses ceased earlier and it seemed imperative that we should get off the public highway at the earliest possible moment. So we toiled up the hill until a kilometre peg told us we were close to Chiasso; then we took a road going off in our direction, to our great relief leaving habitation behind. We crossed the railway and laboured up the hill, very conscious that if anyone behind us was looking we were visible from the toes up. A boy cyclist taking a corner with his hands off the handle-bars nearly sent us flying; but his cheerful whistling was encouraging.

At last we found a deep gully which ran under the road. This was what we needed and at once we jumped into it and became partly covered in the abundant bushes. We climbed for a half-mile or so and decided to stop and eat while there was a little water still available to help wash down our tinned beef. Then we made for the hilltop, from which we could look down in almost every direction. It was a remarkable view and anxious though we were to get on, we rested a little and enjoyed the scene. Far below was Como deep in its basin at the end of the lake..I remembered reading how Garibaldi, after forced marching from Varese, had fought his way up the San Fermo Pass and halting with his men had looked down into Como. It must have been on this spot, for the road was just a little below us. We could see the lake for some distance, bordered on this side by great villas. Above the town a funicular railway ran up to a mountain village, while away to the south and south-west the great plain of Lombardy spread like a carpet.

A deep valley running from Chiasso to Lugano separated us from the snow-covered mountains, reminding us of our own Alps at the other side of the world. In the valley, road and railway ran up towards Lugano; on the other side we could trace a straight line from the snow down to the railway – the frontier fence, and beyond it Switzerland.

We moved on along the ridge from cover to cover, praying that no one would see us from the buildings on the mountainside, which looked like Italian barracks. By mid-afternoon we were still obliged to advance cautiously because of the poor cover. The thin, scrubby trees were sparse and leafless as yet, and the brambles that comprised the only real vegetation did not conceal us. Deciding to rest we dug shallow trenches with the trowel, covering ourselves with dead leaves and trying to sleep; but it was of no use. Before starting we had determined that if we were ever in doubt as to the proper course to follow we would push on, and although we were tired we soon got up and went ahead. We came to a clearing crossed by a road; beyond that was a high wood-covered peak which we made for. We very nearly ran into a party of men repairing an electric power pole; veering off to avoid them brought us much too close to a farmhouse where a man was outside chopping wood. We realized very acutely that our bags looked out of place on a mountain.

Then began the ascent. All the way up, whenever I looked back, I could see the axeman watching us intently. We walked as quickly as we could until we reached the woods, perspiring freely in the great heat. And then, as we lay resting in the shade, a gun fired from the direction of Como. "The alarm!" we said on the instant; but other guns following reassured us. Surely they wouldn't waste all that powder on us.

By that time we were high up, and the compass showed we were south-east of Chiasso station, which we could see quite plainly. According to the map we had to get round to the south-west. We got on to a long ridge and moved very carefully at no more than one and a half miles an hour. By five o'clock we were due south of Chiasso, looking straight into it. We found some deep trenches half full of leaves and settled in for another meal; but we had no water and only one orange between us, so we gave up the attempt. Once we heard voices nearby and went to earth under the leaves until their owners passed. Then we had a second scare. A siren blew, filling the valley; but after a while we concluded it might have been a factory knocking off work.

At seven-thirty we came to the edge of the sparse woods and looked down into a deep valley lying athwart our course. Another wood-covered hill beyond looked forbiddingly steep and high. The valley was almost completely bare; every tree and bush had been cleared away, and occasional trenches on the hill-tops suggested that it was used for the purpose of giving a field of fire. By that time we were terribly thirsty and looked longingly on a square water-hole far below us. The water gleamed in the setting sun. We were very much tempted. Fortunately our attention was distracted by the sight of distant huts and men around them; then a party of men marched in single file along the hillside. When they were met by another party, and each turned back on its tracks, we concluded that they must be the frontier patrols.

There was no sign of a fence anywhere, and after a long watch we decided that the mountain ahead was Olimpino and that the fence ran behind it. There was nothing for it but to wait until darkness and endeavour to get forward between the two patrol areas. Never was there such a leisurely sunset. It may have been beautiful; we were in no state to notice. The reluctant sun hung in the sky, a ball of fire refusing to go down.

Twilight came at last and with it the lights of Switzerland. The bright lights of the railway station and the towns and villages distinguished the neutral state from the state at war. We had not seen a lighted town since Cape Town in 1940 and it was a revelation. I wanted to push on towards it when it was almost dark; but Reg. wisely insisted on another hour's delay.

At last we went down, straight for the water-hole. Reg. had his enamel mug ready and dipped it in. When he raised it something scrambled out – a frog! The hole was stagnant.

The going was rough. We seemed to have got into a narrow rocky defile where the noise of our boots on the stones reverberated alarmingly. Worse still, the reflection from the lights of Chiasso flooded the whole area. For the first time stout-hearted Miles became afraid. He whispered that the combination of light with the dead stillness would make it impossible to avoid detection. "Let us go back to the trenches and hope for better luck to-morrow," he said. I reminded him of our vow to go on; besides, we couldn't hang out another day without water. We had to get on. At the bottom he found a bog in which animals' feet had pressed holes. There was water in some of them, vile water certainly, but we drank it. I am sure that a lot of our troubles later were caused by that drink. Reg. left a scarf there and I a large handkerchief, useful clues when the hunt was up. But there was no going back to retrieve them.

We began to climb. We crept up through very rocky ground expecting to see or hear the patrol above us, but no one appeared. Suddenly a sentry-box seemed to rise out of the ground a few yards in front. For a while I stalked it; but seeing and hearing nothing, walked in and inspected. No one there, and no telephone. We saw a square stone a few feet above ground and Reg. went over to examine it. The next moment the world was full of the sound of bells. We fled. Thirty yards downhill we crept into a small cave under a rock, pulling our coats over us for cover. Nothing happened. Reg. thought he must have struck a trip-wire with his boot. We decided to go back and explore.

We were still under the impression that the frontier was over the hill. We crept back past the sentry-box. While Reg. went up to examine a long pole that was set at an angle against a heavy post, I lay and looked upward to get a view against the light of the sky. At once the truth dawned on me – this was the frontier. The fence was not barbed-wire but high netting, fully twelve feet high and of heavy calibre, tied tightly into the bank and held out from the trees by tightly strained wires so that the slightest touch would ring the bells festooned along the top. I called to Miles, but he was out of sight. I gave the fence a slight shake and he came back at the gallop. . . . "For God's sake!"

I said, "Quick, the wire-cutters." While I held the fence as stiff as I could he cut out a square and I bent back the jagged ends to enlarge the hole.

"Get through," said Reg. I crawled through. He passed the coats and bags up to me, then shot through like a rabbit after them. We raced up the hill into the thick forest.

"Jim, we're in Switzerland!"

I don't know how I felt. I remember uttering a little prayer of thankfulness. My heart was tight-packed with gratitude. Then I dived into my case and hauled out the three-ounce bottle of rum. We drank to our freedom. Out of a lifetime of habit I looked at my watch. It was half-past ten.

CHAPTER EIGHTEEN

Only Brigadiers Hargest and Miles got clean away. Carton de Wiart and O'Connor, whose combined ages totalled one hundred and sixteen years, were recaptured after walking a hundred and fifty miles in seven days. Combe was arrested in Milan, and Boyd, who had jumped a goods train, was caught right on the Swiss frontier.

Once safe in Switzerland, the two New Zealanders set about getting back to England, which meant entering Vichy France and crossing the Pyrenees into neutral Spain. Miles left a few days ahead of Hargest, and was killed in Spain in mysterious circumstances. Hargest reached Gibraltar safely but later he too was killed, while fighting in France after D-Day.

*　　　*　　　*　　　*　　　*

When the British generals escaped in the spring of 1943 the Italian people had the idea that Germany would win the war, and in those days there was little help to be expected from the local peasants. The escaper must make his own way, and consider everyone he met an enemy. But with the capitulation of Italy in the autumn of that year the Italian people discovered that they had always hoped the Allies would win the war. From then on, the escaper could count on help and food from the peasants and his main problem was keeping away from the few remaining Fascists and the German troops.

William L. Newnan, an American Ranger Lieutenant, who tells his story in *Escape in Italy*, knew this, and wisely made his getaway before he could be sent to Germany.

William L. Newnan

We met our dark day at Cisterna, Italy, on February 1, 1944. Cisterna was a natural point for us to attack for this reason: it was astride the Appian Way, one of the three main roads south to Cassino, and had the Allies controlled the Appian Way to Cassino the Jerries would have been very embarrassed, because it would have been very difficult to bring in food and ammunition, and also reinforcements. That is why the Rangers were pushed into Cisterna.

The plan of attack was as follows. The Rangers were to push for Cisterna, supported on their right by elements from the Third Division. The First Ranger Battalion, followed by the Third Ranger Battalion, was to move along the Mussolini Canal, and the Fourth Ranger Battalion was to act as the support. What happened in Cisterna, in brief, can perhaps best be described in football terms – the old mousetrap play. We had the feeling that we had, perhaps, been allowed to penetrate the lines in football and then mousetrapped on either side when we had got through. That was a very dark day for us. The Jerries had a great deal more strength than we thought they had there. As a result, elements of the Third Division, who were to support us by moving up on our right, were stopped entirely and the armoured support that was to have come up to us was stopped also. The net result was that we were left pretty much on our own and after a day's fighting, roughly from a quarter of six in the morning until four in the afternoon, we were entirely out of ammunition and the game was finished. (We had left the Anzio beachhead about one o'clock and moved through the German lines during the night.)

Being captured was quite a shock to all of us because we had been able to visualise very graphically the idea of being badly hurt, or perhaps even being killed, but the idea of being taken prisoner was something that none of us had considered at all. As a result we were temporarily off balance.

We were moved immediately on trucks from the Cisterna area to a town about fifteen kilometres away, and put into a large warehouse. We were taken care of at that time very well, I thought, by the Germans. I believe, from talking to other men, that is the usual experience. Front line troops (because they are faced with the same things that you are, and to-morrow may be in the same position you are in) treat you better than rear echelon troops do.

We had the usual questioning all prisoners undergo and our answer was, of course, "All I can tell you is my name, my rank, and my serial number." When we gave that information and refused to give any more the Jerries questioning us would dismiss us. It was rather interesting in that they had two officers acting in the capacity of questioners who spoke perfect English – very fine English. The old stuff was to say, "Of course this is not military information that we are asking you, but it will aid us and won't take so long for us and you will save us a lot of trouble, and we would appreciate it." And of course, actually, immediately following that remark would come a question of real military importance. But, as far as

I know, our men stuck by their rights – both officers and enlisted men alike – and no information was given.

The next day we were again put on trucks and moved towards Rome and held for a day and a half in an old Interurban roundhouse, well wired and well protected as far as guards and machine-guns were concerned. At this point we picked up some British, Canadian, and French Colonial troops. We stayed there about a day and a half and then were put on trucks and moved to Rome. When we had arrived there early in the morning, we were taken to the old Coliseum, then put off the trucks and marched in triumph through the streets of Rome. As we were marching along I was very interested in watching the Italians because I thought, "I will get an indication here of whether they are friendly or hostile, or what their attitude is" – and it was pretty sober and pretty quiet; I could feel that these people were not at all enthusiastic about our being marched through the city. When we had arrived at the other side of the city we were put back on the trucks and moved further north about fifteen miles, to a camp called Fara Sabina.

This camp was typical of a concentration camp or prisoner of war camp; the barracks were enclosed by two double wire fences about ten feet high and about ten yards apart, and between the fences, at the corners, raised about twelve feet above the ground, were guard posts, each guard post facing the back of the one at the other corner. In addition, on each guard post there were searchlights and along the fence, at intervals of twenty-five yards, a pole with a light on it to give further light. On opposite corners from the guard houses were machine-guns and at the other corners the men were armed with rifles and machine pistols. That seems a rather simple arrangement but with it you can handle a very large number of men perfectly safely. Our food was very, very scanty here and had been all along since we left the front line and the jurisdiction of front-line troops. In the morning we received a cup of burned wheat coffee; at noon two Italian wafers – each wafer four inches square and not quite a half inch thick – and a bowl of very thin soup in addition; and in the evening we would again receive a bowl of very thin soup, and no wafers.

At Fara Sabina we did have water to drink, but no water for bathing and no real sanitary facilities. We met some more British officers at Fara Sabina and there I really had a chance to talk with some of them who had been loose for three or four months in the back country. They told me the Italian farmers took very fine care of them; there was plenty of food and they were quite safe as long as they stayed off railroads, roads, and bridges and out of the towns. So I stowed that information away in the back of my mind as a fact that might be useful sometime.

It was here that I met a "pioneer" British officer. By that I mean simply that he had helped to survey the Anzio landing and had been unfortunate enough not to be taken off by the landing craft. He had been back of the lines for some reason, had tried to get through, and had been hit by our own artillery fire on the way and badly wounded. There was no evident wound on the outside, but a piece of the shrapnel had entered his lung and the next day we got him off to hospital. The Jerries were rather hesitant about moving him, not because of his wound but because they weren't sure he was badly enough hurt to be hospitalized; however we finally prevailed on them.

*   *   *   *   *

We were all loaded on to trucks and told we were being moved two hundred and forty-four kilometres north; and away we went with one can of what corresponds to our C ration for every two men. The Italian C ration was very small, just a little bit of meat, but it tasted pretty good for it was the first meat we had had. We arrived very late that night at a place called Laterina. Unfortunately, on the way up there we were in covered trucks and it was a fine moonlight night; when it did get dark there was no opportunity of leaping from those trucks. They were fairly well guarded and at the end of the column was a small car loaded with Jerries with machine pistols.

Laterina, as I found later, is located about fifteen kilometres north and west of the Italian town of Arezzo. We arrived late at night and our barracks were in quite a mess. We found just stone floors and no bedding for us the first night; so in our barracks we proceeded to tear up some of the cots and burn them for fires and, of course, the Jerries were very upset over that. When they wanted us to stop we pointed out that we were supposed to have stoves and bedding, and here we were freezing, and the devil with them. They were just confused enough to let us get away with it so we did burn fires all night long.

Our bill of fare was just the same as we had received at Fara Sabina, except that there was no water. That is, the water was contaminated, and if you drank it you did so at your own risk; so your soup ration was also your liquid ration for the day. I had been watching the other men to see whether this thin diet was affecting them; as yet I hadn't noticed much effect, and this was already February 8 or 9. We had been prisoners now for eight or nine days.

I hadn't any idea exactly how I was going to leave this place, but we were told that very shortly a Red Cross train was to take all of us north into Germany.

For two reasons I didn't want to go on that trip. For one thing, once in Germany your chances of escaping would be very slim indeed, and secondly, to take that trip was hazardous because our own air force was in complete control of the air, machine-gunning and bombing everything that moved.

O'Reilly was my first scout. He was as fine a fighting man as you will find in any army. I was surprised that he did not come to me with some plan of escape before I left Laterina. I heard of O'Reilly later when I was at Oran waiting to come home. Four Ranger non-commissioned officers drifted into Oran; they had escaped north of Florence. Their story really was epic. When the shipment for Germany was ready the enlisted men had been put into box cars and nailed in. The men in two cars, about a hundred altogether, kicked the sides out of their cars and dropped off the moving train. These Rangers certainly raised Cain in the hills around Florence. They naturally had split up into small groups. O'Reilly had obtained a German machine-gun from a post which they captured. The last they saw of him, he was leaving to make his way home by himself with the machine-gun strapped on his back. He told them he could kill more Germans by himself than in a gang and that he was going to strike off into the hills. They heard later that deep in the hills O'Reilly had found an isolated little town and set himself up there with his machine-gun as king of the district. He was literally living the life of Reilly, with everybody deferring to him.

There were about twelve hundred men gathered together by this time and the thing that set me going was the fact that this camp was not in a good state of repair, because it had not many men in it previously, and was falling apart. By that I mean there were no searchlights on the corners, the guard posts had collapsed, and the fences were not as tight and sound as they could be. But the Jerries were fast putting it in shape. They were setting up new searchlights, stringing fresh wire wherever it was needed, and soon this camp would be as tight as Fara Sabina. They were also putting an additional fence around the officers' barracks and I knew that once that fence was up it would be almost impossible to get out of that camp.

In the mornings there was a customary count of the men, and that gave me the idea that in the confusion of that count I might be able to get away from the officer group, get out of our barracks, and begin looking around for a way to get out of the camp. That is exactly what happened. With twelve hundred men to count, and count accurately, it would mean that starting at eight-thirty it would take the Jerries at least until eleven o'clock or quarter to twelve to complete the count. The count the morning I escaped had particular significance; the night before two officers had escaped, and when that was discovered, in the morning of course, the count was much tighter than usual. It was very cold that morning and we would hop first on one foot and then on the other, trying to keep warm. As yet I didn't know just what I was going to do, but I saw that I had to do something and do it right away.

When the Germans had finished counting our group they moved us off a little to one side, and since I had no insignia on, this gave me an idea; because our group had been counted, the Jerries were no longer paying a great deal of attention to us. Of course they had found the two officers missing in that count. Right near us was a group of enlisted men standing around and I skipped over and joined them. They were only ten feet away and a very casual movement got me over there, and once over of course I was just lost among the men. Standing there with those men and wondering what to do, I noticed that the group, as closely packed as it was, extended to a building – a long shed close to the fence. For some reason I thought I had better get into that building and just hide, because to date the Germans had only made one count a day and if I got in that building I would have until the check was made again the next morning to figure something out. That was the first step – to get into that building. I kept moving from group to group of enlisted men until I had arrived at the building and then ducked into it rapidly.

In the building were several trucks – I would say five or six – that were being repaired. As I stood there for a little while just wondering what I was going to do, one of our own enlisted men came in, and he could see my tense attitude, and he said, "Lieutenant," – my collar was open by that time and he could see my insignia – "are you planning to escape?" I said, "I'm thinking about it." He said, "Could I go along with you?" I said, "No, this is only for one man and it may not even work for me. Now get out of here before you bring some German guards on us." I had no sooner got him out than another drifted in. I used exactly the same formula on him and had to shoo him out too.

I began to look around the building a little bit and I noticed that one of the trucks was without an engine, and it seemed to me that a truck without an engine was a truck that people were not working on. So I went to the truck and opened the cab and climbed in and curled up on the front seat. It was very cold. My teeth were chattering. I had my pocket watch and I said, "Now you just lie here without moving until quarter of twelve; you won't move until quarter of twelve, and the fact that you are so terribly uncomfortable here probably means that you are doing just the right thing."

I hadn't been in the truck more than fifteen minutes when some Italian mechanics, Fascists in German pay who were working on the trucks, came in. They proceeded to work on the trucks and, of course, their presence in there meant to the German guards outside the building that no one was in that building. It got colder and colder in that truck, and I kept lying there, and it seemed years, but finally quarter of twelve did roll around. I slipped out of the truck.

*   *   *   *   *

The mechanics had left for lunch at eleven-thirty. By keeping down low, I could not be seen through the windows by the guards outside. There was a door that opened on the side where the fence was. I went through the door and sat down with my back against the building. The fence was then only about ten feet away and the wings of the building extending out to my left and right just hid me from the guards who were on the inside of the stockade. They were there to herd the prisoners, as you would herd a large bunch of sheep or cattle.

There were Jerries moving around on various duties outside the fence, but they would look in and see me sitting there calmly in the sun with my back to the building and were sure, of course, that the guards inside knew I was there and that it was all right. In other words, it was simply a case of confusion – one person thinking that the other person knew something that he did not. I had counted, as I lay in that truck and had tried to develop some logical plan, on three things, and I had already put one into execution. In a morning count of twelve hundred men – our ranks had by that time been swelled to that number by elements of the Irish Guards, the Forty-fifth Division, the Third Division, and some miscellaneous British officers – there had been a good deal of confusion.

Secondly, guards, like most men, are not apt to be as alert in the day-time as at night. They are frightened a little bit and they are afraid that there might be something in the shadows; at night they are alert and in the daytime they relax. Third, everyone's mind was pretty well concentrated on food at noontime. (Our diet was slim but the diet of the German guards was also slim. They were not receiving very much more to eat than we were.) I counted on those three things and they were working fairly well so far.

Then I almost fell into my own trap. I heard the mess kits rattling for lunch and I could smell the food from the mess hall and I got so hungry that I said, "You'd better call this a day and go and get your food and think about escaping some other time." And then, fortunately, looking at the outside fence, the outer of the two fences. I noticed there was a jagged hole that had not yet been repaired, large enough to let a man through, bending over. I made up my mind that I was going. A couple of strides brought me to the inner fence. I had selected a good strong-looking pole to climb and was over in no time and dropped in between the two fences and ducked through the hole in the outside fence. Of course, by the time I was through the hole in the outside fence I was far enough away from the building so that the wings no longer protected me from the vision of the guards. In fact, when I was on top of the first fence, they could have seen me had they turned around. But they didn't turn around.

Now straight ahead of me, about twenty-five to thirty yards, was a group of buildings. I had selected a time when there were no Jerries on the outside of the fence; at least I couldn't see any of them. They had gone into mess, and the first job was to get those buildings in between me and the guards in the enclosure so they couldn't shoot. I had a hard time stopping myself from running at that point, but I figured that if I was walking casually, but rapidly, even if the guards did turn around they would not know why I was out there. I wouldn't be running, so obviously I wouldn't be escaping; and in any event it would confuse them enough so they might not shoot. But they didn't turn around. I was never faced with that problem.

I had just rounded one of the buildings and got it in between me and the guards when the Italian mechanics that had been eating lunch in that building suddenly walked out. They didn't know what to make of me walking along there; so they called the master mechanic, who came out. He didn't know what to make of me, either, so he began to jabber at me. That was my cue that this walking business was over, and so I bolted on a dead run. Then the Italian master mechanic began to yell and shout and wave his arms; but that meant nothing to the Germans inside the enclosure, because everything was peaceful in there. They couldn't see him; all they could do was hear him; and as only one German in a thousand really understands Italian, they didn't know what he was yelling about.

There was another fence two hundred yards outside the main stockade, and in the old days they would have had a guard out there; but since they were short-handed they didn't, and that was a lucky thing for me. Of course I was over that fence in nothing flat and then just kept running as fast as I could go. Now I hadn't seen the ground out there; this whole process was just one step to the next step. It wasn't well thought out in advance; there was no way of thinking it well out in advance. But on my immediate left was the River Arno. That is, I was near the source of the River Arno – the south spur – and from there it travels on, swings north and then swings west and forms the natural barrier, on which the Gothic

Line is now, and empties into the sea around Pisa. Three or four hundred yards to my right was a highway; so I was caught between those two, and it meant that if I wasn't going to get caught, I had to get out of that. I couldn't simply run right straight ahead. The main thing to do then was to cross this river immediately. Either I would have to swim it, or I would have to ford it.

As I ran along the bank I noticed that the water was breaking white in the river about a hundred yards ahead of me. That meant it must be shallow there – a ford. I went in and it was just about knee deep but very swift and about sixty yards wide. The last four or five feet before I could reach a little bar projecting out from the bank was tough. I was afraid I was going to be swamped, but an Italian farmer working in his fields with his big white oxen saw me and my difficulty, for I was going very slowly across the river; in fact, it seemed as if I was just creeping, and of course I was worrying about the Jerry guards that would soon be after me. He held out his fork to me and I grabbed hold and he pulled me up. He didn't say anything and I didn't say anything; we just understood each other.

And then I took off on a run again, now making for the high ground. Not only making for high ground, but doubling right back on the camp and still keeping the river between me and the camp. I had just reached the high ground about four or five hundred yards from the river and had lain down in some cover when along the bank, trotting from the way I had come, came six Germans, looking for me. They had finally found out what was going on but they couldn't see anything. The Italian across the river didn't tip them off, and they couldn't leave twelve hundred men at the camp with inadequate guards to look for one man; so they had to turn around and go back. That was my cue that I could again start moving with relative safety.

* * * *

I didn't know for sure which direction was which, for that time of year (this was February 8 or 9) the sun doesn't rise due east and travel directly across your head and set due west. It rises somewhere in the east and swings across your front to the south and sets somewhere in the west, but that isn't good enough to travel by. So I just kept blundering along. The first job was to get rid of my uniform or to get something that would cover it up. I hadn't gone more than three-quarters of a mile from the camp, travelling over very wet and rolling ground, with no roads – a good factor – when I saw three Italian farmers, apparently either relatives or brothers, working in the fields. I had to hazard everything, so I decided that I was going to take my chance right then. I walked up to these men; of course I couldn't speak Italian and they couldn't speak English, but they could tell the whole story simply by looking at me.

After standing there for about two or three minutes while both the Italians and I tried to use sign language, they threw their bags over their shoulders and motioned me to go with them. I did. From there, we went, I would say, about a half-mile, still over fields and with no roads anywhere except little dirt trails. When we had got quite near one farmhouse, the other two went on. The one chap led me up to the house, and then went back to the fields and left me. The women and all the children and the dogs rushed out, and the chickens cackled and everything was there to welcome me. They could tell by my uniform immediately that I was either an Englishman or American. Their big term was *Inglese*. They thought perhaps I was an Englishman. So they immediately got out their *vino* and a big loaf of bread, and of course I was mighty darn hungry; so I tore right into it, not having had anything to eat for quite a little while, and not having had anything to drink for a long while, particularly with alcohol in it. I had no more than got down about three-quarters of this bottle than I was all ready to go back and take the prison camp apart. Fortunately I restrained myself, but I was really fit to fight the world at that point. We sat there gesturing to each other. They saw my feet were wet, and insisted on getting me a pair of socks, and dragged out an old pair of trousers, an old mackinaw, an old hat, and a scarf. I sat there until evening, eating and drinking and wondering if the Jerry patrol was really going to wise up and start to comb the country.

Then the man of the house came back. The Italian farmer knocks off about three-thirty and comes in and potters around, straightening his barn up and feeding his cattle like any farmer, but a little earlier than our men do. And about six o'clock he is all done work and eats a very light meal for the evening. I had on a very good combat jacket and I could see the Italian admiring it. I couldn't very well take it with me and when he offered to put me up for the night I immediately said, "Well, now I want you" – this was all in gestures of course – "to have this jacket in exchange for these clothes you have given me." That tickled him to death. He took the jacket and put it away. I started to go out to sleep in the haystack that night, but they missed me and came out and dragged me out of the haystack and put me up in one of their best beds, which was a terribly hazardous thing for them. In other words, I could have been just as lousy as could be and you can imagine what would have happened to that bed shortly. But they were really hospitable souls.

I stayed there two days and three nights. While I was there one of the boys, or rather the boy of one of the other chaps, who was considered the student of the neighbourhood, was called over with his little atlas. He didn't have a really good map of Italy but he did have a school kid's map which had all of Italy on about six inches, and it had some of the towns on it, and they pointed out that I was near Arezzo. Of course I knew immediately about where I was; that is, about two hundred and forty kilometres due north of Rome, because when the Germans moved us from Fara Sabina, they told us they were taking us on a trip of two hundred and forty-four kilometres.

So I had the facts now and I had a map, and then I decided to take off and get somewhere. They insisted on giving me a bottle of *vino* and a loaf of bread, which I carried in a little satchel, and off I went. I had the scarf around my neck covering my uniform so that you couldn't see my shirt, and an old serge hat, the mackinaw buttoned up, and the borrowed trousers on, so that from the distance I could be just an Italian farmer walking along.

* * * * *

I tried to go by a sense of direction and thought I was going south, but after travelling three-quarters of a day and inquiring at a farm house and using the same method that I had used on the first farmers – asking about Rome and pointing where I thought south was – I found out that what *I* thought was south *they* said was north. I wouldn't believe 'em until they dragged out the few maps they had, and finally by pointing to a mountain and learning what its name was, I decided that was north after all.

At that house they said I must come with them, that there was an escaped prisoner in another house; so I was taken over there and not long after I got there a Frenchman was brought to me who spoke very little English but spoke Italian fluently. The war was over for him; he had been one of the French soldiers garrisoned in Algeria that had been taken earlier in the war and he was just going to settle down and become an Italian. He was this farmer's right-hand man. I stayed there one night and they told me that further on down the line I would find an English captain. The Frenchman was going to lead me there. The next morning, bright and early, we started off. When we got to the house the farmer was very suspicious, but I produced my AGO card, that is, the officer's identification card, which the Germans had not taken from me, and I finally convinced him that I was all right. I was taken out in the field near the house and introduced to an English chap (an enlisted man) along with a bunch of Italian youngsters – five or six who were just of draft age and were hiding to avoid the German labour draft. I stayed at that place one night. I tried to get the English chap to go along with me, but he had been holed up there for six months and he was going to wait for the lines to pass over him. He would rather stay right there as he had a pretty good billet.

While I was there I met an Italian who was learning to speak English and was very proud of what he knew and not a bad sort of person at all. He insisted on helping me along all the time and finally, to make use of this chap, who was beginning to bother me a little bit, I had him write out a brief dictionary of the words I thought I would need most going south. He wrote down about fifteen or twenty of these on a piece of paper. Those, in addition to what I picked up, were the Italian words I travelled on the rest of the time.

I remembered my former experience of just blundering around because of trying to guess at directions by the sun, and walking along valleys and getting all mixed up; so I recalled that the Army had taught us in school how to use a pocket watch as a compass. I had a pocket watch that hadn't been taken away, which I could use very easily in this manner; point the hour hand at the sun and then bisect the angle – the smaller of the two angles between the hour hand and twelve o'clock – and get due south. It won't give absolutely due south unless the watch is on sun time (or let's say, set by an almanac as to when the sun rises) but a watch is generally close enough anyhow, and mine was. I could set a south line in that way. I took a peak way off that corresponded with that line and then walked towards that peak in an absolutely straight line over anything in the way. Using my watch as my first sight I set off from this place, and just kept going.

It was very rough country. It isn't what we would call mountains but they are really rugged hills and that time of year it was wet and damp, hard going, not over roads, of course, but over ploughed fields and up and down mountains. It was so hard that I would keep saying to myself – and I still think it was right – "The hard way is the best way, for if it is such hard going for you in here, the Jerries certainly aren't going to be back in here for fun, and they will have to know you are here before they will ever start to come in to get you. You are not just going to blunder into something that you shouldn't blunder into."

I began to perfect a system that I used all the way down. The farmers, as I said before, quit work about three-thirty; so about three-thirty I would begin to look around for a good-looking farmhouse and about that time of day the farmer would just be coming in with his oxen and begin to cut hay out of the rack. Then with my schoolkid's map and a later map that I had picked up, which was a little more detailed, in my hand, I would walk up to him, well knowing where Rome was, and ask him if Rome were in that direction, and I would point south. That would start the conversation. Of course he wouldn't have to look at me twice, and see my good shoes, army shoes, before he knew all about my being an escaped prisoner. Then the question was what kind of prisoner was I – British or American? Pretty soon either he would invite me down to his house or I would invite myself, and then I would produce all my documents and would cause quite a sensation in the house. Naturally these people were cut off from the world, with no amusements. Then the first thing they knew it was getting dark outside, and they had to invite me to stay the night. While they did get up early in the morning, they never had anything to eat at all until around eight-thirty, and I didn't want to leave without any food. That meant the day of travel was from approximately eight-thirty until four o'clock in the afternoon. I travelled only during daylight as the country was too rugged to knock around in at night.

I had talked to the British prisoners and they told me that the old battle line was a very hard one to get through. Thinking it over, I decided the best bet was to make right for Rome, as I was convinced that the Anzio beachhead would be extended shortly. The whole question simply resolved itself into reaching the outskirts of Rome just prior to the time that our boys arrived there and then holing up somewhere and letting the line pass over me. That would be the easiest way; and so I headed straight south for Rome.

I didn't have any trouble except one time, and then I came just about as close to being picked up as I ever want to. I was attempting to avoid the airfield at Chiusi; or rather I thought there was an airfield there. The reason I thought so was that I had had to come down out of the mountains finally, down into the plain by the Arno River, at the point where the Tiber is visible. I really felt unprotected getting out of my mountains and I know why Kipling wrote "Hillmen desire their hills," because when you are in the mountains you are safe. When you are down on the plain you are surrounded on all sides by enemies, or you feel you are.

I could see the bridge crossing the Tiber where the Arno and Tiber nearly join and I knew that would be a place where plenty of Jerries were guarding, so I began to flank it to the west. I was flanking to the west because as I came down due south I was already west of the Arno and Tiber Rivers and to flank anything to the east would have meant recrossing the river. I made a slight error there because Orvieto or Chiusi, I don't know which it is, was guarded by an airfield at Allerona, and Allerona on my map looked as if it was much farther back, much farther to the west than it was. So I flanked right smack into Allerona; not into the town itself, but right into the airfield protecting it.

There was no going back because I had climbed a very steep escarpment and had walked a good two or three hundred yards when I suddenly saw what had happened to me and I simply couldn't turn around. I just kept going ahead and the first thing I knew I was walking over some freshly dug gun emplacements, apparently alternate positions, so that the defences could be shifted in case of bombings. About the time I got by those emplacements I heard voices and ducked down and there came a Jerry patrol going to work. I proceeded a little further, into a cemetery, sat down for a little to collect my wits, looked out, and saw that I was on a bluff that a road was cut through. I was practically at the main gates of Allerona and along the road were Jerry wiring parties, Italian mechanics, and Italian labour gangs. Across the road was a vineyard. My problem then (and I was scared stiff, and didn't know what the devil to do) was to get across the road and into that vineyard for some sort of safety, and then worry about what I was going to do next.

There was nothing to do but go right ahead, so I slipped down the bank, though I didn't like that at all. There was no easy way. I had to drop down a ten-foot bank; a rather strange way for a strange man to appear on a road, by skidding down a bank. I figured that was a danger point, but there was nothing else to do. Of course I felt horribly conspicuous. I was constantly being referred to as a big man. Actually I was the smallest of all the Ranger officers, but in this part of Italy, and even in the north country where men are much bigger, I was considered a large man. Very few Italians were as tall as I. In addition to that, I was wearing my glasses, and in the country they just don't wear glasses. If their eyes are bad that is just too bad; it is God's curse on them. They don't have any glasses. A man wearing glasses and of my height, with good army shoes, although they were covered with mud, was, to my mind, a perfect character to suspect.

I got across the road all right, and there was a little gate into the vineyard. I opened the gate and slipped through, then pretended to be busy working on the vines; but of course people don't do much work on vines that time of year unless they have a pair of clippers in their hands and are clipping and cutting them back. While I was standing there I pulled my pipe out to get nonchalant with it; I had bought the pipe, with a little sack of tobacco, from one of the German guards just outside of Rome for a dollar and a half. I was just getting ready to go across to a little brick house, when, lo and behold! the door opened and ten Jerries walked out of that house. They came right down the path about fifty yards away, paid absolutely no attention to me, and went on to work.

As soon as they were gone I said, "I won't take that path; I will take this one to the right." I took the path to the right, which was going up on to high ground. The path went up to the right and then down into the valley, which the Jerries had just come across, and then up again. I was struggling along up this path nearly to the top, when I saw a fence ahead of me. There was no use stopping then, so I kept on, getting rather fatalistic by that time. I was badly enough shocked the first ten minutes to be no longer capable of being shocked; and inside the fence, when I got to where I could see, was a Jerry sentry walking around a gun emplacement. A bunch of men were sleeping in there on shift. The sentry didn't even stop in his stride – just looked at me, and I looked furtively at him and kept walking.

To the right, on a little bit higher ground, was a quarry where they had been digging stone. I walked on across a flat field and just before I got out of the weeds, which were about head high, I saw another emplacement ahead of me, and suddenly I began to think. "You are doing something terribly wrong to be running into all these emplacements. Even if you are around an airfield you shouldn't run into emplacements so much." I sat down and tried to light my pipe again to think over what the devil was wrong, or if there was anything wrong, or if I was just in a jam, and then I thought, "Well, you *are* stupid." Because coming down the whole trick had been always to stay on high ground for two reasons: first, you could always see from high ground and you could go down either the right slope or the left slope if you were chased, and, second, you didn't have to walk up and down hill that way; you were walking along ridge lines and didn't wear yourself out. But there I was near an airfield, and, naturally, anti-aircraft guns are placed on high points. In following my old method of instinctively seeking high ground, I was getting myself into trouble.

I immediately looked around to see how I could get off this high ground. I didn't want to backtrack. There was about a fifty or sixty-foot drop down into a valley but a good crevice led down. Of course farmers don't climb up and down crevices, that was bad; I didn't want anyone to see me working my way down the crevice; but there was nothing to do but to go down. I did. Almost always I would find that although that country did not have roads, it was just full of little paths. There was a path along the valley floor and I followed it, keeping right to the valley all the time, and gradually it began to rise and took me out beyond these gun emplacements, about a mile and a half beyond, into a little Italian town.

It was the one and only Italian town I ever walked through on my way down, and I had to because the path led right in, and I just took the gamble. I noticed everyone turning and looking at me; I wasn't fooling any Italian. They didn't know who I was, but they did know I wasn't a native. I was protected there too, in a way, because the country was full of men streaming home – Italians from the north who had been put into German labour battalions. They had got sick and tired and had started home. So people didn't pay much attention to travelling men. There were men moving all the time all over the country. They didn't know who I was but I didn't look right to them.

I got out of there in a hurry and kept going south.

CHAPTER NINETEEN

ILLIAM NEWNAN kept on walking until he reached Rome. There he joined the circle of Allied fugitives who were hidden by Italian families until the city was liberated by the advancing American armies.

* * * * *

There is for me no courage in the heat of violent action to match that of the man, or woman, who goes in disguise into the heart of the enemy territory. He knows that if he is caught he will perhaps be tortured and almost certainly killed. He knows too that his Government will be powerless to give him the protection that it gives its prisoners of war. The first story in this book is by John Gerard, who was landed in England in 1588 as a saboteur of ideas. The last is by a man who, having once escaped from German captivity in the recent War, immediately volunteered to go back and work with the French men and women who had helped him in his escape.

George Millar was captured by the Germans early in the war in the Western Desert and handed over to the Italians who sent him to Campo 66 in Italy. Later he was transferred to a monastery camp at Padula, from which he made several unsuccessful attempts to escape. As a punishment he was sent to Campo 5 at Gavi, an ancient fortress and, physically, a most unpleasant camp. There Millar, like so many escapers, found that hard conditions engendered compensating high spirits and comradeship. J. L. Hardy says much the same thing in *I Escape*; and so does A. J. Evans in *The Escaping Club*, the story of his escapes from both the Germans and the Turks. Much that is best in the British spirit flourishes in adversity and it was to the so-called "bad camps" that most of the best escapers found their way.

George Millar had not long been in Campo 5 before the Germans took over from the Italians. With the new guards, who were strange to the intricacies of the fortress, escape efforts were redoubled, and when the Germans gave the order to leave in half an hour for Germany a great number of the prisoners hid in the hope of being left behind. They were all discovered, however, by the methodical search parties.

On the journey into Germany Millar and his friend Wally Binns decided to jump from the train at Innsbruck, but they were too well guarded. The story of how they eventually made their escape is told in Millar's *Horned Pigeon* which, although published later, precedes in time that author's famous book *Maquis*. The two books together are a tribute to those French men and women who refused to accept defeat, and, incidentally, to the British agents who supported them in that refusal.

George Millar

THAT AFTERNOON our train pulled into our destination, a siding outside Moosburg, a small and muddy Bavarian town some twenty-five miles outside Munich. Soon after we arrived there we saw another train exactly similar to our own which was taking other officer prisoners away from Moosburg. Some of the faces that stared gloomily at us through the openings were Padula faces.

They had not got over the shock and disappointment of being in Germany.

There was a cottage beside the siding and two German women, fantastically blowzy and each wide enough to make two well-shaped women, stood in the garden watching us. Looking at them and at the leaden, soggy landscape, I was thankful that I had so far been a prisoner in beautiful Italy.

A party of Russian prisoners, the first that I had seen, swung past us, shouting defiantly at our guards and giving us the clenched first salute or an imitation of our own Army salute.

Once more struggling with the rucksacks and taking turns with the suitcase (we had lost the broom handle), Binns and I trudged along in the van of the tired column of British officers which halted at the imposing oak and barbed-wire gateway of Stalag VIIA. All officers of field rank were taken out of our column to go to more comfortable quarters in the hospital buildings. The rest of us shuffled through the gates, into our first real German prison camp.

This was no beautiful monastery like Padula, no historic fortress like Gavi; it was a huge camp of huts and barbed-wire, more like Campo 66 at Capua, but, being German, fifty times bigger and much better planned.

The first thing we saw – and the spectacle doubled us up with mirth – was a German guard strutting along with a fierce-looking Alsatian police dog held on a long chain.

Stalag VIIA had been built by French prisoner labour. French prisoners of war had been dumped there in 1940, on an exposed flat piece of ground between pine-woods. The Germans had told them: "If you want roofs and walls you must build them yourselves, to our specifications."

The result was a central roadway, one thousand yards long, wide and well-metalled, down each side of which were ranged barbed-wire compounds holding wooden huts. At intervals the central roadway passed through guarded gateways, and the gateway to each compound was also a sentry post. Around the perimeter, where the scrubby pine-woods had been razed for some hundreds of yards to give a field of fire, the German sentry posts were little log cabins raised high on stilts. In fact, at first sight it all looked so efficient that I wondered if Binns had not been right in wanting to get out at Innsbruck.

Near the far end of the central roadway we were halted and then wheeled into a compound. Our small party of officers (the Stalag was a camp for other ranks, and we were only there in transit) was to occupy a corner of one of the wooden huts. Binns and I, opportunists both, were first into the hut, which smelled badly of dirty men. We were met by an unctuous French sous-officier with heavily greased hair, who spoke a little English and called us (translating the French messieurs too literally), "Sirs." We selected bottom beds, near a window. The beds were three-tiered erections of unseasoned deal fixed together in batches of eighteen; that is, with six people sleeping on each tier, in absolute and revolting propinquity. The "springs" were deal boards, and the "mattresses" were of ordinary sacking stuffed with wood shavings and bed-bugs. Each of us was issued with one tattered and verminous blanket.

There were four or five such huts in each compound and a central latrine building designed to provide manure for the Third Reich's boosted agriculture. Each hut was divided into two parts, with a crude wash-house separating them; and at one end there was a slightly more comfortable room occupied by the French sous-officiers who had been there since the camp had opened, and who had been retained to act as interpreters and to explain the running of the camp to new arrivals. They were a cross between guides and what the Germans called "confidence men".

The sight of these Frenchmen filled me with delight. They were what we had been praying for. Wally and I decided at once on our plan of action. I would work among the French, trying to obtain German money, maps, papers, and addresses where we might find help outside the camp. He was to go among the British other ranks who had followed us into the compound, and to buy clothing from them until we both had complete civilian outfits.

Life was interesting in the Stalag, an extremely international prison camp. Although our quarters were bad, the rations proved to be much larger than any we had seen in Italy. There were two reasonably bulky meals a day, meals of potatoes, cabbage soup, and extremely sour and indigestible black bread.

Wally and I, determined to escape before we reached a permanent camp, mercilessly attacked our food reserve to build up our strength. For fuel we chopped up our bed boards, and each morning we cooked a great mess of porridge on a fire made between two stones in the compound. At midday and in the evenings, on the Frenchmen's stove in the "private" part of our hut, we cooked greasy dishes of tinned sausages, bully beef, fried bread, meat and vegetables. Between or after meals we drank our reserves of Ovaltine and cocoa, with quantities of condensed milk and sugar. It was both chilly and wet while we were at Moosburg. The weather gave us an appetite and helped us to store food and energy in our bodies. Morning and afternoon we walked quickly for one hour round the compound. So much for our bodies.

On the morning after our arrival, while I was standing by the gateway to our compound, looking rather wistfully at the queer crowd that trooped past in the central roadway, the German sentry, an elderly man, turned to me and asked: "Are you an officer?"

"Yes," I answered.

"Then you have cigarettes?"

"Certainly," I answered, handing him a Chesterfield. We had just been supplied with such luxuries by the American Air Corps prisoners in the Stalag.

"Well, pass out, officer," he said, opening the gate to my disguised, but unbounded, astonishment. "But don't be too long now."

So all that day I was able to mix with the Poles, Serbs, Croats, Frenchmen, Russians, Americans, Italians, Moors, Senegalese, and Indians who populated this strange community behind barbed-wire.

From these people I picked up various things. Some Poles gave me a small wood saw. A Russian lieutenant, a pilot, gave me a thin stabbing knife which I sold to an American for thirty marks. A Serb gave me a small bottle of what he claimed were knock-out drops for German sentries which I sold to another American for twenty-five marks. He said they made a good drink.

Best organised of all the prisoners, and rather disdainful of the others, were the French. They even had their own cinema, in which German films were shown. The director of the cinema, taking a fancy to my open face and reasonable French accent, gave me three tickets for the show.

In the most unventilated atmosphere that I have ever attempted to breathe, we saw and heard a crude film about two *Luftwaffe* friends who fell in love with the same girl, a night-club queen. This was the first film that I had seen in three years, and I was interested to find that my critical faculty persisted. So much so that if I had not found the audience interesting I should have left the hut.

Packed in front of us were the élite members of the audience. Roughly, fifty per cent of these were low-browed and exaggeratedly manly. And the remainder, whom the hairy ones escorted and squabbled over, were girlish types of young men. Two in front of me were heavily perfumed, had pointed, lacquered finger-nails, and affected the coquettish ways of the cruder Frenchwomen. Most of these "girls", so far as I could see, were French, though a few were Polish and one was Indian. That so many of them were French contradicted in some measure the theory that Latins are normally less addicted to homo-sexuality than the Nordic or Aryan types. Perhaps the fact that French homo-sexuals are so much less in evidence in the outside world than British, American, German and Scandinavian ones is another good mark to be chalked up to the Frenchwoman, who is, generally speaking, the most efficiently attractive woman in the world.

It was noticeable that the section of the audience in front of us was sharply separated from the larger section that sat beside and behind us. The section in front brought its sex to the cinema and took it away afterwards. The remainder, on the other hand, were frankly sitting on the hard benches and enduring the vile atmosphere in order to drag a little sex from the screen. If the blowzy German cinema actress showed the tiniest curves of her puffy breasts some of these men howled their approval, while others, more horribly, greeted it with a voluptuous intake of breath. Towards the end of the performance one of the most dashing of the "girls" in front of us had begun to ogle Binns and myself, and we were extremely glad to get into the dazzling freshness outside the hut.

Since most of the kitchens in the camp were run by Frenchmen, I was often asked to take fatigue parties from our compound to get hot water for "brewing-up". The scullions in these kitchens were usually new Italian prisoners, who, poor creatures, were repaying the 1940 treachery of Mussolini – repaying it to irascible French chefs who were obliged to waste their talents boiling potatoes and *würst* all day on patent German pressure-cookers.

I went whenever possible to the Russian kitchens. The head Russian cook was a colossus, a Georgian. When no other cook in the camp would provide hot water, this man often lit a fire specially to oblige us, although we had no language in common. He used to take the great containers of boiling water, one in each hand, and slap them down on the metal counter between us. I would have to get two British soldiers to carry away each container.

The compounds were separated by double fences of long-pronged barbed-wire stretched on oak saplings fourteen feet high. Between each double fence was an eight-foot wide strip of criss-cross low wire with loose barbed-wire laid on the top. Almost every evening a party of Russians, some of them officers, climbed over this formidable obstacle to visit us. Twice when I watched them climbing German sentries fired either at them or in their direction. The Russians had no leather gloves, and some of them were torn about the hands and bodies. They cheerfully settled down in our hut to eat bully beef and bread and jam, and drink tea. They were very professionally-minded, with a great liking for discussions on the design and equipment of tanks and aircraft, or the weaknesses and strengths of their own and the German army. After tea they would ask us, as though to pay for the meal, whether we wanted lonely, sad songs, or joyous ones. The lonely, sad ones were the best.

These were exceptional men. Only the exceptional Russian prisoners had survived the journey from the Eastern front to Moosburg. They had been packed sixty-five to a cattle-truck. The doors had been shut in Russia and opened anything up to three weeks later at Moosburg. Many of them said that they had been obliged to eat their dead comrades. Their hatred and enmity for our common enemy were very terrible to see, particularly as hatred and enmity seemed to sit ill on these humorous men always ready to laugh at themselves or at us. Some of them had faces unimaginably scarred by wounds that had never been dressed or treated. They swaggered about, apparently unconscious of their man-made ugliness, or else supremely conscious of it, flaunting it like a banner.

The French spoke seriously of the Alsatian dogs that were led around by guards. They claimed that they had photographs secretly taken which showed that the dogs had been set on their comrades and had torn them about the throats and arms. But the Russians only laughed at the dogs; and indeed there was something excruciatingly funny about the strutting German with the ultra-fierce animal on a chain or a leather thong. Sometimes when you passed them the dog would spring at you with bared fangs, only to be dragged back by his admiring jack-booted master.

The Russians told us that shortly before we arrived the Germans turned one dog loose in the Russian compound at night. The following day no trace of the dog could be found, not a tooth, not a hair from its coat. That night the Germans left a *Feldwebel* and two dogs in the compound. Next day one dog was found unharmed. "The other dog and the pig will never be found," said my informant.

I saw that George Sukas was working as I did at Moosburg, making friends with the French. Far from worrying me, this put me in good heart. George was a very intelligent customer, and I felt that I must be working on the right lines. After three days of hard work, long talks about France, French guests for meals, I began to strike oil. I struck it in the person of one Robert Cahin, a Lorrain, a young and wealthy grain merchant from Metz. Cahin was an interpreter. He naturally spoke good German. He had been shut up at Moosburg since the fall of France, with two breaks when he had escaped. Each time he had been picked up near his home.

"It is very difficult at my home," he said sadly. "There are so many Boches in Lorraine, and some of our own people are bad too, though not many."

He and I took an instant liking to each other, which made things easy. Nevertheless, Cahin was most cautious. I saw from the first that he was not quite sure of me, and that gave me confidence in him. On the third day, when Wally had already completed our wardrobes of civilian clothes, Cahin began actively to help.

First he found me German money. It was forbidden in the Stalag to have anything but camp money, but the black market was so developed, and so many of the prisoners went outside each day on working parties, that there was no scarcity of ordinary marks. On the other hand, the civilian marks were highly prized, and it was difficult for two newcomers to get hold of them. We had sold a complete Red Cross parcel to some Poles for 100 marks (a ridiculously low price, but we did not know that then). Now I asked Cahin if he could dispose of my watch. That same evening he sold it for 250 marks to a German officer. Next day he sold two pairs of shoes and some clothing and food for us. I then had 500 marks and Wally had 300 – quite enough money to get us out of the country, we hoped.

I discussed escape again and again with Cahin until finally he took pity on me and spoke of a party of French sous-officiers, all friends of his, who had frequently refused to work on the land or in factories, but who, despite their protests, had been moved to work at a railway siding in Munich. From there they had sent a message to Cahin that if anyone in whom he had absolute confidence wanted to escape he might give that person their address.

Cahin gave me the following instructions:

"When you arrive in Munich, find the main station, the Hauptbahnhof. Face the front of the station, then take the road on the left of the façade which follows the lines of the railway. Shortly after the first street crossing you will see a railway yard in which French prisoners in uniform will be working. Approach them most tactfully when no Boches are watching and ask in French: 'Are you *Arbeitskommando* 2903?' If they answer: 'Yes, 2903 from Moosburg,' you must tell them frankly that you are a British officer sent to them by Robert Cahin."

He explained that the plan these *Arbeitskommando* workers usually followed for getting people out of Germany was to stow them secretly in railway wagons which were sealed in the siding, and which then crossed the frontier unexamined as far as Strasbourg, the main city of Alsace. Although Strasbourg was apparently more German than French, and since the battle of France Alsace and Lorraine had been incorporated inside the frontiers of the Reich itself, the population was mainly pro-French, Cahin believed (and so did I).

Cahin also gave me excellent Michelin maps of Germany from Munich to the Rhine and of Alsace and Lorraine beyond that river. He would accept nothing in return for all his precious gifts.

Not quite satisfied with Cahin's address, I moved about continually among the French in the time that remained at Stalag VIIA, and I succeeded in getting two other addresses. Both belonged to Paris prostitutes imported by the Germans originally to work in Munich factories. I decided that the railway workers were the better bet, since the women would not necessarily have any means of getting us away from Munich.

We now set ourselves to finding a good way out of the Stalag, but all the ways offered to us either by the French or the Americans (the two richest groups of prisoners and therefore the ones who knew most about the venal German guards) were uncertain, and necessitated a good deal of ground work to build them into sound propositions. Neither of us was prepared to throw away all that we had gained in the Stalag on some attempt that might be expected to fail. We had never been so well equipped in Italy.

American prisoners, who at regular intervals bribed the German sentries with an entire Red Cross parcel to let one of their number out, told us that the recapture system at Moosburg was highly developed. The Stalag sat in the middle of an agricultural plain which offered few facilities for hiding, the peasants were unfriendly, and there existed a special pack of police dogs and human sleuths for trailing escaped prisoners.

On our fifth day there John de Jago, who was living in the hospital, went out of the front gate with a party of French prisoners who were going for their fortnightly walk. The Frenchmen hid him among them until they sat down in a wood to rest. Jago was able to crawl unobserved to the other side of the wood, whence he struck the main Munich road. He was dressed in civilian clothes, but in the first town he came to,

Freising, some twelve miles from the Stalag, he was stopped by a plain-clothes policeman and brought back to the Stalag. He was courteously treated by the German commandant, and was given only ten days' cells as punishment.

I had swung more and more to the theory that jumping from a train presented the best method of escape. If you got out of a camp there was an immediate hunt, and the camp had full facilities such as ready constituted and equipped search-parties, telephones, and so on. If you jumped from a train there was bound to be a delay in beginning the hunt, and they might be uncertain at which point you had begun your escape. Wally and I decided that we would jump from the train as soon as possible after leaving Moosburg station. We had been told that we should be going north, so we presumed that we should have to walk some distance to get back to Munich. George Sukas and Buck Palm, I observed (although of course we never discussed the matter with them), had also succeeded with their new French friends. George and Buck were living in hiding in the camp. They wore French uniforms, and they lived in the French compound. They never attended roll-calls. Among the remainder of our group I saw no signs of serious preparation or competition.

Early in the morning of Tuesday, September 28th, our party was told it must move at once to be searched and then to take the train. Carrying our luggage, we marched in column of threes to the big searching hut just inside the gates of the Stalag.

Our Italian rucksacks were innocent enough on the surface, but underneath they contained all our escaping equipment and clothing.

The searching-shed looked efficient, a long bare room with a line of tables down one side, and German N.C.O.s, stiff and smart, standing like *douaniers* behind the tables.

This was a crucial moment for Wally Binns and for me. The first person to be searched, Tony Hay, had a saw and some civilian marks taken out of his socks. But we had a plan.

* * * * *

Accustomed by this time to bribing German sentries at Stalag VIIA, I intended to bribe one more German to get my escaping gear out of the camp. Binns, who had led a more sheltered life inside the Stalag, and who had more nerve, disliked the idea of bribing, and determined to slip the search. Neither of us could have begun to take such liberties in an Italian camp.

There was a general air of polished efficiency about the searching-shed. An officer swaggered up and down the centre of the floor. Poor officer!

Although he shouted and stamped and was absolutely unafraid of his men, he was quite incompetent. His mind was sliding about among the surface do s and don'ts. God bless him!

I was careful to get to the front of the second batch of officers to be searched. From that position I was able to examine the faces of the Germans doing the searching, and I soon picked out the one who looked the most dishonest and perfunctory. As soon as this *Feldwebel* had finished with his first officer I seized my greatcoat and rucksack and hurried across the concrete floor to him.

The German undid the lacing at the mouth of my rucksack. A few handkerchiefs were neatly packed on the top. Delicately moving the handkerchiefs, he found a new packet of Camel cigarettes. As soon as he found them I knew that I was all right.

He shot a quick glance round the searching-shed, then his blue eyes came back to flicker into mine. I nodded very, very slightly. His hand flickered as quickly as his eyes, and the packet of Camels was gone. For the next five minutes his hands, buried in my rucksack, turned my camel-hair blanket over and over, pretending to probe the secrets of my wardrobe.

When I joined the group of prisoners who had been searched I found that several, like Tony Hay, had lost escaping equipment. But Wally had managed, unobserved by the cloddish Germans, to change himself over from the group about to be searched to the group of those who had been searched. The searching took a long time. When we were finally marched out I found that I was sweating and shaking with nerves. So very much had depended on the last hour, and all had gone well.

We were halted in column of threes by the main gates. Wally and I occasionally grinned at each other, like small boys about to get into mischief. Jago came past to say good-bye, on his way to the prison jail-house to do time for his escape. Alasdair (Baron) Cram stood in the file ahead of us, his head swathed in bandages. He had managed to escape from the hospital on the way to the Brenner, but he really had been ill. His illness had got worse in the cold and the wet. Then he had been caught by Austrian volunteers with the letters S.O.D. on their arms. These men belonged to one of the angry sections of the Tyrolean population. With the Italian Armistice they had come raiding across the frontier behind the waves of German troops. They had beaten the Baron shamefully, and had nearly murdered him. The greatest thing about Cram (and he was a very exceptional man) was the philosophic way in which he took his failures. He was smiling and enjoying a conversation with one of the German guards who handed us out our travelling rations, sour bread and a kind of sausage.

Far down the central roadway of the camp I could see an enormous man in extremely tight American overalls. That was Richard Carr, who had changed places with a sergeant in the American Army Air Corps. The sergeant, whose name, funnily enough, was Millar, wanted to see what prison life was like as a British officer. They had completely exchanged identities. The Americans had promised to buy Richard his way out of the camp once our party was well away.

Wally and I ate our bread and *würst* immediately, at the gate and on the way to the station, all of it. We were carrying plenty of food. I saw at once that our time in the Stalag, thanks to Wally's insistence on regular exercise and pressure feeding, had given me back all the feeble strength with which sparing nature endowed me. Wally also felt good. He said that if necessary he would tear the train apart with his hands. But we had all the necessary tools.

When we neared the siding we saw to our disgust that we were to travel in third-class carriages instead of cattle-trucks. Carriages were usually the more difficult proposition for escape, since they always put guards inside them. There were two carriages. The first was divided into small compartments, each capable of holding eight people. The second was divided into two large compartments with a lavatory between them, in the centre of the carriage.

We climbed into one of the small compartments, then, seeing that the brigadier and the more senior officers were doing the same thing, and fearing that the enemy would put a sentry in each eight-seater, we struggled out with our baggage and went to the other carriage. In our compartment there we found three sentries and about eight other officers, all close friends of ours. We immediately saw that the central lavatory might offer good possibilities for a jump.

Before the train started we got down to relieve ourselves on the wheels and to say good-bye to Brigadier Clifton.

"George and I have been trying on and off for twenty months," Wally said. "And this time we'll manage it."

The brigadier gave us a glint from his savage little eye.

"It may not be so easy," he said. "It seldom is."

"The brig. is going to jump for it too," Wally said to me as we climbed back into the train.

"Yes," I answered. "Obviously."

(And he did try, we learned later, but he was shot, wounded, and recaptured.)

This trip went well for us from the beginning.

Our three German guards, instead of distributing their persons about the compartment so that they could control everything that went on, sat together at the end farthest from the lavatory. They were a sleepy trio, and one of them was a weak-chinned Austrian who said that he was very tired indeed of the war and everything else.

Wally and I established immediately with Nugent Cairns, the senior officer in that coach, that we should be allowed to make the first jump. We next examined the window of the lavatory, and found that while it would not willingly open enough to let a man out, Binns, with his great strength, could easily force it when the occasion arose.

Last, and most wonderful of all, the train did not go north, but chugged south towards Munich. We had never expected such a piece of luck. Perhaps we owed it to R.A.F. bombing. It was obvious now that we were going south until we could be shunted on to the main Munich-Kassel line. Our destination, the guards told Wally, was an ancient fortress at Kassel. "Oh, no, it's not," Wally replied in English. Neither he nor I could keep still. All the way to Munich we were on tenterhooks. The train ran slowly, at a speed that would have invited jumping had it not been a bright day with good visibility. And there was scarcely a vestige of cover beside the line. At some points, when we ran through beautiful, but thin, pine-woods, the temptation to jump was almost overwhelming. But common sense prevailed, and we made up our minds to wait for darkness.

A strapping German Red Cross nurse gave us scientific cardboard cups holding sweet ersatz coffee and barley broth in the marshalling yard south of Munich, where we finally halted. Binns and I drank as much as we could hold, hoping that hot stomachs would make us feel sleepy. The German guards, to their disgust, were taken out of the warm carriages and placed in a ring around them. We were told that any officer who so much as put his head out of the window would be shot, and that we would move on, attached to a goods train, at eight o'clock that evening.

We composed ourselves to try to sleep, but we had little chance of doing so. Other people now approached Cairns for permission to escape whenever we left the marshalling yard. Cairns was firm with all of them when I had told him that we were extremely well equipped, and that, as well as having money and maps, we had an address to go to. It began to rain hard, and a brisk south-west wind drove the raindrops fiercely against our windows.

Many of the occupants of the carriage had influenza or bad colds, results of the long and draughty journey from Italy. None of them had stuffed themselves with food as we had both done at the Stalag, and it seemed that only two of them were really serious about facing the elements. They were South Africans, Karl Koelges and Alec Wuth. The former, who had in a former attempt actually reached the frontier wire at Chiasso, was a friend of mine; and, after fighting hard with my strongly selfish nature, I gave him our address in Munich, pass-word and all. Koelges and Wuth very decently agreed that they had less chance than our pair of getting clear away, and we promised not to lock the lavatory door so that they could follow us whenever we had jumped.

We said good-bye to all the others while the train was still in the siding, and bequeathed our rucksacks and the big food suitcase to Tony Hay and his partner Dudley Schofield. Both of them were fevered and ill. Cairns, generous soul, disposed the others about the compartment to mask as much as possible our entry to the lavatory. No sooner had these preparations been completed than the guards climbed in to take their old seat at the end. The train moved out, gathering speed all too quickly, it seemed to me. The time was 8.52.

Binns walked into the lavatory. I crawled between his feet, so that the guards if they were bothering to look would only see one man go in. I shut the door and locked it while Binns, without apparent effort, tore down part of the wooden window-frame and forced the sliding window wide enough to let even his broad body through. In an instant he had placed his two hands on a ledge above the window and had shot his legs through into the night. When I had unlocked the door no part of Binns was visible. I climbed through more gingerly. It was damnably cold, wes and noisy outside. When I let myself down to the full extent of my armt my feet found a step. Feeling round with my hands I caught hold of a door-handle, and crouched on the step beside Wally. The train was going too fast to make jumping at all pleasant. At intervals telegraph-poles whisked past our noses with a blowing noise, like seals coming up to breathe on a pitch-dark night. I was shuddering with cold and fear, and was extremely glad that the powerful and strong-minded Wally was beside me. I reminded myself that the essential was to keep loose when I launched myself. Wally handed me the haversack which was our total baggage for that trip.

"Right! Jump!" he shouted. The crash of his landing sounded like tons of coals going down a chute at London Docks. I threw the haversack after him. Then I jumped.

Instead of hitting something very solid, as I had anticipated, I found myself doing neck rolls down a granite chip embankment. I came to rest in a little gully. The wheels of the train rolled past twelve feet above me. And on the other side a high embankment of loose stones mounted steeply. My eyes were getting used to the dark.

It was a long train. I lay still until the last wagon with its red light had rounded a bend, and suddenly the night was silent. Then I heard the crunch of stones and saw Wally's white raincoat approaching. He had found the haversack.

We climbed the embankment and saw on the other side a large area of allotments. Binns stood, a stocky figure peering out into the rain, his torso leaning slightly forward on his steady hips, his big feet making a wide angle.

"Well, damn your eyes," he said. "We made it."

It was stifling, suffocating, wonderful to be free.

*   *   *   *   *

It seemed a pity that this, of all nights, had to be wet and cold.

"Now, just look what you have done to my nice coat," said Binns, pointing to a dark streak on his shoulder. And I found that my left hand and arm were sticky with blood. There was a fairly deep incision on the wrist, just below the artery. It bled steadily. The hole had probably been made as I jumped by one of the short pointed iron stakes which carried the signal wires alongside the railway. I tied it up with a handkerchief.

"Those allotments are the hell of an obstacle," Binns observed. "And the sooner we are over them the better."

Whereas I was a little light-headed from amazement at finding myself free, he, in his Yorkshire way, was at pains to be more practical and prosaic than ever.

We slithered down a slope and soon were at grips with the allotments, falling into cucumber-frames, climbing absurd fences and trellis-work that broke under us, labouring through sticky, freshly dug earth. The black-out was imperfect, and that helped us to avoid the cottages which were dotted about. At last we were clear of the allotments and in a suburb which reminded me of a quarter of Canterbury where I had once hunted for a murderer. We made our way down a lane, passing a row of bijou residences, and came to a main road. We followed this road for half a mile until we were scared off it by a number of bicycles which flung spray from their tyres as they passed. Then we took to the fields. Away over to our left we could see the lights of the marshalling yard where we had spent the afternoon and evening, and the red glares from the fires of the shunting engines. Now we were travelling on a very small and slippery footpath.

Wally considered spending the night in a large clump of nettles dripping with water. I refused, for the rain-water was already falling down the back of my neck, and I could feel its chill to the base of my spine. We walked on for nearly two hours, searching for some safe place to rest. As we passed a cottage beside a level-crossing a man came out and asked: "Who is that?" We did not answer, but when we were out of his sight we hurried on.

Soon after this we halted under a large tree, an oak, the only natural landmark in that wilderness of railways, bungalows and cabbage-patches. The tree stood beside a lane leading to a small farm. A few yards away was a rusty threshing machine, very ghostly in the darkness and with some small piece of metal on it which swung and clattered dismally in the wind.

Wally, astonishing creature, climbed the fence and, stretching on the mud between the roots of the oak-tree, was soon deeply asleep. Before he allowed himself to sleep, however, he arranged to be called by me at 5 a.m.

There was no chance of my sleeping. If the base of my back is cold and damp, I cannot relax for sleep. And unrelaxed sleep is useless to me.

While Wally slept I walked around the countryside, reconnoitring our route away from that place. Sometimes I walked in fields, sometimes in suburban German roadways with houses and garages and shops on either hand. I moved with extreme circumspection, and in absolute silence. My footgear had come from Harrods in London, a pair of brown half-boots with fleecy linings and crêpe soles. They had arrived at Padula, in my first "next-of-kin" parcel. In prison I had kept them for special occasions, like a first night at the prison theatre, and for escape, because they were at the same time weather-proof and light, and they were silent. I could easily have got more convincingly German shoes or boots at the Stalag, but I had held on to my half-boots (despite Wally's disapproval) on the grounds that in an escape the last reserve lay in one's own powers of running, and I personally cannot run when I am wearing either heavy or uncomfortable shoes.

Now and then during the night I came back to the oak-tree, to look at Wally sleeping stodgily under it. The marshalling yard, some three miles to the south of us, was bright and active all night.

I remember no feeling of fear, only a great exhilaration at being free, and a longing for the dawn and for more positive movement in freedom. In the early morning I saw heavy anti-aircraft shells in the eastern sky, and at intervals German night fighters passed throatily over the Munich defensive area.

Although I walked hard all night in my coat, I was desperately cold, and Wally, when he woke at four o'clock shivered so strongly that he could scarcely whisper. At five o'clock we breakfasted, eating, for warmth more than anything else, slabs of German prison bread and American Red Cross cheese. We drank water from the German water-bottle which I carried in my overcoat pocket.

When we had eaten we set about dressing ourselves to pass into and through Munich. We had jumped in British battle-dress, with coats hiding it and civilian clothes worn beneath it. Our intention had been to bury the battle-dress before going into Munich. But that was now unthinkable. It was much too cold. Instead of discarding it we now changed it round, putting the battle-dress next to our underclothing and hiding it with civilian clothing. I thus had three thicknesses of clothing on my legs. (Long woollen pants, supplied to Padula camp by the British Red Cross, made the third thickness.) But the wind still contrived to cut through the layers of damp cloth and wool.

Waiting for first light, we talked over our movement tactics for the last time. We agreed that we had to forget that we were escaped prisoners; and to try to feel that we were as good as anyone else and has as much right to the pavement as anyone. And that the important impression to give when walking through populated areas was that we knew exactly where we were and where we were going, and that we were in somewhat of a hurry to get there.

Then we set out.

Before we struck the road, Binns, who must still have been cramped after his night of stiff sleep, tripped and fell full length into a muddy puddle. He rose with mud all over everything, and wiping mud from his eyes and nose. This was too much for me. I sat down and howled with laughter. Five hours later I was still unable to prevent myself from laughing uncontrollably when I remembered him rising from the puddle.

I developed in the age of slapstick comedy. And Wally was feeling so serious, so obsessed with the importance of what lay immediately ahead, that he was the ideal recipient for the custard-pie between the eyes. He looked first astonished, then angry and solemn. My laughter infuriated him.

He spent twenty minutes with handkerchiefs and our clothes-brush attempting to put his ensemble to rights; but the mud had added the last irreparable touches to his appearance. He wore a vociferously checked tweed cap, the white waterproof, now dirtied beyond repair and stained on the shoulder by my blood, and below the waterproof appeared a pair of Italian peasant's trousers, loudly striped and patched in several places. His shoes were very pointed, down at heel, and filthy. His shirt was a grey Italian military affair, and his tie, with plenty of silver in it, was the sort of tie that a Whitechapel Jew would keep for weddings. The tie kept slipping round under his right ear.

My overcoat, an Australian military greatcoat which I had tailored myself to look civilian, was too dirty after my jump from the train and also, we felt, too obviously military to wear through Munich. But my clothes were otherwise passable. I had a tweed coat cut on the American model with a belt and a lot of revolting pleats in the back, reasonably good blue trousers, and my English boots. My shirt was a blue checked one sent to me by Anne, and my tie was a dark blue knitted one (it had been khaki, but I had dyed it in Italy with ink and wine).

The one well-made article of clothing, apart from my boots, was my belt. This was of pigskin with a peculiar type of buckle, and I had bought it in Swaine and Adeney's in 1940. I remembered as I tightened it over the two pairs of trousers that when I had been packing to go to the Middle East Anne and Myrtle (the wife of one of the company commanders in my battalion) had particularly admired it. "A very attractive belt but quite useless," Myrtle had said. Now it was the only thing then in my possession which remained, and it bore a peculiar importance for me.

Both Wally and I had shaved before setting out, and both of us had meticulously brushed our hair, yet there was a certain discrepancy in our appearance. I looked like a slightly seedy and impoverished college boy, but Wally, a tough-looking customer at the best, looked like a professional murderer on his way home from a tiring night's work.

We walked for an hour on small deserted suburban roads. Then we came to a park on the outskirts of Munich. Several imposing buildings stood in and around the park and a thin stream of people, obviously going to work in the town, traversed it on the same road as ourselves. Binns announced that he must respond to the calls of nature, so he left me on the road while he cut across the grass to a clump of ornamental trees. I passed an uncomfortable ten minutes on the road, strolling about and conscious of the glances of the German civilians who passed. On the whole they were well dressed, and I was surprised at the number of young men who wore civilian clothes.

It was raining slightly. Eventually Binns came out of the clump of trees, beaming. He said that he had cleaned his shoes and his coat, and perhaps he looked a little better. He carried our haversack. It improved his appearance, gave him some resemblance to a plumber going to work with his tools. It was filled mainly with food. I carried one chocolate emergency ration and my shaving and toilet things in my overcoat pocket so that, if we were separated, I should be quite independent.

Ten minutes' more walking and we passed a tramway terminus with orderly queues of people waiting. We were obliged to walk past a group of six or seven policemen, and immediately beyond them we had the choice of three streets opening from a star-shaped junction. We chose the biggest and walked on purposefully, as though we were hurrying to work.

My wrist was hurting me, and was again bleeding. I carried my coat folded over that arm to hide the blood-stained handkerchief. Wally stumped steadily along at my side, and occasionally I was caught by paroxysms of laughter caused partly by our presence in that prim dumpling of a town, and partly by Wally's pointed shoes which thumped so definitely on the asphalt. Wally was annoyed by my laughter, but the more it annoyed him, the more it conquered me.

Munich is a big place. We walked for miles. For some distance a black Alsatian dog followed us, licking up the spots of blood which occasionally fell from my wrist.

We were beginning to wonder desperately whether we were going in the right direction, when we saw a group of French prisoners who were building a vehicle park on a piece of waste ground. Leaving Wally at a corner, I strolled down a lane towards the Frenchmen, and as I passed one of them I asked quickly: "Which way to the *Hauptbahnhof*?"

"Take a number nine tramcar," he answered. "Going that way." As he spoke an ugly German came out of a hut and glared at me.

"*Français?*" he asked truculently.

"*Oui, monsieur.*"

"Then clear out. I have too much trouble with you pigs." He bounced back into the hut.

"Don't worry about him," said the Frenchman. "He's sore because one of us has pinched his girl. But move on now, there's a good fellow. We don't want any trouble with the police. See you at Henri's one of these evenings."

"Yes, indeed," I said, wondering what sort of place Henri's was. I picked Wally up at the street corner, and we continued. We had, by some lucky chance, been following the correct streets all the way through Munich, cutting straight across two-thirds of the town towards the *Hauptbahnhof*. Now we were able to direct ourselves by the signs on the sides of the tramcars. Wally's feet were hurting him, and he was ready to board a tram. But I dissuaded him. I had no confidence in his German accent. The streets were very crowded now. It was still raining, and we were both colder than ever since we had had no opportunity to melt the chill of the night.

The *Hauptbahnhof*, a large, seedy station of Victorian aspect, with its name sprawling across the façade, had six wood-burning taxis in front of it and a police check on all the entrances. The very sight of it warmed me. It seemed to bring Cahin's promises and plans into the light of reality. Without pausing in front of the station, we walked down the street on the left of it, a rather forbidding street lined with poor grey buildings and cheap eating-houses. Like the majority of main-line railway termini, the *Hauptbahnhof* had stained and fouled its surroundings.

After I had first spoken with Cahin of the French workers in the railway yard I had learned in many later conversations all that he knew of the place where they worked, and when we arrived at the first street crossing I stopped uncertainly. I had expected to recognise the place, but I did not, For one thing there was no café on the corner. For another the street running to the right went under, and not over, the railway. Yet Cahin had always been quite definite that it was the first crossing. I stopped a French *sous-officier* who passed. He said that he thought that *Arbeitskommando* 2903 worked in one of the yards some two hundred yards farther down the street. Wally and I strolled on, keeping a good watch now for policemen.

We made our way down a lane and into the goods sidings behind the buildings on the street we had just left. There were some Russians working there, but no Frenchmen, and the German guards and railway officials eyed us most offensively.

"If we stay here five minutes we'll be picked up," Wally said. We went back into the street. For over two hours we searched round the first crossing that Cahin had so definitely described. Our spirits had fallen sadly. It was still raining. My legs and ankles were beginning to ache from all our pavement pounding. Wally wanted to go into one of the small eating-houses and order coffee but I was afraid.

"I need a hot drink," he repeated. "Just something to warm my stomach. You look like death too." He had been long in the British Army, and had great faith in the recuperative powers of hot drinks.

"All right," I said. "We'll just make one more round, and if we strike blank you shall have your hot drink. But this time we'll go under the railway and try the yards on the far side."

"Huh! If you ask me, those Frenchmen were pulling your leg."

However, he stumped along beside me. We went under the bridge and turned left. But now two policemen were walking behind us, so we slightly increased our pace, and did not dare to look at the railway. We turned left some distance along the railway to cross to the other side by a large bridge, and at the far side of that bridge I had the feeling: "I have been here before." After a good look round I said to Wally:

"Cahin made a mistake. He should have said the second street crossing. This is the place."

"Are you sure?"

"Yes. Here is the café with the menu-card in a brass frame on the left of the door. There is the locksmith's and there the little hotel with the bead curtains."

"Where do we go from here?"

"Four hundred yards farther on. Yes, here is the first entrance to the

railway yard. Here are the iron railings. There are the Frenchmen, un-
loading that truck. We've arrived, Wally . . ."

"We'll be there when they agree to take us in. Too many Jerries about
here for my liking."

Wally stopped at the wide gateway of the railway yard. I went in, and
approached two Frenchmen whose heads alone protruded from the air-
raid trench that they were slowly digging.

"Are you *Arbeitskommando 2903*?"

"Yes, 2903, from Moosburg."

The two of them had stopped digging. They leaned, as though frozen
on their spades and stripped me with the penetrating and analysing eyes of
Latins.

"A droll accent," the smaller of the two remarked to his companion.

"Of course it's droll, my accent," I interrupted. "That man by the gate
is with me." Their eyes swivelled round to bear on Wally's square shape.
Wally was pointedly looking the other way.

"We are British officers, sent to you by Robert Cahin . . ."

"*Mon cher*, you have come to the right place, fetch your friend at once."

They sprang from the trench and violently pump-handled both my
hands.

EPILOGUE

THE STORIES in this book are widely spread in time and space, yet running through nearly all of them is the golden thread of charity and human kindness.

Of those escapers who travelled in company only Casanova was not upheld by the fortitude and humour of his companion. Of those who set out alone on their secret journey only Captain Gwatkin-Williams was not fed, assisted and encouraged by complete strangers. The will to be free is in a man's blood, the inspiration often stems from boyhood reading, but chance can place his precious liberty in the gift of a stranger who has nothing material to gain and everything to lose by helping him.

In no story in this book was the penalty of recapture certain death; yet in nearly every case those who helped the escaper staked their lives.

ERIC WILLIAMS.

Strete, 1953.